Literature in the
First Media Age

Literature in the First Media Age

BRITAIN BETWEEN THE WARS

David Trotter

Harvard University Press

Cambridge, Massachusetts
London, England
2013

Library of Congress Cataloging-in-Publication Data

Trotter, David, 1951–

Literature in the first media age : Britain between the wars / by David Trotter.

pages cm

Includes bibliographical references and index.

ISBN 978-0-674-07315-9 (alk. paper)

1. English literature—20th century—History and criticism.   2. Mass media and literature—Great Britain—History—20th century.

3. Technology in literature.   I. Title.

PR478.M37T76 2013

820.9'00912—dc23   2013006906

Contents

Literature in the
First Media Age

Introduction

THE EMPHASIS OF this book falls for the most part on works of literature published in Britain between 1927 and 1939. I argue that these works can be distinguished from pretty much everything that went before and a great deal that has come after by the sheer intelligence of the inquiries they variously undertake into the technological mediation of experience. After 1927, literary texts began to fill up with communication by telephone, radio, and cinema screening, and with the sorts of behavior virtual interactions made possible. They began to fill up, too, with the look, sound, smell, taste, and feel of the new synthetic and semisynthetic materials that now more than ever before constituted the fabric of everyday existence, and of the technological systems sustaining it. Ralph Waldo Emerson had defined the modern as a breeding of invention upon invention. "No sooner is the electric telegraph devised," he wrote, "than gutta-percha, the very material it requires, is found."[1] Gutta-percha encased the cables that by the end of the nineteenth century were delivering telegraphic communication worldwide. By the 1920s, the telephone apparatus—manifestation of a yet more profound upheaval—had in turn "found" Bakelite, the first-ever wholly synthetic substance. Once again, but more urgently still, and on a far larger scale, the combination of new media with new materials gave writers the chance to reimagine both how lives might be lived and how texts might be written.

Today, we have even less chance of avoiding such virtual and substantive mediations. But the best survivor's guides had all been written by 1940, in response to what already seemed like an irreversible process. Although the devices we communicate with have since then altered out of recognition, in terms of cost, caliber, shape, size, and, above all, versatility, the uses to which we put them remain more or less the same. Communications technology is an attitude before it is a machine or a set of codes. It is an idea about the prosthetic enhancement of our capacity to communicate. The writers who first woke up to this fact were not postwar, postmodern, or post-anything else. Some of the best of them lived and wrote in the British Isles in the period between the world wars.

The First Media Age?

The approach I will take to an understanding of media is by no means original. It derives from the work of Raymond Williams, and has recently been developed to excellent effect by media historians such as William Uricchio and Lisa Gitelman with a view to defining communication technology as an attitude. Media, Uricchio maintains, are not "mere" technologies, institutions, or texts, but "cultural practices" that envelop these and other elements in the "broader fabric" of a particular social order or mentality, including the "lived experiences" of those who produce, define, and use them.[2] Gitelman defines media as "socially realized structures of communication, where structures include both technological forms and their associated protocols, and where communication is a cultural practice, a ritualized collocation of different people on the same mental map, sharing or engaged with popular ontologies of representation."[3] My aim is to investigate the social and cultural realization at a particular moment in history, in literature and elsewhere, of particular structures of communication.

Uricchio notes that during the early decades of the twentieth century three distinct "mass media waves" swept across the Western world in quick succession, "fundamentally altering the exercise of state power, the construction of the citizen, and public memory itself. The cheap rotary press, film, and radio each organized data and the public in distinctive ways."[4] One reason to conceive of the period between the world wars as the first media age is the evolution at that time of a widespread awareness of the multiple coexistence of mass media. The effect of emergent media on the exercise of state power, the construction of the citizen, and public memory had long since been understood. But rarely before had there been reason to regard it as overwhelming. To the more excitable, or more prescient, it began to seem that the hold mass media maintained over the public mind had become a stranglehold. Acknowledging the extent of that effect, criticism has recently sought to address the consequences for literature of an awareness of the sway exercised by the cheap rotary press,[5] and by cinema,[6] radio,[7] and phonography.[8]

One further, indispensable mass medium should be added to the mix: telephony. Invented in 1876, the telephone became at once a sensation, and more gradually, over the next fifty years, an office and household fixture. Historical research has very largely concerned the United States, where the telephone was by 1900 an instrument of business for some, and, more rarely, a middle-class domestic indulgence.[9] Subscriptions increased steadily during the first two decades of the century, and then for a while at a more rapid pace. By the mid-1920s, the government-supported AT&T telephone monopoly, with its Bell research laboratories and Western Electric manufacturing plants, had become "the vertically integrated kingpin of electrically assisted verbal communication." Rapid improvements in service, such as the installation of transcontinental and intercontinental links, nurtured (highly profitable) fantasies of a "communications utopia." In 1929, subscriptions peaked at about 40 percent of the population.[10] In 1908 AT&T had launched an ambitious institutional advertising strategy, which it was to sustain throughout the period, and which became in its scope and themes a model for American big business.[11]

The comparison with Britain is instructive. On January 1, 1912, at a cost of £12,515,264, the General Post Office officially took over the system hitherto run by the National Telephone Company, and with it 9,000 employees, 561,738 subscribers, approximately 1,500,000 miles of cable, and 1,565 exchanges. For the first time, a unified network was available in most parts of the country. The General Post Office (GPO), a government department, had become to all intents and purposes the monopoly supplier of telephone services, and was to remain so until the creation of British Telecom in 1981. A period of rapid expansion followed. During the next three years, 450 new exchanges came into use.[12] It was to be some time, however, before the telephone relinquished its status as luxury item or professional and business convenience. F. G. C. Baldwin concluded his *History of the Telephone in the United Kingdom* (1925) by noting, in a tone of some considerable irritation, that as of January 1, 1924, there were a paltry 26 telephones per thousand persons in Britain, compared with 132 in the United States.[13] A poor show. "While after 1918 the number of telephones per thousand persons continued to increase, with an interruption during the Great Depression and the Second World War, it was not until the 1950s that the rise began to be identified as a major social trend."[14] It is precisely this backwardness that makes telephony in Britain between the wars the perfect case study. The strenuous campaigns mounted to persuade an obstinate public to cultivate telephony provide unique insight into the medium's nature and function at a time when and in a place where it came to exemplify the new form of modern urban industrial living that Raymond Williams once termed "mobile privatization." Williams had in mind the mass-production of a whole range of consumer durables (motorcars and motorcycles, electrical appliances, radio sets, and so on), which were at once domesticating and liberatory in effect.[15] The telephone was marketed as essential to precisely such a form of living. Its onset speaks more directly to our own very much more highly developed state of mobile privatization than that of any other early communications technology.

Telephony has attracted the attention of literary theorists[16] and of historians of early narrative cinema.[17] But a great deal remains to be said about its presence, as technology, system, household fixture, and bodily prosthesis, in British literature and film between the world wars. Chapter 1 provides the first comprehensive account of representations of telephony in British fiction during this period. The eighteen writers whose work I discuss include Samuel Beckett, Patrick Hamilton, Jean Rhys, and Evelyn Waugh. The publicity campaigns of the 1920s, which sought to define telephony as a social as well as a business medium, created a new subject matter for fiction. My primary examples are Elizabeth Bowen's *To the North* (1932) and Virginia Woolf's *The Years* (1938), texts in which family and nation play a less significant part in the lives of some young men and women than the solitary-promiscuous traffic of interactions at a distance made possible by the telephone. The introduction of such traffic into fiction tended to alter the formal balance within it between dialogue and narrative.

Comparable claims have been made, with some justice, for the transformative social and cultural effects of the pivotal nineteenth-century communications technology, the electric telegraph. As Richard Menke has shown with admirable clarity, new media such as the telegraph posed a specific threat to the status of narrative realism. Traditionally, writing had combined the functions of data transmission and data storage. Print publication made this arrangement especially clear, Menke points out, since the mass production of identical texts created "both the possibility of wide dissemination and a supply of backup copies. As long as writing and print held a monopoly on communication across time and space, storage and transmission remained united." The difference with the new media that became increasingly prominent during the nineteenth century was that they decoupled transmission from storage. The telegraph, for example, "replaced physical marks on paper with fugitive pulses of current from afar, on-off rhythms distinct from any particular way of writing them down." We should think of Victorian narrative realism, Menke concludes, "as itself an exploration of the power and the limits of written textuality in an age busy producing alternatives to it." Correlating literary mimesis with the emergence of new media, he restricts himself for good reason to "transmission systems that directly incorporate or adapt *writing*—the post, electric telegraph, and wireless telegraphy—as opposed to photography, the telephone, the gramophone, or cinema."[18] By the time we get to the 1920s, that restriction can no longer be allowed to apply. The telephone was the game-changer: immediate, in ways the telegraph never could be, and before very long ubiquitous, in ways the telegraph never could be, as both a private and a public facility. For the telephone demanded from writers an exploration of the power and the limits of *alternatives* to textuality. And then by 1920 there were all those other media, too, equally ubiquitous, if not equally immediate.

The patents for the first workable television system had been filed in 1884. The "Nipkow disk," a mechanical scanning system that transmitted live images over a short distance, was to shape the development of television into the 1930s. By 1925, C. Francis Jenkins, in America, and John Logie Baird, in Britain, were both claiming dramatic success in their attempts to "see by wireless." In 1927, AT&T went public with its long-distance television system, relaying images over phone lines at the rate of eighteen frames a second.[19] Baird's "televisor" was first marketed in Britain in September 1928. His Television Development Company first broadcast experimentally from a studio in Long Acre on September 30, 1929, transmitting sound and pictures alternately in two-minute bursts to a grand total of around thirty viewers.[20] The "picture" on this occasion was a kind of pale, fizzing, glutinous silhouette approximately the size of a saucer. The first fully fledged BBC broadcast took place on August 22, 1932. Regular coverage of state, sporting, and other events began on November 2, 1936. By that time, cathode-ray technology was producing a higher-definition image than anything mechanical systems could achieve. But the new excellence did not get the chance to establish itself. On September 1, 1939, the BBC's television service was suspended because of the outbreak of war. There were fears that the transmissions might guide enemy bombers to the center of London. Television, in short, completed the already formidable midcentury media "array." There can be no doubt about the extent and effectiveness of that array. "The mass media expanded dramatically in the inter-war years," Richard Overy notes, "and through radio and the cinema newsreel or information film brought issues alive in ways that were not possible before 1914." The number of individuals holding a radio license rose from 2,178,259 in 1927, when the BBC became a public corporation, to 9,082,666 in 1939. It was estimated that by 1935 some 98 percent of the population could listen to at least one BBC station.[21]

There must have come a point, as Julian Murphet puts it in his challenging account of "multimedia modernism," when "the 'accretive, gradual' augmentation of the given communicational media by new, mechanical technologies assumed something like a critical mass, and (quantity becoming quality) began to be thought of and responded to as an integrated *system*."[22] Mass media's critical mass created the conditions for a first media age. But we need to establish how and why that age came about by examining further the nature and scope of the response to that new media system as a system.

The digital media system or culture that took shape during the final decade of the twentieth century has generally been discussed in terms of "convergence": that is, "the flow of content across multiple media platforms, the co-operation between multiple media industries, and the migratory behaviour of media audiences who will go almost anywhere in search of the kinds of entertainment experiences they want."[23] By contrast, the middle decades of the century are generally thought to have witnessed the steady displacement of old (human) forms of communication by new (mechanical) ones. Jay David Bolter and Richard Grusin have defined a process of "remediation" by which the new form incorporates the old as content: the first telephone message was a nursery song.[24] Murphet, approaching the problem from a different angle, describes the "defensive integration" of literature and other traditional arts and crafts during this period under the rubric of a *système des beaux-arts*.[25] It was by maneuvers of this kind that the first media age announced its awareness of itself as a media age.

To my mind, however, the emphasis on old and new—on remediation and dialectical system building—has served to obscure a further and in some ways more profound rivalry: one that arose, as it were, along a vertical rather than a horizontal axis. That further rivalry set old against old and new against new as often as it set old against new. It had to do with the political and aesthetic principles or values the different social and economic functions performed at the time by particular media could be understood to articulate. We need to define those values and principles in terms other than "old" and "new." There is a useful though by no means absolute distinction to be made, where media are concerned, between the representational and the connective. Establishing that distinction will allow me to explore in terms appropriate to the first media age the decoupling of transmission from storage that Menke rightly understands as the challenge new communication technologies have always posed to literature.

Representational media attract the "-graphy" suffix. They involve the storage and deferred release of information: that is, a *writing* in light, in sound, in movement. The record (the writing in light, sound, or movement) makes the image or sound originally captured at another time in another place *present again,* as we watch or listen. The axiom of representational media might be: two places at two times (the place where the image once left its imprint on emulsion, or wax, and the place where it has now been projected). The principle or value articulated by media used to represent

Media forms		
Communication devices		Storage devices
telegraph		photography
telephone		phonography
teleprinter/fax		cinematography
	radio	
	television	
Connectivity		Representation

Media forms.

arises out of that double removal in time and space. Representational media, it could be said, enable us to reflect upon a reflection of our world.[26] The axiom of connective (or "tele-") media, by contrast, is two places at one time. Their primary emphasis has always been on instantaneous, real-time, and preferably interactive one-to-one communication at a distance. Digitalization has of course hugely enhanced the scope of connective media. Connectivity, too, can be understood as a principle or value. Its promise of flexible efficiency produces that close alignment of technique to technology— of what people know how to do to what they are able to do—fundamental to both industrial and postindustrial societies.[27] In such societies, representational media, whether old or new, "literature" or "cinema," find themselves called upon to reinstitute the necessary, desirable lapse between technique and technology: a space for reflection upon reflection.

Of course, the distinction between representational and connective media should not be drawn in absolute terms. Representational media connect, after a fashion, while connective media offer, as Lisa Gitelman puts it, "keenly persuasive representations of text, space/time, and human presence."[28] It is a matter of emphasis, or, rather, of the ways in which a particular medium has been defined and put to use in a particular place at a particular time. No medium is inherently representational or connective. None has remained wholly representational or wholly connective in definition and use throughout its history. But the distinction between emphases will nonetheless help us to establish the nature and scope of the principles or values articulated by the use to which a particular medium has been put in a particular place at a particular time. My primary aim is to demonstrate that the terms I have devised are appropriate to the media system or ecology dominant in Britain between the world wars.

In Britain, and elsewhere, the period between the world wars was a period of intense rivalry, both explicit and implicit, between representational and connective uses of media. Literature and cinema in effect allied themselves, as I show in Chapter 4, against telephony. The period also witnessed the increasing dominance of hybrid media such as broadcast radio and, toward the end of the 1920s, albeit in restricted form, television. Radio began as a connective medium enabling instantaneous, real-time, interactive, one-to-one, telegraphic communication, most often between ship and ship, or ship and shore. It did not establish itself as a broadcast medium until the early 1920s. Even then, while amply representing the world through reportage, chronicle, and fiction, it retained its connective credentials. Like telephony, radio spoke directly to the individual listener in her or his own home. "Listening in" became the term for such absorption.

Similarly, the establishment of television as a radio for the eyes, broadcasting news and entertainment in formats more or less indistinguishable from cinema, did not altogether obscure its potential as a kind of "visio-telephone": a medium of instantaneous, and apparently one-to-one, communication at a distance. David Rodowick has drawn out the phenomenological implications of the fundamental differences between film and video technologies. The cinema screen, he notes, is a "historical expression," a "surface for reflecting the projection of the past as a passing present." In cinematography, as in photography, all parts of the image are exposed simultaneously. Each individual image persists, within the movement induced by projection, as a spatial and temporal whole. The television screen, by contrast, actively produces each individual image, causing it to "become dynamically," in real time, as it is viewed. From the beginning, television viewers or "lookers in" witnessed a representation, more often than not of a talking head. But it was a representation that literally took shape in front of them, because although like film an analog video recording preserves an indexical trace "in playback we are perceptually present to a continually changing causation, the excitation of phosphors traced on an electronic display." The television screen displays signals that "produce an image through sequential scanning." "The different parts of the display correspond to different phases in time such that there is never a moment when the entire image is spatially or temporally present to us."[29] Dynamic becoming, incomplete, without precedent, was television's signature.

The digital interface of a computer screen offers something else again: not just the excitation of phosphors, but interactivity. The computer screen functions as the user's instrument of control in the here and now, rather than the horizon of a universe created once and for all somewhere else at some other time. We view it both actively and passively, as information and as image. "What the digital screen empowers in its alternation between image and information, representation and interface," Rodowick notes, "is action at a distance in the present, that is, in simultaneity or real time regardless of geographical separation."[30] When it came to screens, the first media age had not yet dreamed interactivity. Instantaneity, however, mattered a great deal. Television, like radio, came to be understood, when it was understood at all, primarily in terms of its distinctive (broadcast rather than narrowcast) *liveness*.

Television became television when it started to mean broadcast news and entertainment. The fact that viewers could now actually see what they were looking at mattered less than the fact that they now knew what it meant: which, with sharp variations in content and format, and a massive surge in additional providers, is more or less what it means today. But it wasn't always so. When Baird first marketed his "televisor" sets in September 1928, nobody knew what they were *for.* Earlier that year, visitors to the Ideal Homes Exhibition at the Olympia exhibition center in London had been able to inspect a house containing a similar device positioned not in the living room, as we might now expect, but in the study, where it kept company with the electronic regalia appropriate to a titan of finance: wireless transmitter and receiver, teletext machine, and so on.[31] To the designer of this particular Ideal Home, television clearly meant business rather than pleasure. It meant narrowcast (one to one) rather than broadcast (one to many) communication. And it meant purposeful interactivity, rather than couch-potato indolence.

Baird hedged his bets. The televisor was a window on the world. It showed actual events at the moment of their occurrence. But it also provided the kind of intimate contact at a distance that had hitherto been the preserve of the telephone, the first fully accessible, interactive, real-time telecommunications medium. "Practical television is here!" the Television Development Company announced in August 1928. Their new "dual receiving apparatus and televisor" would be on view for the first time at the Radio Exhibition at Olympia from September 22 to September 29. "The Baird Televisor will show, on your screen, the head and shoulders of the person being transmitted and give a living picture with perfect synchronism of movement and sound."[32] From the outset, then, Baird's "seeing in" set was advertised as an improvement on radio's "listening in" equivalent as a live broadcasting medium. "We can all imagine for ourselves," the anticipatory advertisements prompted, "that the day cannot be far distant when, without leaving our chairs at home, we shall be able to see Ascot in all its excitement and glory, or a Test Match at Lord's (or at Sydney, for that matter)—see, that is, the actual events themselves at the moment of their occurrence, not just moving photographs of them some time afterwards." Television was an "instantaneous process" not to be confused with "photo-telegraphy," the mechanical reproduction of photographs and other records transmitted from a distance. There would be no harm done, however, the advertisers evidently felt, by confusing it with connectivity's benchmark medium, the telephone. The Baird Televisor, we learn, carries sight across thousands of miles of space, "enabling distant events to be witnessed, at the moment of their occurrence, as easily as distant sound is heard by means of wireless telephony."[33] Instantaneity was all. The advent of the Televisor constituted a watershed as momentous as the advent of sound in cinema the previous year, though a good deal less remarked on. The advertisers inadvertently provoke this thought by producing an anecdote comparable to that at the center of Rudyard Kipling's "Mrs Bathurst," a story first published in *Traffics and Discoveries* (1904), and often taken to characterize literature's initial engagement with early cinema.[34] In "Mrs Bathurst," a warrant officer serving in South Africa is driven mad by recognition of the woman he loves in an "actuality" film of a train arriving in Paddington Station in London. He convinces himself that the "blindish" look she directs at the camera is meant for him. Because it projects the past as a passing present, the cinema screen enables him to put his present self back into a past conjunction: at the place he would have had to have occupied, on the platform in Paddington Station, in order to receive the look meant for him only. The Baird television, which deals only in instantaneity, in dynamic becoming, might have spared him the anguish. "A few weeks ago, when the Cunard liner *Berengaria* was 1,500 miles out at sea, the chief wireless operator on board saw his fiancée talking with other people in a room in London. He had not known he was going to see her then, but he recognized her beyond a doubt as soon as her face appeared."[35] The wireless operator and his fiancée both inhabit the moment of the image of her in London appearing on a screen in front of him fifteen hundred miles out at sea. Better informed than Kipling's warrant officer, he is not likely to be driven mad by too much reflection upon a reflection. Such was the difference connectivity made.

That interval of uncertainty, when the new medium had arrived, but nobody yet knew what it meant, saw the publication of a story that makes its rawness palpable. *The Television Girl* (1928), by Gertie de S. Wentworth-James, the veteran author of smirking bodice-rippers with titles like *Pink Purity* and *Crimson Caresses*, features a fabulously authoritative and up-to-date osteopath who in best Ideal Homes style has installed all the latest gadgets in his spacious bachelor apartment, including a "Blair" (that is, Baird) televisor. This device is a telephone with a screen.

> The osteopath went across to the side of the room where, standing on what looked like a large walnut box with a ground glass front (the Blair televisor) was the phone.

> He sat down and took off the receiver in the usual way, then, almost im-
> mediately there appeared on the receiving screen the face of the operator
> (so far, Picadill Exchange was not automatic).

A wrong number fortuitously connects the osteopath to his "television girl," and it is love at first sight. But this is not love at first sight as it might have been imagined in a medieval romance or a troubadour song. For a relationship begun by television is thereafter for quite a while conducted solely by that means. The lovers develop a "televisor playfulness," which takes them and their feelings for each other in unexpected directions.[36] Online works better for romance than offline, is the message. As we shall see in Chapter 1, such (often risky) playfulness was regarded as one of the most important consequence of telephony's transformation, from the late 1920s onward, into a social medium. Wentworth-James, it has to be said, does not in the end have the courage of her own online convictions. For the key that unlocks all this sexual chemistry is in the end not television, but narcissism. Dispiritingly, the television girl turns out to be an osteopath herself: though of course, since she is a mere woman, she will have to give that sort of thing up when she marries her mirror-image.

James Joyce took a different approach, at once declaring intermedial war. "Television kills telephony in brothers' broil. Our eyes demand their turn." In *Finnegans Wake* II.3, a scene from the Crimean War hits the "bairdboard bombardment screen" set up in Humphrey Chimpden Earwicker's Dublin pub with an immediacy beyond cinema's power.[37] *Finnegans Wake* (1934) has been said to belong to the prehistory of cyberspace and virtual reality as "the unacknowledged basis for our thinking about technoculture."[38] The more plausible assumption might be that Joyce kept himself informed concerning the analog technologies of his day. There was no shortage of popular scientific explanation.

> In the latest type of home television receiver the wonderful cathode-ray-
> tube is used. At its narrow end a cathode receives the signals and "fires"
> them in a stream of electrons on to a disc-electrode, which makes the
> stream faster (or "thicker") if a dark shade is coming in, and less intense
> when a light tone arrives. An anode directs the stream on to a fluorescent
> screen at the wide end of the tube. Finally, as the electrons strike the
> screen, they become spots of light and, with incredible rapidity, build the
> picture.[39]

When Joyce termed the "bairdboard" televisor screen a "bombardment" screen, he knew what he was talking about. "Down the photoslope in syncopanc pulses" stream the light brigade at Balaclava, and the electrons in a cathode-ray tube, all elements in each case "borne by their carnier walve." In televisor set and valley of the shadow of death alike, "the scanning firespot of the sgunners traverses the rutilanced illustred sunksundered lines" (*FW* 349). Given his enduring interest in "verbivocovisual" presentation (341), it is not unlikely that Joyce thought of the printed page as a kind of bombardment screen. To adapt Rodowick's account of video imaging: the words at the *Wake,* not one of them ever complete in itself, aspire to "become dynamically" as they are read. The incessant, minute changes of sense and tone to which we are "perceptually present" at a slight distance in real time have superseded the written word as merely historical expression of thoughts that took shape somewhere else at some point in the past. That is just about as close to connectivity as literature was ever to get in the first media age.

When "Mrs Bathurst" appeared, cinema was about to shed its initial tricky approximation to a connective medium and take up the business of representing, on a full-time basis, two places, unequivocally, at two times. Uricchio points out that in the reception of the very first films, little or no distinction was made between the liveness of simultaneity or near-simultaneity—such as press photographs, for example, could achieve—and the liveness of a stored representation's ability to capture movement mimetically. But for all its widespread acknowledgment as a "window on the world," film failed to live up to a "set of temporal expectations in place since the invention of the telephone in 1876." Instantaneity "stood as a powerful anticipation which cinema could simulate but never deliver."[40] Reconstituted as primarily a narrative medium, cinema became during the years immediately after the end of the First World War the preeminent global expression of the principle or value of re-presenting.[41] So it remained, with the addition of synchronous sound from 1927, until at least the 1950s. My digressions from literature into film, in Chapters 3, 4, and 5, and more briefly elsewhere, acknowledge that preeminence. Ultimately, perhaps, it is not so much the emergence in a particular place at a particular time of a critical mass of media forms that makes a media age, as the scale of the rivalry between one form and another. In Britain between the world wars, that rivalry was intense.

One arena in which media titans clashed during that period was the evolution of empire. Since I will not do more than touch on the literature of empire in this book, I should at least indicate how imperial concerns shaped and gave urgency to the debate about technology's transformative effects. By making a spectacle of connectivity, empire raised questions about the nature, function, and status of representational media.

Reconfiguring Empire

By the mid-1920s, advances in shortwave radio had established wireless telegraphy and telephony as the most momentous of all new media, in economic, political, and military terms. Wireless telecommunications became the basis for a new understanding of empire not as the occupation of territory by force, but as the maintenance of a global economic bloc of self-governing states: an understanding enshrined as the Commonwealth of Nations by the Statute of Westminster in 1931. The telephone, international standard-bearer for the principle of real-time interactive telecommunication, had begun to alter fundamentally the exercise both of state power and of public memory, and the construction of the citizen.

The reconfiguration of empire was an outcome of the "time-space compression" that has by David Harvey's account driven the "evolution of the geographical landscape of capitalist activity."[42] The concept of time-space compression, originating in Marxism, indeed in Marx himself, but currently put to a variety of uses, can be taken to address the ways in which human societies have sought to convert distance into durations of shorter and shorter span with a view to the efficient and profitable exchange of goods and information. According to Barney Warf, time-space compression constitutes a mechanism for the production of places as "nodes within increasingly wider networks of mobility and power."[43] Technological advances in aviation and in wireless telegraphy and telephony further honed the mechanism. Telecommunication became, as it still remains, capitalism's essential lubricant.[44]

Connection had long been understood as the key to that enhancement of the mere occupation of territory thought most likely to consolidate Great Britain's commercial and military power in an increasingly competitive world. The British government invested heavily in an "all-red" global submarine cable network connecting the center of empire to its most far-flung peripheries. By 1902, British capitalism controlled most of the world's major commercial cables, while the government had at its disposal a secure means of communication with all strategically significant colonial territories and naval bases.[45] The cable network played no small part in the defeat of Germany in the First World War. Radio, however, was something else.

Guglielmo Marconi's first experiments in the new medium, in the 1890s, had shown that radio waves curve around obstacles, including the earth's surface, and that the distance they travel is proportional to their length and to the strength of the transmitter. During the period up to and beyond the First World War, the great powers and even greater corporations sought continually to outdo each other in the field of long-wave radio transmission. Before the war, the world's most powerful transmitter was located at Nauen, near Berlin; after it, at Sainte-Assise, near Paris. In the 1920s, the General Post Office built a super-station at Rugby capable of reaching Australia or the entire Royal Navy at once, submarines included. It had twelve towers, each 820 feet (250 m) high, supporting an antenna that covered 3.8 square miles (10 square kilometers). Although radio was by now essential to shipping, it remained an adjunct to cable-borne telegraphy in long-distance communication. Cables, though more costly, were more reliable, and more secure. But the demand for communications grew so fast after the end of the war that both cable and wireless companies had as much business as they could handle.[46] The connections to be represented in the mapping of empire were those made possible by a new medium (wireless telegraphy) in competition with an old one (cable telegraphy) and by a surge of investment in a new mode of transport, the airplane, which could itself be conceived, as we shall see, as in some sense a medium.

On February 3, 1920, the *Times* reported that Major General Sir F. H. Sykes, controller general of civil aviation, had given a lecture on the topic of imperial air routes at the Royal Geographical Society to an audience including the Prince of Wales and a generous selection of dignitaries. Sykes's theme was that the British Empire would henceforth be sustained by air rather than sea power, and by the development of telecommunications technologies. The empire, he said, possessed a unique capacity to establish "air depôts, refuelling bases, and meteorological and wireless stations in every part of the world." This network of depots and stations had already taken shape in his mind. "Egypt," he went on, "for some time to come must be the 'hub' or, as I have long called it, the Clapham Junction of the India, Australia, and Cape routes, and the heart of the whole system of their expansion." Winston Churchill, responding on behalf of the Air Ministry, maintained that the impetus given to aviation by war should be kept up during peace.[47] Sykes's lecture provided a template for the representation of empire as connectivity. But how was such a system to be established?

The *Times* took up the cause of time-space compression. Distance, a leading article announced,

> is the chief barrier between the scattered British peoples. But geographical distance should be measured not by the absolute standard of mileage on sea or land, but by mileage divided by the time taken to traverse it. Theoretically the time-mile is now a fraction of a second for aeroplanes, approximately a minute for airships and railway trains, under ninety seconds for light road-transport, and from two to ten minutes for various forms of sea transport.

The smooth and secure functioning of empire required "the quickest transport and the most nearly instantaneous wireless and cable communication."[48] The *Times* had for some time been doing rather more than merely report government initiatives to reinforce or re-create empire through connection. Its proprietor, Alfred Harmsworth, Lord Northcliffe, was at once an imperialist and the chief exponent of the serialized photographic encyclopedia. The ambition of the Northcliffe press was, as Michael North notes, "to construct an empire of information at least as extensive as the British Empire itself."[49] On February 4, 1920, the day after it had reported Sykes's speech about air routes, the *Times* published the map of the route to be taken by an air expedition it had itself funded to blaze a trail the length of Africa from Cairo to the Cape: landing grounds, emergency landing grounds, wireless stations.[50] The flight was undertaken by Alan Cobham, a First World War fighter ace hitherto reduced to providing joy-rides at air shows. The *Times* charted his progress from Cairo to the Cape assiduously. In 1921, Cobham joined the de Havilland Aircraft Company. He made the trailblazing spectacular his business. Indeed, he made time-space compression his business. Speaking at a luncheon given in his honor by the British Empire League in May 1925, he argued for more and better imperial air routes. "By aviation could be effected the quick passage of letters and individuals and acceleration of business. Life could only be judged in measures of time."[51]

The maps accompanying and promoting the flights undertaken by Cobham and other trailblazers represent empire as connection. By the 1920s, Michael Heffernan observes, news media were no longer content merely to describe or picture remote colonial territories. They also became engaged in "actively constructing" the idea and reality of empire as "an integrated space of flows, an abstract concept made real by the telegraph, radio, and aviation networks through which news items circulated between the imperial periphery and the metropolitan core."[52] The newspaper map represents connection as contiguity: as a chain of depots, bases, and stations. The best way to conceive empire's "integrated space of flows"—that "abstract concept"—was to pin it to the earth's surface. Addressing the Imperial Conference in October 1926, Sir Samuel Hoare, secretary of state for air, announced that he and his wife were soon to attempt the new Cairo-to-Karachi route. The next step, he thought, should be an extension to Bombay and Calcutta. And how about Rangoon? "If, in the not remote future, links can be inserted in some such way as I have suggested, a long chain of great tensile power will have been forged across the Empire's framework."[53] Hoare's remarks show not just that political and economic connection could be imagined concretely, but that concreteness itself had taken on an important political and economic function. Empire's "space of flows" would only ever be fully known as a paradigm of global integration if and when it became fully contiguous throughout that space, fully tensile: one link clasping, and flexed against, the next.

Contiguity proved a tall order, but not an impossible one. Imperial Airways, established by multiple merger in 1924 with a working capital of £1 million, two government-appointed directors on a board of ten, and the promise of £1 million of subsidies over the next ten years, took on the task of developing the major empire routes. Regular passenger services from Croydon airport reached Delhi in 1929, Cape Town in 1932, Brisbane in 1934, and Hong Kong in 1936.[54] Imperial Airways posters of the 1930s show an inverted Y with its base in London and its stem forking at Cairo: in one direction, the route stretches down through Entebbe, Nairobi, and Salisbury (Harari) to Johannesburg and Cape Town; in the other, across to Baghdad, Basra, Karachi, and Delhi, and then down to Rangoon, Bangkok, Singapore, and beyond. Cairo, Sykes's Clapham Junction, was regarded as the key link in the chain. Rather, the idea of Egypt, or of "the Egyptian," overwhelmingly familiar in Britain since Howard Carter had reopened King Tutankhamen's tomb on November 29, 1922, anchored a whole way of thinking about connection—about empire as an integrated space of flows. From the outset, Imperial Airways posters insisted on empire's capacity to integrate time as well as space.

Integrating time as well as space. Imperial Airways poster, 1924.
© Science Museum / Science & Society Picture Library.

Subsequent posters were to favor scenes such as an airliner approaching a pair of sharply etched pyramids from the general direction of Karachi (snowcapped peaks), by way of Baghdad (minarets). These spaces and times had somehow to be held within a single glance if the system they constituted was to be understood as a whole. Martin Stollery notes that the promotional films made by Strand for Imperial Airways in the late 1930s often include planes over pyramids: the ancient engineering feat now viewed afresh in all its grandeur courtesy of a modern one.[55]

Passengers alone did not create contiguity. There were simply not enough of them. From the outset, civil aviation had required subsidy. Postal services soon became instrumental in its growth, offering lucrative contracts to private carriers between selected cities. Air mail became at once agent and emblem of connectivity. On one hand, it greatly reduced the amount of time monetary orders spent in the mails, thus accelerating capital's invisible flow;[56] on the other, it was easy to visualize as a series of linked physical actions (publicity material often featured the transfer of a bulging mailbag from van or launch to plane). Air mail was a chain of events anyone could initiate simply by placing a letter in a letter box. During the 1930s, Imperial Airways rebranded itself in spectacular fashion by securing a contract to carry *all* the British Empire's mail at a flat rate of a penny halfpenny per half ounce. The Empire Mail Scheme, launched on June 29, 1937, made use of a fleet of twenty-eight state-of-the art flying boats, which became the company's best and boldest advertisement. To be sure, they carried more passengers in even greater luxury. But their raison d'être was to deliver packets of information rapidly and reliably. The Empire Mail Scheme didn't just represent connection. It converted a particular mode of transport into a telecommunications medium (a topic I explore at length in Chapter 5). Nevertheless, we should not necessarily assume that air travel created a "discontinuous geography of collected rather than connected points."[57] There was nothing at all impalpable about the links forming the Empire Mail chain.

Palpability was a quality not easy to associate with the new media of wireless telegraphy and telephony, which set about compressing time-space during the 1920s, as a supplement to, or in competition with, cable. In 1921, the *Times* could still envisage a "chain" or girdle of stations "connecting the communities of the Empire by geographical steps of about 2,000 miles each."[58] The long-wave station built at Rugby had physical presence enough and to spare. However, Marconi and his research engineers had been working with bandwidths under 200 meters. They knew that radio waves could be intensified by reflection, and that because the reflector had to be proportional in size to the square of the wavelength, the method would only work for shortwave radio. Using a parabolic reflector made of wire, they were able to direct much of the transmitter's energy toward a receiver equipped with a parabolic antenna. In May 1924, Marconi announced that messages transmitted from Cornwall using his "beam" system had been received by engineers in Australia, India, South Africa, and North and South America. Shortwave radio was a great deal cheaper than long-wave, and it transmitted at up to 200 words per minute, faster than long-wave, faster even than cable. The British government signed a contract with Marconi to build shortwave stations in Canada, Australia, South Africa, and India. These stations were owned and operated by the General Post Office. The BBC's Empire Service began broadcasting on shortwave on December 19, 1932.[59] For a variety of reasons, commercial, political, and technical, shortwave radio did not simply displace long-wave, any more than wireless transmission displaced transmission by submarine cable.[60] In fact, an Imperial Wireless and Cable Conference held in January 1927 recommended the merger of all British communications interests. The plan was approved by Parliament in August 1928. In April 1929, the new conglomerate, Imperial and International Communications, assumed control over 253 cable and radio stations, and more than half the world's cables. Each point on the network was now linked to all the others by at least two separate channels of communication. Cable and Wireless, as it was from 1934, had become as monumental a "pillar" of empire as Imperial Airways.[61]

Shortwaves do not curve around the earth's surface. Instead, they bounce off the upper layers of the atmosphere, reappearing far from their origin by means of a "skip" effect. They make it hard to imagine contiguity as a principle of connection. This is one data-flow that cannot be mapped without interruption from point to point across a network. Shortwave radio exemplified the dilemma confronting representational media from the mid-1920s onward. Representing connectivity had just got a lot harder. Maps of the period that display the imperial cable and wireless network tend to show radio beams curving delicately around the earth's surface to their remote destinations, as though the transmitters were all long-wave. There could be continuity in fantasy—in representation—where there was now none in fact.

For representation was indeed the issue, or *an* issue, where the oddly unspectacular spectacle of connectivity was concerned. The reconfiguration of empire in the late 1920s both produced and was produced by the emergent genre of British documentary film.[62] Bursts of long-distance conversation and signal galvanize Basil Wright's languorous *Song of Ceylon* (1934) like little else.[63] The job of representational media was to render palpable again a connectivity that had become at once more necessary than ever before and more abstract.[64] The literature of empire seems only to have put its shoulder to this particular wheel intermittently. The focus of E. M. Forster's propaganda for connection shifted from mentality and class to race. "The nations *must* understand one another, and quickly," he declared in concluding his "Notes on the English Character" (1920), "and without the interposition of their governments, for the shrinkage of the globe is throwing them into one another's arms."[65] *A Passage to India* (1924) largely concerns the ultimate failure of colonizer and colonized to throw themselves into each other's arms. The schoolmaster Fielding allies himself with Dr. Aziz, with the aspiring lower middle class, with India, by defending Aziz against the charge of raping Miss Quested in the Marabar Caves, at the cost of complete social ostracism. But Aziz's acquittal changes nothing. When Fielding returns to India in part 3 of the book, after a period of leave spent in Britain, he does so as a married man and a state official: the novel's conclusion acknowledges that he and Aziz will never again be firm friends (or, if you prefer, that they will not become lovers). The acknowledgment may be the reason why, in the final chapter of part 2, Forster goes into considerable detail concerning Fielding's journey back to England via Egypt. Retracing the chain of empire, link by link, Fielding becomes absorbed in, and into, its logic. The connection at issue is not between one race (or class, or mentality) and another, but between links in the techno-administrative chain that makes empire palpable. When Fielding embarks on an official tour through Central India "to see what the remoter states were doing with regard to English education," in part 3, he does so as a link in the chain.[66] The connection Forster had famously urged in *Howards End* (1910) was to be between the world of sensibility and moral concern, where "personal relations" count for most, and the world of "telegrams and anger."[67] But in the interim it was the telegrams that had done the connecting. *A Passage to India* just about acknowledges as much. In that respect, it was pretty much alone in the literature of empire.

From Energy to Information

There is a further context for the evolution of connective media in the historical sequence that leads from the nineteenth-century sciences of energy to the twentieth-century sciences of information. This context requires consideration not just in itself, but as a way to start to define how literature, specifically, set about representing connectivity.

Introducing an important collection of essays on the cultural consequences of the supersession of sciences of energy by sciences of information, Bruce Clarke and Linda Dalrymple Henderson explain that the development of an efficient steam engine at the beginning of the nineteenth century resulted both in the technological reorganization of industry and transport, and in a new research emphasis on the mechanics of heat.

> At mid-century, the development of thermodynamics was consolidated in the modern energy concept. The mathematics of probabilities adopted in the statistical methods of both social and physical sciences carried thermodynamics toward a logic of order and randomness that later unfolded throughout the twentieth century in the forms of quantum mechanics, cybernetics, information theory, and the subsequent and ongoing expansion of computer sciences and communication technologies.

By the late nineteenth century, Clarke and Henderson add, electromagnetism had joined thermodynamics in challenging current conceptions of physical reality. Inventions such as X-rays announced radiant energy in the form of electromagnetic waves. "The discovery of radioactivity and the identification of the electron subsequently kept the thermodynamic and electromagnetic themes of energy in the forefront of the public's imagination well into the twentieth century." And not just the public's imagination, either. The scientific and technological discourse of energy pervades the manifestos and self-explanations broadcast by avant-garde writers and artists of the period. It became, Clarke and Henderson conclude, a "basic impetus for artistic and literary modernisms."[68] There is, of course, a danger in identifying a movement the nature, scope, duration, and value of which remain to this day so variously and so vigorously in dispute with a particular discourse, scientific or otherwise. Literary Modernism should not be reduced to a preoccupation with energy. It is, however, the case, as I intend to show, that what looks very much like a preoccupation with energy did give way, at some point during the 1920s, to what looks very much like a preoccupation with something else altogether: call it information, or connectivity.

There can be little doubt that the people who were there at the time, in London and other major cities during the years immediately before and immediately after the First World War, thought a lot about energy. "We might come to believe," Ezra Pound observed, "that the thing that matters in art is a sort of energy, something more or less like electricity or radioactivity, a force transfusing, welding, and unifying."[69] Pound invoked the idea of electromagnetism to claim that the imagination "gives light where it meets resistance."[70] He was by no means alone among his contemporaries, as Tim Armstrong has shown, in conceiving literary production as a form of incandescence that lights up the reader.[71] Scholarship has not yet quite established electrical energy as the formula for Modernism—that is, for literary and artistic experiment ca. 1910 to ca. 1925. But it seems at least reasonable to assume that scientific and technological discourse contributed to a reanimation of the ancient rhetorical sense of the term as vigor of expression: in Sir Philip Sidney's phrase "that same forcibleness, or *energia,* (as the Greeks call it), of the writer."[72] Much attention has rightly been devoted to the reception of the manuscripts of the sinologist Ernest Fenellosa, which Pound published in 1920 as *The Chinese Written Character as a Medium for Poetry.* Pound thought that he (or Fenellosa) had found in Chinese script a system of representation in which meaning is ascribed not so much to objects as to the lines of relation or force between. A poetry developing such a system could be said to have associated itself with science rather than with logic. "Valid scientific thought consists in following as closely as may be the actual and entangled lines of force as they pulse through things."[73] Technology, too, had its part to play in the Imagist or Vorticist poetic arising out of this renewed interest in the Chinese written character. As Christopher Bush has shown, the concept of the ideograph as electrifying sign was a modern Western invention prompted in no small measure by the emergence of representational media such as photography and phonography. The ideograph's beauty was that it at once united idea and image, and kept them apart. It promised, Bush concludes, "new, seemingly impossible combinations" of motion and stasis, autonomy and contingency: in short, "a language approaching the condition of photography."[74]

Jean Toomer's "Her Lips Are Copper Wire," a poem written around 1920 under Imagist auspices, and subsequently included in *Cane* (1923), the mixed-genre inauguration of the Harlem or New Negro Renaissance, richly demonstrates ideography at work.

> whisper of yellow globes
> gleaming on lamp-posts that sway
> like bootleg licker drinkers in the fog
>
> and let your breath be moist against me
> like bright beads on yellow globes
>
> telephone the power-house
> that the main wires are insulate
>
> (her words play softly up and down
> dewy corridors of billboards)
>
> then with your tongue remove the tape
> and press your lips to mine
> till they are incandescent[75]

According to Michael North, Toomer had been struck by Richard Aldington's claim that to be successful, an Imagist poem would have to include phrases that gave him a "shock of illumination." "Her Lips Are Copper Wire" literalized the metaphor. Electricity jumps the gap between lovers, and that between text and reader. "The incandescence is not simply sexual," North adds, "because its glow is the glow of words released from inhibition."[76] The parenthesis about billboards, for example, owes its meaning at least in part to its (liberated) position on the page. The poem's method (its "images," the freedom of its words) can be read back into its subject matter: the brightness of the lamps, the billboards, the lips pressed to lips. Toomer does appear to want his text to approach the condition of photography's shock effect, its flare of immediacy.

It remains, of course, a text. The ideograph also keeps idea and image apart. As Karen Jackson Ford points out, the association established in "Her Lips Are Copper Wire" between human bodies and technological apparatus in fact generates a "figurative conflict" between moisture and electricity, sound and sight, nature and culture.[77] The shock of illumination the poem delivers is less photographic than one might at first think. And that is by no means the end of it. There is a good deal of emphasis throughout *Cane* on the full lips of those who still feel their African ancestry most intensely. And yet the poem's final word, "incandescent," derives from the

Latin *candescere,* which means to become white. The lips pressed electrically to lips are thereby whitened. This parting etymological rather than visual shock may or may not have had something to do with Toomer's reluctance to consider himself a Negro writer. Either way, it demonstrates ideography at work.

Generally speaking, though, it does seem fair to conclude that "Her Lips Are Copper Wire" is a poem significantly preoccupied with electrical energies of one kind or another. Information, including information conveyed by electricity, does play a part. Someone needs to telephone the powerhouse to ensure that the system does not crash. But telephony itself is very much not to the point, because it is a process requiring insulation, and insulation is what the speaker wants less of. An apparatus enabling communication at a distance *cannot* be of interest when the urgent priority is to press lips against lips. We get a sense, here, of the awkwardness that is always liable to arise whenever a metaphor derived from the transfer of energy coincides with one derived from the transfer of information. The telephone call is not a shock still waiting to happen. Rather, it is an inertness, a non-shock: an act that, by requiring perfect insulation in order to take place at all, insulates itself perfectly from the rest of the poem. When it comes to phone calls, the tape had better not be removed. This is one metaphor that resists any attempt to gather it up into incandescence. The near-photographic poem's dead spot is the message transmitted by telephone.

Where the energized Modernist text ever so slightly fades out, information advances. That advance into consciousness, and into literature, depended on profound social and cultural change. It depended on the emergence during the first half of the twentieth century of bureaucratic structures of "generalized control,"[78] and of a new class of clerical and other clean-collar service workers whose job was information management (and who were known, not incidentally, to amuse themselves by moviegoing).[79] If the discourse network of 1900 anchored itself in the "symbolic terrain" of the typewriter, as we have been told, that of 1930—no longer, perhaps, in any meaningful sense a *discourse* network—was largely built upon the telephone exchange.[80] The telephone, as Lee Sproull and Sara Kiesler note, had a huge "organizational impact." "It led," they add, "to new occupational roles: telephone operator, telemarketer, call girl."[81]

The hope has long been that information might "constitute a new regime," as Katherine Hayles puts it, "an economy of exchange not bound by the laws of conservation formulated for energy in the nineteenth century." Information, unlike energy, proliferates endlessly without prohibitive cost. "Operating in the economy of information, one can dream that social position and economic class will cease to matter, that one could even loosen the constraints of living in a single body located at a single position in space and time." One can dream: until physical time and space, not to mention class, gender, race, and so on, "reassert their inevitability." Several preoccupations take shape at the point where freedom encounters constraint (or constraint freedom): how to articulate the human body with its enabling prostheses; how to conceive subjectivities "reconfigured for a regime of information." Furthermore, in that regime, "struggles for possession yield to issues of access, narrators characterized as speaking or writing voices shift to decoders and encoders, and flat signifiers are transformed into accordion structures whose expansions and contractions across multiple levels are regulated by coding rules."[82] The signifiers that will concern me here (even when they belong in *Finnegans Wake*) are print's flat signifiers. Like Menke, I aim to explore the power and the limits of written textuality in an age busy producing alternatives to it. But the other two preoccupations outlined by Hayles—with the body and its prostheses, and with subjectivities reconfigured for a regime of information—arose vividly in literature between the wars.

Hayles traces the shift from an energy to an information regime by examining three variously transitional stories: Henry James's "In the Cage," written in 1898, and two post–Second World War texts, by Philip K. Dick and James Tiptree. In each case, the regime of information looks like an escape route, the basis for a viable and wildly appealing alternative existence, but turns out to be another version of constraint by class, gender, race, mortality, and so on. James's caged telegraph girl uses her expertise in codes to reconstruct, and possibly to prepare the way for participation in, the glamorous extramarital affair Captain Everard is conducting with Lady Bradeen, as a way out of engagement to timid Mr. Mudge, the grocer. But she realizes that Everard, having exploited the knowledge she freely offers him, would only ever exploit her, too, if she were freely to offer herself. That knowledge is not in itself substantial enough to provide the basis for a viable existence. "At the close of the nineteenth-century," Hayles observes, "the regime of information had not penetrated far enough into the social infrastructure to maintain itself as a separate space."[83] If her analysis of the texts by Dick and Tiptree is anything to go by, the prospects for the transcendence of economic, social, and physical constraint through telecommunication had not improved greatly by the 1960s. My argument here, by contrast, will be that telephony had by the late 1920s sufficiently penetrated the infrastructure of British society to create a "separate space" in which, as I shall show, access to information really did matter. The traffic of interactions at a distance that I investigate in Chapter 1 scarcely amounts to transcendence. But it did provide, especially where young, independent women were concerned, the basis for a viable and appealing existence. By 1930, Britain was no mere shrinking island.[84] The interest Bowen, Woolf, and others took in such developments amounted to a good deal more than the adoption of a "cosmopolitan style."[85] As we shall see in Chapter 1, it amounted to a gradual and enduring redefinition of community.

The proof of this assertion lies not only in the establishment of telephony as a fully fledged social (as well as business) medium, but also in the fundamental change in attitudes to transport that is the subject of Chapter 5. For centuries, the term "communication" referred equally to the movement of people and goods and to the movement of information. Since the rapid development of air and automobile transport during the 1930s, however, the second meaning has increasingly supervened on the first. Cultural historians have on the whole understood mechanized transport as a representational medium or imaging system: a platform for the production of views. In the period between the wars, the genre that took greatest advantage of this platform to extend its range and diversity was travel writing, a genre now increasingly associated with literary Modernism. But a more fundamental change concerned the recognition that, for millions of the commuters worldwide, if not for tens of thousands of tourists, and the odd backpacker, transport meant connecting one place to another with a minimum of fuss. The recognition generated a new, and not especially Modernist, literary mode: transit writing. Even those writers who understood that transit had brought into being a new supranational class and habitat found it hard to represent as anything other than a scandalous negation. That is certainly true of Graham Greene's *England Made Me* (1934), a subtle reflection on the new internationalism made possible above all by mechanized transport (by cars and planes). Kate Farrant is assistant to and mistress of Erik Krogh, an international capitalist based in Stockholm; her brother, Anthony, a feckless drifter who has failed at empire and now needs his sister to find a job for him. Kate tells Anthony that "there are no foreigners in a business like Krogh's; we're internationals there, we haven't a country."[86] That deracinated way of life strikes Anthony (and perhaps Greene himself) as so perverse that it is almost impossible to imagine. Greene's figure for it is incest, the ultimate taboo: all the passion in this novel occurs between brother and sister (between a brother and a sister who have cut themselves off from the shaping energies of an allegiance to nation and family). Or almost all the passion. At the end of the novel, Krogh, losing Kate Farrant, has nobody to turn to except his faithful sidekick Fred Hall, another deracinated Englishman who has given himself over to perversity, if not perversion, in the name of finance capital. In 1935, the leading Modernist architect Le Corbusier had published a rather excitable book about aircraft that celebrates the "almost miraculous emancipation" this new mode of transport had brought about. "The airplane," Le Corbusier reminds us, "flies straight from one point to another." The grid or diagram imposes itself on the map, establishing a regime in which the possession of energy matters a good deal less than access to navigational and other codes. I don't know whether or not Greene had read Le Corbusier's book before writing *England Made Me*. But the flight Le Corbusier sketches from Amsterdam north across Holland and Germany to Copenhagen and on to Malmö is the flight taken by Fred Hall in order to stand loyally at Krogh's side.[87] Hall finds the commute a "comfortable dull way of travelling," but abstract, merely connective, and lacking "the atmosphere of third-class Pullmans to Brighton, the week-end jaunt, the whisky and splash, peroxide blonde."[88]

Other writers—Bowen and Woolf, again, but also Eric Ambler, Robert Byron, Christopher Isherwood, D. H. Lawrence, Wyndham Lewis, Kate O'Brien, Edward Upward, and Evelyn Waugh—found ways in which to imagine subjectivities reconfigured for and by transport understood as a connective medium. Transit writing, furthermore, does some reconfiguring of its own, in 1930s fiction. Appearing paratextually, as a kind of narrative feint, it obliges us to regard the text as operating on more than one level. We have not quite arrived at the "accordion structures" of which Katherine Hayles speaks, but we are getting there. It would be wrong, however, to ignore either the unease Greene obviously felt at the apparent withering away of allegiance to nation and family, or the difficulties that beset him when he had to represent what had begun to take their place. There was in the 1930s no great wave of enthusiasm, either among writers or more generally, for transcendence through telecommunication. The erasure of traditional communities by ribbon development and other forms of suburbanization created a need for face-to-face encounter that could not be met by listening to the radio or calling someone on the phone. In Britain, sociability became a political issue. In Chapter 5, I argue that sound cinema, evolving after 1927 in competition with radio, above all, but also with telephony, created an opportunity both to imagine a particular kind of talk as a moral and political value, and to incorporate this talkativeness into a social logic of space: an understanding of coexistence, of cross-class cooperation, of community, even. The result was a remarkable Popular Front moment, in American, British, and French cinema. I explore that moment by way of Greene's film reviewing, and of novels by Patrick Hamilton, J. B. Priestley, and Storm Jameson. But it seems to me that its most complex outcome was the cinematically inflected representation of sociability in a series of novels that set out to describe collective rather than individual identity: Henry Green's *Living* (1929), Dot Allan's *Hunger March* (1934), Harold Heslop's *Last Cage Down* (1935), John Sommerfield's *May Day* (1936), and George Buchanan's *Entanglement* (1938). These novels imagine an informal social solidarity—a certain kind of space, neither wholly public nor wholly private, primed for a certain kind of talk—which might become, in the fullness of time, the basis for formal political solidarity. What is at issue in this fiction is a sociability more casual and more egalitarian than the relationships between benefactor and client discussed by Bruce Robbins in his important study of welfare-state stories, but one no less productive of a commitment to the common good.[89] What is at issue, to put it more broadly still, is the future of the idea of the social in a society shaped increasingly by mobile privatization and its connective technologies.

The texts I discuss in Chapters 4 and 5 all explore subjectivities reconfigured, whether in enjoyment or in resistance, for a regime of information. They all understand that energy alone will no longer cut it. The concept of Modernism—the energy addict's aesthetic—has been extended instructively to encompass the literature of the period up to and including the Second World War.[90] But it does not have a great deal to tell us about those encounters with connective media that persuaded some of the best writers of the time to an understanding that energy alone would no longer cut it. My argument is that the response of representational media like literature and film to connective media like telephony and mass-transit systems offers as good a way as any of investigating the process by which, from the mid-1920s onward, a regime of information gradually superseded a regime of energy. Connective media demanded something other than Modernism.

Of all early-twentieth-century writers, none did electro-vitalism quite like D. H. Lawrence. In chapter 23 of *Women in Love* (1920), Ursula Brangwen, massaging the back of Rupert Birkin's thighs, creates "a rich new circuit, a new current of passional electric energy, between the two of them, released from the darkest poles of the body and established in perfect circuit."[91] By the time the novel had appeared, however, Lawrence was already writing the poems that were to make up *Birds, Beasts, and Flowers* (1923). One of the best of these, "Bare Almond-Trees," begins in Imagist fashion by picturing the wintry trunks as "iron implements twisted, hideous, out of the earth," but then takes a different direction. The fineness of the stems as they curve up in a parabola into the air reminds Lawrence of some other kind of implement altogether.

> Have you a strange electric sensitiveness in your steel tips?
> Do you feel the air for electric influences
> Like some strange magnetic apparatus?
> Do you take in messages, in some strange code,
> From heaven's wolfish, wandering electricity, that prowls so constantly
>   round Etna?
> Do you take the whisper of sulphur from the air?
> Do you hear the chemical accents of the sun?
> Do you telephone the roar of the waters over the earth?
> And from all this, do you make calculations?[92]

Like Toomer's "Her Lips Are Copper Wire," this poem has a telephone in it. The difference is that Lawrence wants to know how the apparatus works. His lines do not seek to discharge an energy they have stored metaphorically. Instead, they cautiously extend their own length in search of answers, flexing multisyllabic technical terminology: sensitiveness, influences, apparatus, electricity. The trees interest him in so far as they might be thought to transmit and receive messages in code. By the end of the stanza, the shift of emphasis from energy to information has become explicit. Lawrence's almond trees are calculating machines.

By 1923, there was plenty of strange apparatus around, in the form of radio towers and swaths of telephone wire. Some of it entered painting, photography, and film in the shape of a kind of non-ideographic ideograph: an image that looks as though it might reveal the history of its own consti-

After the Balloon. Frame grab from *M* (1931, Nero-Film AG, dir. Fritz Lang).

tution as meaningful, but doesn't. In Edward Hopper's 1928 watercolor *Adam's House*, the telephone pole with its bands of dependent wires fills the space between buildings, masterful, in its way, yet expressionless. The closest equivalent I can think of to Lawrence's bare almond trees is a photograph by Tina Modotti, whom he met in November 1924 in Mexico City, *Telephone Wires, Mexico* (ca. 1925): a sheaf of wires thrusts up and away from its merely mechanical point of anchorage, as dense as information flow itself. In Fritz Lang's *M* (1931), murdered Elsie Beckmann's ball bounces softly down a slope, while the balloon the murderer has bought for her rises into the air until it strikes some telephone wires. Lang holds the shot of the wires for an instant after the balloon has disappeared.

The shot is strikingly inexpressive, in a film packed to the brim with significant detail. Like Modotti's photograph, it is an image of pure connectivity. By representing connectivity, these images give up on energy's effortful production of a meaning that might simply be the meaning of effort itself. They give up on Modernism. For a long time now, debates about the literature of the first half of the twentieth century have largely concerned the poetics and politics of representation, with Modernism widely understood as having shaken representation's principles up like little else before or after it. Those debates will no doubt continue. But we need also to consider, with equal if not greater urgency, what happened to representation when it came under challenge from a different set of principles altogether. That is the debate that will shape literature and culture today.

Plastics

It is important not to lose sight of the second of the two preoccupations prompted, as Katherine Hayles points out, by the prospect of freedom through information: how to articulate the human body with its enabling prostheses. Telecommunication media disembody and etherealize. But the more ethereal the medium, the more abjectly concrete its user interface. The digital age is the age of keyboards, touch screens, and game consoles. During the period between the world wars, connective media, transforming cultures and societies worldwide, still found themselves brought down to earth, re-embedded in senses they did not claim to enhance: in touch, taste, and smell. Telephony, as most people encountered it, was not in fact at all an impalpable mode of connection. Domestically, and in the office, or the hotel bedroom, it was a creature of wiring, an apparatus. The apparatus, furthermore, if not the wiring, was there to be touched, and in some cases no doubt smelled, as well as seen. "Comfort isolates," Walter Benjamin observed; "on the other hand, it brings those enjoying it closer to mechanization." The main example he gave of this enhanced closeness was a new kind of telephone, "where the lifting of a receiver has taken the place of the steady movement that used to be required to crank the older models."[93]

In Chapters 2 and 3, I consider the representation of technology's closeness in literature and film as one strand in a more general acknowledgment of the consequences of the technological mediation of experience. I describe the expression of that acknowledgment as a form of "techno-primitivism." All primitivisms, of whatever era, require an understanding of the ancient in relation to the modern. Techno-primitivism operates within and upon the abstractions particular to technologically mediated experience by means of an awareness of synthetic and semisynthetic *substance*. That awareness could itself be considered "primitive," despite its focus on plastics, in so far as it drew primarily on the evidence of senses that nineteenth-century psychophysiology had classified as primitive, and which twentieth-century communications technology sought to transcend: touch, taste, and smell.

My hypothesis is that representation rearmed itself, during the late 1920s and early 1930s, with a new knowledge, not just of narrative space, but of material substance. In order to grasp the extent of that knowledge, we need a (selective) plastics timeline.

Modern comfort of all kinds was made out of many substances, including the wholly natural (such as shellac, used to make phonograph records), at one end of the spectrum, and the wholly artificial (Bakelite), at the

Natural	Semi-synthetic	Synthetic
ca. 2000 BCE–now: amber		
ca. 2000 BCE–now: horn		
ca. 2000 BCE–now: tortoiseshell		
ca. 2000 BCE–now: bitumen		
1770s: Rubber from Amazon basin becomes widely available in Europe and North America		
	1839–1970: Vulcanite	
1843–ca.1945: gutta-percha		
1850–1950: shellac		
	1862–1980: cellulose nitrate (celluloid)	
	1892–now: viscose rayon	
		1910–now: phenol-formaldehyde (Bakelite)
	1927–now: cellophane	
	1928–now: cellulose acetate	
		c.1930–1949: urea-formaldehyde
		c.1930–now: PVC
		c.1930–now: polystyrene
		1935–now: Perspex
		1938–now: nylon
		c.1938–now: polythene
		1941–now: polyester fibres
		1942–now: fiberglass

A plastics timeline. Adapted from Susan Mossman, ed., *Early Plastics: Perspectives, 1850–1950* (London: Leicester University Press, 1997).

other. But it is probably true to say that Western societies between the world wars were transformed by, and in the image of, the *semi*synthetic: rubber, above all, and versions of celluloid—essential, of course, in film-making. It was the tensions built into the idea of the semisynthetic that provoked the most far-reaching inquiries into the consequences of techno-logical change. The future imagined by Aldous Huxley in *Brave New World* (1932) involves new forms both of connectivity—"boxes where you could see and hear what was happening on the other side of the world"—and of techno-primitivist representation: "pictures that you could hear and feel and smell, as well as see." In contrast to television, cinema is under-stood as the medium best adapted to "primitive" sensation. That is why it is called "the feelies."[94]

Chapter 2 describes how Lawrence, H. D. (Hilda Doolittle), and Rad-clyffe Hall chose not so much to exorcise those tensions as to exercise them in creating versions of the "modern woman" (Connie Chatterley, Julia Ash-ton, Stephen Gordon). The modern woman, it turns out, should more strictly be thought of as ancient-modern, since what sets her free, within limits, is her awareness, through touch, taste, and smell, of substance; or, rather, of the stark contrast between the organic and the inorganic, be-tween nature and culture, built into the substances modern comfort now required. In Chapter 3, I show how the search for flexibility in building and other materials overtook Modernist architecture's fondness for plate glass. To be sure, Modernism itself had already unsettled that fondness. For Virginia Woolf, for Marcel Duchamp, for the genius behind the rede-sign of the Coca-Cola bottle, glass's great virtue lay not in its transparency, its status as both medium and barrier, but in the unique fashion in which it broke, or could be imagined to break. In *Jacob's Room* (1922), Woolf used the fact that objects made of glass do not necessarily lose their identity as objects when broken to explore the (almost) impervious vulnerability of a privileged young man. However, the development around 1927 of new semisynthetic plastics such as cellophane and cellulose acetate established standards of flexible transparency that glass could never hope to match, hard though the manufacturers tried. The world could now be *filmed,* or felt in the viewing; and not just on film. This chapter, unlike the others, will concern itself more or less exclusively with poetry. The "synthetic" En-glish variously devised by W. H. Auden and Hugh MacDiarmid in the po-litical 1930s throve on the narrowness of the gap separating adhesion (to place and time) from adherence (to a party line).

I stop in 1939, as I explain in my Conclusion, because world war was a one-off (or two-off) event that changed everything for the duration. After it, a media age of a different sort took shape under the auspices of television, while the introduction of the mainframe computer into the workplace prepared the way for information's current dominance over energy. The literature I study in this book is neither for nor against technology. It articulates, on our behalf, as well as on that of its original readers, the consistently altering attitude that technology is. When I say that it articulates, I mean, of course, that it expresses distinctly something we might struggle to express at all. But I also have in mind, more remotely, the medical sense of the term. The literature of the period joins together, or reassembles, the disparate elements of a media array. It understands that cinema, radio, telephony, television, and the rest exist in (often rivalrous) conjunction.

What might literature's "attitude" to technology's attitude have been? I am going to argue that, in eschewing "hot" Modernist experiment, literature developed, in skeptical alliance with technology, a philosophy and a style best thought of as "cool." In their illuminating history of the term, Dick Pountain and David Robins define cool as a "new secular virtue," the official language at once of a private or subcultural rebelliousness deviously recalibrated from generation to generation, and of worldwide commodity fetishism.[95] Various genealogies of cool have been proposed, ever more speculative in tendency as they reach back into the nineteenth century and beyond. The term itself, although current in isolated fashion in African American culture in the 1930s, did not enter into the general definition of an avant-garde until after the Second World War.[96] I will not be claiming, then, that the writers I discuss were self-consciously advocates or exponents of cool. But I do believe that they confronted, more directly than previous generations had had reason to, the problems to which cool was later to be proposed as an answer. According to Pountain and Robins, cool provides the "psychological structure" by means of which the "longest-standing contradiction in Western societies"—that between the need to work and the desire for play—may yet be resolved.[97] The writers I discuss did their bit to help create such a "psychological structure."

If Modernist energy generated heat, then coolness is a quality we have come to associate with the attitudes and behaviors, cultural or otherwise, endemic to an information age. In the most comprehensive recent account of the topic, Alan Liu defines cool as a manner of living in a world structured by technological and other systems. Liu's main concern is with the fate of the arts and humanities in an information age, and I will not attempt here to summarize his rich and complex argument. What I will do, instead, is draw attention to the metaphor he develops intermittently for the role cool might be thought to have taken in addressing the contradiction described by Pountain and Robins, between the need to work and the desire for play. The metaphor is that of slack. I rehearse it now as a way to think about some of the issues that will arise in this book.

For Liu, cool arises within and in some measure against the demands and protocols of that "knowledge work" that shapes and sustains the global, networked, postindustrial economy. "Structured as *information designed to resist information*," Liu writes, "cool is the paradoxical gesture by which the ethos of the unknown—of the archaically and stubbornly unknowable— struggles to stand in the midst of knowledge work." Of what does that "gesture" consist? Cool demonstrates that the alignment between technique and technology that has been the premise of both industrialism and postindustrialism need not be precise, or complete. Technique, in short, can be diverted, momentarily, as it slackens, or slacks off. Technique, the exercise of free will, reveals its true potential as the "same-yet-different *representation* of necessity": not (only) as obedience to the laws of nature and their social enforcement, but as a "reflection upon those laws." Liu's immediate examples are drawn from Web design. But his reiterated conclusion has a broad resonance. Slack, he argues, is a "hidden reserve that insinuates into each of the stray and informal intervals of work an archaism making possible an *act of judgment.*" What interests me in these formulations is their reliance on the concept of archaism. They arise directly out of Liu's engagement with an anthropological study of the South American Guayaki (or Aché) people.[98] In short, the study of cool is knowingly primitivist, and for good reason.[99] The good reason is that cool finds itself prefigured in the techno-primitivism that, I will argue, did so much to shape British literary culture in the period between the world wars. Literature, in a most precise sense, insinuated into the stray and informal intervals of work an archaism enabling an act of judgment. My major claim is that the techno-primitivism informing this literature constitutes not just an anticipation of cool, but a way to think about what cool is, and why we need it.

A pattern has emerged from these preliminary soundings. The advent of synchronous sound in cinema, the marketing of a television or "televisor" set, the crescendo of the campaign to define telephony as a social medium, the Imperial Wireless and Cable Conference that recommended the merger of all British communications interests, the invention of a further range of semisynthetic plastics such as cellophane and cellulose acetate: all these developments took place in or around 1927. If there was a year in which the world "changed," for literature at least, it may have been 1927, rather than 1910, as Virginia Woolf thought; or perhaps 1926, which saw the first-ever general strike in Britain. "Only from about the year 1926," T. S. Eliot claimed, "did the features of the post-war world begin clearly to emerge—and not only in the sphere of politics. From about that date one began slowly to realize that the intellectual and artistic output of the previous seven years had been rather the last efforts of an old world, than the struggles of a new."[100] Eliot was offering, in 1939, his "Last Words" as editor of the *Criterion,* as the end-stop not only of a magazine, but of a phase in literary history. In his 1937 memoir *Blasting and Bombardiering,* Wyndham Lewis arrived at a similar conclusion. The world changed for him, he wrote, in 1926, "when politics came on the scene." In this book, I will argue that what came on the scene in 1927, or thereabouts, was not so much politics as an awareness that the technological mediation of experience had become both widespread and irreversible. Of the two transformations, it may have been the latter that in the end proved most consequential. Lewis sort of acknowledges as much in the rather surprising warmth with which he greets the emergence of W. H. Auden as a public figure. "Is he *the new guy who's got into the landscape?* No: but he's got the technique of a new guy. I like what he does. He is all ice and woodenfaced acrobatics."[101] Auden, techno-primitivist to the core, as we shall see, could be considered cool. Like all techno-primitivisms, Auden's took shape within and against the increasing intensity of the technological mediation of experience. To gauge that intensity, we need to turn our attention to the moment when the world's first fully accessible real-time telecommunications technology "came on the scene." It is time to get to the phone.

ONE

☷|☷

Telephony

THE AIM OF THIS CHAPTER is to describe how telephony changed the social and cultural game in Britain between the world wars, and literature's game, too. Telephony could be said to have introduced into the experience of the increasingly self-confident middle classes an idea of *connective sociability:* connecting in order to connect, connecting in order to stay connected, at a distance. Since the connections it made put one person's privacy directly and immediately in touch—but not, of course, in *touch*—with another's, the new sociability would have to be understood as somehow subsuming the social as constituted by face-to-face encounters in a public or semipublic space, rather than merely bypassing it. According to what rules were such exchanges to be conducted? It is a question whose urgency has scarcely been diminished by the global proliferation of social media today.

Literature seized eagerly on the paradoxes of connective sociability. Instantaneous, palpable intimacy at a distance, such as letter and telegram could not provide, added a shape to the repertoire of directions it was possible to imagine a life assuming: neither upward into marriage and renown, nor downward into the abyss, as in so much nineteenth- and early-twentieth-century fiction, but straight ahead at the given level, by a kind of pulsation or stoical to-and-fro, taking liberties wherever and whenever possible. Furthermore, telephony had significantly enhanced the status of dialogue in fiction; and that enhancement laid bare, at the very furthest limit of the uses that the medium's industrial and state sponsors were minded to envisage, a solitary-promiscuous erotics of connection, and, almost as disturbing, a kind of clannishness. These are my topics.

38

Commenting on approaches made to the postmaster general by a delegation of telephone manufacturing interests in July 1932, a *Times* editorial observed that the "special irritation which commonly accompanies this form of social intercourse"—people still did not know how to use the technology, and, even when they did, it could not be relied on to work properly—would soon be a thing of the past. "The future of the industry will then depend upon the increased sociability of the public. As a nation English people do not feel the same urge as do Americans to ring up strangers, or to assist in the general spread of information." Sociability has been redefined, for the telephone-renting classes, as a peculiarly unsociable, or at any rate unsocial, exploration of linked privacies: one that does not require the participants to represent themselves to each other physically, morally, or politically. What kind of fun is it, exactly, to "assist in the general spread of information"? What national benefit might flow from such assistance? The editorial writer acknowledges that there is something missing from the idea of connective sociability he or she has put forward, but blames it all on the Post Office.

> The eager would-be telephoner, who installs a machine and practises with a real friend, finds the Post Office gives him two enormous volumes of possible people to ring up, but has no suggestions, beyond avoiding "Hello," as to what can be said to this almost bewildering assemblage of fellow-players. Although it is in a position to learn almost everything, bit by bit, about its subscribers, it offers no hints to the timid newcomer about what subjects are welcome to which particular people.

Already, it seems, there was some awareness of the capacity of connective technologies to produce information about those who use them (meta-data): a capacity that today's social media exploit to the full. The *Times* had some suggestions about producing meta-data. The telephoner needed to get a sense of who his or her fellow players might be, and of what rules they might habitually play by. "A great many people, particularly unoccupied women with mornings to fill, would welcome general chat with strangers, as they welcome talk in a train, and it should be a simple matter to reserve a special type in the Directory for those who would welcome new telephone friends." To begin with, this sentence basks in the prospect of a benign normality: the housewife who fills her morning with general chat of the kind customarily conducted in a familiar semipublic space such as the railway carriage. By its conclusion, however, it has to more ambiguous effect proposed a special classification in the directory for the minority of subscribers wishing to indicate that they would welcome new telephone "friends." Such subscribers might furthermore benefit from the introduction of a "gently crooning bell, for purely social ringing."[1] Like the radio jazz crooner, the social bell murmurs its invitation into the listener's receptive ear. It all sounds more like a brochure for an online dating agency than a recommendation to the Post Office. Literature was to make merry with such implicit acknowledgments of the abnormality of the connectively sociable. In the fiction of the period, people who make regular use of the telephone are sometimes very odd indeed.

It might help, in getting at that oddness, if I were briefly to align my distinction between representation and connectivity with terms proposed in recent work in the history of media and the social anthropology of material culture. In a 1975 essay that drew on the groundbreaking work of Raymond Williams, James W. Carey compared "transmission" and "ritual" views of the purposes of communication. The ritual view, Carey suggested, should take as its focus the communicative "maintenance of society in time"—"not the act of imparting information, but the representation of shared beliefs."[2] In so far as it represents shared beliefs, communication can be said to result in community. The question to be asked of the *Times*'s players, when they respond to the gently crooning bell, is whether or not they are up for some ceremony, for a little "maintenance of society in time."

By Williams's account, and Carey's, the history of the emergence of machines amounts as much to a social and cultural as to a technological history. To say that a machine "works" is to say a great deal more than that it can be operated. According to Roger Silverstone and Leslie Haddon, this is particularly the case when the machines concerned are communication devices. The distinctiveness of all such devices depends upon their "double articulation" both as technology (object, machine, delivery system) and as medium (expressive enablement of the "habits, beliefs, and procedures" that keep a society going).[3] This double articulation as technology and medium ensures that there is no transmission without ritual, though the scope for ritual will depend on the extent to which a given medium has been defined primarily for technological use. How much scope for habit, belief, and procedure is there in the welcome given, as the *Times* imagined it, to a new telephone friend?

Media, Lisa Gitelman argues, are "socially realized structures of communication." They include both "technological forms" and the "protocols" expressive of a variety of social, economic, and material relationships that "gather and adhere" around that "nucleus" of technological forms. Telephony, for example, must be understood to include the salutation "Hello?" and the monthly billing cycle, as well as the wires and cables that connect one instrument to another.[4] There *is* ritual, then, or scope for habit, belief, and procedure, in telephony: though the *Times* was not alone in hoping for some juicier alternatives to "Hello?" My primary concern in what follows will be with the ways in which the socioeconomic relationships expressed by this particular structure of communication materialize in and as a relationship with the technological form itself. Silverstone and Haddon argue that appropriation into the routines of everyday life should be understood as the means by which new technologies are "cultivated." These technologies objectify the distinctive pattern of differentiations (male/female, adult/child, owner/employee, shared/unshared) constituting a specific "domestic geography."[5] Cultivation is that excess in our definition and use of a particular communication device that always and everywhere makes of its mere functioning a ritual or small drama. It constitutes a protocol whose nature, scope, and development can be understood historically. Using a plow, we cultivate the soil. Using a telephone, we cultivate acquaintance of different kinds, for a variety of purposes, and, at the same time, the instrument itself, to which we have in the process become to a greater or lesser degree attached.

The telephone probably comes as close as any communication device can come to single articulation, as technology rather than medium. But there is culture in the technology. Transmitting a message is always in some small measure a ritual act. That so much interactivity at a distance should suddenly have become available, in the 1920s and 1930s, provoked thought—and not just in the design and sales departments—about the ways in which people represent themselves to each other when interacting. As Gitelman puts it, "Media represent and delimit representing, so that new media provide new sites for the ongoing and vernacular experience of representation as such."[6] Steady improvements in the quality and reach of the telephone service in Britain from around 1925 created a new "site" for the vernacular experience of representation. The constraint upon that site—from the point of view of representation, of ritual, of the maintenance of society in time—was that the technological form constituting it allowed only for the connection of one privacy to another at a distance. As I have already suggested, telephony requires us to reanimate Raymond

Williams's term for the dominant tendency in the modern urban industrial life of the period. It *was* "mobile privatization."[7] Attachment to the telephone, unlike attachment to radio, say, or to television, or to the gramophone, radically privatized experience; although then, as now, the connection of one privacy to another might provide the means for the creation of social networks. Literature, plotting mobile privatization from within, found the paradox of connective sociability impossible to resist. Before addressing its indulgence of that paradox, I need first to tell the as yet untold story of how telephony came to prominence in middle-class life in Britain between the world wars.

Secure, Intelligible Communication

In the late 1920s, technological advances in the reproduction of sound transformed telephony more or less out of recognition, thus making it possible for the first time to grasp the specificity of the kind of talking customarily done by this means. In February 1934, the writer and activist Naomi Mitchison planned to visit Vienna in order to report on the most recent and bloodiest episode in the Austrian civil war, the siege of city council housing estates such as Karl-Marx-Hof. "Sam definitely wants me to come over. I rang him up last night—it was funny telephoning right across Europe, and the voice at the other end as clear as though it came from Bloomsbury; it made one's ordinary Newtonian space-time ideas shrivel a little and go unreal." It was the medium's efficiency that brought home to Mitchison the "unreal" absoluteness of the time-space compression entailed in its use. In the 1930s, telephony astonished by its clarity. Clarity made it hard to ignore the emergence of a new, and perhaps uniquely valuable, kind of talk. It also carried risks of its own, as Mitchison found out when calling her husband from Vienna. "Yesterday I telephoned to Dick, who had little news—and it was, in a way, unpleasant to be so apparently near and yet unable to speak plainly of urgent things for fear of overhearing."[8] The "apparent nearness" afforded by telephony could have been nearness to persons other than the one she meant to talk exclusively to. The danger might lie in interception, of course. But there had long been an anxiety that, since clarity on the line required clear enunciation, the call might be overheard by someone standing close to the caller. The specificity of this new kind of talking was understood to involve a negotiation between the two sorts of nearness of which Mitchison had become aware: nearness to an intended listener a long way away, and to an unintended listener or listeners in the immediate vicinity, or somewhere along the line. We need to take account of the social and material construction of each sort in turn.

Jonathan Sterne has shown that research leading to the telephone played a crucial role in the lengthy process by which sound became between about 1750 and about 1925 both an "object" and a "domain of thought and practice." The outcome of this process was an insistence on hearing as a physiological process, a receptivity that could be enhanced through aural "technique." The new understanding made it possible to design a whole range of prosthetic devices that would enhance that receptivity yet further. Vital experiments with the "phonautograph," the telephone's direct ancestor, enabled Alexander Graham Bell and others to isolate the ear's tympanic apparatus or function—which receives vibrations from the air and transmits them to the inner labyrinth—and to build technologies around it. "Even today," Sterne observes, "every apparatus of sound reproduction has a tympanic function at precisely the point where it turns sound into something else (usually electric current) and when it turns something else into sound."[9] The most palpable of the advances made during the 1920s— and one good reason why Mitchison heard the voice at the other end "as clear as though it came from Bloomsbury"—was the development of ever more sensitive microphones.

Tympanic function became, in the design and marketing of the telephone, more than a function. It became a principle or value. Telephone engineers in the 1920s concerned themselves, as Bell had in the 1870s, not with the vibration's particular origin or causes, but with its effect in general. The aim was to ensure that what needed to get through invariably got through. In 1929, W. H. Martin and C. H. G. Gray wrote in the *Bell System Technical Journal* about a new system that Bell engineers had recently devised for rating the "transmission performance" of telephone circuits. "From the standpoint of telephony," Martin and Gray proposed, "the major importance of a difference between the original and the reproduced sounds is determined by its effect on 'intelligibility,' that is, the degree to which the latter sounds can be recognized and understood by the listener when carrying on a telephone conversation."[10] Intelligibility became the measure of the effectiveness of interaction at a distance. "Fundamentally," R. H. Chamney observed in the *Post Office Electrical Engineers' Journal* in 1934, "the telephone exists for the transmission of speech with sufficient volume and intelligibility to enable conversation to be carried out between any two points." Intelligibility had been improved dramatically by the elimination of "parasitic" noise. "It is hard perhaps to realize that less than ten years ago it was almost an adventure to call from London to Aberdeen."[11] Hefty articles in the *Times* sought to explain how recent developments had established telephony as the benchmark for intelligibility in one-to-one communication at a distance.[12] In Stuart Legg's General Post Office film *The Coming of the Dial* (1933), a dazzling *Ballet mécanique*-style montage of objects in rotation introduces an eminently sober account of the tests undertaken by engineers to improve the quality of transmission. Where telephony led, in the reproduction of sound, other media followed: phonography, radio, and, as we shall see in Chapter 4, film.

You did not have to be a sound engineer, of course, to be aware of what was happening. Writers, like everyone else, went to the movies, bought gramophone records, and listened to the wireless. What Virginia Woolf remembered most vividly about the first broadcast she made, in April 1927, was "being shut up in a soundproof room, with a red light over the door, and a notice to say that if one rustles one's manuscript thousands will be deafened."[13] British fiction was about to confine itself and all who spoke in it to a soundproof room. Characterizing the first generation of novelists after Joyce, David Lodge singles out their decision to "foreground" dialogue— a decision he associates directly with the increasing prominence of the telephone in everyday life.[14] Dialogue came forward, as it were, while other modes of representation receded. In a 1950 BBC broadcast, Henry Green asked how literary art might best "create life, of a kind, in the reader." His answer: "Of course, by dialogue. And why? Because we do not write letters any more, we ring up on the telephone instead. The communication between human beings has now come to be almost entirely conducted by conversation." Dialogue in fiction had above all to be intelligible to the reader, whether or not it was an "exact record of the way people talk." Green might have been paraphrasing Martin and Gray. What mattered, to novelist and sound engineer alike, was intelligibility. For Green, the new criterion meant a change in technique. He proposed to write a novel "with an absolute minimum of descriptive passages in it, or even of directions to the reader (that may be such as, 'She said angrily,' etc.)."[15] Green's radical technique grasps telephonic communication as a new kind of talk by paring away the devices that embed it for us in time and space, in bodily appearance and expression. For him, as for Mitchison, it made Newtonian ideas go unreal.

In a series of BBC talks given in 1956, Elizabeth Bowen spoke of a certain "stylized" dialogue as the primary means by which contemporary novelists like Green and Ivy Compton-Burnett kept character "in evidence" or "in play."[16] Sexual intercourse and murder always excepted, she wrote elsewhere, "dialogue is the most vigorous and visible inter-action of which characters in a novel are capable. Speech is what the characters *do to each other*."[17] Green would have agreed. While Bowen's mention of Compton-Burnett reminds us that it was perfectly possible to foreground dialogue without showing any interest at all in telephony, there can be little doubt that enhancements of the medium's efficiency did prompt attention to the new kind of talk, and to the ways in which it might be thought to have adjusted the relation between technique and technology, free will and necessity, desire and obligation.

Consider the following passage from Richard Aldington's *Death of a Hero* (1929), a semiautobiographical novel set during the First World War. George Winterbourne, just back from the front on a fortnight's leave, has been met at the station by his wife, Elizabeth, and taken home. Pretty much his first thought, however, is to contact his mistress, Fanny.

Winterbourne washed, and worked desperately hard with a nail-brush to get out the dirt deeply and apparently ineradicably engrained in his roughened hands. He got a little more off, but his fingers were still striated with lines of dirt which made them look coarse and horrible. He rang Fanny up from a call-box.

"Hullo. That you, Fanny? George speaking."

"*Darling!* How are you? When did you get back?"

"Two or three days ago. Didn't you get my letter?" Fanny lied:

"I've been away, and only found it when I got back just now."

"It doesn't matter. Listen: will you dine with me tonight?"

"Darling, I'm *so* sorry, but I simply can't. I've an appointment I simply must keep. *Such* a bore!"

"Such a bore, as you say! Never mind; the visitation can't last long, and it doesn't matter, darling. When can we meet?"

"Just a moment: let me look at my memorandum book."

A brief silence. He could hear a faint voice from another line crossing his: "My God! you say he's killed! And he only went back last week!"

Fanny's voice again:

"Hullo. Are you there, George?"

"Yes."

"Today's Wednesday. I'm awfully busy for some reason this week. Can you see me on Saturday for dinner?"

"Must it be as late as Saturday? I've only a fortnight, you know."

"Well, you can make it lunch on Friday, if you prefer. I'm lunching with somebody, but you can come along. It'd be nicer to dine alone together, though, wouldn't it?"

"Yes, of course. Saturday, then. What time?"

"Seven-thirty, the usual place."

"All right."

"Good-bye, darling."

"Good-bye, Fanny dear."[18]

Aldington, as though anticipating Henry Green's admonition, has cut "descriptive passages" and "directions to the reader" to a minimum. By appearing to capture each utterance verbatim, however banal it might be ("Hullo. Are you there, George?"), while failing to indicate what it might signify to either participant, or to us, he creates a gap between information and meaning. We have more than enough information about the exchange, but we don't know what it all means. That, roughly speaking, is George's position with regard to Fanny, who has taken full advantage of the protocols of telecommunication in order to prevaricate. Her consultation of the memorandum book is precisely the sort of "slack" that the telephone expert can introduce into the relation between technique and technology: between the requirement to provide in response a further element of information, and the desire and the ability to endow that further element with unexpected significance, if only by delaying its production. Aldington rather over-emphasizes the significance of the delay by the melodrama of crossed wires ("And he only went back last week!"). But the fiction of the period was to generate plenty of examples of coolness on the phone.

With regard to the representation of telephony, however, *Death of a Hero* remains a transitional text. The system that connects George to Fanny is very much of its (First World War) era. It does not work properly. Malfunction generating ironies of one kind or another is very much the note of the relatively rare representations of telephony in the classic texts of British and Irish Modernism. The consequences of secure, intelligible telecommunication were just about the last thing on the Modernist mind.

In the first of the three scenes set in a London restaurant that compose Wyndham Lewis's play *The Ideal Giant* (1918), John Porter Kemp portentously expounds to a male companion his theory of the artist as "the Crowd at its moment of heroism." During the second scene, he phones his friend Rose Godd from a "dark recess" set into the wall of the restaurant. His new theory has to do with the manias that constitute genius. The telephone's abstraction of spoken discourse from its environment has engendered (or at least done nothing at all to control) a maniacal monologue, a monomania. The monologue, however, proves rather less monological—rather more interactive—than Kemp had bargained for. When Rose Godd shows up at the restaurant the next day, in scene 3, it turns out that in response to his telephonic injunction to act at all costs she has in the interim murdered her father.[19]

A call may convey crucial information, as in Ford Madox Ford's *A Man Could Stand Up—* (1926), when Edith Ethel Duchemin tells Valentine Wannop where Christopher Tietjens is, or none at all, as in *The Tunnel* (1919), the fourth volume of Dorothy Richardson's *Pilgrimage,* when Miriam Henderson, now working for a dentist in Wimpole Street, fields a wrong number.[20] In both cases, the rich evocation of embodied consciousness through free indirect style further obscures the content of an exchange itself already rendered opaque by fizzing static and circumambient noise. Modernist phones simply do not work, in the most basic technical sense; even when they do work, they don't, because their working is itself an estrangement, a disconnection.[21] A noteworthy estrangement, of course. "The event immediately acquires symbolic proportions," Sara Danius quite rightly says of the narrator's telephone conversation with his grandmother in Marcel Proust's *The Guermantes Way* (1921).[22] A telephonic literature began when, and only when, the event ceased to function as the catalyst for ironies extraneous to its successful completion in its own terms.

Successful completion depended not only on improvements in the reproduction of sound, but also on guarantees of privacy. Intelligibility had to be secured against interception and overhearing. From the outset, the effort to secure it created new physical spaces as well as new protocols: a reinscription of the boundary separating the private from the public sphere, whose urgency and force indicate just how thoroughly that boundary had been eroded. "Today," trumpeted the *Daily News* on April 1, 1891, "the new Telephone line between London and Paris is open to the public." A person with eight shillings to spare could now gossip happily with anyone in Paris she or he could find to gossip with for a period of up to three minutes. What most preoccupied the *News,* however, was not the science behind this latest technological triumph, but the material construction of the "chamber" in which calls were to be made. The marvel lay as much in the erection of a barrier in London as in the lowering of one between London and Paris. We learn that the person in London wishing to call Paris "steps into a little sort of padded sentry-box, the door of which is edged with india-rubber."

> When this closes upon him he is hermetically sealed, and might rave himself hoarse without conveying the faintest sound to anyone outside. There is a pane of glass in the door, so that the officer in charge could see the inmate of the box, though unable to hear him. On stepping in, the interior of the little cupboard is in darkness, but the telephoner by sitting down on the seat establishes connection, and an arc light instantly blazes out until he again rises, when it goes out till the next comer takes his seat. The telephone box is a wonderfully compact and all but perfect little institution, the only drawback being that it is entirely unventilated, and the person sitting in it is literally hermetically sealed up.[23]

As the repetition of the phrase "hermetically sealed" makes clear, the emphasis in this early assessment of the new method of telecommunication was on enclosure. The guarantees offered concerning privacy had literally to be ironclad. There had always been a degree of excess in the construction of privacy in public by physical as well as social and cultural means. The box had to be sealed, yes. But *hermetically* sealed, so that one could scarcely breathe inside it? While the requirement for clear enunciation may have eased somewhat, by the 1930s, anxiety about being overheard had not. By that time, secure, intelligible telecommunication had been achieved. But what was its purpose?

Marketing Telephony

During the 1920s and 1930s, the impetus toward an expansion of the telephone system in Britain did not derive directly from the General Post Office, but from the Telephone Development Association (TDA), a pressure group created in 1924 to represent the interests of the private sector cable and equipment manufacturers.[24] The TDA operated with the support of, but no direct connection to, the GPO. According to a memorandum submitted to the postmaster general on December 9, 1924, its principal object was "to popularize and extend the use of the telephone and to secure its recognition as an effective ally to business and a genuine, indeed indispensable, factor in social and domestic life." The memorandum frankly acknowledges the difficulties entailed in marketing interactive real-time communication at a distance. First, there is no commodity as such: "the one part visible to the average man or woman (the actual thing we call a telephone) is a comparatively simple instrument, and the rest is unseen." Second, the promise of instantaneous contact might prove hard to sustain. For the placing of a phone call via an operator differs from face-to-face service in that it always involves a hiatus, as the customer awaits completion, during which seconds can seem like hours.[25] The gradual introduction of automatic exchanges in Britain during the period enabled the Post Office eventually to live up to the grand promise of immediate interactivity at a distance. The stark pauses and interruptions that had rendered the phone calls in Modernist fiction so maddeningly opaque became a thing of the past. The most likely reason for a pause or interruption was now not technological failure, but a lapse—deliberate or otherwise—in medium-specific protocol. Hesitation, or background noise, or reluctance to answer in person: these factors had acquired social, moral, and even sexual meaning.[26] But such interactivity, even or especially when successful, still had somehow to be represented.

The TDA's indefatigable secretary, H. E. Powell-Jones, wasted no time in making himself felt. The script survives of a radio broadcast he made in June 1925. He began by observing that there were at that time in Britain about the same number of wireless receiving sets (1.3 million) as there were telephones. The tactic, clearly, was at once to appeal to the cultural and technological enthusiasms of the radio audience, and to point out what each individual member of it might be missing.

You evidently all welcome a regular or occasional voice from the world outside your own doors. But you are only half way round the circle, for you can't have, without the telephone, the tremendous additional satisfaction of talking back. And you can't pick out just the one individual, relation, friend, sweetheart, doctor, tradesman, whose voice you want to hear, whose ear you want to gain, just at that particular moment. You can receive a message but you can't give one.

The telephone, unlike the radio, was interactive and private. Powell-Jones went on to complain, in what was to become a familiar litany, that when it came to the number of telephones in use Britain lagged behind not only America, but countries such as Australia, New Zealand, Norway, Sweden, and Denmark, while struggling to hold its own with Iceland and Hawaii: "We as a nation have not yet learnt to appreciate the telephone, to visualize it as one of the essential services of modern life."[27] A *very* poor show. But how was this essential service of modern life to be understood or seen as such? Visualization remained a key term throughout Powell-Jones's voluminous exchanges with the various parties involved in promoting telephony.

In its first major campaign, a series of advertisements run in the London *Times* in June and July 1926, the TDA chose to present telephony as a way to generate wealth by transforming the means of communication. "More telephones—and telephones more frequently used—mean brisker business, increased efficiency and greater national prosperity." The emphasis on nation became explicit in the images accompanying each text, which visualize telephony as a material apparatus of cables and exchanges, an incorporative network. Overhead wires ("The Nerves of the Nation") snake across open countryside, connecting market town to factory, or festoon a scene of enterprise and bustle set outside the Bank of England building in central London, the heart of economic empire.[28] Secure, intelligible telecommunication was to be understood—visualized—in and through its connective effects, as a social and political value. The network—the system, the interlinked assemblage of cables, wires, exchanges, and booths—looms large; the user is nowhere to be seen. Image and text attempt to convert interactive telecommunication directly into nationhood. That was how AT&T had chosen to present telephony to an American public since 1908.[29] But this was a nation conceived almost exclusively as a commercial enterprise. In James Carey's terms, the initial TDA campaign amounts to a transmission rather than a ritual view of the purposes of telecommunication. It figures telephony as a technology rather than as a medium expressive of the "habits, beliefs, and procedures" that, as Silverstone and Haddon observe, keep a society going.

What was missing from it was any concerted attempt to develop a protocol of cultivation for telephony. But the TDA seems to have realized early on that a technology built for instant one-to-one communication could not be sold—in Britain, at least—as an instrument of system-building alone.

Departing from the American model, its campaigns began to visualize the individual user in her or his individuality. Already, on January 20, 1925, Powell-Jones had sent the GPO the brief synopsis of "a cartoon film illustrating in a popular and vivid way some of the benefits derivable from the installation of a telephone in a private house of the lower middle class type," which the TDA proposed to exhibit at more than fifty theaters nationwide. The script consists of three familiar domestic scenes: at breakfast, a husband, thinking that he will miss his train, calls a taxi; later, his wife, staring out of the window at heavy rain, orders a joint from the butcher; later still, she climbs a pair of steps to hang some curtains, slips, falls, and lies helpless, until her daughter and a telephone materialize simultaneously.[30] Here, the telephone does not generate wealth, or build a nation. Instead, it puts one person instantly in touch with another at a distance, and so resolves a series of major and minor emergencies. The emphasis has shifted from the telephone as technology to the telephone as medium. But it should be noted that this medium is not as yet a *social* medium in any meaningful sense. For the exchanges it permits are purely functional. The TDA had as yet shown no interest in the ways in which people might represent themselves to each other, except in a professional capacity, while interacting. The telephone, it seems, was to be cultivated primarily for use in an emergency.

How much effort and resource should a government department put into selling? Tensions between the GPO and the TDA crystallized around the need to create new markets. A GPO memorandum dated January 4, 1931, states that the TDA, in recommending the postmaster general to undertake a "telephone 'push,'" had referred with evident approval to the shoe manufacturers' practice of spending a large proportion of the cost of an item in selling it. It was felt that the GPO would not be justified in expenditure on any publicity other than that necessary to bring its existing services to the attention of potential subscribers. It should not undertake newspaper advertising. The TDA, however, soon came back with another suggestion. How about a national poster campaign? On February 5, 1931, G. E. P. Murray wrote on behalf of the postmaster general to the secretary of the treasury, arguing that if the current rate of expansion were to be maintained, devices other than canvassing and special literature might become necessary. "If there is to be any striking growth of the telephone service in this country," Murray observed, "it will have to be by the extension of the telephone habit to social strata in which it has hardly as yet begun to develop; and the experience of commercial firms seems to prove that constant reiteration of a particular idea in the press and as street hoardings exercises an important influence on the minds of the public." He requested permission to contribute £5,000 to a TDA poster campaign. On March 10, 1931, the Treasury sanctioned the expenditure, as an experiment. As far as I am aware, the posters do not survive. But the file contains a selection of possible slogans consistently emphasizing the practical domestic value of interactivity in matters both of convenience ("The telephone saves time and trouble") and of emergency ("Presence in absence—secured by the telephone"). Their rhetoric addresses the individual consumer directly in and through her or his most urgent needs and desires: "You are wanted on the telephone"; or, "Can a telephone call reach *you*?"; or, "Are *you* on the telephone?"[31] Such injunctions seek to bind technique to technology, free will to (moments of) necessity.

The British Telecom (BT) Archives contain a selection of pamphlets and flyers produced by the TDA during the late 1920s and early 1930s.[32] The emphasis throughout is on the practical domestic value of interactivity at a distance. What matters above all is the rapid and intelligible transmission of a message to the individual most likely to be able to act upon it without further delay. In 1925, the ideal user had been the businessman implicitly present at either end of each vital link in a system; by 1935, it was the housewife explicitly present in the home.

This flyer is thoroughly representative in that it envisages an array of functional interlocutors, from tradesman and box office clerk to doctor and police officer. In 1935, as in 1925, the requirements of secure, intelligible transmission remain paramount, even though the scene has shifted from office to home. Under the circumstances envisaged, indeed, any pause for ceremony—for the "maintenance of society in time"—might well prove fatal. Even the most sociable of the housewife's potential interlocutors—the husband in his office, the friend in her home—have a function attributed to them.

The telephone prevents anxiety by putting the housewife instantly in touch with "powers greater than her own." More potently still, it eases her out of that "womanly feeling of loneliness." Still, it is hard not to conclude that ceremony has at least begun to make itself felt, however tentatively, within the array of functions. Facebook this isn't. But there had been a change of emphasis. By the early 1930s telephony was being marketed as a medium for gossip. To cultivate your telephone was, perhaps, to engage in

The Tradesman · The Doctor · The Friend · The Police Station · The Office · The Box Office

WONDERS OF THE TELEPHONE

III.—The Happy Eyes of the Telephone-Wife

They twinkle and glow, those clear bright eyes of hers, because they are the windows through which all the sunniness of her nature shines out —unclouded by the worries of domestic life.

For her, one simple contrivance has reduced those worries to insignificance.

She is the Telephone-Wife, the wife for whom a thoughtful husband (or her own mother-wit) has provided a telephone. It is her ally and helpmeet to cope with harassing occasions.

That womanly feeling of loneliness! Thanks to the telephone, husband or friend is ready at hand.

That fear of burglars at night, or of fire, or of sudden sickness! Down the telephone lies the quickest path to aid.

For those workaday affairs— whether with butcher or baker or candlestick - maker ; for social occasions, foreseen or impromptu, whose going - right means pleasure and wifely pride, whose going-wrong means worry and the shame of failure —the telephone is her standby.

Her servant in big things and little, a breaker of isolation, a leaper of distances, a link with powers greater than her own — the telephone gives her that sense of care-freedom which her cheery eyes reflect.

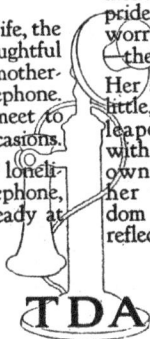

TDA

Issued by THE TELEPHONE DEVELOPMENT ASSOCIATION, Aldine House, 10-13, Bedford Street, London, W.C. 2.

The housewife explicitly present in the home. "Wonders of the Telephone." TDA flyer. Mary Evans Picture Library.

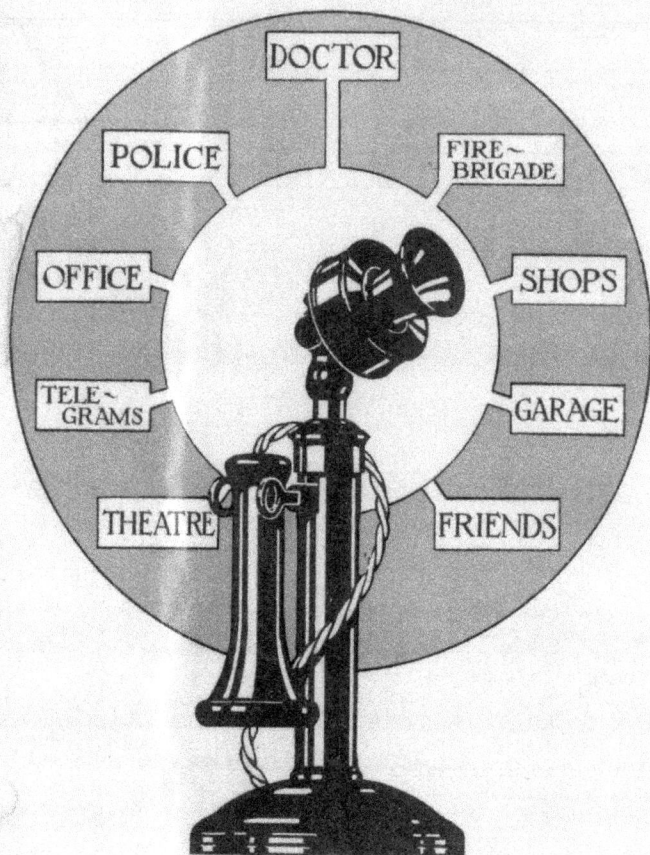

The array of functions. "The Telephone and a Few of Its Many Uses." TDA flyer. Courtesy of BT Heritage. Post 84/8.

connective sociability. We remember the hopes fondly held out by the *Times.* "A great many people, particularly unoccupied women with mornings to fill, would welcome general chat with strangers, as they welcome talk in a train, and it should be a simple matter to reserve a special type in the Directory for those who would welcome new telephone friends."[33]

Connective sociability, then as now, created an archipelago of privacies. In America, AT&T, although increasingly orientated toward the domestic rather than the business market, still put the emphasis on the collective, describing "the telephone—and, by extension, itself—as the restorer of community." "It Belongs to Main Street," affirmed a 1937 advertisement showing a phone on a desk, and beyond it, through the window, a familiar bustling small-town scene.[34] *Far Speaking,* a promotional film exhibited in 1935, begins in 1877 with a husband persuading his wife to install a telephone and ends, after sixty years of technological progress, with the couple speaking to their granddaughter in Japan. Telephony connects generation to generation, enabling gestures of mutual love and respect: the "maintenance of society in time," indeed. The TDA's campaign, by comparison, assiduously promoted the radical privatization of experience. And it did so, furthermore, by continuing to characterize telephony as a technological form rather than a medium. For example, the design of the instrument itself, unlike the design of radio sets, continued to owe a great deal more to engineering than to fashion. From 1930, an instrument that combined transmission and reception into a single unit held to mouth and ear began to replace the older candlestick model. It was called a "hand-microphone." By 1938, about half the phones in use in Britain were hand-microphones.[35] But that was it. GPO engineers firmly resisted attempts to modify the instrument's basic shape by the addition of notepad, mouthpiece, or magnifying glass. The whole thing, they protested, would simply topple over.[36] Whether candlestick or hand-microphone, the instrument simply exuded function.

Although the TDA remained active well into the 1930s, and indeed beyond, there is evidence to suggest that the GPO was devoting further resources to publicity on its own account. When it did so, it was in terms already established by the TDA campaigns. For example, an A3 poster found loose in the April 1929 issue of the *Post Office Electrical Engineers' Journal,* and no doubt meant for wider distribution, advised potential users to "Telephone It" under circumstances as diverse as a dinner reservation and a raging inferno. The "it" to be "telephoned" was always an urgent request rather than an attitude or a feeling. In April 1932, the GPO mounted an extensive display of equipment and installation methods at the Ideal Homes Exhibition at Olympia whose underlying motif was that "Every home needs a phone."[37] In July 1938, the *Journal* noted that the GPO's Public Relations Office had been responsible for an "upward trend" in publicity, through press advertisement, film, and "interesting exhibitions in very many towns in the United Kingdom."[38] The *Post Office Telephone Sales Bulletin*, launched in July 1935, struck very much the same note in the advice it gave month after month to telephone canvassers.[39] Protection—against disaster, inconvenience, and loneliness—remained the central theme.

It is probably true to say that the campaign for telephone development undertaken by the TDA and the GPO Public Relations Office during the period between the wars constitutes the first ever public advocacy of the principle of interactivity at a distance as a basis for the proper organization of (middle-class) social and cultural life. The starkness of that public advocacy—its entailment of a widespread "mobile privatization" of experience—was the challenge confronted by those writers who could not help noticing that there were phones more or less everywhere: 1,280,725 in March 1925; 1,892,658 by March 1930; 2,371,697 by March 1935; and 3,364,294 by September 1939. The GPO had celebrated the installation of London's millionth phone in 1937, and of three million phones nationwide in 1938.[40] Any novel, play, or film that showed the telephone in use thereby became itself a new instance of the protocol of cultivation. It had certainly occurred to GPO canvassers that novels, plays, and films might actually have a powerful effect on what people thought phones were for. The sort of popular entertainment in which phone calls had a disheartening tendency to bring bad news was not considered helpful. In the January 1936 issue of the *Post Office Telephone Sales Bulletin*, E. Dunnill, a sales representative from the South Midland District, attributed the irritation and mild panic often felt by subscribers to the telephone's association with "something unpleasant" in newspaper headlines like "Sound of Shot over Telephone" and "Fatal Telephone Message." Nor did literature help. In novels, he claimed, a telephone call is usually bad news. He made the point by fabricating a passage in an imaginary novel.

> Suddenly the silence was shattered by the blatant whirr of the telephone bell.

> "Who can it be . . . at this time?" whispered Sonia, apprehensively.
>
> Peter never answered. He crossed the room and picked up the receiver.
>
> "Yes, this is Mayfair 1292—Yes . . . What! Half-an-hour ago? My God!"
>
> Sonia saw his face, white, tense, tortured. Then he replaced the telephone.

Films and plays, Dunnill added, were not much better. One could only hope that the GPO's increasingly successful publicity campaigns would dispel this "sinister atmosphere."[41]

The publicity campaigns promoting telephony went to remarkable lengths to suppress its articulation as a medium in favor of its articulation as a technology. Rather, they found in a particular understanding of function as that which makes a suburban family tick just enough medium— enough expression or enactment of habits, beliefs, and procedures—to render the technology visible without, as it were, fleshing it out. But the inclusion of gossip among potential uses for the telephone rather powerfully indicated that there might be another and altogether more unpredictable ritual aspect to interactivity at a distance. Gossip will not order a taxi, or a joint of meat. It is one of the ways in which we most vividly represent ourselves to each other for representation's sake, as a ritualized strengthening of habit, belief, and procedure. Gossip put the sociability into connection. When the writers of the period took to representing telephony, they represented the (self-)representation it allows. They articulated it as a medium with greater enthusiasm than the TDA had ever shown. But they did so precisely *not* in order to claim for real-time interactive telecommunication the function of comfort and reassurance. That womanly (or in some cases manly) "feeling of loneliness" was indeed to be eased thereby, but not in ways the TDA had thought of. The easing literature had in mind, as I have already intimated, took the form either of a transgressive erotics of connection, or of a clannishness that had little to do with happy suburban families.

Telephone Sex

Roland Barthes once chose a telephone call to exemplify the "cardinal function" in narrative, the hinge point or risky moment at which the protagonist is obliged to choose between mutually exclusive courses of action.[42] The directedness of a narrowcast medium leaves no doubt as to whose choice it is, while its instantaneity makes a decision imperative. The protagonist's identity is suddenly, and with horrible explicitness, *on the line.* Such calls flexibly find out the right person, and more often than not prove efficient in obliging her or him to act. Barthes had Ian Fleming's James Bond stories in mind when defining narrative's cardinal function, and parallels could easily be found, as Dunnill's observations remind us, in the sensational fiction of the interwar years. In sensational fiction, the phone call could be said to provide a kind of meta-commentary, its usefulness in art mischievously reproducing its usefulness in life (if only to deliver bad news). And there were other kinds of fiction, some even involving the delivery of good news, in which it played an important part.

In George Orwell's *Keep the Aspidistra Flying* (1936), Gordon Comstock finally calls a halt to his stubborn attempt to live an unrespectable bohemian life when he discovers that his girlfriend Rosemary is pregnant. His carefully nurtured hatred of conformity and commercialization stands no chance against the prospect of fatherhood. Free will's skirmish with necessity has ended in (probably fortunate) defeat. All he has to do now is to call Rosemary and tell her that he will reapply immediately for his old job in an advertising agency. "He felt as though some force outside himself were pushing him. There was a telephone booth nearby." The mechanism of the phone booth, with its prescribed sequence of actions, at once effects and stages (or restages) his capitulation. "He pressed Button A. So the die was cast." In a nineteenth-century novel, this valiant if tardy act of commitment would have required an epic journey, or an equally epic letter; but it is if anything all the more decisive for its brief duration. "He came out of the booth. So that was that. He had torn it now, right enough."[43] Tearing it, one way or another, is what a phone call does. Here, as in sensation fiction, the velocity of the narrative event—one minute Gordon is walking along the street, the next he is virtually a husband and father, and the novel is to all intents and purposes over—merely reproduces the velocity of a decision taken under duress. Telephone protocol has short-circuited the protocol appropriate to courtship. That may be Orwell's point. But there were plenty of writers who sought to represent, rather than merely to reproduce, connectivity, and in doing so to expose the representation within it.

In 1936, John Grierson, the driving force behind the GPO Film Unit, described the telephone as the very "essence of modern life." "However much it pesters me," Grierson wrote, "it is nothing less than my liberty of voice." The purpose of the GPO films about the telephone, he went on, was to represent the device as "securing wide and intimate contacts in a world where wide and intimate contacts are necessary to the modern ordinary life."[44] It would be hard to imagine a more emphatic manifesto for mobile privatization. Grierson's insistence that the contacts thus secured should be both wide and intimate suggests, however, something a good deal more promiscuous than the TDA had in mind when encouraging housewives to call the butcher. By 1936, telephony had for a long time featured in explorations of the nature and scope of sexual desire, in art, and no doubt in life as well. The erotics of connection provides a route map to some of the most adventurous writing of the period.

Patrick Hamilton's *The Midnight Bell* (1929), later republished as the first volume of the trilogy *Twenty Thousand Streets under the Sky* (1935), largely concerns a waiter in a London pub, and his infatuation with an unattainable, waif-like prostitute. Bob wants Jenny as a waif, and as a waif only. She knows that prostitution pays, and will continue to pay until she is a waif no longer, and, what's more, that he will continue to pay her to be a waif until he has exhausted his hard-earned savings, at which point she can resume her full-time career as a prostitute. Telephony, combining distance with intimacy, immediate access with ample scope for deception, locks them into their double bind. For these are people who understand each other only too well.[45] Bob first encounters Jenny, at her most waif-like, when he waits on her in the pub where he works. Eager to "connect with her again," he spends his time off loitering on her Soho beat. After a couple of further meetings, and some initial outlay on his part, she concedes a phone number. Telephony, he thinks, will put her "at his mercy." "At any rate she could not elude him. She was accessible at the end of a line, and he could indulge his whim and pleasure in the matter of ringing her up." An invitation to call her at eleven on Monday morning, sealed with a kiss, creates the pattern of his desire. "Why was he so taken up with all this, and what his next move was in this so original and bewitching relationship, he did not know. And, since the telephone had entered into it, he had no need to know at present. He had her at the end of a line, and could think it all over during the week-end."[46] Bob's not knowing, or not needing to know, is in fact a kind of knowledge: at the end of a line is exactly where he wants to have her. The erotics of connection has subsumed the erotics of face-to-face encounter, rather than merely bypassing it.

In order to cultivate his acquaintance with Jenny, Bob has first to cultivate telephony's technological form. Slipping out of the pub, he sets off for the phone box at nearby Great Portland Street station, his head full of the promise of close contact at a given moment. "The walk would take him about three and a half minutes, and he calculated to connect with her on the stroke of eleven" (*TTS* 91). "He saw with annoyance that it was one of those new ones, with Press Button 'A' and 'B,' and a lot of instructions. He had to read them all over again. He had only used one of these once before, and he didn't like them. He put in his two pennies and lifted the receiver" (92). The details of Bob's mechanical embarrassment bring home to us the extent to which his relationship with Jenny has been not just facilitated, but brought about and given shape by a prior relationship with a particular technology. Hamilton wants us to understand, furthermore, that the technology in question is a new one. This phone box is bang up-to-date (Gordon Comstock will have had several years in which to get used to Buttons A and B). When Bob finally gets through to the boardinghouse in which Jenny has a room, the voice that greets him is that of an "elderly woman" (92), the landlady, who undertakes to see if Jenny is home. The connection made has already fallen short of any conceivable intimacy, since it has been made with a semipublic space policed by authority, a hallway or lobby. It is a connection, furthermore, already weighted with economic necessity. "He had expended a pound sterling on her being in" (92). She isn't, of course. In her (alleged) absence, the landlady becomes in Bob's eyes a "loathsome" (93) monster whose primitive, mangled English brutally cancels the technology's promise of immediate close contact. As Hamilton imagines it, the relation between technology and technique, between the telephone system and the expertise required to use it properly, is one that sets the contemporary and the archaic in exquisite tension. That tension might contract into a double bind, or it might ease slightly, creating scope for virtuosity.

A second, fruitless attempt follows, the next afternoon (94–95), and then a third, on Wednesday at eleven. This time, it is the phone box, with its "stale smell and heat" (96), that appears primitive, a throwback, while Jenny arrives in a flurry of "vivacious spontaneity." "It made him go all funny with pleasure" (97). The technology has delivered on its promise of close contact at a given moment. Jenny's voice "came into his ears like siren's music, at once soothing and exciting, wrapping him round with fervid delights" (98). The balance of pleasure has shifted dramatically, though not, we suspect, the balance of power. For Jenny, no doubt as a result of long experience, has cultivated telephony rather better than Bob. Her telephone technique, which includes, of course, manipulation of the monstrous landlady, has created a degree of slack or give in its relation to technological necessity that permits a virtuoso performance of waif-dom, "at once soothing and exciting." Even after her abrupt departure from the lodging house has put an end to the "halcyon days of phoning" (160), she is able to maintain exactly the degree of control it had enabled her to establish from the outset, rationing "piquancy" (116) to perfection. "She had 'played him up' throughout—that was all" (165).

Hamilton did not attribute to the telephone any Griersonian "liberty of voice," at least when it came to the fulfillment of male heterosexual desire. In *Hangover Square* (1941), George Harvey Bone puts a call through to *his* blond siren, Netta, at the end of the novel's second part, and she lifts the receiver at the beginning of the third. Telecommunication structures relationship, and the text. Rather, it structures and is structured by the terrifying psychotic episodes that convert Bone into a remorseless killer.

> In the line of telephone booths there were a few other people locked and lit up in glass, like waxed fruit, or Crown jewels, or footballers in a slot machine on a pier, and he went in and became like them—a different sort of person in a different sort of world—a muffled, urgent, anxious, private, ghostly world, composed not of human beings but of voices, disembodied communications—a world not unlike, so far as he could remember, the one he entered when he had one of his "dead" moods.

The feeling of disembodiment induced by telephony and psychotic episode alike is also a feeling of power, a dangerous intoxication.

> *Brr-brr!* . . . *Brr-brr!* . . . He was on the table by her bed, breaking into her privacy, adding another complication to the mysterious complications already prevailing! It was very thrilling to have got right into her flat, right into her bedroom, disguised as a bell, merely by paying twopence; but the suspense was horrid.

During the suspense, Bone's primary relationship is with the mechanism, not the person who may or may not answer his call. He examines the instructions concerning the "engaged" tone closely: such is the form necessity has taken, in a mediatized culture.

> *Brr-brr!* . . . *Brr-brr!* . . . There was the longed-for click—a click which relieved the tension in his heart in rather the same way as the click in his

head relieved him from one of his "dead" moods—and he heard her say
"Hullo!" . . . [47]

If entering the booth had initiated the sexual and affective equivalent of
one of his moods, then the lifting of the receiver brings it to a conclusion
satisfactory to him in so far as it maintains the fantasy of intimate access.
The phone call has given Bone his clearest insight yet into the structure
both of his desire for Netta and of his psychosis. Once he has decided, after
further mortifying experiences, to allow the psychosis in effect to determine the desire by extinguishing it—and her, and his rival, Peter—he cul-
tivates telephony as the means to, or the medium of, that determination.
He coolly plots his murders by phone (*HS* 185–86, 189, 272). Hamilton
may even intend a grim pun on this proficiency. Bone has understood that
cultivation requires a performance, an excess of technique over technology. "He had got to be natural, to pretend to be hurt. They'd think there
was something phoney if he wasn't" (186). "Phoney," an American colloqui-
alism, predates telephony. It had more recently come to designate the
period of the war between the German invasion of Poland, in September
1939, and that of Norway, in April 1940. In the novel's penultimate chapter, Neville Chamberlain announces the British response to the invasion
of Poland on the radio as Bone tidies up the crime scene in his own crazily
punning way: "Netta, the net. Netta—the net—all complete and fitting in
at last" (275). Telephone users, in the fiction of the period, can be very odd
indeed.

Even if they are not very odd—to the extent, say, of wishing to marry
each other—they still play by a new (and still slippery) set of rules. One of
the most spectacular literary experiments in telephony was that attempted
by Evelyn Waugh in *Vile Bodies* (1930). Adam Fenwick-Symes and Nina
Blount conduct their on-off engagement more or less exclusively by phone.
What engages them, and perhaps renders them engaging, as something
new in fiction, is precisely the on and off of the engagement itself: life's
straight ahead at the given level, neither rising nor falling. Both, we can
safely say, possess expertise in the relevant protocols. They appear to have
cultivated telephony since birth. That expertise contrasts vividly with their
ignorance of the protocols concerning courtship. To put it bluntly, their
exchanges involve an excess of information and a deficit of meaning. Adam
either tells Nina that he has money, and that they can marry, or he tells her
that he has no money, and that they cannot marry. In either case, he does

not know what he is talking about. In either case, it is impossible to understand what he means by offering this information, and what she means by taking it precisely at face value. They may, or may not, "love" each other.

As the engagement between Adam and Nina unravels, so the informational content of their phone calls becomes increasingly exact, and increasingly obtrusive, as though that is all it can now amount to. In chapter 12, Adam explains to Nina that in order to pay his hotel bill he has sold her to his rival, Ginger Littlejohn.

> Adam went to the telephone-box . . . "Hullo, is that Nina?"
> "Who's speaking, please? I don't think Miss Blount is in."
> "Mr Fenwick-Symes."
> "Oh, Adam. I was afraid it was Ginger. I woke up feeling I just couldn't bear him. He rang up last night just as I got in."
> "I know. Nina, darling, something awful's happened."
> "What?"
> "Lottie presented me with her bill."
> "Darling, what *did* you do?"
> "Well, I did something rather extraordinary . . . My dear, I sold *you.*"
> "Darling . . . *Who to?*"
> "Ginger. You fetched seventy-eight pounds sixteen and twopence."
> "Well?"
> "And now I never am going to see you again."
> "Oh, but Adam, I think this is beastly of you; I don't want not to see you again."
> "I'm sorry . . . Good-bye, Nina, darling."
> "Good-bye, Adam, my sweet. But I think you're rather a cad."[48]

The point about this exchange, of course, is that it speaks for itself. Whatever it is that Adam and Nina still feel for each other, and about each other, will not survive the enumeration of pounds, shillings, and pence. We might note, however, the lengths to which Waugh has gone to inform us, through italicization, of the exact tone in which the two participants keep each other informed. The absence of meaning could not be more stark. What is perhaps most striking about the novel, and marks it as Waugh's most adventurous, is the extent to which it has been given over, in form as well as content, to the new kind of talk. Never more so than in chapter 11, which consists entirely of the transcription of two phone calls, one confirming that Adam has no money, the other that Nina will therefore marry Ginger instead (*VB* 154–55). Chapters are a generic convention that break the flow of narrative information into meaningful episodes.[49] Waugh has subordinated storytelling to the requirements of the new kind of talk.

Patrick Hamilton was by no means the only writer of the period who thought it appropriate to represent the new kind of tele-talk from the point of view of dependence or a frank appraisal of necessity: from the point of view of the prostitute, demimondaine, or déclassé singleton obliged to sell her body. These women work the phone: their mastery of its protocols enables them to sell themselves more successfully than they would otherwise have been able to do, and so keeps starvation at bay. In approaching the fiction that describes them in action, I want to resume my (that is, Alan Liu's) understanding of cool as a display of virtuosity that introduces an element of "give," "slack," or "play" into the otherwise determined relation between technique and technology. Jenny, in *The Midnight Bell*, is *cool*, for better or worse. Working the phone, she plays hapless Bob up.

Hamilton's sirens answer, or fail to answer, the call; Jean Rhys's make it. None more effectively than Julia Martin, in *After Leaving Mr Mackenzie* (1930). On her return to London, after leaving, or being left by, Mr. Mackenzie, her protector in Paris, Julia rents a room in a cheap hotel. She has brought with her the London phone number of a shabby-genteel businessman called George Horsfield. Julia most certainly operates from the side of necessity.

> She made anxious calculations and decided that with about another couple of pounds she would be all right.
> The thing was to keep calm and try everything possible.
> She found Mr Horsfield's card in her bag.
> At the telephone she became very nervous. Mr Horsfield was not able to hear what she was saying, and this made her still more nervous. The man at the bureau was looking at her. Julia fixed him with a cold and defiant stare.
> "Oh, yes," said Mr Horsfield. "Yes, yes . . . Of course . . ."
> Then there was a long pause while he was making up his mind.

Telephone protocol requires a vigorous disengagement from the public or semipublic realm of face-to-face encounter, either by stepping into a booth, or by a barrage of cold and defiant stares. It delivers in return an intimacy at a distance that could not be achieved by face-to-face encounter in the private realm. Had Julia called on Mr. Horsfield, whose address she knows, he might well have considered her presumptuous. Once on the line, however, he is hooked. A telephonic pause is no pause at all: for the line remains open, the expectancy at the other end of it palpable.

> He wished he could remember more clearly what she looked like. Then, as invariably happened, he gave way to his impulse.
> "Hullo," he said. "Are you there?"
> "Yes," said Julia.
> When he asked her if she would dine with him that night she answered: "Yes," smiling at the telephone.[50]

I would suggest that Mr. Horsfield has in fact given in not to impulse, but to technological necessity, or rather to Julia's expert technical manipulation of technology. The smile she gives the instrument itself is the slack in the system, the moment of self-awareness, which restores her dignity. She has played Mr. Horsfield up, achieving by telephone what she fails to achieve through face-to-face encounter when, at the beginning of the next chapter, she visits her rich uncle in his palatial home and is indignantly rebuffed. Julia is cool, for better or worse.

Rosamond Lehmann's *The Weather in the Streets* (1936) begins with a phone call. Olivia Curtis, who has left her husband, shares a small and congested London house with her friend Etty, getting by as best she can. The phone almost always rings for Etty. On this occasion, it is Olivia's mother, with the news that her father has caught pneumonia. The train journey to Tulverton throws her into the company of the local grandee, Rollo Spencer, now prosperous and fashionably married, whom she had known well when they were younger. They embark on an affair that takes place in a parallel universe of assignations and muffled identity. Now the phone rings for her.

> The telephone rang in the morning. I was just going out.
> "Look here." He always said that on the telephone. "What are you doing tonight?" He was always guarded on the telephone, crisp, off-hand, he never spoke for long—only to make quick arrangements. He never said anything nice.
> "Well, I was having dinner with some people, and going to a film or something."
> "I see."
> "But I could get out of going—"
> "Well, I've got to dine in myself."

He was always like that on the telephone—non-committal—grudging, it sounded: rather putting-off till I got accustomed and could tease.

"Oh . . . It doesn't seem much use then . . ."

"I was rather wondering if we could meet afterwards? I can get away by ten. We might have supper or something? Unless you're fixed up?"

"I'm not fixed up. That'll be fine."

It was a funny sort of half-hearted invitation . . . [51]

Once again, telephony does not so much facilitate the relationship as express it. Rollo's preference for the brisk exchange of necessary information makes it plain that he will always in the final analysis think, speak, and act from the point of view of necessity, as he perceives it. The most powerful feeling he possesses, more powerful even than his desire for Olivia, is a sense of obligation to his class: he will not leave his wife. Olivia, by contrast, learning how to tease him for his brusqueness, creates a little slack in the relation between technique and technology. That slack is her independent being: an expression of desire, a contempt for orthodoxy that will never quite amount to a politics. Rollo's funny sort of halfhearted invitations enroll Olivia in an intermittent, clandestine union that can never be made public (that is, social). Sometimes they have lunch in restaurants off the beaten track, which require less by way of concealment. "It came nearer to being a public relationship, a reality in the world there than anywhere else. Almost, the split closed up" (WS 163–64). Almost, but not quite. A telephonically regulated intimacy will never wholly subsume the social. Hence, perhaps, the measure of disgust it continues to induce in Olivia.

Telephony acquires in her mind—and therefore in the novel—a powerful association with obscenity. Invited to dine with Rollo's parents in their mansion, shortly after the encounter on the train, she tries to bring home to him, and to herself, the extent and depth of the social gulf that separates them. So much of her experience, she feels, simply will not have come his way. "Most particularly not those evenings alone in Etty's box of a house, waging the unrewarding, everlasting war on grubbiness—rinsing out, mending stockings for tomorrow, washing brush and comb, cleaning stained linings of handbags; hearing the telephone ring: for Etty again; and the ring before, and the next ring" (WS 77). In Olivia's mind, use of the telephone belongs unequivocally to grubbiness, understood as a grinding routine of make do and mend, a perpetual confrontation with a particular

kind of necessity. It soon acquires a further and more exotic layer of physical and moral dirt when Rollo's sister Marigold takes her off for a chat in
the mansion's "telephone room," where members of the family go to "put
their secret calls through." And not just members of the family, according
to Marigold, who is nobly revolted by the stink of the footman's hair oil on
a leather armchair. "She took up the receiver from an old-fashioned instrument screwed to the wall behind the door, and gave a London number."
She wants to find out if her husband is at home; the butler informs her that
he has been unavoidably detained in the country (99). This is a different
kind of dirt, but no less dirty for its difference. The secret room, with its
old-fashioned instrument and its feudal stench, expresses not so much liberty of voice as the furtive regulation of desire by an alternative necessity,
that of the maintenance of power and privilege. It speaks of a *requirement*
to transgress, a duty, almost. Marigold quizzes Olivia about lesbianism,
about her friendships with "queer people" (106). It is that duty to transgress
that Rollo will fulfill when making his quick arrangements by phone. Because his desire for Olivia is in its way merely dutiful, it will in the end
yield to other, yet more pressing duties. She, for her part, lives the TDA
dream, or, rather, beyond it, at its furthest limit. Telephony's provision of
immediate contact at a distance has indeed delivered her from "that womanly feeling of loneliness." In so far as she is *not* driven by necessity, or has
at least introduced some slack into her acquiescence, Olivia, too, can be
considered cool.

Perhaps the closest equivalent to the plight of the lovers in *The Weather
in the Streets* is that of the lovers in William Gerhardie's deadpan tragi-
comedy *Of Mortal Love* (1936). Gerhardie has flitted in and out of our
understanding of literature between the wars, mostly out. He made a precocious Modernist splash with *Futility* (1922), published when he was still
an undergraduate at Oxford, and *The Polyglots* (1925). Both involve over-
seas adventures (one in Russia during and immediately after the Revolution, the other in Japan) during which it becomes increasingly hard, for
protagonist and reader alike, to distinguish the exotic from the absurd, and
vice versa. The very few worthwhile accounts of Gerhardie's early fiction
quite rightly stress its literariness. Randall Craig, for example, has examined the aggregate or cellular structures of *Futility* and *The Polyglots* as a
development of and beyond the impressionism of James, Conrad, and Ford
Madox Ford. In these novels, Craig argues, art systematically mediates
life, its purposefully purposeless point of view a "welcome relief from the

impenetrable confusion of twentieth-century existence."[52] By this account, by no means inaccurate in itself, Gerhardie might appear to have been little more than an amanuensis to Eliot and Joyce. However, his third novel, *Doom* (1928), marked a decisive change of approach. From then onward, his fiction was to be set either in mundane contemporary England, or in some variety of utopia, or alternatingly in both. *Of Mortal Love*, which concerns an affair between a composer and an unblushingly promiscuous married woman, remains sober in tone throughout, neither exotic, nor absurd, nor sold on literature as a welcome relief from the muddle of existence. The composer does not compose much of note during the course of it, and certainly not himself. The affair begins, in effect, when the married woman's husband installs a telephone, thus rendering her accessible to her admirers through a medium other than chance encounter. It is thereafter largely sustained, like that between Olivia and Rollo, by phone calls. If there is anything aggregate or cellular going on, it has to do with the multiplying of means of communication: no letter can be considered complete without a follow-up phone call. Communication at a distance, connecting in order to feel connected, is in fact what both parties most fervently desire: nothing upsets them quite like the husband's threat to sue for divorce, since they really do not want to be present to each other any more often than adultery strictly demands.

Gerhardie, it would seem, knew that there was already in British writing a tradition of experiment prompted by the telephone's increasing penetration of public and private life. Several exchanges indicate a more than passing awareness of the most adventurous chapter in *Vile Bodies*.[53] *Of Mortal Love* provides some evidence to support my claim that by the late 1920s, media awareness had become the new Modernism. Gerhardie, however, remained too conscientiously Modernist to entertain ideas of cool. For his lovers, it all ends badly.

It was the "queer people" who most vividly constituted the limit of the TDA dream. Christopher Isherwood's achievement in *Mr Norris Changes Trains* (1935) was to reconfigure the erotics of connection as a parable concerning innocence and experience. For innocence, the world is all information; for experience, it is all meaning. The new kind of tele-talk, abstracting information from meaning, and content from form, put into question the moral and political advantage traditionally held to accrue to experience. Its cultivation of knowing innocence somehow nullifies that advantage. Young William Bradshaw, the novel's protagonist, is literally and metaphorically an innocent abroad. By contrast, old Arthur Norris, whom he first encounters on the train to Berlin, appears to have almost unbounded reserves of meaningful experience to draw on. It is not long before he has delivered an elaborate lecture on the "disadvantages of most of the chief European cities."[54] As their acquaintance develops further, in Berlin, so the breadth and depth of Norris's worldly wisdom impresses itself ever more sharply on his ingenuous young friend. But that is not all there is to him. Bradshaw's first impression, when asking him for a light in the train, had been of the panic in his light blue eyes, a panic that experience has done little to alleviate. "Startled and innocently naughty, they half reminded me of an incident I couldn't quite place; something which had happened a long time ago to do with the upper fourth form classroom" (*BN* 1). The panic in the light blue eyes sends Bradshaw himself back to school, back to a world before (adult) experience. Who exactly is the innocent, here? Norris's panic intensifies abruptly when his passport is examined at the German frontier. His "acute misery" does not look like the fruit of experience (8–9).

When Bradshaw visits Norris in his Berlin flat, in chapter 2, he is shown into the sitting room by a young man who immediately retires, leaving the door ajar. "From somewhere just outside I heard him say, presumably into a telephone: 'The gentleman is here, sir.' And now, with even greater distinctness, Mr Norris's voice was audible as he replied, from behind a door in the opposite wall of the sitting-room: 'Oh, is he? Thank you.'" (*BN* 16–17). This "little comedy" of telecommunication between adjacent rooms in a far from palatial apartment, a performance "so unnecessary as to seem slightly sinister" (17), ensures that the friendship between the two men will from the outset be mediated; indeed, that mediation is its essence. The next five chapters all open with a phone call, as Isherwood, like Waugh, gives narrative over to the new kind of talk.[55] The purpose of these calls is to make arrangements, or to gather information. They are a plot device. But they also contribute to the parable by defining innocence as an information habit. "When once Arthur had started telephoning," Bradshaw observes, it was difficult to stop him. "I used often to lay the receiver on the table for a few minutes knowing that when I picked it up again he would still be talking away as fast as ever" (26). Norris, for all his worldly wisdom, is the innocent party in all this. He remains profoundly inexpressive, as only innocence, dedicated to conveying information for information's sake, can remain inexpressive. Then, in chapter 8, the phone rings without answer (96). Norris has absconded. Bradshaw leaves for London. But physical proximity is of no consequence in an essentially mediated relationship. "I thought of Arthur often; so often, indeed, that correspondence seemed unnecessary. It was as though we were in some kind of telepathic communication" (112). When both fetch up in Berlin again, the parabolic function once assumed by the phone calls reverts to metaphor. "We regarded each other with the amusement of two people who, night after night, cheat each other at a card game which is not played for money" (163). He could almost be describing Adam and Nina's engagement, in *Vile Bodies*. In both cases, the exchange of (largely false) information has become an end in itself. Relationship defaults again and again to a mutual knowing-innocence pact. Feelings such as anger, apology, and remorse, so often the catalyst of meaningful self-expression in literature as in life, just fizzle out. "It was no good; we had returned to our verbal card-playing. The moment of frankness, which might have redeemed so much, had been elegantly avoided" (205). Norris's worldly wisdom has from the outset been an innocent performance: all (largely false) information, and no meaning. Encountering him has not provoked in Bradshaw the transformation that bildungsroman demands. He has learned that experience is reversible, which is a kind of knowledge gained, but a kind not exceeding innocence. Bradshaw's relationship with Arthur Norris is not sexual. But their verbal card-playing, often conducted at a distance, is the very stuff of the erotics of connection.

It is tempting to compare this telephonic-telepathic performance with those put on by the various "pseudo-couples" who crop up in the literature of the period: the pairs of mismatched yet inseparable male protagonists so prominent in the fiction of Wyndham Lewis and Samuel Beckett. The term is Beckett's. "Two shapes then, oblong like men, entered into collision before me," reports the narrator of *The Unnamable*. "They fell and I saw them no more. I naturally thought of the pseudocouple Mercier-Camier."[56] Fredric Jameson has argued that the pseudo-couple became in Modernist writing from Flaubert to Beckett a "structural device for preserving narrative as such." In his view, the modern plotless novel, with its antihero and its compensatory weight of "abstract stylization," was a result of the extinction of the traditional passions and interests by ennui and anorexia.[57] It is certainly true that Isherwood found in the phone call a structural device for preserving narrative as such, when the conventions of bildungsroman and romance would no longer do the job. The device brought with it its own weight of abstract stylization. For Isherwood, however, telephonic-telepathic pseudo-coupling was also, and more importantly, a way to think about existence in an information age: a pathology more precise, and of a greater interest today, than whatever might be indicated in this context by terms like ennui and anorexia.

Furthermore, telephonic-telepathic pseudo-coupling did not have to be homosocial in orientation. It might include heterosexual (or indeed homosexual) experience, provided that such experience fell short of self-expression. Beckett's Murphy and Celia form a pseudo-couple as compelling as Mercier and Camier, their innocent information-habit reignited at the beginning of the novel by a phone call that would not have been altogether out of place in *Vile Bodies* or *Mr Norris Changes Trains*. The presence of a telephone in the ramshackle room Murphy rents is explained by the fact that the previous occupant had been a prostitute. "The telephone that she had found useful in her prime, in her decline she found indispensable. For the only money she made was when a client from the old days rang her up." Beckett embeds connectivity in the flesh, in the immediacy of the instrument's sound and heft.

> The loud calm crake of the telephone mocked him. At last he freed a hand and seized the receiver, which in his agitation he clapped to his head instead of dashing to the ground.
>
> "God blast you," he said.
>
> "He is doing so," she replied. Celia.
>
> He laid the receiver hastily in his lap. The part of him that he hated craved for Celia, the part that he loved shrivelled up at the thought of her. The voice lamented faintly against his flesh.[58]

This, too, does more than preserve narrative as such. It is a thought about existence in an information age: something that will prove beyond Murphy's ability.

It is a quarter of a century since Valentine Cunningham pointed out that British fiction of the 1930s is "cluttered with cinemas, wirelesses, newspapers."[59] I have gone some way toward showing that we should add telephones to the list. The point, of course, is the manner rather than the fact of their substantial appearance in British fiction from the late 1920s onward: the shape they gave to the plotting of mobile privacy, particularly where young independent women were concerned. In Rose Macaulay's *Keeping Up Appearances* (1928), young, independent Daisy Simpson, from a suburban London working-class background, masquerades socially as her own younger, prettier, more popular, genteel sister Daphne, and by profession as Marjorie Wynne, columnist for the *Sunday Wire,* and (by the end of the novel) best-selling author of *Summer's Over.* Daisy's "undoing" is precipitated, in the penultimate chapter, by two phone calls requiring her to renew commitments she no longer feels able to sustain, one from her fiancé Raymond, the other from the *Sunday Wire.* Macaulay, like Beckett, stresses the palpable intrusion. "The telephone-bell rang, suddenly and sharply (for this is the way in which telephones always ring). Sitting up in bed, Daisy gave it nervous attention." The call is from Raymond, who proposes to pick her up at seven that evening. Her command over telephone protocol enables her to deduce from his tone that he has lost interest in her, but will not admit it. "The bell rang again. It was like a chorus of noisy cicadas chirping—the same cadence and rhythm and impertinent contempt of the repose of others." It is the *Wire,* commissioning this week's article, on the "modern girl" and romance. There is too much telephone, too much ease, too much nonchalance, too much coolness, in the way in which these communications have been undertaken: a fatal preference for information over meaning. In terminating both relationships, however, Daisy has no intention of turning her back on the advantages yielded to a young independent woman by intimacy at a distance. The final chapter finds her on a liner bound for America, "passported" as Daphne Daisy Simpson. Feeling, to begin with, like a near-suicidal Daisy, she is nonetheless approached during the voyage first as Marjorie Wynne, by some female fans, then as Daphne, by someone who used to know her aunt. She realizes, not uncontentedly, that she will have to continue to masquerade as both.[60] In a sense, those phone calls are the "doing" rather than the undoing of Daisy. She has found out about herself prosthetically. For the time being, at least, she will continue to feel and know by means of the further artifice of a passport bearing the name "Daphne Daisy Simpson."

Much the same could be said of another journalist, Rosamund Miller, in Walter Allen's *Blind Man's Ditch* (1939). Rosamund, a self-confessed "bitch," goes to great lengths to keep herself free of "emotional entanglements."

> She thought of what she had: her own flat, decorated and furnished as she liked it; the telephone at her bedside: her independence. She wasn't jeopardising this for anybody: it has been too hardly won. She thought of the telephone at her bedside as the symbol of her independence. A telephone

was a good thing. You could ring up people when you were bored; or people rang you up. But at the end of the telephone you were safe from contacts; you had control of the situation; when the conversation was no longer amusing, when the person at the other end began to trespass on your privacy, you rang off, and that was the end of it. She wanted human contacts to be as simple as that: when you'd had enough you put the receiver back on its rest.[61]

It is a manifesto for the first media age, and for the cool the age demanded. Rosamund's creator, we might note, evidently thinks rather better of her than she does herself. Telephony cut both male and female writers some narrative slack. It enabled them coolly to propose destinies—for independent young women in particular—that they might otherwise have struggled to imagine.

Connective Sociability: Bowen and Woolf

The novels so far discussed in this chapter certainly did their bit to advance the TDA's slowly developing emphasis on telephony as a social medium, if not, perhaps, in ways the TDA would have approved of. They dwelt in crisp detail on the emergent protocols surrounding the technological form. But the genre's enduring concern with sexual transgression, combined with a more recent sense that the telephone had become the weapon of choice among adulterers and prostitutes, left little scope for the housewife who on a rainy day calls a taxi to take her to the shops. Phones are for sex, in the fiction of the period, out of desire, or necessity, or both. Addressing the will to promiscuity, as it informs (to a degree) the lives of men and women of different ages, backgrounds, and ambitions, these novels themselves become (to a degree) formally promiscuous. They do not, however, by the same token, have a great deal to say about connective sociability: connecting in order to connect, connecting in order to stay connected, at a distance. That is an omission richly made up for by Elizabeth Bowen, in *To the North* (1932), and by Virginia Woolf, in *The Years* (1938).

To the North is knowingly a novel of modern life. "The age of speed," Bowen said, "came into being around me." She endowed her protagonists accordingly with an enthusiasm for transport. "Zestfully they take ship or board planes: few of them even are *blasés* about railways. Motorcars magnetise them particularly."[62] High-velocity motion and locomotion pervade

To the North. The widowed Cecilia Summers shares with her sister-in-law Emmeline a house in St. John's Wood, a demurely fashionable area in North London, and a certain restlessness. Both love to travel, and, it could be said, travel to love. Emmeline runs a travel agency whose slogan is "Move Dangerously," while we first encounter Cecilia on a transcontinental express, about to pick up a Byronic young man call Mark Linkwater. The novel's opening gambit proves deceptive, however. Cecilia soon loses interest in Mark; it is Emmeline who falls for him, suffers the inevitable betrayal, and contrives to kill both of them in a motor smash. Cecilia, in the meantime, has become engaged to sensitive, reliable Julian Tower. Speed sounds modern. But the equation between fast driving and fast living adds little to *To the North* apart from a brand of sensationalism patented by Michael Arlen, in *The Green Hat* (1924), whose glamorous protagonist seeks redemption by aiming her Hispano-Suiza at a tree. By 1932, speed as an end in itself was already old news in fiction. Emmeline's is a traditional romantic sensibility given the full romance treatment, the "splinter of ice" at its heart "bombed out" by Byronism, rather than simply left to thaw (*TTN* 47). *To the North* brings itself bang up-to-date in subtler fashion.

In her absorbing account of Bowen's fiction, Maud Ellmann points out that the "vast relay systems" that enmesh the protagonists of *To the North* are as much those of communication as those of travel. "The transport of messages via post, telephone, and telegraph," Ellmann argues, "combined with the transport of persons via motorways, shipping routes, and flight paths, has the effect of alienating speech and motion from the human will." Thus far, her analysis conforms to the media-theoretical paradigm that conceives of communication technology as a generalized historical given. But if we set that paradigm aside and concentrate instead on the protocol of cultivation defining the effectiveness of a particular device during a particular phase of its development, we can build upon the crucial distinction she has drawn between Cecilia's habits and Emmeline's. "If Cecilia fuses with her telephone, Emmeline fuses with the 'shadowy nets' of transportation: the railways, airlines, and shipping routes whose schedules she knows by heart."[63]

Cecilia's primary relation to telephony determines the "trajectory" of her actions in the novel. It is a relation itself determined, socially and spatially, by the strenuous efforts made from the outset to secure the medium's intelligibility against interception and overhearing. Those efforts reinscribed the boundary separating the private from the public sphere. In order to establish a context for Cecilia's telephone habit we need to return to the TDA, and in particular to its deliberations on the subject of domestic architecture. On November 25, 1929, the association's secretary, H. E. Powell-Jones, wrote to F. H. S. Grant at the GPO to report that perusal of American publicity material concerning the wiring of houses for telephony had convinced him of the need to attempt something comparable. He had already approached the Royal Institute of British Architects (RIBA). "I visualized, for instance, that if we could get every architect to include and indicate as a matter of course the site for a telephone, and perhaps one or more extensions, in the plans of every house designed to cost more than £x, it would be a definite help in the direction of getting more development." RIBA, however, objected to the use of their name for "anything that might appear as advertising": "we had to deal with the suggestion that, if they did anything for telephones, they would have to do in like measure for cement, bricks, Frigidaire, and so forth. I think we did eventually bring them round to the point of view that the telephone service ought to be regarded in a very different category from these." Grant replied on November 30, 1929, saying that the GPO engineers were already at work on an appropriate booklet, and that both RIBA and the TDA would duly be consulted.[64]

The TDA printed ten thousand copies of *Facilities for Telephones in New Buildings: For the Use of Architects, Surveyors, Engineers and Builders* (1931). The pamphlet dealt with four types of building—office, hotel, house, and apartment block—in each case offering advice on how to preinstall a "comprehensive and flexible system of run-ways."

> The telephone is entering more and more into domestic and social life. The rate at which telephones are being installed, even in small residences, makes it a matter of reasonable certainty that the time is not far distant when the telephone will be regarded as indispensable, not only in the homes of the well-to-do but in social circles embracing all grades. The three-roomed flat and the villa residence of six or seven rooms are already well within the scope of telephone development.[65]

On July 26, 1934, D. G. Freestone of the engineering department wrote to the public relations department to say that *Facilities* was not reaching the "builders of small and medium class property" and to suggest rewriting section 4, on dwelling houses, "in a less formal style," to be reissued as a separate pamphlet.[66]

The telephone in the home was a mode of one-to-one communication requiring some limited measure of general accessibility. According to the TDA booklet, the entrance hall was the location most frequently chosen in domestic dwellings, with a shelf or recess provided for the instrument.[67] As a liminal area, the entrance hall was secluded at once from public attention and from too exclusive a privacy. It secured the listener against both the world indoors and the world outdoors. To be sure, the entrance hall could be a drafty place in winter, as the *Post Office Telephone Sales Bulletin* pointed out, and there was never anywhere to sit; while conversations could easily be overheard by people passing through, or in the next room. But the alternatives were not much of an improvement. The best solution was to locate the telephone bell and the main receiver in the hall, with one or more extensions in other rooms.[68] All this bears directly on the care with which Bowen describes Cecilia's cultivation of telephony. The house in St. John's Wood Cecilia shares with Emmeline has the bell and main receiver in the hall, with an extension in her bedroom. Although she always checks the telephone pad for messages on her way into the house, she prefers, like Daisy Simpson in Rose Macaulay's *Keeping Up Appearances*, the bedroom extension to make and receive the calls that sustain her solitary-promiscuous lifestyle. While she sleeps, the phone stands like a sentinel beside her bed, guarding her and her privacy.[69] The conditions have been established for the exercise of connective sociability.

In chapter 14, Cecilia receives a call during a lunch party from Julian Tower, the sensitive and reliable man she cannot quite bring herself to marry. We hear every word of the distinctly uneventful conversation. So, it turns out, might all her guests have done. Going out into the entrance hall to take the call, she has left the dining room door open. Realizing as much, she slams the phone down on Julian's Gordon Comstock moment. "Silence sent a sharp vibration across the wire. Julian, hanging up, stared a moment more at the dumb black instrument, then touched a bell for his secretary." Bowen allows time for Julian to resume his day at the office, before returning to the lunch party to note that Cecilia's guests, who could in theory have heard everything she said to Julian, in fact raised their voices as if by agreement once the exchange began, and thereafter upheld a "strenuous conversation" (*TTN* 114–15). Bowen constructs an intradiegetic point of audition—the place from which a person present on the occasion would have heard something of what Cecilia and Julian said to each other—in order to establish its irrelevance. She lets us hear what Cecilia's guests have chosen not to hear (and could in any case only have heard indistinctly). The boundary separating public from private has been reinscribed by social rather than physical means: by politeness, rather than a stout door. The instability of this guarantee—its reliance on a protocol we cannot suppose to be universally observed—draws attention to the paradox built into the idea of connective sociability. How can it sustain its subsumption of the social understood as face-to-face encounters in public or semipublic space?

The only reflection Julian's call provokes in Cecilia is a reflection not about any message he might have for her, but about his relation to the medium. "She thought he was really bad on the telephone" (*TTN* 114). Yet in calling merely for the sake of calling, Julian has in effect announced his allegiance to her way of life. It is almost as though he is parodying in advance one of the TDA's favorite scenarios, in which an office worker calls his wife at home in order to relieve her of that "womanly feeling of loneliness": no doubt the TDA would have made allowances for a certain amount of manly fatuousness. Cecilia's relation to the medium is harder to establish. This is the moment in the novel at which we begin to suppose that she will after all marry Julian. But no such commitment can be decisive if one's first closeness is to mechanization itself, to the medium. On the afternoon of the lunch party, Cecilia, alone in the house, gives herself over once again to the telephone's "positive silence" (132). The silence comes to an abrupt end while she is sunk in thoughts of her dead husband, Henry, and of Julian. Hearing the bell ring downstairs, she plugs in her bedside phone. We never learn the identity of the caller who thus takes the opportunity to ask her out to dinner, an invitation she gladly accepts, while at the same time appearing to reassure the caller, who surely cannot be Julian, of her availability. "No, I'm alone, so happy: you know I am always happy alone" (134). Cecilia, unlike Julian, is good on the telephone. The network this social medium has established on her behalf, while including Julian, would appear to extend well beyond him, and well beyond the luncheon guests. There is something troubling about the way in which it has been constituted, by a linking of private spaces that circumvents the socially validated protocols of courtship through the exercise of very particular skills, through technocracy. A community exists, clearly, though not one founded on any discernible moral or political basis. Cecilia's happiness could be a foretaste of telephony's Facebook effect.

If the telephone was indeed to secure "wide and intimate contacts in a world where wide and intimate contacts are necessary," as John Grierson

hoped, then it could not afford to respect national boundaries and the pi-
eties clinging to them. In April 1921, the *Times* announced a "New Era"
for the medium, an era of "Talking Round the World," with a story about
links between Washington, DC, Catalina Island, and Havana. London,
too, might yet become the center of a global network. An Imperial Communications Advisory Committee was set up in 1929. The *Times* reported
new links to Latvia, by cable, in June 1930, and to Argentina, by radio, and
then Uruguay and Chile, by cable, in December. The aim, readers were
told in September 1931, was a "World-Wide Conversation." "The Importance of the International Exchange in London as the switching centre
for the world," one commentator remarked in May 1935, "cannot be over-
emphasized." Perhaps the most telling item of all is a full-page feature in
the *Times* of February 2, 1932. The feature consists for the most part of
photographs of agricultural life in England in the 1880s. But shoehorned
in at the bottom of the page is an image of Prime Minister Ramsay Mac-
Donald in his study in 10 Downing Street, inaugurating the new radiotele-
phone service to South Africa.[70] I have already touched on the part played
by these developments in the reconfiguration of empire as a Commonwealth of Nations. I want to focus here on the ways in which telephony's
expansiveness might be thought to have reconstituted community, of a
kind, within the nation.

   In *To the North*, Lady Waters remarks that the age is not just restless,
like all ages, but "more than restless," because "decentralized" (*TTN* 170).
When Harold Nicolson waxed sentimental about empire, Virginia Woolf
thought instead of the effects of transport and communications technologies. "'But why not grow, change?' I said. Also, I said, recalling the aeroplanes that had flown over us, while the portable wireless played dance
music on the terrace, 'can't you see that nationality is over? All divisions
are now rubbed out, or about to be.'"[71] By this account, the dance music
relayed to a terrace rubs out the divisions that establish national identity,
substituting for them popular perceptions of difference within a global order.
But Woolf knew that the wireless had more than one social and political
use, and that when *not* playing dance music it might well be doing nationalism's work. She remained deeply suspicious of broadcast media. In "The
Leaning Tower" (1940), she spoke of the menace in Hitler's voice on the
radio and went on to criticize the didactic or "loud-speaker" strain that in
her view compromised the poetry of Auden and his followers.[72] In wartime, the spectacle of fighter planes overhead made her hope that the thrill

provoked was not just a "communal BBC dictated feeling."[73] I will return more fully in Chapter 4 to the "loud-speaker" qualities of broadcast radio. But I want simply to suggest here that Woolf may have found telephony a more reliable solvent of communal dictated feeling than radio.

The Years tells the story of the Pargiter family from the 1880s to the 1930s, with a particular emphasis on the social and economic transformation of the lives of (mostly) middle-class women during that period. Woolf thought she had failed in her attempt to "give a picture of society as a whole," to turn her protagonists away from "private life" and so "exhibit the effect of ceremonies."[74] But it is worth noting that the women the novel is most concerned with begin it in the patriarchal family home and end it living independently in rented rooms. Its politics—its feminism, even—have to do with the radical "mobile privatization" of experience: with solitariness and promiscuity. Woolf knew very well how to use telephony's expansiveness to reconstitute community, of a kind, within the nation. On one occasion, she had tried to set Julian Bell up with Sylva Norman, author of *Nature Has No Time,* which the Hogarth Press published in 1929.

> Julian dines with us tonight to meet Miss Sylva Norman whom I fetched up from complete nonentity on the telephone last night. Another marvel of science. There she was in 10 minutes after we thought of her saying she would LOVE to come [. . .] They will dine with us; & that is what I am ripe for—to go adventuring on the streams of other peoples lives—speculating, adrift.[75]

It was the telephone's power to fetch someone (anyone) up from "complete nonentity" that *enabled* what Woolf then herself felt ripe for: that sense of adventuring, of speculation, of pleasurable drift, but at a distance, since the stage upon which the action took place would be other people's lives. Telephony was cool.

The measure of the change thus brought about is the fact that the section of the novel devoted to the "Present Day" opens with the rapid reintegration of North Pargiter, who has made a success of farming in Africa, not so much into family life or into the metropolitan heart of empire, as into a network of single women of different generations connected primarily by the telephone. The London to which North has returned is a system of intersecting flows of information rather than a community made known in and through ceremony. North's first visit is to his seventy-year-old aunt

Eleanor, who lives alone in a flat in central London. Here, he finds himself in company (too much company), including "that very talkative man, her friend Nicholas Pomjalovsky, whom they called Brown for short." After a brief conversation with Eleanor, he drives away, her final words to him drowned by the roar of his "little sports car." Face-to-face encounter is the very least of the modern metropolitan condition he has come back into. The memory of Eleanor's pleasure in her new shower bath absorbs him. "But the cars behind him hooted persistently; they hooted and hooted. What at? He asked. Suddenly he realised that they were hooting at him. The light had changed; it was green now, he had been blocking the way. He started off with a violent jerk. He had not mastered the art of driving in London."[76] The issue for him is not old-fashioned speed, as it had been for Emmeline, in *To the North,* but *traffic:* one solitariness brought promiscuously into contact with another at a distance. Traffic, Walter Benjamin noted in 1939, implicates the individual in a "series of shocks and collisions."[77] Woolf's understanding is, if anything, more radical. What concerns her is the subordination of flows of energy to flows of information. North knows perfectly well how to control his vehicle. He is not yet quite ready for *system:* for the predictable alteration of signals, for the semaphore of horns. Traffic has begun to refashion him.

North's cousin Sara is on the telephone when he arrives at the door of the room she rents in a lodging house somewhere close to the Tower of London. He hears himself described as "my cousin from Africa." "That's me, North thought. 'My cousin from Africa.' That's my label" (Y 281). Sara is in fact speaking to Brown, the man he had met in Eleanor's flat. Brown has a largely notional existence in the novel (his given name is Pomjalovsky, which no one can pronounce). North can just about recall what they had talked about. But Brown remains for him a network effect rather than an interlocutor, and in that respect exemplary. "After all these years, he thought, everyone was paired off; settled down; busy with their own affairs. You found them telephoning, remembering other conversations; they went out of the room; they left one alone" (286). Woolf's semicolons enact the cellularity enforced by mobile privatization.

North will be able to revise—that is, to edit—his own telematic and notional existence ("My cousin from Africa") once he has learned how to cultivate acquaintance through technology rather than the soil through plowing. An opportunity soon arises. When the telephone in Sara's room rings, and she refuses to answer, he promptly takes her place at intersec-

tion in the system of flows connecting one member of the dispersed Pargiter family to another.

> "Hullo," he said, answering the telephone. But there was a pause. He
> looked at her sitting on the edge of her chair, swinging her foot up and
> down. Then a voice spoke.
>   "I'm North," he answered the telephone. "I'm dining with Sara . . . Yes,
> I'll tell her . . ." He looked at her again. "She is sitting on the edge of her
> chair," he said, "with a smudge on her face, swinging her foot up and
> down."

> Eleanor stood holding the telephone. She smiled, and for a moment after
> she had put the receiver back stood there, still smiling, before she turned
> to her niece Peggy who had been dining with her.
>   "North is dining with Sara," she said, smiling at the little telephone pic-
> ture of two people at the other end of London, one of whom was sitting on
> the edge of her chair with a smudge on her face.
>   "He's dining with Sara," she said again. But her niece did not smile, for
> she had not seen the picture, and she was slightly irritated because, in the
> middle of what they were saying, Eleanor suddenly got up and said, "I'll
> just remind Sara." (Y 292–93)

Repetition makes it apparent that North has answered the phone twice:
first the sound of the bell, then the caller. Answering it twice, he has in
effect answered to the technology itself, first of all, and then to the person
using it. That is his first lesson in cultivation. Comfort, in Benjamin's formula, brings those enjoying it closer to mechanization.[78] The delay enforced by the need to answer twice enables North (like Cecilia) to convert
the experience of interactivity into the experience of representation. The
"telephone picture" he creates of Sara on the edge of her chair is both what
carries over from one locus to another, thus establishing North in a new
identity, and what has enabled Woolf (like Bowen) to advance her story by
discontinuities in narrative time and space.[79] The scene thus discontinued
will resume a few pages later with equal abruptness. " 'That's Eleanor,' said
North. He left the telephone and turned to Sara" (305). In the interim,
North's representation of Sara, which captures his solitariness, too, his
willingness to dwell on the smudge on a face, has begun to circulate promiscuously as a representation. Its circulation is a bit of culture arising out of,
but inseparable from, technology. Peggy does not get the picture until she,

in her turn, lifts the receiver to call a taxi (the TDA would have approved). She has perhaps been reading Gertie de S. Wentworth-James's *The Television Girl,* for the experience prompts her to note that the addition of a camera would significantly advance the further development of interactivity at a distance. "'One of these days d'you think you'll be able to see things at the end of the telephone?' Peggy said, getting up" (295).

Enlisting among the ladies who phone, North has made himself known far more effectively than he is able to do subsequently at the long-drawn-out family gathering that concludes the novel. Neither family nor empire can any longer represent him to himself. He has been caught up without estrangement in the solitary-promiscuous traffic of interactive privacies established in and through telephony. Reconstitution in and by solitary-promiscuous traffic prompts in him a diatribe against contemporary politics with its "reverberating megaphones" and "marching in step after leaders, in herds, groups, societies, caparisoned" (*Y* 369). North's one real achievement at the party is to pick up a young woman whose identity, like that of Cecilia's midnight caller in *To the North,* is withheld from us (332, 335). Bowen and Woolf radicalized the protocol of cultivation set out in the telephone publicity campaigns by severing it, first, from pure function, and second from family as well as from nation. Their novels render an idea of connective sociability that, although scarcely utopian, does enable groups of more or less "queer people" to determine in collaboration the trajectory of each individual life. They grasped the (ambiguously social) medium in a technology otherwise dedicated to the furtherance of mobile privatization. It is a theme I will return to in Chapter 5, when I discuss the reinvention of transport as a telecommunications device.

One further aspect of Woolf's representation of telephony in *The Years* deserves brief consideration, both to tie its interest in the clan of outsiders back into the erotics of connection imagined by Hamilton, Isherwood, Lehmann, and others, and to point forward to the rather different perspectives I will offer in Chapters 3 and 4. It strikes me as significant that the "telephone picture" North paints of Sara in *The Years* should have as its catalyst and focus a smudge on a person's face: the body revealed not just as matter, but as in some measure abject.

After North has taken the phone call from Eleanor, and passed on to Sara the message that they should get ready for Delia's party, he begins to recite a poem, Andrew Marvell's "The Garden." As he reaches the end of the poem's second verse, with its celebration of a "delicious solitude" apart from society, they hear the sound of footsteps outside. The harshness of their shared response to this sound, a harshness of which Woolf seems barely in control, is startling.

> "The Jew," she murmured.
> "The Jew?" he said. They listened. He could hear quite distinctly now. Somebody was turning on taps; somebody was having a bath in the room opposite.
> "The Jew having a bath," she said.
> "The Jew having a bath?" he repeated.
> "And tomorrow there'll be a line of grease round the bath," she said.
> "Damn the Jew!" he exclaimed. The thought of a line of grease from a strange man's body on the bath next door disgusted him. (Y 306)

The reiterations leave us in no doubt that something has arisen that is of greater moment than a quarrel with a neighbor. Sara encourages North to continue, prompting him with the line about delicious solitude. But he can't. The fear of physical contamination reinforces, and is in turn reinforced by, the fear of racial difference. Compounding racial with social difference, Sara explains that the Jew is Abrahamson, in the tallow trade, and engaged to a pretty girl in a tailor's shop.

> They could hear the sounds through the thin walls very distinctly.
> He was snorting as he sponged himself.
> "But he leaves hairs in the bath," she concluded.
> North felt a shiver run through him. Hairs in food, hairs on basins, other people's hairs made him feel physically sick.
> "D'you share a bath with him?" he asked.
> She nodded.
> He made a noise like "Pah!" (Y 307)

This, surely, is the dark side of mobile privatization. Solitary-promiscuous telephonic community has been constituted in direct opposition to the idea of the strange man's body in the bath in the next room. The social, cultural, and sexual exclusions that found this community will have to be reiterated interminably if it is to survive the pressures of physical proximity. Some kinds of smudge fit adorably into the telephone picture, it would seem, while others do not. The tallow-trading, Jewish grease on the bath—like the footman's hair oil on the armchair, in Lehmann's *The Weather in the Streets*—will have to be brought sickeningly up again and again.

Woolf and Lehmann stretch decorum to its limit in order to dramatize the force of the exclusions it may take to build a network, or conduct an adulterous affair. There were, as we have seen, other versions of what networking might require of its participants (those "fellow-players," as the *Times* had put it). "Neither Cecilia nor Mark had nice characters," we learn in the opening chapter of *To the North* (*TTN* 10). Emphatic though her assessments of who is good or bad on the telephone may be, however, Cecilia does not trade in social or racial discrimination. These other versions of solitary-promiscuous networking tend to investigate the sorts of smudge that might be regarded as integral to telephony, rather than its antithesis. The telephone picture is often in itself a dirty picture. In Christopher Isherwood's *Goodbye to Berlin* (1939), Sally Bowles, pictured by the narrator, puts in a call to her latest pickup. "As she dialed the number, I noticed that her finger-nails were painted emerald green, a colour unfortunately chosen, for it called attention to her hands, which were much stained by cigarette-smoking and as dirty as a little girl's" (*BN* 268–69). We remember that Aldington's George Winterbourne had worked desperately hard with a nail brush to get the dirt out of his hands before going out to a phone box to call his mistress.

The telephonic act involves clamping a prosthesis to one's face. This physical closeness or mutual contamination produces a new (networked) identity. Recall Julia Martin, in *After Leaving Mr Mackenzie*, smiling at the telephone. In *To the North*, Cecilia's first instinct, on returning to London, is to reestablish her network.

> Cecilia resumed home life at high pressure: before she was into her bath two people had rung up to know whether she had arrived. Then—as she could not bear to miss anyone—she was called twice from her bath to the telephone, and stood steaming and talking, while patches of damp from her skin came through her wrapper. It would have been sad to return unnoticed. (*TTN* 27)

The patches of damp are a smudge integral to telephony: like the grubbiness of the house in which Olivia and Etty live, in *The Weather in the Streets*, they enact, or express, the never quite complete absorption of body into network. Cecilia's failure to attend to them, like Sally Bowles's failure to attend to her filthy, nicotine-stained fingers, alerts us to connective sociability's failure to transcend social and physical circumstance. We remember them even as the resumption of networking produces once again a new identity. "Cecilia felt herself crystallize over the wire, and recklessly made an appointment for tea" (*TTN* 29). Crystallization over the wire, and as often as not into recklessness: that is how telephony changed the social and cultural game. The crystallization, however, would never be complete. The pulses traveling down the wire were surrounded by more material substance than they could ever hope to absorb—to convert alchemically into pure information. That disparity, or disproportion, was something cool could exploit. In Chapters 2 and 3, I will consider the material substance not just of the body enfolding a mechanism like the telephone, but of the mechanism itself: of all the mechanisms that together constituted a process of mobile privatization reliant on connective media. I will try to define the proto-cool—the techno-primitivism—that arose out of a new awareness of new (that is, semisynthetic) material substances.

TWO

※|※

Techno-Primitivism

THE TELEPHONIC COMMUNITIES imagined in *To the North* and *The Years* are, despite (or perhaps because of) the pioneer spirit that sustains them, in some ways unforgiving, or harshly exclusive. There was something sectarian about all that crystallization into recklessness. The Bakelite cannot have helped. Marketed as impervious to heat, moisture, and electrical discharge alike, the material out of which most telephones were by then made lent its dourness to the virtual encounters they enabled. The GPO did its best to reinforce the impression by decreeing that you could have one in any color you liked, as long as it was black. Bakelite, invented in 1910, was the almost pure product of chemical formula. It is a thermosetting rather than a thermoplastic substance, and once molded into a shape stays that way. The molecules form a three-dimensional structure with cross-linked bonds that will not break down on reheating, although at very high temperatures the structure may collapse altogether. There is no give or play or slack in Bakelite. Although the protocols surrounding telephony allowed for displays of virtuosity—for cool, in short—the material interface between user and technological system did not. This was one device that could not be customized. Such obduracy was far from the rule, however, when it came to the technological mediation of experience in general. By 1930, there was a wide range of equally innovative but altogether more malleable materials on the market. Combinations of organic and inorganic substance, these thermoplastic materials proved as supple metaphysically as they were physically. Under their auspices, the various interfaces enabling the human body to withstand or gain some purchase on its environment, through touch, sight, and locomotion, became a source of pleasure, as well as of knowledge and power. In the longer term, an understanding of the virtues of suppleness fed back into the design and promotion of those connective media that had at first prided themselves on their status as technology *rather than* medium.

In this chapter I want to suspend for a while the question of connectivity in order to concentrate on the give or play or slack provided by a particular semisynthetic thermoplastic material, one no longer new, but nonetheless susceptible, as we shall see, to adventurous marketing. By the 1920s, rubber was a substance universally assimilated into everyday experience. Elastic in its essence, unlike Bakelite, rubber in turn elasticated the human body's contact with the technological and other systems controlling its environment.

I have chosen to concentrate on rubber because it was, among all plastics—the term designates a wide range of almost infinitely versatile polymer-based synthetic and semisynthetic solids—the one most widely understood as being at once ancient and modern, exotic and mundane. Rubber began as a natural plastic, but proved of little use industrially until, in the late 1830s, someone (in fact, two people separately) worked out how to combine it with sulfur at a high temperature, a process known as vulcanization. Thereafter, it gradually became ubiquitous. Electrification and the motorcar, the two most spectacular consequences of the second industrial (or techno-scientific) revolution, and between them the stimulus to momentous social and cultural change, both ran on rubber. And yet this substance that variously coated, supported, and interlined the miracles of modern engineering (both civic and homely) was itself, or had once been, palpably a product of nature. Chemistry transformed it, endowing it with suppleness and strength, but not out of recognition.

The imaginative opportunity rubber's hybridity represented, of exposing the archaic in the contemporary, the raw in the cooked, was not one a literary culture high on primitivism was likely to pass up. However problematic the assumptions it might be thought to encode, primitivism has long been, and still remains, a key term in inquiries into the wide range of cross-cultural encounters constitutive of literary Modernism, and into the proposals for social, moral, and aesthetic regeneration so enthusiastically derived from them. For if civilization has been identified "with mechanisms of censorship and with the debilities associated with distance from the 'natural' order," Tim Armstrong notes, "then primitivism ostensibly offers a route back to the 'original' and whole self; a vitalist self at one with its sexuality and being."[1] Modernism, thus understood, once again aligns itself with a science of energy: the science in this case being ethnography, which discovered in "primitive" cultures a vitality absent from "civilization."

The idea of primitivism has recently been put to productive use in developing Edward Said's argument that, whatever the map might indicate, there was nothing at all remote about empire: on the contrary, colonial business thoroughly informed metropolitan culture, right down to the "minutiae of daily life."[2] Primitivism can be understood, then, as the "vernacular" by means of which writers and artists "presented" the tension between sameness and difference inherent in everyday cross-cultural encounter, as John Marx has shown in his engaging study of the mutual reinforcement of two familiar Modernist narratives: that of reverse colonization, or the intrusion of matter from far-flung colonies into the recesses of the metropolitan household; and that of the displacement of feminine sentimentality by female sexuality.[3] Primitivist ideas also mediated the construction of queer sexual identities in the years after the First World War.[4] Indeed, the current consensus in Modernist studies would seem to be that Modernisms of all kinds make themselves and are made from the outside in, and that the local (wherever it may take place) "conducts the charge of the imperial and racial."[5] Electricity, indeed.

Primitivism would not be a bad way to describe rubber's fleeting appearance in two early twentieth-century texts dedicated to experiment. The Professor, in Joseph Conrad's *The Secret Agent* (1907), "grasping lightly" the "india-rubber ball" that will detonate his bomb, has grasped and been grasped as the power of utter insignificance, of absolute reduction: of the archaic in the contemporary.[6] "Jingling on supple rubbers it jaunted from the bridge to Ormond quay." The sight of Blazes Boylan's "jauntingcar," en route for the Ormond Hotel, and ultimately for 7 Eccles Street, has cut Leopold Bloom down yet further, at a low moment in the "Sirens" episode in James Joyce's *Ulysses* (1922).[7] Assonance ("supple rubbers") cradled by alliteration ("Jingling . . . jaunted") thickens style itself, reducing rhetorical form and function (what the carriage looks like, what its particular mode of progress at this particular time on this particular day might imply) to something close to sound. What more is there to say about Boylan than that he, too, represents the comic-brutish return of the archaic within the contemporary?[8] Both the Professor and Blazes Boylan could be said to constitute an energy absent from civilization's civilities.

On the face of it, there is not a great deal more to say than that about rubber's equally fleeting appearance in the three texts that will most concern me here: D. H. Lawrence's *Lady Chatterley's Lover* (1928), Radclyffe Hall's *The Well of Loneliness* (1928), and *Bid Me to Live*, by H. D. (Hilda Doolittle), begun as early as 1918, first published in 1960. All three could justly be described as primitivist in emphasis. When it comes to the rubber in them, however, the emphasis alters. I want to argue that the primitivism that crossed and thereby constituted so many narratives of the displacement of feminine sentimentality by female sexuality was itself crossed and thereby reconstituted, in these three versions of it, by a further *techno*-primitivism: one operating within and upon technologically mediated experience by means of a strong awareness of synthetic and semisynthetic substance. That awareness could itself be considered "primitive," despite its focus on plastics, in so far as it drew primarily on the evidence of senses that Victorian psychophysiology had classified as primitive: touch, taste, and smell. It bears comparison with, but cannot be reduced to, sexual fetishism.[9] In so far as it was an awareness of substance, and perhaps of the information encoded in synthetic or semisynthetic substance, rather than an awareness of energy ("the charge of the imperial and racial"), it was no longer Modernist.

I will begin to define the nature and scope of techno-primitivism proper by means of a case study of the most notorious of all stories concerning the displacement of feminine sentimentality by female sexuality. *Lady Chatterley's Lover,* though scarcely central to current understandings of early twentieth-century literature in English, remains the focus for productive inquiry into the cultural politics of sexual expression.[10] And there seems to be complete agreement among critics with regard to the primitivism of this text, and of its author's later writing in general.

During the First World War, Lawrence finally became convinced that Europe was in the process of destroying itself, and that renewal—if renewal were still possible—could only come from sources in a mentality at once beyond and before the civilization it had brought about. In works like *Fantasia of the Unconscious* (1923), *St Mawr* (1925), *The Plumed Serpent* (1926), and *Mornings in Mexico* (1927), he drew a stark contrast between a white European and North American civilization rendered lethally sterile by its commitment to Christian-Platonic idealism and doctrines of scientific-industrial "progress," and that of aboriginal peoples whose custodianship of ancient intuitive and animist modes of consciousness had encouraged momentous if ultimately futile resistance to colonial expansion. After the war, he traveled to Italy, Ceylon, Australia, and New Mexico in search of the few remaining custodians. His letters of this period express both contempt for Western attitudes and ways of life in toxic decline, and uncertainty about what the available alternatives might add up to.[11] A good deal of the contempt was reserved for what England had become. So it is not surprising that the novel he wrote when he decided once again to write about England, *Lady Chatterley's Lover,* a novel instinct with the melancholy of his final return to his "native Midlands" in September 1926,[12] should lapse into polemic, or that the utopia reflected faintly back from its polemical *furor* should exist in imagination at once beyond and before what England had so palpably become in his eyes.

Lady Chatterley's Lover has been said to derive its force from the contrast it draws—often and furiously—between "contemporary industrial reality" and a "lost sexual wholeness."[13] It advocates in an "explicitly evangelistic manner" a return to "a preindustrial, a precivilized, indeed a primeval, world" (the ancient woods in which Connie and Mellors achieve consummation representing "that lost territory of a wild, authentic existence where the life of the body is still possible").[14] Lawrence thought and wrote at all times within the "classic paradigm of modernist primitivism."[15] His was a primitivism of the most conventional kind, forever rooting out alternatives to techno-industrial modernity, either in ancient England or in a contemporary elsewhere. That is not the whole story, I think, or indeed the most interesting part of it.

To begin with, we need to grasp the extent to which Lawrence's primitivism was a rhetoric, or, rather, a set of interlocking rhetorics that can be said ultimately to cancel each other out. In a letter written on July 16, 1926, a couple of months before he embarked on the first version of *Lady Chatterley's Lover,* Lawrence once again gave voice to the hatred he felt for "our most modern world."[16] Tin cans and "imitation tea" feature prominently on his list of things not to like about being most modern. Tin cans often featured on such lists, either as litter or as culinary shortcut, in both cases signifying degeneracy. For "modern world" was then and still remains an expression held at the arm's length allegory requires. It is a tableau well stocked with emblems. But imitation tea is a nice touch, all the same, because it recovers the starkness of the contrast between the organic and the inorganic that knowing you are most modern always involves. Unlike some allegorists, Lawrence could not help describing in luminous expository detail what he meant conscientiously to hate before he dissolved it in emblem. Like the other iconic banned books of the period between the world wars—*Ulysses, The Well of Loneliness*—*Lady Chatterley's Lover* has long since ceased to be notorious. Unlike them, it has not yet acquired a different kind of fame. But what it does best, better than any other novel of its time, better than most published since then, is to describe the modern world as it was, and in some measure still is. It describes the modern world from the point of view of a polemic that, while apparently overreaching description altogether, in fact makes better room for it.

To be sure, primitivism of a conventional kind has been inscribed in the topography of the tale, consistent through all three versions of it. The hut and the cottage where Constance Chatterley undergoes her rite of passage, redeemed from feminine sentimentality by male sexual tenderness, constitute a liminal space deep in the heart of old England: a sacred realm distinct from the equal and opposite profanities of crumbling manor and brash suburb. That much is obvious. The topography, however, has been overlaid with polemic, indeed is in some sense constituted by polemic, and polemic's faint reflection back as utopia. When Lawrence rewrote the novel for the second and last time between November 23, 1927, and January 8, 1928, he thickened it discursively. As Frieda Lawrence put it, the first version came as though "out of his own immediate self," but in the third he was "also aware of his contemporaries' minds."[17] Working-class Parkin in the second version became gentlemanly Mellors in the third, more bookish, more articulate, more dominant (more like Lawrence himself, in short). As David Ellis points out, many readers have "complained that the increased discursive element, together with a much stronger strain of denunciatory rage in the reflections of the gamekeeper, obscure the lyrical celebrations of sexual intercourse which make the second version so impressive."[18] In his comprehensive study of the making of the novel, Derek Britton notes that Lawrence went out of his way in revision to reduce and qualify the original's "pastoral lyricism."[19] The displacement of Connie's old feminine sentimentality by a new female sexuality now requires a journey not just from one place to another, but from one discourse to another. Lawrence's is a discursive primitivism, adjusted both to age-old mythic structure and to what was going on in the minds of his contemporaries.

The novel's initiating rhetoric, fueled by hatred of "our most modern world," flickers in Mellors's explanation of why Connie Chatterley is the woman for him. The great thing about her, he says, is that she is not "all tough rubber-goods-and-platinum, like the modern girl." She has a tenderness that has "gone out" of the "celluloid women of today."[20] Before long, Connie herself will in turn, and without reference to Mellors, describe Sir Clifford and his set as celluloid nonentities, unappealingly tough and "india-rubbery" in appearance and manner (*LCL* 194). Connie and Mellors, speaking with one voice, are fully united by hatred before they are fully united in sex. Platinum, india rubber, celluloid: all have been dissolved in metaphor. This shared vituperation has a peculiar autonomy and denseness, even by Lawrence's standards. It is an aporetic discourse, numbed by its own vigor. It has no diagnostic value. If it proposes anything, it proposes an end to diagnosis, and a consequent reversion to the "primitive" in discourse itself: the exchange of one set of metaphors for another, of an address to the minds of one's contemporaries for an address to one's immediate, archaic self. In liminal space, in the heart of old England, Connie and Mellors devote themselves to dialect, to the vivid naming of body parts and functions. "'What is cunt?' she said" (178). Or, to reframe her question in fully primitivist terms, as Mellors in effect does by phallic insistence during the second night they spend together at the cottage, "What or where in the human body is 'before' and 'beyond' cunt?"

Embarking on the short journey from all-mod-cons Wragby Hall to the ancient forest that contains the gamekeeper's hut and cottage, Connie gets ready to swap signs made in anger for signs made in tenderness: celluloid and radio sets for forget-me-nots woven into pubic hair. The danger in such exchanges is that the second performance will simply cancel out the first, without either transforming it in the process or cutting loose from it altogether. The result is stalemate. In an essay on John Galsworthy's *Forsyte Saga* written while he was completing the second version of *Lady Chatterley's Lover*, Lawrence argued that even those characters in the *Saga* who rebel against the power of money merely confirm it by their rebellion. Bosinney, the young architect who has a passionate affair with Irene Forsyte, is merely an "anti-Forsyte, with a vast grudge against property." The thing a man has a grudge against, Lawrence added, "is the man's determinant."[21] How true might that be of Mellors?

Connie, I believe, is a different matter. In September 1927, shortly before he began the novel's third and final version, Lawrence finished translating a collection of short fiction by Giovanni Verga that was to appear as *"Cavalleria Rusticana" and Other Stories*. In his preface, he made the case for a "formlessness" in fiction that would more fully capture what happens in the transition from one deed or mood to another. "A great deal of the meaning of life and of art lies in the apparently dull spaces, the pauses, the unimportant passages."[22] The dull space he himself created around Connie is the space of her movement between Wragby Hall and the gamekeeper's hut and cottage. In that space, description flourishes. The most important change of emphasis, as Lawrence revised the novel heavily on two separate occasions, concerns Connie's emergence in these unimportant passages as a particular kind of modern woman.

It is the specificity of her understanding of the things she takes with her when she leaves for the forest that bids fair to protect her not only against emblematically celluloid Sir Clifford, but also against emblematically supple and rooted Mellors: a pair of rubber-soled tennis shoes, a lightweight mackintosh, perfume by Coty. There is of course a narrative reason for her to avail herself at such a time of these particular accessories: truants need shoes that do not squeak, an overcoat keeps off the chill night air, perfume can mask as well as entice. But the accessories acquire a further salience in the text because the journeys undertaken involve a complex negotiation between the self-consciously contemporary and the self-consciously archaic. The condition of that salience is rhetorical rather than narrative. On each occasion, a rant against the most modern world's artificiality provides a context for the description of these products of modern artifice: a description that flares briefly, before being extinguished in the depths of the forest by a counter-rant in the form of a celebration of archaic sexuality. The emphasis thus laid lightly in that brief flaring on modern artifice creates the possibility of a story different not only from what has gone before, but also, we may begin to suspect, from what is to come. It gives shape to an attitude unlikely to flourish either in the big house or in the gamekeeper's cottage.

I am going to suggest that Lawrence, whose temperament and prose style might be thought to tend perpetually to the condition of molten lava, was in fact, when the mood took him, an advocate of cool. The definitions of cool I have drawn on thus far are of course definitions for the twenty-first century. But if Lawrence's novel is also for the twenty-first century, as I have claimed, it could be said in some way to prefigure those definitions, as indeed might some of his other writings of this period. In *The Virgin and the Gypsy*, written in 1926 and in some respects a dry run for *Lady Chatterley's Lover*, the two protagonists demonstrate their mutual affinity by displays of coolness. His has to do with the way he moves, hers with the "nonchalance" she exhibits from the moment of her first encounter with him. "Nonchalance" was one of the contemporary translations of *sprezza-tura*, the doctrine of the well-rehearsed concealment of effort first put forward by Baldassare Castiglione in his *Book of the Courtier*.[23] She has, we later learn, "that peculiar calm, virginal contempt of the free-born for the base-born." The gypsy, a vagabond allying himself with the bohemian element of the aristocracy, coolly exploits the slack in the social system: "he was too much master of himself, and too wary, to expose himself openly to the vast and gruesome clutch of our law. He had been through the war. He had been enslaved against his will, that time."[24] This class-based under-standing of nonchalance as the exclusive possession of aristocrat or vaga-bond was, however, already out of date. In revising *Lady Chatterley's Lover*, Lawrence removed from the novel the last traces of the propaganda for a new aristocracy that had driven his writing in the years after the end of the First World War. Connie's rebellion will be private, apolitical, con-sumerist. Mellors, like the gypsy, moves well. But, as an ex-blacksmith and horse-whisperer turned game warden, he is, like the gypsy, an anachronistic figure: an exponent and advocate of artisanal technique as an alternative to technology. It is Connie who, for better or worse, speaks most directly to the twenty-first century.

In chapter 13, Connie, having dined with her husband, and roundly con-demned him in her own mind as a dead fish of a gentleman with a celluloid soul, slips out of the house to spend the night, for the first time, in Mellors's cottage. She puts on "rubber tennis-shoes, and then a light coat" (*LCL* 195). Unimportant descriptive passages such as this constitute the slack in narra-tive's system. Lawrence establishes by means of their matter-of-factness a view of the modern world not determined by any "vast grudge" against it. The tennis shoes (as such, enough to guarantee a silent exit) only became *rubber* tennis shoes in the novel's second version. I have often wondered why. The answer to that question lies in the history of the production and marketing of rubber.

A Brief History of Rubber

The industrial exploitation of natural rubber, a substance familiar to the indigenous peoples of the Amazon basin for centuries, dates from the sec-ond half of the eighteenth century. The name given in English to latex extracted from the *Hevea brasiliensis* tree derives from its original function in Western culture: rubbing.[25] Small blocks of a substance thereafter known as rubber turned out to be a distinct improvement on bread crumbs when it came to erasing pencil marks.

For pencil marks were the least of it. In 1785, François Blanchard crossed the English Channel in a balloon varnished with a mixture of rubber and turpentine. By the 1820s, further uses had been devised for this versatile natural product, from belts for driving heavy machinery, through buckets, cylinders, pipes, and a wide range of mattresses and cushions, to gaiter straps and elastic bands. However, rubber in its natural state still posed major—indeed, insuperable—problems from the point of view of manufacture. It became sticky when hot, and brittle when cold. It took the intervention of chemical science to convert a useful if unreliable natural product into an industrial necessity. In 1838, the American inventor Charles Goodyear managed to stabilize raw latex by mixing it with sulfur and white lead. A Londoner, Thomas Hancock, who may or may not have got hold indirectly of one of Goodyear's samples, obtained a British patent for the process of "vulcanization" in 1843. Goodyear's U.S. patent, which dates from the following year, gained him little benefit; he died in poverty. Vulcanization, Hancock was later to note triumphantly, brought about an "extraordinary change" in raw latex, rendering it at once durable and elastic. He and Goodyear had between them devised a method by which sheets of pure rubber "could be immersed in a sulphur bath, and changed to any required degree, from the softest and most elastic up to a state of hardness similar to horn, and capable of being wrought with carpenters' tools, or turned like ivory and ebony on a lathe."[26] The "changed" substance, which became known in its hardest and most durable form as Vulcanite, was used in the manufacture of dental plates, matchboxes, penholders, and jewelry. "Vulcanite may be regarded as the first truly semi-synthetic plastic, since it is made from a natural material, rubber, which has been chemically altered, its composition and properties being changed by the addition of sulphur under controlled conditions."[27]

Vulcanite could be thought of as rubber *over*-stabilized: a substitute for or imitation of wood, stone, and metal, remarkable only in so far as it gave rise to the particular form and function imposed during the process of manufacture. Rubber at its most supple, by contrast, did what no traditional substance could do.[28] Gutta-percha, a relative of rubber drawn from the *Palaquium* tree native to Malaysia, turned out to possess excellent insulating properties. Wire insulated with gutta-percha was laid across the Hudson River at Fort Lee in August 1849 for the Morse Telegraph Company. Other submarine cables soon followed, including that laid across the Atlantic by the *Great Western* in 1866. Rubber made modern connectivity possible. During the same period, the gradual introduction of electric lighting, inside and outside the home, and electric traction, in factories and underground railways, further increased the demand for the material sharply, though no more sharply than the fitting of tires, solid at first, but from 1888 pneumatic, to horse-drawn carriages, bicycles, and, from around 1900, the automobile. Rubber had become ubiquitous in daily life. In John Lethaby's fantasy sketch, "A Rubberless World," first published in 1910, a particularly sulfurous London fog dissolves the very element or condition of modern urban life. Boot heels subside, papers once held together by elastic bands tumble apart, a doormat dissolves into a "film of smoke-coloured fluff." Worse is to follow. "But now, in a flash, we saw that motor lorry and brougham, bus and bicycle, had been stripped clean of their rubber tyres, and jolted, banged, shook, and rocked from side to side of the muddy road."[29]

By 1910, a further momentous transformation was under way in the production and marketing of rubber, this time geopolitical rather than scientific. During the nineteenth century, Brazil and the countries that share the Amazon basin were the only major exporters of natural rubber, for the most part through Para, the port of the Amazon delta. Brazilian or Para rubber was wild rubber, the trees tapped where they stood in the jungle between early June and late January, by methods that did progressive damage to their ability to yield latex. This was an era of low production, high wage costs, and high prices.[30] By the end of the century, tropical Africa provided an alternative source. The supply of wild rubber from these sources was just about sufficient to meet the worldwide demand created by electrification and the craze for bicycling. Congo rubber became a focus for fierce debates about imperialism.[31] In chapter 23 of E. M. Forster's *Howards End* (1910), Margaret Schlegel, by no means an enthusiast for empire, visits Henry Wilcox at the offices of the Imperial and West African Rubber Company. "She was glad to go there, for Henry had implied his business rather than described it, and the formlessness and vagueness that one associates with Africa had hitherto brooded over the main sources of his wealth."[32] Lethaby's stories are mostly set in Africa or South America. All that was about to change.

In 1876, at the request of the India Office, Henry Wickham, an Englishman living in Brazil, obtained seventy thousand *Hevea brasiliensis* seeds and sent them back to Britain. Twenty-seven hundred plants were germinated from these seeds at Kew Gardens and sent on to Ceylon (Sri Lanka) and Singapore, where they were to form the basis of a systematic attempt to establish rubber plantations. Twenty years or so of discontinuous experiment ensued. At the turn of the century, however, the rapid expansion of the motor industry in the United States and elsewhere created a massive global demand for rubber that simply could not be met from Africa and South America.[33] Investment in rubber plantations in Ceylon and Malaya, and in the Dutch East Indies, began in earnest. Initial high returns ensured a steady flow of capital.[34] In 1907, a Rubber Growers Association (RGA) was founded in London to protect and develop the interests of British firms operating in Southeast Asia. By October, sixty companies and thirty-four individuals had become members; an executive committee was formed, together with committees for each of the various countries in which plantations had been set up. During the association's early years, discussion centered for the most part on proposals concerning the management and supervision of Malay estates: labor supply, hospital provision, drainage works.[35] By 1914, the supply of cultivated rubber from the British and Dutch East Indies had outstripped the supply of wild rubber from Africa and South America. In that year, Malaya exported 47,600 tons and Ceylon 15,800, while 12,900 tons came from the Dutch East Indies and elsewhere. The total amount of wild rubber produced in Africa and South America was 48,586 tons. By 1922, the output of cultivated rubber worldwide had risen to 373,700 tons (214,000 tons of it Malayan), while that of wild rubber had dropped to 26,874 tons.[36] The era of high production, low wage costs, and falling prices had set in. If empire informed metropolitan culture in Britain during the 1910s and 1920s, it did so to a large extent by means of the trade in plantation rubber.

It was the steady and apparently irreversible fall in the price of rubber after 1910 that made this ultramodern substance the focus of a techno-primitivism as formative in commercial practice as it was in literature. By 1921, the bottom had fallen out of the market, and the British colonial authorities persuaded Malayan rubber producers to take part in a scheme to restrict production. An export quota was set for each plantation. In the event, the so-called Stevenson Committee restriction enjoyed some initial success, but competition from the Dutch East Indies and elsewhere soon

drove prices down again. The scheme came to an end in 1928.[37] The underlying problem—an overinvestment in capacity, coupled with a reduction in demand brought about by technological advances in the automobile
industry—required a different solution. New uses had to be found for rubber. In 1921, the RGA created a publicity department, under the control of
the propaganda committee, whose function was to develop "press propaganda advocating the use of rubber for all conceivable purposes," as well as
closer links with manufacturers.[38] By May 1923, the propaganda fund set
up at the same time had received contributions totaling £40,000.[39] The
propaganda committee's deliberations with regard to publicity, as recorded
in the *Minute Books*, provide crucial insight into the selling of the *idea* of
rubber to an ignorant or skeptical public.

The most significant initiative undertaken by the publicity department
during the 1920s concerned the exploitation, primarily for the leisure
market, of the "crudeness" of crude rubber. After collection, the coagu-
lum from *Hevea brasiliensis* was prepared for export either as crepe or as
ribbed smoked sheet. Unlike sheet, crepe underwent a "tearing or disinte-
grating action" in the mills that produced its characteristic corrugations. In
the early 1920s, it represented about 25 percent of output from the British
East Indies.[40] Crepe rubber did not require vulcanization before use. The
material out of which a commodity was to be made could be prepared on
the plantation itself, by "native" artisanal labor, rather than in a factory in
Europe or the United States, by chemical process. Maximum profits were
thus ensured for the grower, whose interests the RGA had been brought
into being to protect. At a propaganda committee meeting on October 3,
1921, there was extensive discussion of the recent arrival on the market of
a new item that seemed likely to open up "a large field for consumption of
rubber": crepe soles for shoes and boots. Naturalness, or the degree of the
chemical alteration of a crude substance during the process of manufacture, was definitely on the agenda. Although it had always been necessary
to "compound rubber with mineral matters for practically every purpose,"
a "minimum percentage" of raw material could nonetheless be established.[41] The great thing about crepe was that the proportion of raw material to added mineral matters in any commodity made from it was very
high indeed. The RGA saw this predominance of naturalness as the perfect opportunity to develop a new and distinctive field for rubber products.
It sounds like the ultimate techno-primitivist challenge. How, then, to
design and market a luxury synthetic item whose very luxuriousness connected it back to its origin in nature?

The solution was the sports shoe. On November 7, 1921, the propaganda committee reported that shoes with crepe soles had been sent to tennis professionals for testing.[42] In December, the Pure Plantation Rubber Products Co. Ltd. began trading at 40 Fenchurch Street, in central London; one hundred thousand circulars were sent out.[43] By the following July, demand had exceeded supply. Striking while the iron was hot, the propaganda committee prepared folders for distribution to golf, tennis, bowls, and cricket clubs, in order to "produce a demand which will compel manufacturers to manufacture shoes with crêpe rubber soles in the next few months for next summer's stock."[44] In May 1923, a decision was made to concentrate RGA resources on "publicity for crude rubber products," and especially crepe rubber soles.[45] The propaganda committee must have been very pleased to receive confirmation of the material's "high standard of hygienic merit" in a report from the Incorporated Institute of Hygiene that came up for discussion on October 1, 1923. It was, the report noted, "very durable," and of a "firm and *gristly* texture." "It is finally milled at the plantations and undergoes no further manufacturing process so that it is cheap and also retains the natural resiliency and flexibility of pure, natural rubber."[46] Of course, you could have *too much* naturalness. Concerns raised by the local propaganda committee in Kuala Lumpur about the advisability of promoting unvulcanized rubber, "especially in the tropics where rubber quickly becomes tacky," came up at a council meeting on June 4, 1923.[47] But tacky in Kuala Lumpur might well mean resilient and flexible in Brighton or Scarborough.

Sports shoes and boots could be characterized as the medium for a rekindling of hitherto dormant energies and aptitudes. Crepe rubber had proved to be the "ideal sole" because, according to an advertisement placed in the *Times* in June 1924, it "responds to every foot movement, braces up the muscles, and at the same time affords a perfect grip." "The cushion of 'live' rubber lessens fatigue and makes walking a pleasure, adding hours to endurance and a spring to every step." Furthermore, the "special process" of plantation finishing meant that nothing had been done, chemically or otherwise, to "impair the natural live quality and nerve of the virgin product." The implication was the "live" or "virgin" quality of crepe rubber— its "nerve"—would refresh and reinvigorate the wearer of shoes fashioned from it, while at the same time ensuring that he or she could henceforth get a "perfect grip," with the aid of its "peculiar gristly texture," on the earth's surface.[48] In August 1923, George Cummings, professional walking champion of the world, set out to walk from London to York in crepe-soled shoes. He was to be paid £100 by the GPA, with a further £150 if he beat

George Cummings and entourage. Still from *London to York on Foot*. British Pathé Gazette, 1923.

the equestrian record for the distance set by Mr. Tyrwhitt-Drake on a horse called The Sheik. On the way, Cummings had periodically to commend his footwear for its "durability, resilience, absence of road-shock, etc."[49] A Pathé Gazette newsreel film shows him on his way out of Trafalgar Square, and then bustling along a country road past some mildly apprehensive cattle, accompanied by a publicity car, an entourage of cyclists, and a man on horseback.

In September, Harrods mounted a special display featuring his footwear, and his staunch testimonials to its durability, resilience, etc.; six hundred pairs of the same brand were sold within a week.[50] Crepe rubber had by now become very strongly associated with golf and tennis shoes in particular. The June 1924 *Times* advertisement claimed that leading players in both sports had worn crepe-soled shoes "exclusively" for the past two years. Images of the material's distinctive gristly texture began to proliferate. From April 1923 onward, the Fortmason Golf Shoe, previously visible in advertisements in sober profile only, turned up its corrugations for all to see.[51] In April 1924, the Chairman of the Straits Rubber Company told its fourth annual general meeting that the crepe rubber sole was the most important of the new uses that had been found for the material: "it is firmly established for sports footwear in this country, and from all accounts it appears likely to become quite as popular in the United States of America." Its extension to ordinary footwear was "only a matter of time."[52]

It did not quite work out that way, at least not in Britain in the 1920s. Periodic attempts were made to broaden the material's appeal. In May 1925, a letter headed "Natural Crêpe Rubber (Plantation Finished) for Everybody's Everyday Wear" was sent to footwear manufacturers soliciting their cooperation.[53] In October 1925, the propaganda committee agreed to co-fund a Morton Bros. campaign to "popularise crêpe soled footwear among the working classes" through advertising in magazines such as *Police Chronicle* and *Railway Review*.[54] Trials involving naval cadets and postmen apparently came to nothing.[55] The larger reluctance could perhaps be blamed on national character. "There is considerable prejudice against the use of rubber footwear in this country which requires to be got rid of before the public generally will buy overshoes." A proposal that steps should at once be taken to explain the "medical advantages of rubber footwear from the point of view of the British climate" does not seem to have received funding.[56] When it came to "stunts," the propaganda committee's elixir, there was simply no substitute for a (preferably genteel) sporting hero. In July 1924, the committee had high hopes that the Wimbledon championships would be won that year by "wearers of crêpe rubber soles," since (disobliging Americans apart) practically every player of repute had endorsed the "natural product."[57] In December 1924, Mr. H. de V. Hazard's crepe-soled boots performed admirably during an ascent of Everest, except for a certain "slippiness" on wet, smooth surfaces; while Captain J. Noel, in charge of the filming party, was equally full of praise. Alas, the timing of Hazard's success proved unfortunate. His testimonials had no sooner been formulated than the winter sports season came to an end, and the newspapers promptly lost interest in the topic of adhesiveness.[58] Still, stunts there had been, of a kind. The committee was able to report that the International Shoe and Leather Fair held at the Royal Agricultural Hall in October 1924 had featured a large portrait of His Royal Highness the Prince of Wales wearing golf shoes with crepe rubber soles.[59]

Vulcanized rubber was a modern semisynthetic substance. By putting the emphasis on an unvulcanized version, "virgin" product of colonial abundance, the RGA cleverly sold reinvigoration to the (literally) well-heeled metropolitan middle and upper classes: a bit of wildness on golf course and tennis court. Its crepe rubber campaign amounted to techno-primitivism in action. We need now to consider how such an emphasis might have found its way into literature, or at least into *Lady Chatterley's Lover.*

Rubber Tennis Shoes and Other Accessories

Lawrence added Connie's denunciation of Sir Clifford as "tough and india-rubbery" to the novel's third and final version. It is followed in chapter 13 by dinner, during which they discuss Proust, and then the passage describing what she has decided to wear on her excursion to Mellors's cottage in the forest, where she will for the first time spend the night. "Connie returned to her room, threw her pyjamas on the tossed bed, put on a thin night-dress and over that a woolen day-dress, put on rubber tennis-shoes, and then a light coat, and she was ready" (*LCL* 195). In the second version, the shoes are "rubber-soled shoes."[60] I hope that I have already done enough to suggest why Lawrence might have thought that the association of rubber soles with tennis would find an echo in the minds of his contemporaries. While there is of course no absolute guarantee that the shoes he imagined Connie wearing on this occasion have crepe rubber soles, the likelihood, given the additional detail of their purpose, and the prominence throughout the period during which the novel was written of the publicity campaigns surrounding the use of such shoes for such a purpose, is that they do. There is a different primitivism at work here, one that no longer looks before and beyond techno-industrial civilization, and Lawrence makes sure that we know it.

In chapter 15, after she and Mellors have met at the hut in the woods in which they first made love, Connie dances naked in the rain. "She slipped on her rubber shoes and ran out with a wild little laugh." By adding in the novel's third version that Connie has chosen to rehearse for Mellors's benefit the "eurhythmic dance-movements" she had learned in Dresden, Lawrence confirms that this is indeed a thoroughly modern primitivism. "It was a strange pallid figure lifting and falling, bending so the rain beat and glistened on the full haunches, swaying up again and coming belly-forward through the rain, then stooping again so that only the full loins and buttocks were offered in a kind of homage towards him, repeating a wild obeisance" (*LCL* 221).

The dance, as modern in style as the shoes Connie dons to perform it, is a response to yet another of Mellors's rants against the "industrial epoch" and its reduction of men and women to "labour-insects" (*LCL* 220). Techno-primitivism is cool, however, because, as we might guess from the strangeness of the pallid figure stooping before him, ancient practices echo to its modern beat. In April 1927, after completing his first revision of the novel, Lawrence undertook an extensive tour of Tuscany, in order to examine the famous painted tombs and other vestiges of the ancient Etruscan civilization in which he had for a long time taken an interest. By the end of June, he had written pretty much all he was ever to write of his posthumously published *Sketches of Etruscan Places.* The ease, naturalness, and "abundance of life" revealed to him by the tomb paintings became the latest in a series of antidotes to modern commerce and empire. So, another gang of happy, conquered sensualists. Except that what he most liked about this lot was their sprezzatura, their apparent "carelessness." In a poem written in 1920, he had imagined the men of "old Etruria," naked except for "fanciful long shoes," transacting "forgotten business" with "some of Africa's imperturbable sang-froid."[61] In 1927, it was the friezes representing dance that most delighted him: men clad only in sandals and a kind of scarf, a woman who "throws back her head and curves out her long strong fingers, wild and yet contained within herself," all equally caught up in the "archaic earnestness of insouciance."[62] Connie, naked except for her no less fanciful shoes, dances herself "ruddy": the flesh tone Lawrence most readily attributed to his old Etrurian men. Techno-primitivism has brought her to her senses. It recovers the starkness of the contrast between the organic and the inorganic involved in being most modern.

After the dance, rubber's enabling substance is granted ghostly reanimation in a thoroughly unimportant passage that nonetheless attains a remarkable comic-lyrical intensity.

He took the old sheet and rubbed her down, she standing like a child. Then he rubbed himself, having shut the door of the hut. The fire was blazing up. She ducked her head in the other end of the sheet, and rubbed her wet hair.

"We're drying ourselves together on the same towel, we shall quarrel!" he said.

She looked up for a moment, her hair all odds and ends.

"No!" she said, her eyes wide. "It's not a towel, it's a sheet."

And she went on busily rubbing her head, while he busily rubbed his. (*LCL* 222)

The actions described, like the sentiments they give rise to, are entirely mundane. The steady reiteration of "rubbed" casts over them, by summoning from within the substance Connie has so recently put to eurhythmic use a memory of its original function in the West, a glow that itself never exceeds the mundane. It is an oddly (that is, comically) beautiful moment, and one that could not have been conceived without the tennis shoes. Connie has brought with her into the ancient forest a gadget that releases her not only from modern metropolitan gentility, but also from the forest. She can be old-new simply by wearing a certain kind of shoe in a certain way. This particular rite of passage has more passage to it than rite.

An important catalyst for Lawrence's decision to revise the novel for a second and last time was his encounter in Florence on November 17, 1927, with Dikran Kouyoumdjian, a Bulgarian-born Armenian who had adopted British citizenship. Under the pen name of Michael Arlen, Kouyoumdjian had published a sensational best seller, *The Green Hat* (1924), which trains a lugubrious prurience on jazz, drug taking, and sexually transmitted disease. The fast-living heroine, Iris Storm, turns out to be a good sort in the end. She sends her lover back to his wife and commits suicide by driving her Hispano-Suiza into a tree. Lawrence had little time for the novel, but thought of Iris Storm as an exemplary modern heroine. "And there is the heroine who is always 'pure,' usually, nowadays, on the muck-heap! Like the Green Hatted Woman."[63] He liked Kouyoumdjian, and put him in the final version of *Lady Chatterley's Lover* as Michaelis, a hugely successful playwright courted and condemned by the "smart set" his plays describe. Connie has an affair with Michaelis before getting to know Mellors. His introduction imparts a "new moral character" to Connie, as Derek Britton has pointed out; it makes her the "archetype" of the modern woman, seeking sexual satisfaction wherever she can find it.[64] Lawrence, of course, continued until his death to comment in the severest terms on the modern woman.[65] Connie is rather the archetype, in her rubber tennis shoes, of the modern old-new woman.

The first and more or less last thing we are told about Iris Storm, as the narrator looks down from the window of his apartment into the street, is that her hat is "bright green, of a sort of felt, and bravely worn: being, no

doubt, one of those that women who have many hats affect *pour le sport.*"
Closer inspection at street level reveals a tall woman who somehow gives
the impression "that she had just been playing six sets of tennis."[66] By the
mid-1920s, sport had become a major fashion and mass media event.[67] To
dress and act *pour le sport* was one way to be modern. The narrator spots
a second. "Her hair, in the shadow of her hat, may have been any colour,
but I dared swear that there was a tawny whisper to it."[68] Sport combined
with tawniness was the formula for the complete modern primitive. Tawny
designates a composite color (brown with a preponderance of yellow or
orange), and it could be applied to a person whose skin was somewhere
between white and black: a person like Ciccio, the young Italian circus
performer who redeems Alvina Houghton from spinsterdom, in Lawrence's *The Lost Girl* (1920). Tawny-skinned Ciccio gazes lingeringly at
Alvina out of "tawny" eyes. When he touches her from behind, it is as if
"some unseen creature had stroked her with its paw." Sitting beside this
"dark-skinned foreigner" on a tram, Alvina is reminded of "the woman
with the negro husband, down in Lumley."[69] Hollywood adopted tawniness with enthusiasm. Ciccio's nearest female equivalent was María, the
working-class Mexican heroine of *The Tiger's Coat* (1920), from a 1917
novel by Elizabeth Dejeans, whose youthful joie de vivre redeems a jaded
Californian tycoon, Alexander McAllister. In the novel, Marie (as she is
there) has Ciccio-like tawny eyes and Iris Storm–like luxuriant tawny
hair, the "gold in her hair" resembling "the yellow streak in a tiger's coat."[70]
In the film, a local artist, commissioned to paint her portrait, remarks that
she has the "tawny skin of a tiger." María was played by the Italian actress
and model Tina Modotti, later to become a celebrated photographer and
political activist. Lawrence met Modotti in November 1924, in Mexico
City, where she was then living with the American photographer Edward
Weston, who took two portrait photographs of him. Thanking Weston for
these, on December 19, 1924, Lawrence suggested that *Vanity Fair* might
like some of his "less startling nudes" (the more startling ones were of
Modotti), and sent her his regards ("Greet the Signora").[71] Back in the metropolis, of course, you did not have to be naked to appear tawny. Bradley
Furs would be happy to provide you with a coat in "Natural Tawny Russian
Coltskin, collared with mink," a bargain at thirty-two guineas.[72] Beneath
her green hat, Iris Storm wears a "light brown leather jacket—*pour le
sport*—which shone quite definitely in the lamplight: it was wide open at
the throat, and had a high collar of the fur of a few minks."[73]

Connie Chatterley, examining her own body in the mirror after the gamekeeper has first aroused her interest, notes, not altogether disapprovingly, that her skin is "faintly tawny" (*LCL* 70). The rubber tennis shoes subsequently add the proper note of *pour le sport*. Of course, Connie is not Iris Storm, or Jordan Baker, in *The Great Gatsby*, the golf champion who remembers wearing as a sixteen-year-old "shoes from England with rubber nobs on the soles that bit into the soft ground,"[74] or any other modern primitive whose primitivism runs skin-deep only. My point is simply that Lawrence's modernization of Connie, in the third and final version of *Lady Chatterley's Lover*, had as profound an effect as the transformation of Parkin into Mellors. Lawrence went out of his way to identify her as modern by equipping her with modern synthetic and semisynthetic substances that not only regulate her passage to and from ancient woodland's sacred realm, but in and through that regulation bring her to her senses (to senses whose proper functioning will immunize her against Mellors as well as Sir Clifford). It may be that the emphasis put on the comb she uses to tidy her hair before returning home after her first night at the cottage constitutes a further identification with the semisynthetic. By the 1920s, all cheap combs were made of celluloid.[75] Even more striking is the "little bottle of Coty's Wood-violet perfume, half-empty," she leaves among Mellors's things after her second night at the cottage. "She wanted him to remember her in the perfume" (264). Spraying perfume on your lover's shirts does not seem like the coolest thing you could possibly do, and Connie herself subsequently dismisses the gesture as childish. The devil, however, is in the detail, as it always is in this novel. The manufacturer's name is an addition in the final draft. Coty did not in fact manufacture a perfume called Wood Violet. As Lawrence was revising, in January 1928, Coty launched L'Aimant (The Magnet).[76] But wood violets feature earlier in the novel (114). As with the tennis shoes, Lawrence has chosen for Connie a combination of old and new: the natural *in* the synthetic, rather than before or beyond it. Connie's strong awareness of synthetic and semisynthetic substance—an awareness coolly established by description alone—saves her both from Sir Clifford and from Mellors: from too much civilizing, and too little.

I hope I have been able to show that *Lady Chatterley's Lover* was conceived, in its third version at least, as a rather more topical text than we have for the most part taken it to be. One consequence of the lengthy ban it endured was to obscure the extent of its topicality. If we take full account of the ways in which Lawrence engaged with the minds of his contemporaries, we can grasp in that engagement a bold accommodation to some aspects of modern techno-industrial reality that is not without consequence for our understanding of his work, and that of other writers of the time. The colonies would not be "far enough," Mellors says at one point, for a new beginning. He knows that the "industrial epoch" has no recoverable before or beyond. "I'd better hold my peace, an' try an' live my own life" (*LCL* 220). But it is Connie, I think, who lives her own life. Connie is modern literature's most fully rendered techno-primitivist.

Touching Rubber, Smelling Rubber: H. D. and Radclyffe Hall

There were of course many other versions of the narrative of the displacement of feminine sentimentality by female sexuality in the literature of the period, and in some of these, orthodox primitivism did much of the displacing. I want now to discuss two texts that, although by no means as systematic in their techno-primitivism as *Lady Chatterley's Lover*, did nonetheless acknowledge in passing the tension between nature and culture, between the archaic and the contemporary, that characterizes rubber as a substance.

Bid Me to Live was autobiographical and therapeutic in intention. Its cast of characters includes H. D. herself (Julia Ashton), evidently, as well as her then husband Richard Aldington (Rafe Ashton), Aldington's lover, Dorothy Yorke (Bella), the musicologist Cecil Gray (Vane), and Lawrence (Rico), for whom and in opposition to whom she was then writing her poems, and who bid her to live. Like Connie Chatterley, Julia Ashton emancipates herself by abandoning the utter profanity of modern civilized existence in favor of an ancient sacred realm: in this case, one at England's edge, rather than in its center. Provoked by Rico, she leaves London, the scene of personal and collective trauma, to live with Vane in a cottage in Cornwall, close to where Lawrence had recently been living. "It was not England. Rico had said that." Rico also advises her to look out for inscriptions, for vestiges of the primitive such as the Druid circle high on the hill, and the path made by donkeys taking tin from the mines to Phoenician ships. Julia regards the path as "hieratic writing," like a screen in a temple in Egypt. "She felt that every casual stone was laid here, there, for a reason. Phoenicians, Rico had written, made this track, and in making this track, they had trod into the soil more than the countless imprints of ancient sandals or thonged leather shoes." Julia, again at Rico's behest, feels herself a priestess, a seer.[77] So forceful is her embrace of the "pantheistic, healing powers of nature residual in the magical environs of Cornwall," as Suzette Henke puts it, that the novel can without undue strain end on a note of "expectancy and resurrection."[78] But we also need to take account of the role played by the decisive men in Julia's life, Vane and Rico, in defining Cornwall as a sacred realm. Musicological Vane is no Mellors, rampant in hut and cottage alike, but Julia's emancipation as a writer, if not as a woman, does appear to depend on Rico's willingness to needle her and lecture her. Did H. D. imagine, as Lawrence was to, a female techno-primitivism capable of qualifying male primitivism?

Chapters 2 and 3 of *Bid Me to Live* turn on, or reiterate, or circle around Rafe's departure for France, at the end of a period of leave. Julia wants to accompany him to the station.

> "I'm coming with you."
> "No," he said, "no."
> She sorted out her clothes, shook out her garter-belt. "Stop," he said.
> He snatched the web of elastic and silk from her. It was a pretty belt, she had made it for this, salvaged the elastic straps from an old pair, sewed on the old buttons. He flung that silk and faded elastic with the tight sewed-on buttons, that fastened at the back, across the room.
> "You're not going out in this fog." (*BMTL* 26)

The garter belt, lovingly made with this precise occasion in mind, and now flung across the room, seems destined to symbolize rupture and breakdown, the end of the affair. Julia, however, getting up after Rafe has gone, methodically redeems the garment from symbolism.

> What was it that happened? It was as definite as putting on a dress, as pulling up stockings, as fastening the garter-belt and tightening the stocking-web into the rubber-lined garter-catches, four. Automatically, you did these things, without thinking. A form of automatic mood flowed over her with the second cup of tea, it would embrace her, enfold her with the first puff of the cigarette, her morning cigarette, after the cup of tea. She was a creature of habits, she moved in a room to a sort of precise rhythm, the garter-belt, the stockings were attributes of a dance, they were attributes. (40–41)

The feel of rubber has helped to restore Julia to automatism, which is what she most needs in herself at this juncture. Recollection of the feel of rubber enables H. D. to write the paragraph that halts, temporarily at least, the narrative's vertiginous downward spiral into trauma.[79] Unlike Connie Chatterley's tennis shoes, the garter belt can scarcely be said to carry Julia over into a sacred realm of some kind. Like them, however, it arouses awareness of an unresolved tension between the contemporary and the archaic.

For Julia's affair with Vane, begun after Rafe's departure for France, is framed throughout in terms of natural substance, of stone, and wood, and iron: of materials that require shaping, in manufacture, but cannot be transformed out of recognition by chemical process. In London, Julia and Vane find themselves out in the street during an air raid. "They started back against the iron railing. She felt the iron of the rails run furrows through her coat, as she registered a final nerve-shock" (*BMTL* 110). Shock is figured as the force not of the bomb blast's chemical heat felt all at once from in front, but of an environment fashioned industrially out of natural materials steadily working its way into her body from behind as the plow furrows the soil. Julia has to unfasten from the railing fingers that seem to belong to someone else altogether. "She felt as if she were glued there or held there by some magnetic force" (113). Trauma, here, is a kind of re-naturalization, but one brought about by the infliction of chemistry.

In Cornwall, returning from a wet and windy walk to the cottage she shares with Vane, Julia finds herself once again transfixed. "She was glued to the inner side of the wooden door, like a door in a barn, an old inn or a church. He laid his hand on her coatsleeve" (*BMTL* 154). Trauma makes itself felt, now, not so much through the touch of modern male sexuality from in front as through the touch of the primitive from behind. "The very wood of the door was part of the ancient grove, over the other side of the Druid circle that she had not yet had time to get to. The stone, the wood of this house were part of the rock outside, the cliff, the trees descended no doubt from some old Druid oak-circle" (154). If there is a man involved at all, here, it is two parts of Rico to one of Vane. Julia's response to enforced re-naturalization is to go upstairs to dry and brush her hair and put on some new clothes. "She fastened one fresh, warm, soft stocking, felt the icy rim of her wet skirt, knife-cold against the other bare leg" (155). The garter belt's rubber-lined contemporaneity has done its bit to unglue her from the archaic. It has also done its bit to unglue H. D. from a fantasized D. H. Lawrence.

The second text I want to investigate with regard to its sadly neglected dabbling in rubber is Radclyffe Hall's *The Well of Loneliness*, the period's most notorious celebration (if that is the right word) of lesbian sexual-romantic fulfillment. *The Well of Loneliness* is a novel of erotic sites rather than of erotic events. Sarah Chinn asks why Hall only ever allows lesbian sexuality to express itself fully at the Villa del Ciprés on the Canary Island of Tenerife, which Stephen Gordon and Mary Llewellyn rent for a blissful holiday during which they finally become lovers. Neither Morton, the Gordon family estate, nor Stephen's homes in London and Paris, staunchly maintained by the proto-invert Puddle, nor, indeed, the bivouacs of the ambulance corps she joins during the First World War, have been able to sustain such an expression. "In fact," Chinn points out, "Europe as a whole cannot bear the lightness of a lesbian sexuality that is not freighted with anxiety, decadence, self-doubt, and strict self-control (or its complement, anarchy)." Instead, Hall constructs a liminal space, a sacred realm remote from modern profanities, where Stephen and Mary consummate their love by going native. Stephen can study lesbian identity by reading Richard von Krafft-Ebing's *Psychopathia Sexualis* in the library at Morton, or by frequenting Valérie Seymour's louche salon in Paris, but nothing follows from this knowledge. Tenerife enables her finally to test the truth of Krafft-Ebing's claim that the more archaic a culture, the less it operates within the heterosexual matrix. "This is the world that gives permission to lesbian sexuality, even as it allows Stephen and Mary (and Hall) to imagine that the sexuality permitted is not lesbian but something else, something 'primitive and age-old as Nature herself.'"[80]

The Well of Loneliness strikes me as more thoroughly persuaded by its own primitivism than either *Lady Chatterley's Lover* or *Bid Me to Live*. But it does contain an episode that suggests that Hall, too, delighted to discover the archaic within the contemporary, rather than beyond it, and that she was led to this discovery by rubber's heady fusion of substance and formula, nature and culture. In chapter 33, Stephen, who has moved to Paris in order to enjoy its relative freedom from constraint, nonetheless steers clear of Valérie Seymour, that freedom's most effusive embodiment, while working on her next novel. On one of her long walks, she stumbles across the Passage Choiseul, a faintly seedy arcade in the Bourse area. The arcade boasts a range of attractions, including a patisserie and a stationer (Lavrut), each equipped with intoxicating odors, as well as "that shamelessly anatomical chemist's, whose wares do not figure in school manuals on the practical uses of rubber." To Stephen, it seems like a repository of "imprisoned thoughts."

> Stephen's thoughts got themselves entrapped with the others, but hers, at the moment, were those of a schoolgirl, for her eye had suddenly lit on Lavrut, drawn thereto by the trays of ornate india-rubber. And once inside, she could not resist the "Bracelets de caoutchouc," or the blotting paper as red as a rose, or the manuscript books with the mottled blue borders. Growing reckless, she gave an enormous order, for the simple reason that these things looked different.[51]

The chemist's shop strikes the modern note. But it is the touch and smell of india rubber that intoxicates Stephen, that re-naturalizes her, converting her back into the schoolgirl she once was. This glimpse of the archaic within rather than beyond the contemporary frees her more effectively from constraint than anything else that happens to her in Paris, though not as effectively as Nature itself will do, courtesy of the Villa del Ciprés.

The episodes I have discussed from *Bid Me to Live* and *The Well of Loneliness* belong with Lawrence's "unimportant passages." Neither can be said to prove decisive in the displacement of feminine sentimentality by female sexuality. But their very unimportance enables the articulation of an attitude—a techno-primitivism—that the text as a whole cannot fully endorse.

Bad Smells: Woolf and Orwell

To Stephen Gordon, the smell of rubber is a perfume. But it was not always so. In 1825, Charles Macintosh discovered that naphtha drawn from coal tar stabilized raw latex into a liquid that when spread between two layers of fabric made for an excellent waterproof material. Macintosh gave his name to a whole range of rubberized silk or cotton garments—or almost gave his name, since mackintosh with a "k," the variant spelling, is now standard. There was a problem, however. Rubberized cotton stank. So severe had this problem become, by the end of the nineteenth century, that there was considerable reluctance to admit mackintosh wearers onto omnibuses.[52] G. K. Chesterton had no difficulty in discerning the "primitive"—the delightfully nonmetropolitan—in rubberized cotton: "There is a wild garment that still carries nobly the name of a wild Highland clan: a clan come from those hills where rain is not so much an incident as an atmosphere.

Surely every man of imagination must feel a tempestuous flame of Celtic romance spring up within him whenever he puts on a mackintosh."[83] Others were not so convinced. When Henry, the bookish clerk in Katherine Mansfield's story "Something Childish but Very Natural," boards a commuter train one evening, he is disturbed to find that the carriage "smelt horribly of wet india-rubber and soot."[84] Something a bit *too* natural, perhaps. Rubber's "mackintosheriness," as H. G. Wells put it, could be understood as the smell of decomposition: the raw reasserting itself inside the cooked.[85] This return of the "bad" primitive within a characteristic modern garment provided a reason for literary displays of lack of cool.

Mackintoshes remained highly fashionable throughout the 1920s and 1930s, and steps could be taken to avoid their less congenial aspect. "Women are learning that the thick rubber waterproof coat is uncomfortable for its lack of ventilation," a 1920 guide to hygiene noted, "and they are discarding it for a light weight and rainproof cloth."[86] Some women, it seems, did not learn. Readers of Virginia Woolf's *Mrs Dalloway* (1925) have long wondered at the ferocious intensity of the feelings provoked in Clarissa by Doris Kilman, her daughter's history teacher and constant companion. At times, the object of those feelings appears to be not so much Miss Kilman herself as her "green mackintosh coat." The color of this coat is striking enough. But that is not all there is to it.

> Year in, year out, she wore that coat; she perspired; she was never in the room five minutes without making you feel her superiority, your inferiority; how poor she was; how rich you were; how she lived in a slum without a cushion or a bed or a rug or whatever it might be, all her soul rusted with that grievance sticking in it, her dismissal from school during the War— poor embittered unfortunate creature![87]

Woolf could perhaps have stopped after the remark about perspiration. The problem with Doris Kilman is that she *smells*. The mackintoshery stench she obtusely brings with her into the house is the mark of her outsiderdom. That grievance stuck in her soul might almost be a source of gangrene. The sentiment is Clarissa's, of course. But Woolf, introducing the smell before the emotional pathology, has let the revulsion conceivably felt by her more fastidious readers loose in the text.

Mackintoshes housed the "bad" techno-primitive: that residue of nature that no degree of artifice could ever wholly expunge, since it was itself artifice's product. Or so it seems, at least, to George Bowling, in Orwell's

Coming Up for Air (1939). Bowling, a middle-aged insurance agent, leads a desperate half-life in the company of a more or less comatose family in the heart of suburbia: Ellesmere Road, West Bletchley. There is not much in his experience that is *not* synthetic. Bowling's story begins on the day he equips himself with a new set of false teeth. Before that happens, he has had to endure a breakfast featuring a boiled egg and a piece of bread with Golden Crown marmalade, which according to the label "contains 'a certain proportion of neutral fruit-juice.'" "This started me off, in the rather irritating way I have sometimes, talking about neutral fruit-trees, wondering what they looked like and what countries they grew in, until finally Hilda got angry." Lunch in London, on the way to the dentist, provides yet further mortification. The "rubber skin" of his frankfurter bursts as he saws through it with his ancient false teeth, filling his mouth with "horrible soft stuff" that tastes like fish. The sensation unleashes a memorable outburst against the ersatz in all its forms.

> It gave me the feeling that I'd bitten into the modern world and discovered what it was really made of. That's the way we're going nowadays. Everything slick and streamlined, everything made out of something else. Celluloid, rubber, chromium-steel everywhere, arc-lamps blazing all night, glass roofs over your head, radios all playing the same tune, no vegetation left, everything cemented over, mock-turtles grazing under the neutral fruit-trees. But when you come down to brass tacks and get your teeth into something solid, a sausage for instance, that's what you get. Rotten fish in a rubber skin. Bombs of filth bursting inside your mouth.

Lawrence's tin cans are missing from this list, but even without them the allegory alert sounds immediately. By the time the mock turtles have started to graze under the neutral fruit trees, like refugees from a poem by Wallace Stevens, there is no contrast left between the organic and the inorganic. Even the something else has been made out of something else. Bowling's tirade is in a direct line of descent from Mellors's denunciation of the "tough rubber-goods-and-platinum" type of "modern girl." It prompts him to a comparable withdrawal from the most modern world into an ancient realm in the heart of England: in this case, the market town of Lower Binfield, in which he grew up. For him, however, there will be no escape from rotten fish in a rubber skin, as there had been for his distant fictional precursor, Wells's Mr. Polly. Bowling's return home to Ellesmere Road is first and foremost a renewal of acquaintance with the "bad" techno-primitive. "I fumbled with the key, got the door open, and the familiar smell of old mackintoshes hit me."[88] The subsequent row with Hilda is steeped in the smell of the familiar, the smell of family: of a nature that artifice has produced, in regard to which it is no longer possible to behave coolly.

It could be that "bad" techno-primitivism is just out-of-date techno-primitivism. After all, the fashion in cool changes constantly, at the very least from generation to generation, and often at shorter notice than that. During the first thirty years of the twentieth century, the turnover in versions of the "new woman" was very rapid indeed.[89] Doris Kilman, her soul rusted with grievance, may simply have had her chance, in Clarissa Dalloway's eyes, and Woolf's. Or consider Miss Frances Haymer, in William Plomer's *The Case Is Altered*, a high-end thriller published by the Woolfs at the Hogarth Press in 1932. The novel's topic is shabby gentility on the skids. "A generation ago," we learn, Miss Haymer had enjoyed a significant reputation as an intrepid explorer. When travel became commonplace, she lost her public. Although she has "grown old with a good deal of bravura," the bravura itself is largely prosthetic.

> To look at her you would say that when she went to bed her toilet must be almost a dissolution; so carefully got up each morning, she must end the day by an equally careful disintegration, almost a dismemberment; the removal of hat, wig and shoes would at once take cubits off her stature; out would come teeth, off bracelets and stays, and with the removal of that perennial velvet band, down would tumble a cascade of chins. Heaven alone knows what supports and safety-pins, screws, straps, skewers and stanchions might not hold the old girl together.[90]

Plomer's description of decrepitude is self-consciously retro. It glances back at Wyndham Lewis's account of "veteran gossip star" Lady Fredigonde Follett at her toilet, in the prelude to *The Apes of God* (1930), which itself glances back at the figure of the Honourable Mrs. Skewton, in Charles Dickens's *Dombey and Son* (1848), who lives upon the "reputation of some diamonds, and her family connexions."[91] All three women are more artifact than person: they have to be taken apart at night by their maids, and reassembled in the morning. Plomer supplies Miss Haymer with a rubber-tipped walking stick, a device technologically beyond Mrs. Skewton, if not Lady Follett, but nonetheless by 1932, it would seem, a period piece. When she walks in Kensington Gardens, she points vigorously with her stick, "its rubber end fastening on the landscape like a huge tentacle."[92] The device, as much perceptual as pedestrian in function, expresses the rabid curiosity that is her primary characteristic. This, too, is a bad, and an old-fashioned, techno-primitivism. Some uses of rubber were clearly not conducive to cool, especially if they retained an association with the prewar era. In the second chapter of Joyce's *Finnegans Wake*, Dublin publican Humphrey Chimpden Earwicker meets a "cad with a pipe" in Phoenix Park, scene of the murders of Lord Frederick Cavendish and Thomas Henry Burke on May 6, 1882. As a result of this meeting, rumors begin to circulate about an "alleged misdemeanour" involving some young girls. I have always thought that Earwicker does not do himself any favors by showing up in a "rubberised inverness."[93] Connie Chatterley, of course, is neither bad nor old-fashioned in *her* techno-primitivism.

Listening In

It is striking that Lawrence attributed a productive techno-primitivism to women far more readily than he did to men. No man in Lawrence's fiction tries harder to renew himself through technology than hapless Sir Clifford Chatterley, especially after the arrival of a new nurse and companion, Mrs. Bolton, has provoked in him a resurgence of energy. "Somehow, he got his pecker up" (*LCL* 107). Thereafter, the single-minded development for profit of his researches into the "technicalities of modern coal-mining" (108) encourages him to think of himself once again as "lord and master" (109) of all he surveys. But this outward self-renewal has the effect of delivering him inwardly into a state of complete dependence upon Mrs. Bolton, which is also a state of complete dependence upon technology. His interest in the radio, mentioned in passing in the second version of the novel, takes center stage in the third. It is established at the beginning of chapter 10 that he no longer wants company at Wragby, or the sort of wide-ranging intellectual debate he had once warmly encouraged. "He preferred the radio, which he had installed at some expense, with a good deal of success at last. He could sometimes get Madrid, or Frankfurt, even there in the uneasy Midlands" (110). Radio is the novel's emblem of technological *system*, of that to which there is no conceivable outside. Later, when Connie wonders whether one could "go right away, to the far ends of the earth," Lawrence comments tartly that one could not. "While the wireless is active, there are no far ends of the earth. Kings of Dahomey and Lamas of Thibet listen in to London and New York" (281). Even more than his researches into the technicalities of mining, Clifford's researches into the technicalities of radio constitute an attempt to master a system, in order to claim his share of the power yielded by its autonomy, its apparent transcendence of individual human failings.

Considerable technical expertise was required to operate the radio sets of the mid-1920s, as newspaper articles on the difficulties of reception made plain.[94] Clifford has mastered the uneasy atmospheric conditions around Wragby, in a feat roughly equivalent to, though a good deal less demanding than, his new command over the technicalities of modern mining. Once mastered by him, however, the radio exercises over him a mastery of its own. The loudspeaker "bellowing forth" hour after hour reduces him to trance-like imbecility. He seems neither willing nor able to reflect on whatever reflection of the world it is that the broadcasts have to offer. "Why do people like to listen for hours on end to the impersonal blare of their loud-speakers," Henry Cantril and Gordon W. Allport were to ask in an academic study of the psychology of radio, "or is the blare for them not so impersonal after all?" For Lawrence, as for Cantril and Allport, the loudspeaker's blare or bellowing forth is literally "unspeakable": it articulates nothing. But he, too, understood that the blare does not strike the devoted listener as impersonal. Radio, Cantril and Allport continue, is a new and highly effective "method of communication." "It reaches a larger population of people at greater distances than the other mediums, and it reaches them both instantaneously and cheaply. Through its own peculiar blend of personal and impersonal characteristics it relates the speaker and the auditor in a novel way." The crowds or "clusters of people" gathered by radio are not "congregate" but "consociate."[95] Clifford has given up congregation, and the active engagement it requires, for the blankness of consociate tele-connection. To put it another way, his radio technique "expresses" not himself, but the technology that relies on it. For him, there will be no slack or play in the system.

Technology enables both Clifford's outward self-assertion and his inward surrender. He has become, as Lawrence floridly puts it, "one of the amazing crabs and lobsters of the modern industrial and financial world, invertebrates of the crustacean order, with shells of steel, like machines, and inner bodies of soft pulp" (*LCL* 110). This is not cool. In cool, steeliness without does involve an acknowledgment of the pulp within: acknowledgment, rather than expression or disavowal, being what emotion most needs. Clifford, attempting to acknowledge emotion coolly, at once expresses and disavows it. This "astute and powerful practical man" worships his wife "with a queer craven idolatry, like a savage" (111). Idolatry, whether ancient or modern, occurs when technique expresses only the "technology"— the system, whether social, political, or mechanical—that relies on it. It is the mirror image of the disavowal of system preached by Mellors. Clifford, like Mellors, although to opposite effect, practices a *bad* techno-primitivism. For obvious reasons, the sprezzatura arising out of physical suppleness, of which both Mellors and the hero of *The Virgin and the Gypsy* avail themselves, is not an option for him. Theirs is a bad techno-primitivism not in itself, but because it no longer works. His is a more complicated failure. All techno-primitivisms establish a relation between the archaic and the contemporary. Those that work involve an understanding of difference, in that relation, as well as similarity. Clifford's radio worship merely repeats his worship of Connie. Both are craven, and the repetition of the one in the other reinforces their cravenness.

That Connie is herself at the point of establishing just such a relation becomes clear later in the chapter, when, in the evening of the day after she has first had sex with Mellors, she once again seeks him out at the hut, "to see if it were really real" (122). Clifford's radio habit, reintroduced into the narrative as a further "unimportant passage," becomes the context for her first significant re-naturalization of culture. She asks Clifford whether he would like Mrs. Bolton to play something to him.

> "No, I think I'll listen in."
>
> She heard the curious satisfaction in his voice. She went upstairs to her bedroom. There, she heard the loud-speaker begin to bellow, in an idiotically velveteen-genteel sort of voice, something about a series of street-cries, the very cream of genteel affectation imitating old criers. She pulled on her old violet-coloured mackintosh, and slipped out of the house at the side door.
>
> The drizzle of rain was like a veil over the world, mysterious, hushed, not cold. She got very warm as she hurried across the park. She had to open her light water-proof. (122)

Lawrence is again very precise in identifying the contemporaneity of Clifford's habit. Adepts of the new BBC cult were indeed said to "listen in," rather than merely to listen, as though extravagantly purposeful in their absorption. On this occasion, he also specifies the broadcast's content. Parodically techno-primitivist, the loudspeaker bellow reproduces a series of vulgar archaic street cries with "genteel affectation." Lawrence may even

intend a dig at Frieda's ex-husband, Professor Ernest Weekley, who had
already featured as a clergyman fanatically afraid of the unconventional in
The Virgin and the Gypsy. Weekley tends to disappear from the D. H.
Lawrence story after divorcing Frieda in 1914. But in 1926 he did crop up
in correspondence as the father of Frieda's two daughters. This, Lawrence
reminded Lady Cynthia Asquith on April 15, is the Ernest Weekley "who
writes about words and gives radio lectures on words."[96] The BBC's evening programs for February 10, 1926, had included Mr. Arthur Somervell's
setting of Tennyson's *Maud* sung by Mr. Dale Smith, and a talk by Professor Ernest Weekley on "The Romance of Words: Catchwords and Clichés,"
a "matter of more than passing importance to those who listen and those
who broadcast what is heard."[97] There was a further, indirect link. Lawrence and Weekley were both founding subscribers to *Word-Lore: The
"Folk" Magazine,* which commenced publication in January 1926, describing itself as "a unique repository of valuable and out-of-the-way records
concerning a picturesque past that is rapidly fading out of remembrance."[98]
The picturesque past bellowed futuristically forth from a loudspeaker is
the epitome of bad techno-primitivism.

Clifford's subjection to radio demonstrates just how hard Lawrence
found it to imagine men as cool. Men were absolute, in his philosophy,
women relative (as cool is). To put it more charitably, Lawrence understood
how men had become caught up in masquerades of earnestness, to adapt
his own term for the performative dimension he discerned in many kinds
of "most modern" behavior.[99] There is technique in such masquerades, of
course, but it has no other purpose, Lawrence may have thought, than to
keep the performance going, to sustain the system that rewards a show of
perpetual earnestness. The Etruscan tombs subsequently taught him that
the only thing you should be in earnest about is insouciance.

Connie, slipping out of the house, slips insouciantly out of the masquerade. The parodic techno-primitivism Clifford so avidly and so haplessly
listens in to provides as obtrusive a rhetorical context as any of Mellors's
rants against the modern world for a reassertion of cool. In the novel's second
version, the old mackintosh Connie pulls on had been blue.[100] In revising,
Lawrence re-naturalized the garment, as he was to re-naturalize Connie's
synthetic perfume, by associating it with a woodland flower. He then gave
this natural association a further technological twist. Connie's mackintosh
has become through revision a *light* water-proof of the kind women were
being encouraged to wear for reasons of hygiene. Nature, however, has the

last word. Connie, it turns out, is not ashamed to sweat a little (but only the right amount, we assume) in her hurry. Rubber's mixed constitution has enabled Lawrence, in this most telling of unimportant passages, to capture the subtlety and robustness of an emergent techno-primitivism. Connie's taste in rainwear, her inhabitation of a garment, has introduced some give—some slack, some play—into the relation between technique and technology, free will and necessity. Connie is cool.

THREE

⚛

Thermoplastic

IN CHAPTER II of *Lady Chatterley's Lover,* Connie Chatterley tours the Midlands mining community presided over by her husband, Sir Clifford, and his fellow coal magnates. What she has seen provokes her to meditate bitterly on the industrialization not only of a landscape, and of the class relations inscribed in that landscape, but of subjectivity itself: "Men not men, but animas of coal and iron and clay. Fauna of the elements, carbon, iron, silicon: elementals. They had perhaps some of the weird inhuman beauty of minerals, the lustre of coal, the weight and blueness and resistance of iron, the transparency of glass. Elemental creatures, weird and distorted, of the mineral world!" Connie envisages a new act of creation: the industrial making of a second (human) nature, which might be thought to have superseded the first, and with it, perhaps, the very idea of a world given rather than made. What Lawrence could be asking, through her, is whether this new act of creation had not for the first time in history made it necessary, rather than merely plausible, to conceive individual as well as collective identity materially in all its aspects: social, political, moral, spiritual. For Sir Clifford and his set seem to Connie no less weird and distorted than the miners who work for him: *their* element, she notes, is celluloid, or india rubber: that is to say, plastic.[1]

Already, there is a story here, in broad outline, a story about British culture and society caught between industrial revolutions, and about the class politics of that uneasy transition from steam-powered past to chemical future. The industrial proletariat will continue to belong to coal, clay, iron, and glass, to natural substances extracted from the earth. These are resources as national as they are natural. The miners, fauna of the elements, continually re-naturalize mechanical industrial process, root it in soil and rock—that is, in the nation—through the arduousness and risk of their efforts at its furthest limit: at the coal face, where the machines either cannot operate, or require painstaking guidance. The coal face is the site of an epic encounter between obdurate muscle and obdurate mineral element, mediated by a tool of equal or greater obduracy. Yet because the encounter takes place underground, in conditions of physical as well as social and political invisibility, and because its product disappears at once into furnace and kiln, its epic quality endures only in the medium of a perverse poetry of identification such as that conjured by Connie Chatterley's rapid survey from the window of a limousine, or, a few years later, by George Orwell, in *The Road to Wigan Pier* (1937). The miners, Orwell wrote, "look and work as though they were made of iron. They really do look like iron—hammered iron statues—under the smooth coat of coal dust which clings to them from head to foot."[2] The limousine window, however, like the poetry it on occasion gives rise to, constitutes a mediation of a different kind from the miner's pick and shovel, a mediation permitting a different kind of encounter.

For glass is surely the odd element out in Connie's list. Luster, weight, resistance: these qualities might well be regarded as characteristically proletarian, from the point of view of a wealthy middle-class woman in a limousine. But transparency? What might she hope to see through the window abruptly let into these statuesque elemental creatures seen through a window? The transparency of glass is on her side of the encounter, not theirs. Seeing through and into is a power and a pleasure she wants so badly to experience that she must find it even in the most unlikely places, among creatures of coal and iron and clay.

Because it enables, enhances, and preserves vision, glass has the capacity to shape and express a person's most powerful and most intimate relation to the world in a way that coal, clay, and iron, whether in raw or in manufactured form, do not. In scrambling her list of proletarian qualities, Connie has in effect described the imminent supersession, as key social and cultural infrastructure, of one kind of material substance by another: of coal and iron, which convert energy into work, by glass, which establishes itself as medium and barrier in the space between a person (of a certain class, mostly) and the world. All three substances are the product of the first industrial revolution. Glass, however, was the one that in its standard functions most closely prefigured the thermoplastics with which Connie associates the

British ruling classes: products of the second industrial revolution, natural substances made over by chemical formula. What she has half articulated is the politics of that supersession. For territory, traditionally the very ground and guarantee of political power, does not and perhaps cannot contain the entirety of the production of thermoplastics. The plastics factory, like the laboratory, but unlike the coal mine or iron foundry, could be anywhere in the world, or at least anywhere where capital already is. *Lady Chatterley's Lover* proposes that British cosmopolitan ruling-class identity will soon be more fully expressed by mobile, plastic mediations than by any residual allegiance to natural resource and nation-state. Unlike thermosets, thermoplastics can be reheated, and made to flow into other shapes.

There are long- and short-term perspectives in play here. In the longer term, the history at issue in texts like *Lady Chatterley's Lover* concerns the social, political, and cultural consequences of the introduction of a range of material substances that you could see better through, or feel yourself feel with (glass, rubber, celluloid). Prosthesis would soon rule, if it did not already. Power would depend on control over prosthesis. Connie's abrupt switch from coal, clay, and iron to glass expresses a widespread anxiety concerning the consequences for individual and collective identity of the new regime of cognitive-perceptual prosthesis: a world in which glass mattered more than coal and iron. One popular response to that anxiety was primitivism: the derivation of new capabilities from ancient skills, from an aboriginal creativity mightily reinforced by the first industrial revolution. This long-term perspective is not my main concern, but I need to dwell briefly on some of its promptings.

In 1931, John Grierson, head of the Empire Marketing Board Film Unit, recruited Robert Flaherty to direct a documentary about industrial Britain. Flaherty, as much anthropologist as filmmaker, had made his name with *Nanook of the North* (1922), which details the hardships of Eskimo life. Flaherty's brilliant impressionism and virtuoso handling of montage proved too great an extravagance for the august Empire Marketing Board. Edgar Anstey was hired to instill some shape into Flaherty's fragments, which he did largely by adding an assertive commentary. Although there is not an Eskimo in sight, the story told in and about those fragments remains to a significant degree primitivist. "In the metabolism of the Western world," Orwell was to observe, "the coal-miner is second only to the man who ploughs the soil."[3] *Industrial Britain* begins with the latter. "The old

order changes," we are told, "giving place to the new." The power behind
the new order is coal. Deep underground, we watch miners strip to the
waist and start hacking at a seam with their picks. Where the workings are
too narrow and confined for machinery, they "have still to use this primitive method of hewing coal." The miner's methods, then, are neither wholly
new nor wholly old. They constitute a modern tradition. The wholly new,
by contrast, exists aboveground, in the "world that coal has created," or,
rather, as the film repeatedly insists, *behind* the world that coal has created, behind the drab factories and drabber estates. If you look behind the
factories and estates, "you will find that the spirit of craftsmanship has not
disappeared." The wholly new turns out to be the wholly old revived. We
are in a pottery, watching a potter work as, we are told, ancient Greek pot-
ters worked; and then in a glass foundry, where the man filling the glory
hole "works a trade as old as the pyramids." Unlike the miners at the coal
face, both men are named. As its technological component intensifies, so
labor has to be rooted for ideological purposes ever more conclusively both
in an aboriginal creative effort and in a knowable identity. By now the film
has shown us the "modern aspect" of the glass industry. Foundry men delicately fashion the lenses "without which it would be impossible to conceive
the modern world": lenses for microscopes, for telescopes, "for the camera
that made this picture, for the projector that is throwing it on the screen."
This is matter transcending its status as matter, becoming pure prosthesis,
no more and no less than an extension of human powers. The images, however, tell a different story. The anthropologically minded Flaherty has shot
the gigantic, multifaceted, multilayered lens built for lightship or airfield
use as though it were a prehistoric monolith.

   Primitivism, reimagining medium as object, sutures the break introduced into social and cultural history by the mass production of cognitive-
perceptual prostheses infinitely more powerful than anything hitherto
available. "You find that the man does not change," *Industrial Britain* sol-
emnly concludes, "whatever else changes." In order to take proper account
of the consequences of that break, I will describe still-Modernist glass
writing as both an acknowledgment of and resistance to the new regime of
pure prosthesis, whose core value was transparency. To put it another way:
still-Modernist glass writing was a writing preoccupied with the coal face
or glory-hole energies that go into the making—and the breaking—of
artifacts. Information's ideal transparency held little allure for the glass-
minded among the writers of the time.

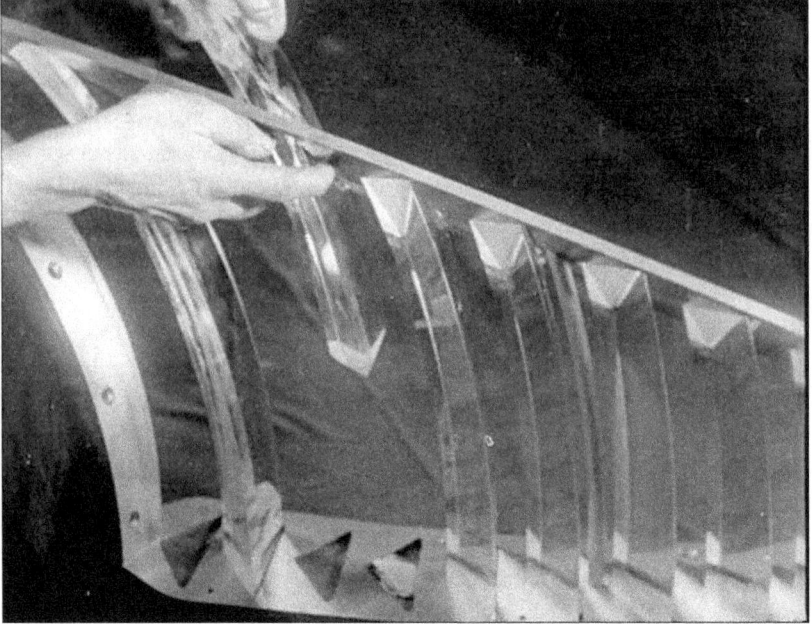

Lens as monolith. Frame grab from *Industrial Britain* (1931, Empire Marketing Board Film Unit, prod. John Grierson, dir. Robert Flaherty).

The bulk of the chapter will however concern itself with the shorter-term perspective: the supersession, during the mid-1920s, of glass by thermoplastics, and then of one kind of thermoplastic by another, as a way at once to conjoin and to separate self and world. For the period between the world wars was the age not of plastic in general, but of particular plastics such as cellophane, or waterproofed viscose sheet, a derivative of cellulose. By the late 1920s, cellophane was just about the most glamorous new substance you could feel yourself feeling with.

Jeffrey Meikle has described in exemplary fashion how plastic, more or less pervasive from the late 1930s in public and private experience alike, acquired for postwar generations the status of "emblem of modernity."[4] The discourse of an "age of plastic"—an era of unprecedented opportunity or of unprecedented deprivation, according to taste—began almost as soon as there were plastics to celebrate and deplore, and is still going strong today. Drawing on Meikle, scholars have begun to examine the cultural connotations of materials such as cellophane.[5] However, in getting to grips with their arrival on the scene in the period between the world wars, we need to avoid the assumption that they were once widely understood, and should still be understood, in some uncomplicated fashion, as a "sign of the new."[6] The whole "age of plastic" discourse, which developed in the 1920s and flourishes to this day in cultural theory and cultural history, is thoroughly misleading.[7] While a plastic like cellophane, for example, could be configured to signify the new in the context of an avant-garde opera, say, or a song by Cole Porter, it did not do so in and of itself.[8] My aim here will be to historicize the overlapping and mutually definitive appearances on the market and in social and cultural view of thermoplastics of different origin and composition. To that end, I draw where appropriate on the social anthropology of material substances.[9] What matters most about the substances I shall pay most attention to is that they were *compound* substances. Their compound quality provoked further expressions of the techno-primitivism that can be said to distinguish the literature of the period from that of earlier and later periods. The chapter concludes with a brief account of the simultaneous acknowledgment in poetry and sculpture of a wholly synthetic substance (Perspex, or Lucite) whose absolute artificiality threatened to rule out altogether any appeal to the primitive. By the late 1930s, as we shall see, techno-primitivism had become a hard act to sustain.

I shall concentrate to a great extent on poetry, an art often regarded, in view of its connections with song and chant, as more "primitive" than prose fiction. The example set by Pound and Eliot had if anything accelerated poetry's self-conscious return to origins.[10] For them, the wholly new in literature was not at all unlike the wholly old. By no means the least mindful of that example, among their contemporaries, were W. H. Auden and Hugh MacDiarmid. In the 1930s, Auden and MacDiarmid, while never less than wary of each other, developed simultaneously, albeit to very different effect, a politics and poetics of adhesion. I take the term "adhesion" from Virginia Woolf's *The Waves* (1931), where it defines Jinny's physical and moral absorption into the pulsating, opportunity-laden world created by the recent refurbishment of Piccadilly underground station. Jinny is promiscuous, and indeterminate: this underground world is the laboratory bench at which she habitually resynthesizes herself, makes herself over again and again, like Prufrock fed on a diet of Nietzsche. "Therefore I will powder my face and redden my lips. I will make the angle of my eyebrows sharper than usual. I will rise to the surface, standing erect with the others in Piccadilly Circus."[11] Like Connie Chatterley, Jinny finds herself among subterranean elementals, among animas (though not of coal, iron, and clay). Unlike Connie, she adheres to these inhabitants of a second nature, of a universe made over technologically. She sticks to and with them.

According to the *OED*, to adhere is to become or remain firmly attached to a substance, by absorption into a glutinous surface, or by grasping; to adhere is also to act as a close companion, partisan, or follower. We tend perhaps to speak of adhesion when we mean the former, and of adherence when we mean the latter (though the terms are virtually interchangeable). For Auden—more Jinny than Connie—the problem was that there were people whom one already stuck to, because one was like them, because one liked them; and there were people, who might well not be the same people, whom one must learn to stick with, through an act of will, if change was to happen. Was adhesion always already an indissoluble ideological adherence, not to be broken even by dramatic changes of heart? Might counteradherence to a new doctrine or a new class generate its own adhesiveness? MacDiarmid—more Connie than Jinny—hoped that adherence to the new would once and for all dissolve any old adhesiveness. But he knew that it would not. Both, like Connie and Jinny, are techno-primitivist. Adherence, we might note, is a function of energies released, often apocalyptically, or as a return to origins. Adhesiveness, by contrast, is what information often does. We get stuck in it, or stick with it. Auden and MacDiarmid wanted to know what information does.

Glass Writing

Glass, a combination of sand and other minerals fused at a high temperature, fulfills a variety of functions, from intricately wrought decorative object to ubiquitous feature of the built environment. Glass manufacture was an ancient technology radically overhauled during the nineteenth century. Isobel Armstrong has shown in convincing detail that the period between 1830 and 1880 witnessed the emergence of an "environment of mass transparency" and of a corresponding "glass consciousness." "In the nineteenth century," Armstrong argues, "glass became a third or middle term: it interposed an almost invisible layer of matter between the seer and the seen—the sheen of a window, the silver glaze of the mirror, the convexity or concavity of the lens." The glass consciousness informing so many Victorian texts understood that interposition dialectically as at once medium and barrier. "The experience of contradiction," Armstrong concludes, "was built into everyday life."[12] During the first decades of the twentieth century, further changes in the methods, and in particular the scale, of its production made glass newly available, in architecture above all, and newly spectacular.[13] The plate-glass walls with which some of the most influential architects of the period chose to sheathe some of their most innovative buildings (or projects for buildings) became the embodiment of the international style's vision of the radiant city of the future. Two principles inform these buildings: (a) their self-manifestation as structure rather than mass; and (b) the transparency they propose, the dissolution of the boundary separating interior from exterior.[14]

The international style has not been to everyone's taste. In Armstrong's view, the new architectural emphasis on structure and transparency destroyed the productive dialectical tension built into glass's existence as at once medium and barrier. "Transparency encourages a simple dualism, or, what is the opposite form of the same thing, the collapse of seer into seen."[15] Anne Friedberg is by no means the only cultural historian to have denounced the "spartan Le Corbusier and Mies glass boxes of High Modernism."[16] I am not sure that this is entirely fair. Mies van der Rohe's 1922 Berlin skyscraper project was neither spartan nor boxy. On the contrary, its "fat, rolling, exterior curves" (in the words of one critic) take a frankly indecent interest in the possibilities of the diaphanous.[17]

Transparency, moreover, had acquired a *political* value. Hannes Meyer's "Project for the Palace of the League of Nations, Geneva, 1926–7" sought to release this new "supranational organization," with its commitment to debate rather than blitzkrieg, from the "straitjacket" of traditional architecture. "No back corridors for backstairs diplomacy," Meyer explained, "but open glazed rooms for the public negotiations of honest men."[18] Unsurprisingly, neither plan made it off the drawing board. But that should not prevent us from acknowledging the force of the utopian aspiration bound up in the transparency glass might be supposed to enable.

To be sure, the more one thought about it, the less plausible the aspiration became. Walter Benjamin was a great admirer of Paul Scheerbart's staunchly utopian *Glasarchitektur* of 1914. "To live in a glass house is a revolutionary virtue par excellence," he declared in his 1929 critique of surrealism. "It is also an intoxication, a moral exhibitionism, that we badly need."[19] So far, so Mies. But Benjamin's subsequent thoughts about living in a glass house fell, with a nudge from Bertolt Brecht, under the general heading of a reflection upon the "Destructive Character" in modernity. "Objects made of glass have no 'aura,'" he noted in "Experience and Poverty"

(1933). "Glass is, in general, the enemy of secrets. It is also the enemy of possession." Had you entered the "bourgeois room of the 1880s," he went on, you would have found absolutely no spot in it on which the owner had not left a mark of some kind. Modern architects, by contrast, building in iron and glass, had created rooms in which it was very hard to "leave traces."[20] Politically, Benjamin abhorred secrets and possessions: but the traces they left fed his imagination like nothing else. He developed his own politics and poetics of adhesion.

Of course, it was not just buildings that needed looking into. The health and hygiene movements that caused such a stir in Europe and North America from the turn of the century onward had an equal stake in transparency: in the transparency of the human body to inspection. They found an icon in the Glass Man, an anatomical model created for the 1930 International Hygiene Exhibition in Dresden, and shown again at "The Wonder of Life," in Berlin in 1935.[21] The Glass Man consisted of a human skeleton and an array of wax-work organs, the whole wrapped in a see-through "skin." Gazing upward in rapture, his arms outstretched, the Glass Man transparently embraces the future.

It is perhaps laboring the point a little to add that the Glass Man constitutes a "bad" techno-primitivism. The fit between the modern technological miracle of molded glass and the ancient genetic miracle of an aboriginal Aryan purity is too tight to allow for reflection upon either.

The Glass Man was soon joined by a Glass Woman. They were just what Nazi propaganda had been waiting for. During the 1930s, the Glass Couple toured the international exhibition circuit as an advertisement for eugenic programs, and a symbol of Aryan superiority. The glass buildings and the glass bodies articulate a widespread aspiration toward a future in which the social and political order would have been rendered transparent, for better or for worse. As far as I am aware, few writers took an enduring interest in this aspiration, though I sometimes wonder about the figure Wallace Stevens found for his ideal poet-philosopher in "Asides on the Oboe," in *Parts of a World* (1942).

> The central man, the human globe, responsive
> As a mirror with a voice, the man of glass,
> Who in a million diamonds sums us up.[22]

Stevens's version of a "central man" has generally been thought to derive from Emerson or Schopenhauer. I have not come across any evidence to

Transparently embracing the future. *Der gläserne Mensch.* Deutsches
Historisches Museum.

suggest that he had seen or read about the Glass Man of the hygienists. He could in theory have done so, since one went on display in a museum in Buffalo in 1934.

But thinking through glass did not necessarily involve thinking about transparency.[23] Glass, the *OED* tells us, is "in its ordinary forms transparent, lustrous, hard, and brittle." My argument will be that on the whole Modernist writers found in the brittleness of glass a metaphor more appropriate to their purposes than they did in its transparency. Those purposes might, of course, be apocalyptic. Toward the end of Lawrence's *Women in Love*, Rupert Birkin gazes at Gerald Crich's frozen corpse, "curled up as if for sleep, yet with the horrible hardness somehow evident. It filled him with horror. The room must be made warm, the body must be thawed. The limbs would break like glass or like wood if they had to be straightened."[24] Images of broken glass increasingly pervaded the photojournalism of the 1930s and 1940s. They cropped up in literature, too, from *Ulysses* to Blitz fiction.[25] For breakage had become the primary manifestation of apocalypse; and apocalyptic thinking was the means by which Modernism fed its addiction to energy. But I want to concentrate here on the possibilities that one writer in particular discerned in the material's brittleness.

In order to define those possibilities, I will touch on two other glass icons, or rather two other glass events, of the period (for we do need to consider the energies released both in making and in breaking). The first is Marcel Duchamp's *The Bride Stripped Bare by Her Bachelors, Even,* also known as the *Large Glass,* of 1915 to 1923. My concern is not so much with the work itself as with an event that overtook it. In 1927, both panes in the *Large Glass* shattered in transit from an exhibition in Brooklyn. When Katherine Dreier, its owner, finally brought herself to tell Duchamp what had happened, he chose to understand the mishap as the work's "chance completion," and spent months meticulously repairing it.[26] The *Large Glass*'s chance completion could be said to have restored it from brokenness to breakability. The other icon I have in mind is the Coca-Cola bottle. Again, my concern is not so much with the icon itself as with an event that overtook it: the redesign accomplished in 1915. By that time, the Coca-Cola Company had a serious problem: imitation. The bottles in which Coca-Cola had been marketed until then had straight sides, with a label applied: they were easy to copy. In 1915, Coca-Cola commissioned the Root Glass Company in Terre Haute, Indiana, to design a bottle so utterly distinctive that if broken it could be identified by touch as well as sight from each individual piece. The heavy, fluted container the company came up with, known as the hobbleskirt or Mae West model, fulfilled the brief to perfection. The transformation in the product's image from the late 1890s to the early 1930s was spectacular: it represents one of the most effective exercises in rebranding in corporate history.[27]

The differences between these two objects, one a unique work of art, the other an endlessly replicated commodity, scarcely need restating. But each has something to say about the nature and scope of glass as a material, and therefore about the nature and scope of the fantasies that might be invested in its use. Built into each object is an awareness of the breakability of the material out of which it has been made. Things break, ideas break: but to imagine them as breakable is not necessarily to imagine them broken. It could be to imagine them as not needing to be unbreakable in order to remain what they are.

There were Modernist writers who thought, if not about Marcel Duchamp or Coca-Cola bottles, then about breakability: none, perhaps, more intently than Virginia Woolf, in *Jacob's Room* (1922), generally regarded as her first fully experimental work of fiction. For Woolf, breakability defined the peculiar pathos of young men.[28] *Jacob's Room,* narrated by a woman ten years older than the protagonist, has for its "centre" or "magnet" a "young man alone in his room." At one point, the narrator observes Jacob and his friends through the open window of his room in Trinity College, Cambridge.

Was it to receive this gift from the past that the young man came to the window and stood there, looking out across the court? It was Jacob. He stood smoking his pipe while the last stroke of the clock purred softly round him. Perhaps there had been an argument. He looked satisfied; indeed masterly; which expression changed slightly as he stood there, the sound of the clock conveying to him (it may be) a sense of old buildings and time; and himself the inheritor; and then to-morrow; and friends; at the thought of whom, in sheer confidence and pleasure, it seemed, he yawned and stretched himself.

Meanwhile behind him the shape they had made, whether by argument or not, the spiritual shape, hard yet ephemeral, as of glass compared with the dark stone of the Chapel, was dashed to splinters, young men rising from chairs and sofa corners, buzzing and barging about the room, one driving another against the bedroom door, which giving way, in they fell.

Then Jacob was left there, in the shallow arm-chair, alone with Masham?
Anderson? Simeon? Oh, it was Simeon. The others had all gone.[29]

Glass features in this scene not as transparent—the window is open, and
Jacob's looking out not the main issue—but as brittle. In true Modernist
fashion, its breaking serves to dramatize an explosion of energies, both
physical and psychic. If Jacob has won the argument, then someone else
must have lost. The brittleness of glass enables Woolf to understand the
hurt that may nor may not have been sublimated into buzzing and barging
horseplay, the hurt that inheres in all such rivalrous friendships, and is yet
unlikely to destroy them (though it might). The collective shape glimpsed
through the open window has been broken, but remains identifiable in
each of its pieces. Who stays behind? "Masham? Anderson? Simeon? Oh,
it was Simeon." That, at least, is the reasonable expectation. Woolf imagines the group not needing to be unbreakable in order to remain what it
is. There is hopefulness in that expectation—soon to be extinguished by
Jacob's death in war.

Glass, however, was about to become less brittle. In its manufacture, the
emphasis began to shift in the mid-1920s from transparency to robustness
and flexibility. In H. G. Wells's *Marriage* (1912), a sympathetic plutocrat
had addressed the scientist-hero in the following hearty fashion. "Business has hardly begun to touch substances yet, you know, Trafford—
flexible glass, for example, and things like that. So far we've always taken
substances for granted."[30] By 1928, an article in *Popular Mechanics* could
claim that flexible glass was now readily available for a range of uses.[31] In
1936, Pilkington Brothers were advertising glass that "will bend before it
will break."[32] The truth was that glass manufacturers were having to adapt
fast because they faced intense competition from the plastics industry.
Glass was about to be superseded, in some functions, by thermoplastics: by
a material substance that had no brittleness to protect from explosions of
energy.

Applied Transparency

Celluloid, a combination of nitric acid, camphor, and cellulose derived
from sources such as cotton, was the first artificial plastic. Although materials with similar properties had long been in use at the time of its introduction during the 1860s, these were all mixtures or modifications of sub-

stances that possessed some plastic properties in their natural state. Celluloid, on the other hand, as Robert Friedel observes, "was produced from an omnipresent fibrous material changed by the action of very common acids and then made tractable by the addition of a crystallized resin. None of the original ingredients of celluloid suggested at all a hard, transparent, mouldable product."[33] Cellulose nitrate (celluloid) rapidly found a market as the basis for a competitively priced, durable, and decorative imitation of materials used in the manufacture of items such as dental plates, knife handles, combs, buttons, and billiard balls. During the final decades of the century, it became associated above all with washable collars and cuffs, and with photographic film. The collars and cuffs were less in evidence by the 1930s. Beckett's Murphy declares his unfitness for modern life by brightening up an ancient suit with "a perfectly plain lemon made-up bow tie presented as though in derision by a collar and dicky combination carved from a single sheet of celluloid and without seam, of a period with the suit and the last of its kind."[34] His is clearly the most old-fashioned of techno-primitivisms.

The widespread use of celluloid in photography, and in the manufacture of a variety of domestic objects, drew attention to the material's disadvantages as well as to its advantages. The instability of its elements (nitrate, camphor) caused a good deal of understandable anxiety. There was no shortage of stories about exploding billiard balls. Celluloid did not in fact explode on impact: but it *was* liable to burst into flames. Manufacturers had frequently to quell a popular prejudice to the effect that a shirt with celluloid buttons and collar was a funeral pyre waiting to happen.[35] More disturbing still, celluloid was now also the material out of which dolls were made. Other objects likely to catch fire included the film in film projectors. The history of early cinema is in no small measure the history of buildings ablaze.[36] Kodak began to produce safety film in 1909. In the period immediately before the First World War, safety film became a feature in the marketing of home entertainment systems such as the Pathéscope, a "scientifically perfect yet extremely simple machine using only NON-INFLAMMABLE FILMS and generating its own electric light," which would, it was claimed, allow the "absolutely safe and flickerless projection of the World's most life-like, interesting, and topical pictures."[37] But these types of film shrank and tore easily, so that the image quality deteriorated rapidly: the studios lost interest. Safety film did not become the industry standard until the 1950s. In Alfred Hitchcock's *Sabotage* (1936), it is only by special dispensation that young Stevie is allowed to carry his cans of film onto a bus. As it happens, Stevie's cans do no wrong: but Hitchcock blew him up anyway. Although there was more cooked than raw in celluloid, the substance's instability provided a constant reminder of the limitations of the synthesizing process.

The second half of the 1920s saw the development of new resins in competition with celluloid and Bakelite. What seems to have driven these advances was an emphasis on improvements in transparency. For once plastic had matched glass for transparency, it would be possible to exploit its existing virtues (robustness and flexibility) more fully. The new thermoplastics available by the end of the 1920s (cellulose acetate, cellophane) altered the terms of the interpositions glass had made possible by adjusting a material's properties as medium to its properties as barrier. They produced a new relation between subject and object. What they had to offer, in short, was an *applied* transparency: one that, in surrounding or coating people and objects the better to protect them, or to show them off, took its shape from them. The sense of touch predominates in the way cellulose acetate was marketed during the early 1930s. It was said to be indispensable, for example, in the manufacture of "coverings for hand-rails" and "transparent wrapping paper."[38] Cellulose acetate took the place of cellulose nitrate as the absorptive middle layer in the safety glass used for automobile and airplane windshields, a huge and rapidly expanding market. Companies like Triplex Safety Glass advertised widely, in the *Times* and elsewhere. The traffic jam in Louis MacNeice's "Birmingham" features "Chromium dogs on the bonnet, faces behind the triplex screens."[39]

Here is the thing: the Dresden Glass Man and Glass Woman were not made out of glass at all. They were made out of a new transparent and flexible plastic called Cellon.[40] Cellophane, too, was to prove exemplary as a form of flexible transparency used in the packaging of cigarettes and other commodities. It clung to that which it proofed. "Say, I must be transparent" is Cary Grant's response, in the Paramount comedy *I'm No Angel* (1933), when Mae West tells him that she always knew he was mad about her. "Honey," she agrees, her hands all over him, "you're just wrapped in cellophane." Cellophane informs and is informed by that which it adheres to.

The development during the late 1920s of effective methods of applying transparency is the context for Michael Powell's wonderful early celluloid comedy, and comedy of celluloid, *The Love Test* (1935). *The Love Test* follows generic formula obediently enough: boy gets girl, boy loses girl, boy gets girl again.[41] But the boy and girl in question are chemists working at a laboratory that has been commissioned by the Union Celluloid Company to devise a means of flameproofing its products. It is worth adding that the enthusiasm for plastics old and new during the early 1930s ensured that the flammability of cellulose nitrate remained a matter of vivid public concern. In February 1935, the *Times* reported that, when touring the British Industries Fair at Olympia, Her Majesty the Queen had spent a good deal of time at the stand of a firm that, in answer to a challenge she herself had issued during a similar visit two years previously, was now manufacturing safe celluloid dolls.[42] Flammability is not, of course, a mark of the natural; but failure to eradicate it was seen as science's failure, a failure fully to synthesize.

In *The Love Test*, the space in which the scientists and their managers work is divided between the managing director's office and staff common rooms, which encourage hierarchical gendered behavior, and the relative social and gender equality of the laboratory. We are introduced to this space, and the divisions within it, during a short sequence early on in the film, which begins and ends in the managing director's office but has in between explored other areas, most notably the laboratory, by means of a fluid tracking shot. At first, the emphasis is on glass: the picture window separating office from laboratory, the porthole in a door, spectacles, a whole array of bottles and flasks. These interpositions are more barrier than medium. Powell immediately opposes to them a vantage point that is more medium than barrier. A beautifully conceived tracking shot that coasts coolly around the laboratory, coating the space and its occupants in transparency, literally *filming* it, serves as prelude to and foretaste of a narrative that will endorse a comparable plasticity of social and sexual attitude. This is a film about the synthesizing of heterosexual romance. In one remarkable cross-cut sequence, the managing director's secretary visits the hero in his apartment, and, removing her gum, teaches him how to kiss passionately: while the heroine, in *her* apartment, is concurrently made over from starchy egghead to femme fatale by the glamorous woman who lives next door. Editing wittily elides the perfume flasks on the neighbor's dressing table with the flasks of chemicals on the hero's desk. It is the heroine who (at last!) asks the hero out to dinner: his gaze, when he arrives to collect her, smolders appropriately—but still falls short of the intensity of that bestowed by the neighborly makeover artist, as she closes the door of her apartment on this heterosexual mating ritual. Powell's tracking shot finds in the unbrokenness of its own sinuous tactile passage beyond the panoptic glass partition a kind of insouciance, a comic composure hinting at utopia (the "feelies," indeed!). Once through the glass, it no longer has to worry about barriers, or the explosions that break them. It enters into the thermoplastic spirit. The doll we see may shortly burst into flames, but by the end of the film a use will have been found for properly applied heat. There was in the insouciance of the thermoplastic spirit the basis, at least, for a politics and poetics of adhesion: for cool, we might say.

Thermoplastic Writing: The Audenesque

Is there anything like such insouciance in the literature of the period? The place to start might be the opening paragraph of W. H. Auden's "Consider this and in our time," written in March 1930, a poem that, while it does not develop a new aesthetic, could be said to indicate the need for one, and to do so by expressing a certain dissatisfaction with glass as an enabling material.

> Consider this and in our time
> As the hawk sees it or the helmeted airman:
> The clouds rift suddenly—look there
> At cigarette-end smouldering on a border
> At the first garden party of the year.
> Pass on, admire the view of the massif
> Through plate-glass windows of the Sport Hotel;
> Join there the insufficient units
> Dangerous, easy, in furs, in uniform
> And constellated at reserved tables
> Supplied with feelings by an efficient band
> Relayed elsewhere to farmers and their dogs
> Sitting in kitchens in the stormy fens.[43]

What we are asked to consider, here, is the lure of transparency, and the power-knowledge it produces: the view seen through plate-glass windows a mundane version of the transcendental panorama available to hawk and helmeted airman. But transparency is no sooner proffered than withdrawn. The poem's production of and immediate withdrawal from this view brings to mind a scene set in a somewhat similar Sport Hotel, in Hitchcock's *The Man Who Knew Too Much* (1934). Hitchcock, too, proffers a panoramic view of the massif through the plate-glass window of the hotel's ballroom, and then immediately tracks back from it, amid a whirl of dancers. As the camera withdraws, the event it has withdrawn from surges in from both sides to fill the gap it has left.

In Auden's poem, the instruction to consider and admire yields immediately to a contrary instruction to circulate and mingle: activities that necessarily involve a surrender of the commanding heights. The contrary instruction, like a camera tracking backward through a crowd, rapidly loses its ability to command. Broadcast radio, connecting Alp to fenland, playboy to farmer, drowsily usurps the disciplinary gaze enabled by viewing platform and telephoto lens: we no longer have to jump to it. Too much has been made of the poem's initial peremptoriness, Rod Mengham notes, as symptomatic of a "dictatorial tendency" in 1930s writing. It may continue to evoke a "feeling of dominance"; but what prevails is an awareness of the variety in the scene it unfolds.[44] By the end of its first paragraph, the balance of rhetorical power between syntax and meter has already shifted subtly. For seven of the paragraph's thirteen lines, syntax lords it over meter, not allowing a pattern to form in the ear that might distract from or resist declarative utterance. In the remaining six, meter reasserts itself: the poetic line, shrugging off syntax and punctuation, becomes in effect the primary unit of sense. Lineation lines the world. Auden has put his faith in description in an almost geometrical sense. Geometrically, to describe is to delineate, to trace the outline of a figure. The paragraph's conclusion invites us not to inspect the world as though from behind a window, but to feel ourselves *filming* it, as Mae West films Cary Grant, applying desire to it. It did for a moment look as though the original instruction to consider and admire might produce a request for adherence: adherence, possibly, to the overthrow of the society and culture about to be described. What follows, instead, is a series of gestures of adhesion, the last of which locates us firmly in the current media age, as radio relays the efficient band to farmers and their dogs sitting in kitchens in the stormy fens.

To summarize, crudely: glass mattered in late-nineteenth-century literature and culture on account of the productive tension built into its existence as at once medium and barrier, as Armstrong has shown, and in early twentieth-century literature and culture on account of a brittleness seeming to invite the ferocious energies unleashed by apocalyptic fantasy. By 1930, glass no longer mattered so much, because other substances had begun to articulate a relation to the world neither tense nor hotly explosive, but instead coolly seeking out by adhesion the slack in the system. A flexible transparency became the cool gesture at what might come next, after energy's heat death.

Does the shift of emphasis enacted in the poem's first paragraph tell us anything at all about the ways in which Auden's work could be said to "mature" during the 1930s, beyond, as Michael O'Neill puts it, an "early, electrifying stylistic brilliance"?[45] Clearly, the peremptoriness persisted, in his poems, as a response to the widely felt need to take a stand politically. In "August for the people and their favourite islands," for example, Auden called upon Christopher Isherwood to take up once again his "strict and adult pen" and "Make action urgent and its nature clear" (EA 157). That Isherwood's strict and adult pen should be required at all, however, indicates the durability of the attachment to be overcome. The poet feels that attachment as strongly as the people he writes about; indeed, he is strongly attached to their attachment. Should we then regard adhesion to "Our freedom in this English house, / Our picnics in the sun" (137), as Auden himself seems half inclined to, as mere nostalgia? Nostalgia is a feeling not always thought to make for maturity, though it is enhanced by maturity, by growing up and growing old.

I would argue, on the contrary, that the determination to (as it were) film the world announced at the end of the first paragraph of "Consider this and in our time" constitutes a nostalgia (literally, a homesickness): but a nostalgia for the present, rather than for the past. Auden's pen was to become strict and adult by making *passion* urgent and its nature clear. The aesthetic his poem requires—which could be said to arise dialectically out of peremptoriness—is an aesthetic of adhesion.

Passion, or passivity, has on the whole not been the note discerned in the early, electrifying Auden. We need here to take into account Robert Crawford's ambitious argument concerning the (Modernist, in his view) poetries of knowledge developed during the interwar period, by Eliot, Pound, and others. "Modernist verse," Crawford argues, "so nurtured by and alert to academic channels as well as to the relationship between knowledge and power, is very much a poetry of the governing of knowledge."[46] Evidence adduced for this claim includes Eliot's conversations and correspondence with Norbert Wiener, the founder of cybernetics, the science of regulatory systems; both had taken Josiah Royce's Harvard graduate course on types of scientific method. According to Crawford, Eliot's conception of poetry is cybernetic. *The Waste Land* should be "read" as an exercise in the regulation of certain kinds of knowledge. My feeling is that the argument rather too easily conflates analog and digital methods: the scholarly footnote and the database. I shall return later, in a discussion of Hugh MacDiarmid's "On a Raised Beach," to the general question of the emergence of a poetry of knowledge, and of its imputed Modernism. I want first to take up Crawford's recruitment of Auden's *The Orators: An English Study* to the cybernetic cause. First published in May 1932 under Eliot's auspices, *The Orators* was thought to update *The Waste Land*. It is a text compounded of poetry and prose in more or less equal proportion, written during the period of the establishment and consolidation of radical regimes in Italy, Germany, and Russia, and concerning the human impulse to lead or be led. Its protagonist is an Airman who denounces the bourgeoisie as the Enemy and plots violent revolution.

"*The Orators*," Crawford remarks, "is probably the first poem to include diagrams, to mention 'Cyclostyle copies' or 'the screen of a television set' or the 'Vickers 163.' Its engagement with forms and technologies of information is part of its poetic excitement."[47] Whether we regard it as a poem or not, we can certainly agree that *The Orators* draws on scholarly research. Following Peter Firchow, critics have noted its debt to essays about shamanism published in 1930 by Auden's friend John Layard in the *Journal of the Royal Anthropological Institute of Great Britain and Ireland*.[48] But does it constitute a database? The diagrams are interspersed with poems of meticulous formal regularity, including a sestina, while the journal entries give way altogether, in book 3, to a set of six odes. The substantial nod to technologies of information is countered by, and perhaps could even be said to give rise to, a return to poetry's enduring capacity for sensuous apprehension. The reference to television, for example, exemplifies nostalgia. The Airman recalls that his first memories of his uncle were "like images cast on the screen of a television set" (*EA* 84). Similarly, the references to radio—"the voice, of the announcer, maybe, from some foreign broadcasting station" (62)—belong to the litany of vaguely familiar circumstance designed to make us feel homesick for the present, for the here and now. So too with other sorts of prosthesis. "The working mouth, the flimsy flexing knee, the leap in summer in the rubber shoes, these signal in their only codes" (85–86). Auden would have known what Connie Chatterley was about. The early poems are not electrifying at all. They constitute a thermoplastic rhetorical event sustained by astute techno-primitivism.

That, perhaps, is where the scholarly interest in shamans came in, as an attempt not at cybernetics, but at adjustment to life in the first media age. Douglas Mao has audaciously compared Auden to Wyndham Lewis, whose *The Revenge for Love* (1937) I will discuss at length in Chapter 5, as liberals against liberalism: that is, as writers who prized the exercise of critical intelligence, above all, and sought to diversify and defend it as an essential safeguard as much in regimes promoting tolerance as in those promoting autocracy. The fascist coup planned by the Airman would almost certainly stamp out critical intelligence altogether. As Mao notes, however, the "surrender of eccentricity, romance, plans, secrets, and practical jokes" that reabsorption by the "liberal mainstream" entailed did not strike Auden as much of an improvement. At least, not in 1932. For while Lewis continued to regard liberal democracy as fraudulent through and through, Auden began to believe that the "prevailing order" might yet prove acceptable "so long as it provided room for the dissenters who would help it to evolve." He had not abandoned all hope that modern democracies might offer a "shamanic role" to "their queers, their highbrows, their neurotic children," and, presumably, their poets.[49] The (highbrow) dissenter as shaman: Auden was set up for techno-primitivism. His investment in the orality of metrical language may have led him to declare that the speech of the peasant was more vivid than that of the university graduate, but he also thought that the wireless and the talkies had produced a "revival of the spoken word" (*EA* 307). All he needed to put techno-primitivism into effect was an aesthetic of adhesion. The difficulty throughout would be to avoid the sort of bad or parodic techno-primitivism represented by the "genteel affectation" of the BBC program about street cries that so enthralls Sir Clifford Chatterley.[50]

Another term for an aesthetic of adhesion, as this took shape in the 1930s, would be the Audenesque. The Audenesque can be defined most precisely through its distinctive use of the definite article to enlist the reader in the construction of a (more or less) shared fictional world.[51] It was already fully effective in book 2 of *The Orators*, "Journal of an Airman," which catalogs the shortcomings of Enemy (that is, bourgeois) behavior.

Three kinds of enemy walk—the grandiose stunt—the melancholic swagger—the paranoic sidle.

Three kinds of enemy bearing—the condor stoop—the toad stupor—the robin's stance.

Three kinds of enemy face—the fucked hen—the favourite puss—the stone in the rain. (*EA* 81)

Eliot emended "fucked hen" to "June bride" before publication: but neither detail would seem to have any necessary connection with bourgeois physiognomies.

In this catalog, the definite article does all the work. It suggests that bourgeois faces look like something specific (a fucked hen, a favorite puss), but relies on the reader to complete the proffered identification: to bring to mind from his or her own experience a particular face that might be thought to resemble a fucked hen or a favorite puss. "These are excellent descriptions," Auden's friend Stephen Spender commented, "of the kind of people whose pictures we see in society newspapers."[52] They are excellent descriptions for those among Auden's readers who follow the society newspapers and can complete the identifications proffered by the definite article. The definite article (like demonstratives such as "this" and "that," unlike the indefinite article) is a specifying agent, which serves to identify a particular individual or subclass within the class designated by the noun it precedes. But the demonstratives differ in that they themselves provide part of the information needed to identify that particular individual or subclass: they position it along a scale of proximity, and their associations of intimacy or distance survive even if we cannot identify what they refer to. When Madame Sosostris, in *The Waste Land*, refers to "this card," we know it is one she will be playing close to her chest; when the typist thinks about sex ("Well now that's done"), we know it is something she is glad to put behind her.[53] The definite article, by contrast, has no semantic content to speak of and does not so position the individual or subclass it refers to. Its relative neutrality allows greater scope for interpretation. If Auden had compared the bourgeois walk to "this" grandiose stunt or "that" paranoiac sidle, the relevance of our own familiarity with grandiose stunts and paranoiac sidles would have been severely curtailed. *The* grandiose stunt and *the* paranoiac sidle are a different matter: we all know them, if we have been following the society newspapers. The definite article makes possible a collaborative filming of elements of a known world. It wraps the enemy walk and the enemy face in cellophane: the better to display them, and, it could be, the better to preserve them.

The method lent itself to caricature. "The weakness of the Enemy captions," Spender observed, "is that they apply to the people whom one doesn't like. One's own little set draws closer together."[54] The members of the "little set" wanted change, but knew that they themselves, in so far as they avidly read the society newspapers, were part of what had to be changed. Caricature gave them something to distance themselves from without undue loss of sleep.

> It's farewell to the drawing-room's civilised cry,
> The professor's sensible whereto and why,
> The frock-coated diplomat's social aplomb,
> Now matters are settled with gas and with bomb. (*EA* 208)

Who is going to miss any of that? Gas and bomb, by contrast, require no further collaborative identification by means of the definite article. They are absolute facts. Auden invokes an über-rationality that has not only resigned itself to the imminent deployment of gas and bomb by others, but would also, in the ultimate act of adherence to revolutionary or counter-revolutionary doctrine, consider deploying them on its own behalf. However, it would be wrong to suppose that the aesthetic of adhesion built into Auden's use of the definite article, in this poem and more generally, serves merely to identify a world ripe for destruction. After a riotously camp rehearsal of the day of judgment, the poem concludes with a gentle goodbye to "the house with its wallpaper red" and "the sheets on the warm double bed" (209). These, too, have been wrapped in cellophane: as we complete the work begun by the definite articles, we can feel ourselves feeling them. Stuck to the sheets on the warm double bed, we know exactly what we are going to miss most.

We need to acknowledge just how various are the adhesions that Auden's poems of the 1930s propose. In "August for the people and their favourite islands," he demands from Isherwood a strict and adult reckoning, an über-rationality, but in his own voice cleaves unashamedly to the people as they are, and to the islands they have every right to favor.

> Lulled by the light they live their dreams of freedom;
> May climb the old road twisting to the moors,
> Play leap-frog, enter cafés, wear
> The tigerish blazer and the dove-like shoe. (*EA* 155)

Auden remains as warmly attached to the most modern tigerish blazer and dove-like shoe as he does to the ancient road twisting to the moors. He has understood the passions they express. "Certainly our city," written in spring 1936, adds a further absolute fact to gas and bomb—germ warfare—while at the same time invoking the über-rationality apparent in the actions of those who have turned their face toward the "really better / World": Stalin, complicit in the death of Maxim Gorki; Freud and Groddeck at their "candid studies." But Auden has also seen the future in the city's present condition,

cathedral and slum notwithstanding: "Here is the cosmopolitan cooking /
And the light alloys and the glass" (165). A sonnet written in 1933 reflects
that it is good to sunbathe on a roof side by side with your lover:

> . . . and good to see them passing by
> Below on the white sidewalk in the heat,
> The dog, the lady with parcels, and the boy:
> There is the casual life outside the heart. (149)

Enjambment neatly enacts a shift of attention away from the roof's *locus
amoenus* down into the street, as we wait to discover who "they" are. The
strength of Auden's heartfelt commitment to the futures built into the "casual life outside the heart" should not be underestimated. It was a nostalgia
for the present.

Auden's poems of the 1930s propose (at least) three versions, or visions,
of the future: gas, bomb, and germ warfare; candid studies, or über-
rationality, up to and including political assassination; and popular dreams
of freedom. They assemble these versions, I have argued, not by collage,
but dialectically. Adhesion to the world as it is provokes by its own excess
adherence to a doctrine whose explicit aim is to transform that world utterly. The doctrine, in turn, sticks; or *should* stick. Given the strength of
the poet's lingering attachment to modern democracy, we may doubt
whether it will.

The ultimate test of this dialectic of adherence and adhesion was the
civil war that erupted in Spain in 1936. Auden's "Spain 1937" is a propaganda piece, unashamedly panoramic and peremptory. So absolute is Re-
publicanism's appeal that adherence to it resembles the product "not so
much of will," as Edward Mendelson puts it, "as of something very much
like unconscious instinctive nature."[55] Auden imagines International Brigade members migrating to Spain "like gulls or the seeds of a flower." But
he cannot let the metaphor rest there. The next stanza describes freedom
fighters clinging "like burrs" to the long expresses that lurch through the
"unjust lands." The balance within the figure has tilted, from a concern
with moral and political adherence to a concern with physical adhesion.
The more peremptory and more abstract its injunctions, the closer the
poem sticks to stickiness, to what it might actually have felt like ("the theo-
logical feuds in the taverns"), or now feels like ("the expending of powers /
On the flat ephemeral pamphlet and the boring meeting"), or might yet
conceivably feel like ("the winter of perfect communion," but also, mundanely,

"the bicycle races / Through the suburbs on summer evenings") to inhabit a more or less identifiable world (*EA* 210–12). "Spain 1937" films past, present, and future with equal abandon. Too much proclamation—"To-day the struggle"—generates as its antithesis a carnival of collaborative inquiry into the minutiae of the casual life past, present, and future. When the carnival in turn eventually recedes, there is nothing for it but to proclaim a new and singular awareness of absolute cosmic indifference. "The stars are dead; the animals will not look . . ." (213). We cannot know what adherence to doctrine will deliver us over to. All the more important, then, that a poem proclaiming adherence to doctrine should at the same time adhere to a continuation of the casual life. The heat death announced here is that of literary Modernism.

The Audenesque, as is well known, did not confine itself to poems by W. H. Auden. In Graham Greene's *England Made Me* (1935), a subtle and provocative inquiry into international styles of one kind or another—economic, political, architectural—the Stockholm HQ of the mildly sinister Krogh corporation consists of "five floors of steel and glass." Krogh, whose credit on the exchanges stands a point higher than that of the French government, finds himself as he enters the courtyard of the building "watched through the glass by an accountant over his machine, by a director from his chromium balcony, by a waitress drawing the black leather blinds in the staff restaurant." He ascends alone to his room on the top floor. "He was enclosed now by a double thickness of glass, the glass wall of the lift, the glass wall of the building; the office, like an untrustworthy man, emphasized its transparency." As in Hannes Meyer's Project for the Palace of the League of Nations, there is nothing to hide behind, nothing to stick to: *an* accountant, *a* director, *a* waitress. The heroine, Krogh's assistant and lover, tries in vain to create a "home from home" for her irreparably English brother somewhere amidst the five floors of steel and glass. "But she was handicapped; she couldn't build up his London inside the glass walls of Krogh's as a seaside landlady can construct Birmingham with the beads, the mantel ornaments, the brass-work in the fender."[56] Homesickness fatally attaches Anthony Farrant to "his London," to an array of definite articles.

In this chapter, I have examined some of the ways in which two writers in particular sought to blur the sharpness of the distinction Greene drew between past and future, the national and the international, the definite and the indefinite, concealment and transparency, touch and sight. Woolf,

thinking through glass, came upon the idea of breakability, as a way to negotiate, though not to prevent, the consequences of brittleness. Hers was a
Modernist preoccupation with energy and what happens to it. Auden, ex-
ploiting the definite article's collaborative reach for all it was worth, developed an aesthetic of adhesion comparable to the coolest of tracking shots.
He was the first poet of the first media age.

After Scottish Modernism

There has recently been a good deal of interest in the idea of Scottish Modernism, as a way to think more variously both about writing in Scotland in
the first half of the twentieth century, and about the politics of Modernist
literature and culture. "Popularly known in its own time as the 'Scottish
Renaissance,'" Margery Palmer McCullough observes, the work of writers
such as Hugh MacDiarmid, Lewis Grassic Gibbon, Edwin Muir, Nan
Shepherd, and others "is increasingly being recognized today as a Scottish
manifestation of literary modernism." The main aims of the interwar Scottish Renaissance, McCullough continues, were "to remove Scotland from
the provincial North British status it had acquired as a result of the political union between Scotland and England and to recover a distinctive and
modern cultural identity as well as, in the longer term, political self-
determination." In its reliance on small magazines for propaganda and
publicity, and in its championing of the Scots vernacular on political as well
as aesthetic grounds, the movement found allies or counterparts in Ireland, in Europe more generally, and in the United States.[57]

In keeping with my argument as a whole, I shall concentrate here on
what happened *after* Scottish Modernism: on the development, in Mac-
Diarmid's later work, and in the final volume of Lewis Grassic Gibbon's *A
Scots Quair,* of a synthetic (or strictly speaking, semisynthetic) English
idiom as a techno-primitivist practice. MacDiarmid and Gibbon raised the
stakes. They advocated a politics and poetics of adherence to militant
international communism. They, too, wanted to know—but with greater
urgency—what doctrine might entail once it had been fully adhered to;
and they, too, found the experience of adhesion to the world as it is utterly
compelling. For there was no shortage of Audenesque nostalgia for the
present in what happened after Scottish Modernism.

Synthetic Scots was a reaction against the increasing standardization of
English during the early decades of the twentieth century. It was not a

language, but a literary rhetoric: an assemblage of past and present Gaelic derivatives, and Scots vocabulary and mannerisms, said to express the character of everyday Scottish speech and behavior more closely than English. Between 1919 and 1929, MacDiarmid took root in Montrose, a small town on the east coast of Scotland situated between Aberdeen and Dundee. As Robert Crawford has shown in a meticulous account of that period, absorption in the life of the community by no means precluded absorption in international politics, and in the latest news of ambitious literary experiment in English and other languages. MacDiarmid read *Ulysses* and *The Waste Land* avidly and with fierce attention.[58] "A Drunk Man Looks at the Thistle," his most ambitious poem in synthetic Scots, first published in 1926, was at least in part a "direct response to *The Waste Land* and to its political and cultural agenda."[59] The invention of synthetic Scots enabled him to fuse, as Crawford puts it, the "immediate and vernacular" with the "transnational and synthetic practices of modernist writing."[60]

The most astute readings of "A Drunk Man" have understandably sought to define it as a variation upon Modernist difficulty. MacDiarmid's synthetic Scots undoubtedly constitutes a "dense and resistant medium," as Ian Duncan notes. Like many Modernist texts, the poem reminds us that "language stands in a relation of materiality to literature (since language is what literature is 'made of'), even if that materiality, too, is ultimately figurative." Where it departs from those texts, however, Duncan concludes, is in its "specification of that materiality as a national—which is to say a historical—problematic."[61]

In May 1933, anxious about the alcoholism into which separation from his first wife, Peggy, had plunged him, MacDiarmid left Scotland for Whalsay, in the Shetland Isles. The next year, he joined the Communist Party of Great Britain. Geographically, he had moved even further from the metropolitan (Modernist) center, right out to the social and political edge, and into the most austerely local of localisms. He was to convert this uttermost isolation into a yet more strenuous transnational political and literary practice. The change that reconfigured his work from *First Hymn to Lenin and Other Poems* (1931) was, as Alan Riach has put it, a change not only of attitude, but of technical procedure, a "change into a different kind of poetry altogether."[62] The medium of the epic "poetry of knowledge," which culminated in *In Memoriam James Joyce* (1955), was synthetic English, not synthetic Scots. That fact alone might encourage us to ask whether the later poetry really does belong to something called "Modernism," Scottish or otherwise.

Robert Crawford has argued that during the 1930s MacDiarmid, "aware of (though tangential to) the knowledge-world of the modern universities, evolved in his prickly and restless fashion a cybernetic poetry attuned to the work of Eliot, Pound, and Auden, yet reaching beyond theirs in provocative and striking ways." The poetic idiom he was in search of would be "tooled, artificial, and brilliant." Its products, Crawford adds, seem "like nothing so much as material turned out by a computer database, bibliographical printout." We might say that they deal in information rather than in meaning. The perforated-card technology crucial to the development of computers derived directly from that of the Jacquard loom still in use in factory weaving in MacDiarmid's day, and a potent source of metaphor. Yet the way in which his later verse constitutes a "braiding or weaving of scientific and other kinds of knowledge" was far in advance of the hardware and software extant when it was composed. For Crawford, this remains a *Modernist* cybernetics. MacDiarmid's later cybernetic poetry emerged out of, rather than in contradistinction to, his experiments with synthetic Scots. Both were "powered" by a lexical and lexicographical acquisitiveness that set the poet in some measure against his audience, in Modernist fashion. The strategy, in both cases, was "a journey away from the most publicly accessible standard English language into productive but remoter acoustic and lexical corners."[63] Crawford's metaphor is itself thoroughly Modernist in its assumption that energies can only ever be renewed by voyages of discovery culminating in an exotic encounter with the nonstandard: by primitivism, in short, since the remote so often manifests itself, in the literature of the period, in the guise of the archaic.

There is some evidence to suggest that MacDiarmid meant to distinguish firmly between the remote and the archaic. "Charles Doughty and the Need for Heroic Poetry" (1936) reflects on the condition of any language that could be said to have "deserted its native basis and over-adulterated its vocabulary," so disabling itself from the "expression and elucidation of the Ur-motives of its people"—that is, for "the perspectives of modern life and the horizons now opening before us."[64] So far, so Modernist. According to MacDiarmid, the people's Ur-motives *are* the horizons opening before it. If that was the case, then the new heroic poetry, British or Soviet, would have to follow Doughty's example in *The Dawn of Britain* (1906), an epic poem in six volumes that, as one early reviewer put it, "might almost be taken for a publication of the Early English Text Society."[65] In order to express and elucidate the people's Ur-motives, MacDiarmid proposed, Doughty "had to abandon modern English and use a large infusion of Anglo-Saxon words and native syntactical forms." Following Doughty's example, Robert Graves, too, "went 'back to Skelton' and used the old native rhythms, and Auden and other young poets today are following that lead, and that accounts for their communist tendency." That MacDiarmid should go on to compare the hostility with which *The Dawn of Britain* was greeted to the rejection of epic works by Joyce and Pound, and of his own experiments in synthetic English in *Stony Limits and Other Poems* (1934), would seem to support Crawford's argument. To go back to Skelton, or back beyond Skelton, is to go forward. It becomes increasingly clear, however, that Doughty's primary relevance, as far as MacDiarmid is concerned, is to a specific literary and political enterprise in which he himself no longer takes a direct interest. The essay concludes with the lukewarm remark that the books about Doughty he has been reviewing

> should be carefully read by all those who are concerned with the problems of the Scottish renaissance, as showing in detail how all the difficulties involved in the reintegration and full modern use of Scots were solved to great poetic purpose in a kindred medium; and bearing no less effectively on the issues involved in the future use and development of Scots Gaelic as a literary medium.[66]

MacDiarmid himself was by now working almost exclusively in that "kindred medium." It would not have been appropriate for him to express and elucidate the Ur-motives of the people whose first and only language was English by going back to Skelton. His synthesizing of the English language was to take a different form altogether.

In an interview given in March 1960, MacDiarmid himself gave the clearest possible explanation as to why his own work had never resembled, and could not resemble, *The Dawn in Britain.*

> My reason for writing my later poetry in English now is simply that the revived Scots I wrote my earlier work in is not sufficiently flexible yet—it will take a generation or two of people writing Scots, following the line that I struck out on, before we can make Scots available again for scientific purposes. After all, Scots ceased to be used before the advent of the Industrial Revolution and we have an enormous leeway to make up.[67]

Poetic language *after* the Industrial Revolution had to be, in some measure at least, the language *of* Industrial Revolution. Synthetic Scots could not yet be regarded as a language of Industrial Revolution because it was lacking in flexibility. The task MacDiarmid set synthetic English was not to elucidate an Ur-motive, or to prove dense and resistant, in Modernist fashion, but rather to describe the world as scientifically understood. How?

It all depends, of course, on what you mean by "synthetic." As Ian Duncan points out, the term can denote either the product of artifice (something inorganic, and without discernible origin in human labor) or the resolution, temporary or permanent, of opposing theses. Critics, mindful, no doubt, of MacDiarmid's own often proclaimed contradictoriness, have on the whole understood the poems of the Montrose period as synthetic in the second sense rather than the first. According to Duncan, for example, the synthetic Scots of "A Drunk Man" enacts a failure to overcome resistance through totalization: that is, a failure to synthesize.[68] It would also be true to say—and again supportive of Crawford's argument for continuity—that MacDiarmid never ceased to imagine synthesis philosophically. In his autobiography, *Lucky Poet* (1943), for example, he wrote with warm approval of Jakob Wasserman's consistent attempts to make a "synthesis of life" based firmly on his own "visible contacts" with it.[69] But I want to argue, nonetheless, that he did not regard the idea of chemical synthesis as out of bounds for a poet. To put it with a slight difference of emphasis, he was the writer of the period who did most to grasp how life had already been resynthesized in various ways as a result of the Industrial Revolution, before anyone began to think about it philosophically. From that point of view, the key poem, which constitutes a turning point or watershed in his career, and which he himself regarded as "one of the very best things" he had written, is "On a Raised Beach."[70] First published in *Stony Limits*, the poem proposes to link the "insensate world of matter," as Roderick Watson puts it, with MacDiarmid's "vision of the need for a ruthless dialectical materialism."[71] It is the nature and scope of that link that will concern me here.

The speaker of the poem stands, sits, or lies flat on the stones forming the raised beach at Croo Wick, on the uninhabited island of West Linga, which was visible from MacDiarmid's cottage on Whalsay. It is a poem "on," or about, the raising of physical matter not so much into the object of philosophical meditation as into its supplementary or alternative subject: the source or ground of an "argument" concerning ontology more powerful than the arguments philosophy has thus far put forward. The speaker wishes to achieve a position—"It is necessary to make a stand and maintain it forever"[72]—that might be dialectical materialism's position, from which the entire history of human consciousness to date will appear as insignificant as it must already do to stones that were in existence long before that history began, and are likely to remain in existence long after it has come to an end. The absoluteness of the stand made ("maintain it forever") has somehow not merely to echo, but to reproduce, the absoluteness of the impersonal, un-sourced imperative ("It is necessary") that went into its making. Only when we speak with the robust complexity of a stone will we speak truly about our-selves. The method MacDiarmid devised for this task in the relatively plain-spoken first version of the poem (*CP* 1458–65) was an extreme primitivism.

> Iconoclasts, quacks. So these stones have dismissed
>   All but all of evolution, unmoved by it,
> As the essential life of mankind in the mass
>   Is the same as their earliest ancestors' yet. (1458)

Returning to an origin, primitivism maintains, we return to essence: to that point of view from which everything that has happened since looks like mere iconoclasm, or quackery. Getting back to stone, we get back to an origin earlier even than the "earliest ancestors," an essence more essential even than their parade of autochthonous culture. Charles Doughty would surely have approved of the speaker's attempts to "try" the stones he con-templates with the old Norn words (Norn was a North Germanic language once spoken in Orkney and Shetland, as well as parts of northern Scotland): *hraun, duss, queedaruns, kollyarun, kolgref, hurdifell*, and so on (1460). Getting back to the old words, we get back to the world at its oldest. Insis-tence on the local in both word and world anthropologizes the encounter, characterizing contemplation as fieldwork. Should we think of the poem's first version as a manifesto for Norn Modernism?

If this is a manifesto, it is one that does not convince its author. The Norn words will not "serve" him, he says, over this "hurdifell," or rocky hill. But then "No other language can" (1460). For no other language even knows what a hurdifell is. The manifesto registers an impasse.

> I pile these words together as Nature piles a raised beach,
> But they are not meaningless. They are carefully chosen and apt.
> Dictionaries are open to all; but these words are not easily
>   capped. (*CP* 1460)

The declaration might sound like Walt Whitman if it did not also sound, in its approximation to couplet form, a bit like Alexander Pope, who favored the word "apt," though never as an end rhyme. "Capped" is indeed the "apt" word insofar as it can refer to the placement of a stone as well as to demonstrations of superiority. But finicky neoclassicism does not quite cut it, as MacDiarmid knew, if you are trying to get at the essence of stoniness. By stone's standards, poetic language must be reckoned mere iconoclasm or quackery. Primitivism will not work. But there is really no alternative to it.

Norn Modernism survives intact into the published version. Its announcement is now rapidly succeeded, however, by a disavowal of the most influential of all Modernist returns to origin and essence, *The Waste Land*. The speaker claims that the words he has assembled amount to "no heap of broken images" (*CP* 427). In revising the draft for publication, MacDiarmid had already introduced into it a stern critique of the whole primitivist project. F. R. Leavis concluded his assessment of Eliot, Pound, and Gerard Manley Hopkins in *New Bearings in English Poetry* (1932) with the confident assertion that the newest bearing of all in English poetry was that given by the work of Ronald Bottrall. According to Leavis, Bottrall's preoccupation with the modern world more closely resembled Eliot's than Pound's. Bottrall's world, like Eliot's, was one in which "the traditions are bankrupt, the cultures uprooted and withering, and the advance of civilization seems to mean death to distinction of spirit and fineness of living." However, the conclusion to his most complex poem to date, "The Loosening," appeared to Leavis to offer grounds for cautious optimism concerning both the modern world and English poetry.

> The poet glimpses here a recovered spontaneity, a re-adjustment to life, an ability to ride it easily, analogous to the buoyant, prelapsarian "naturalness" of the farm-girl who

> > Poised herself like a falcon at check
> > Amid the unfooted ploughland,
> > Laughter splashing from her mouth and
> > Rippling down her brown neck;
> > Not passion-rent she
> > But sensing in the bound
> > Of her breasts vigours to come, free
> > As air and powered to make her one
> > With the stream of earth-life around.

Must we despair of attaining a new naturalness at the far side of the experience of disharmony?[73]

MacDiarmid cut and pasted this primitivist nonsense into his poem, barely troubling to distinguish by quotation mark between the poet's maudlin fantasy and the critic's lazy tolerance of it (*CP* 425).[74] His aim was to stigmatize not a particular poet, but the fantasy of a return to origin and essence embedded in contemporary literary culture. It would be wrong, the speaker continues, to "indulge in these illustrations," instead of "just accepting" the spectacle of the stones (425). Just accepting, however, is easier said than done. MacDiarmid proposed to do it by means of a synthetic English that had to accept, among other things, that it could not get back to anything like stoniness. "On a Raised Beach" is a poem to be read prosthetically, with dictionary in hand, or on screen. There is no implied "native speaker" to whom this odd utterance might conceivably make immediate sense.

The published version begins and ends in synthetic English. Here is its beginning.

> All is lithogenesis—or lochia,
> Carpolite fruit of the forbidden tree,
> Stones blacker than any in the Caaba,
> Cream-coloured caen-stone, chatoyant pieces,
> Celadon and corbeau, bistre and beige,
> Glaucous, hoar, enfouldered, cyathiform,
> Making mere faculae of the sun and moon
> I study you glout and gloss, but have
> No cadrans to adjust you with, and turn again
> From optik to haptik and like a blind man run
> My fingers over you, arris by arris, burr by burr,
> Slickensides, truité, rugas, foveoles,
> Bringing my aesthesis in vain to bear,
> An angle-titch to all your corrugations and coigns,
> Hatched foraminous cava-rilievo of the world,
> Deictic, fiducial stones. (*CP* 422–3)

The speaker, close enough in attitude and tone to the poet to be regarded for the sake of convenience as male, finds himself on a raised beach, somewhere, whose process of production (lithogenesis) he wishes to explain. He reaches for a foundation myth. Conceived as discharge after birth (lochia), or the shrine in Mecca enclosing a black ruby brought from heaven (Caaba), the beach might allow us to retrace our metaphorical steps back to an all-explanatory origin. But it cannot be so conceived. For a start, some of the stones that constitute it are not black, but "cream-coloured." How unheavenly is that? And, indeed, how un-Shetland? According to the 1933 geological survey of Shetland, which MacDiarmid drew on, the islands of Whalsay and West Linga, composed mainly of gneiss and schist, with intrusions of granite, are over 420 million years old.[75] Caen stone, by contrast, is a lightish-yellow Jurassic limestone quarried in Normandy and used extensively in the construction of Romanesque churches. MacDiarmid has explicitly synthesized his beach. So, while the hard c sounds encasing foundation myth (Carpolite/Caaba) persist strenuously, in "Cream-coloured caen-stone," and then in "corbeau," the argument's ground has shifted. These variously colored and variously sourced stones require description, in the first instance, rather than mythology. Mention of caen stone sets off a little flurry of terms, from "chatoyant" onward, that derive from French or Old French. A graceful pentameter balances celadon and corbeau, bistre and beige. Lineation lines the world. Like Auden, MacDiarmid has put his faith in description in an almost geometrical sense. He "films" the world. Unlike Auden, however, he films it defiantly in French, thus finally laying Doughty's ghost to rest. Synthetic English does not claim to express the people's Ur-motives. Instead, it selects, according to sound as much as sense, from the dictionary. Furthermore, in choosing French words to describe the color of a stone sourced in Normandy, it could be said to mock the very principle of primitivism. There is no getting back to an origin or essence by way of synthetic English.

However, this display of elegance (of *poetry*) at once overreaches itself, into grandiose alternative mythology: the stones "enfouldered" (charged as with thunderbolts), reducing sun and moon to smears of light. The dictionary cannot be blamed for this spasm of stone worship. So who or what *is* to blame? MacDiarmid seems to have felt that the sentence had reached a pivot, or limit, for he introduces himself into it in the guise of a man stood on a bank of stones: a late-Romantic poet determined to apply his "adverting mind" to the least tractable of wildernesses, like Shelley among the "primaeval mountains."[76] "I study you glout and gloss": to study something "glout and gloss" is to study it sullenly, with little hope of epiphany, and by the book, by explanatory rendering—or, it could equally be, by attention to surface gleam. Etymologically, "glout" neighbors "gloat," so the thought is that there may be satisfaction as well as gloom to be found in the study of stones.

There is a return in progress, a getting back not so much to first principles (lithogenesis) as to last: to what remains after science, superseding mythology, has itself reached a limit, has come to grief, or to gloom. A cadrans is an instrument by means of which the angles of gems are measured in the process of cutting and polishing. The speaker has no cadrans—no technology—with which to "adjust" the stones he studies glout and gloss. So he proposes to "turn again / From optik to haptik," as the line turns by enjambment. MacDiarmid invokes the distinction made by the art historian Aloïs Riegl between the two kinds of visual experience: the optical, which delivers a survey, an account of (and accounting for) distinguishable objects in deep space; and the haptic, which feels its way along or around a world conceived as an infinitely variable surface, alert to texture rather than outline.[77] Previously, the speaker had brought words from afar to identify the colors of a particular kind of stone, itself an import. Now he will like a "blind man" run his fingers over individual stones, feeling for shape just as his speech feels for or toward the end of a line, its edge or contour. The poem seeks to enact rather than to describe: each word in succession, wherever it has been drawn from, inching along a surface, "arris by arris, burr by burr." "On a Raised Beach" is MacDiarmid at the feelies. We might say that it constitutes a manifesto for techno-primitivism: a primitivism operating within and upon technologically mediated experience by means of those senses that had long been classified as primitive: touch, taste, and smell. The poem's mediating technology is the cadrans of the dictionary, its primitivism a residual conviction that language might yet hold fast to the world. Still, we cannot very well ignore the deliberately classicizing terms MacDiarmid has used both to herald this conviction as a turn from "optik" to "haptik," and to boost its final flourish: "Deictic, fiducial stones." If these stones are to be known as both direct and sure in their demonstration, it will not be by feel alone. As Connie Chatterley's rain dance had demonstrated, the primitivism in techno-primitivism rarely lasts long. MacDiarmid has even fewer illusions on this score than Lawrence. The speaker declares that he has brought his "aesthesis" to bear "in vain."

A deictic is a sign that points to its referent, a demonstrative, like "this" or "here" in English. In *The Waste Land,* Eliot had used "this" and "here" to indicate and enact closeness to a transcendental source of truth: notably, of course, the red rock under whose shadow the prophet is beckoned, in "The Burial of the Dead." MacDiarmid's stones are a stark, deterrent black and white, rather than a warmly inviting red. The speaker announces deictically—"This not discommendable obstinacy"—his admiration for a deixis more absolute than mere words could ever accomplish. The stones ob-stinate: they *stand against,* as the dictionary tells us, the man who studies them glout and gloss. They will not permit epiphany. The only way in which the student can summon a comparable obstinacy is by not discommending, or rather, by instructing others not to discommend, for the text that follows this acknowledgment resembles a lecture or a sermon rather more closely than it does a meditative lyric poem. As Catherine Kerrigan observes, the poem's middle section is written in a "discursive style," which although "peppered with geological terms, Biblical and literary allusions, and scientific references," is nonetheless "readily accessible."[78] In its rehearsal of evolutionary theory, its interventions into literary-critical debate, and its cheerful cutting and pasting, "On a Raised Beach" serves as a prolegomenon to the later academic, data-based "poetry of fact" about which Crawford has written; though it is a poetry of fact, I would argue, distinct from, and indeed in reaction against, the primitivist synthetic Scots project of the Montrose years.

Poetry, it seems clear, will not be reinvigorated either through Norn Modernism or through hapticity. Instead, it becomes obstinate by ceasing—almost—to be poetry. The concepts that dictate the terms of the poem's remainder are rhetoric and song. Rhetorical figures such as chiasmus contract the meditation into sound bite:

> What happens to us
> Is irrelevant to the world's geology
> But what happens to the world's geology
> Is not irrelevant to us. (*CP* 428)

The function of the line break in this passage is to fall in so emphatically with syntax that there is no need for punctuation. So emphatically, indeed, that the structure of chiasmus and other such figures can be felt to indicate (deixis!) or to enact the structure of a song (impersonal, collective, even, and so not just poetry) appropriate to the universe. The "kindred form" the speaker declares himself conscious of

> Is the beginning and end of the world,
> The unsearchable masterpiece, the music of the spheres,
> Alpha and Omega, the Omnific Word. (428–29)

Song, exceeding mere poetry, as dialectical materialism exceeds mere philosophy, should seek to outlast, as it has preceded, individual human consciousness, like rock. It should be alpha and omega. Or, failing that, it should be a full set of rhetorical figures. Rhetoric, as communication's matrix, precedes and outlasts individual human consciousness. It shapes thought, as lithogenesis has shaped the universe. Significantly, the allusion here is to a poet—an English poet, we might note—for whom rhetoric and song were indistinguishable, John Milton. In book 7 of *Paradise Lost*, Raphael describes to Adam how God created the universe out of chaos:

> Silence, ye troubled waves, and thou deep, peace,
> Said then the omnific Word, your discord end . . .

It is at the beginning of this book that Milton magnificently invokes his muse, Urania,

> whose voice divine
> Following, above the *Olympian* Hill I soar,
> Above the flight of *Pegasean* wing.

The invocation establishes the account that will shortly follow of the creation of the universe as song transcending poetry, rhetorical throughout (note the chiasmus):

> Standing on earth, not rapt above the pole,
> More safe I sing with mortal voice, unchanged
> To hoarse or mute, though fallen on evil days,
> On evil dayes though fallen, and evil tongues;
> In darkness, and with dangers compassed round,
> And solitude; yet not alone, while thou
> Visit'st my slumbers nightly, or when morn
> Purples the East: still govern thou my song,
> *Urania*, and fit audience find, though few.[79]

The condition of darkness and solitude, with more than a hint of encompassing dangers, is one MacDiarmid recognized as his own, as he too sought a fit audience, though few, for "On a Raised Beach."

The rhetorical figure that seems most trenchantly to have captured dialectical materialism's song—its claim to stand as alpha and omega—is epanadiplosis, which begins and ends a sentence with the same word. The
"reality of life" is not hard to know, the speaker maintains.

> It is nearest of all and easiest to grasp,
> But you must participate in it to proclaim it. (*CP* 432)

Synthetic English returns, in the poem's conclusion, but not as a return
from optic to haptic. It returns as an invocation of rhetoric, as that which
synthesizes thought into something like a statement about lithogenesis.

> Diallage of the world's debate, end of the long auxesis,
> Although no ébrillade of Pegasus can here avail,
> I prefer your enchorial characters—the futhorc of the future—
> To the hieroglyphics of all the other forms of Nature.
> Song, your apprentice encrinite, seems to sweep
> The Heavens with a last entrochal movement;
> And with the same word that began it, closes
> Earth's vast epanadiplosis. (433)

Synthetic English has found in rhetoric the "technology" that will supplement and decisively ratchet up its inaugural reimmersion in the senses: a
man on a beach touching stone. Tutored by lithogenesis ("apprentice en-
crinite"), dialectical materialist song replaces one rhetorical form (auxesis,
or Romantic hyperbole) by another: diallage. Diallage is a rhetorical figure
by means of which various arguments, each having been considered fully
in its own terms, are brought to bear on a single point. It is also a kind of
rock: grass-green pyroxene. Tutored by the dictionary, synthetic English
could be said to enact song's lesson from stone, by bringing the preoccupation with varieties of knowledge that has sustained the poem thus far to
bear on a single point. The term "diallage" derives from the classical Greek
for interchange. Since this is a book about the cultural consequences of a
revolution in telecommunications technologies, I cannot help hearing in
the term an allusion to the widespread advertisement of new automatic
dialing systems at the time when the poem was written (though I will not
go so far as to imagine a telephone booth on West Linga). Like Milton,
though to very different effect, MacDiarmid has learned not to rely on
Pegasus. Poetry does survive the switch to diallage, as demonstrated by
the gently satirical half-rhyme on "began it, closes" and "epanadiplosis,"

which brings the speaker's oratory to a surprisingly un-apocalyptic conclusion. But it will henceforth be unequivocally a poetry of fact. "On a
Raised Beach" is not just techno-primitivism's manifesto, but one of its
masterpieces.

My focus in this chapter has been on poetry (or on poetry rhetorically
sublated into song). But it is worth pointing out that a version of techno-
primitivist diallage shaped to a significant degree at least one novel by
MacDiarmid's friend and collaborator, Lewis Grassic Gibbon, whose literary English synthetically incorporates modern Scots idiom and usage.[80]
Gibbon's most famous work, and greatest achievement, is *A Scots Quair*
(quair = book), a trilogy published over three years as *Sunset Song* (1932),
Cloud Howe (1933), and *Grey Granite* (1934). The trilogy chronicles the
life of its heroine, Chris Guthrie, through three marriages, in three different milieux: village, small town, and city. *Sunset Song* concerns the choice
the young Chris must make between life on the land (her Scottish identity), and the English part of her, which draws her away from home toward
books and education; at the end of the novel, her husband is killed in the
First World War. *Cloud Howe* describes her second marriage, to a Chris-
tian Socialist minister, Robert Colquohoun, who also dies, of natural
causes, at the end of the novel. In *Grey Granite,* which Gibbon dedicated
to MacDiarmid, Chris has moved to the city of Duncairn (loosely modeled
on Aberdeen), where she runs a boardinghouse, while her son Ewan becomes increasingly radicalized, joining the Communist Party and taking
part in strikes and demonstrations. *Grey Granite* has four parts, each
named after an element of the eponymous rock: Epidote, Sphene, Apatite,
Zircon. The various narrative "arguments" concerning the interest we
might or might not take in each of the main characters have been brought
to bear on the single point of the nature and scope of political commitment, and of the stoniness it has often been thought to require. The challenge, for Gibbon, was to evoke both sympathy for and judgment upon the
über-rationality Ewan brings to his role as champion of the proletariat.
Ewan's rationality is the enduring granite in him, a "not discommendable
obstinacy" comparable to that MacDiarmid found in the "Deictic, fiducial
stones" at Croo Wick.

Chris Guthrie could be said to study her son as the speaker in "On a
Raised Beach" studies the stones at his feet, "glout and gloss": "Queer
loon that he was, lovely loon, on even him change working its measure as
sunlight on granite bringing out the gleams of gold and red through the

cold grey glister."[81] In order to render the change that works its measure even on hard-as-granite Ewan, without privileging in Modernist fashion the fluidity of his individual consciousness, or anyone else's, Gibbon devised a narrative strategy comparable to MacDiarmid's literary and philosophical investment in the rhetorical figure as matrix. Its main innovation is a use of "you" that defines and expresses a specific culture's reflection upon itself, but also always potentially includes the reader, who feels him- or herself thereby addressed, engaged in debate: with Ewan, of course, the single point on which the various arguments have been brought to bear.

> Ewan cried *Hello, Bob!* And you said *Hello,* and *Ewan, I'd like to speak to you sometime.* And he said *Right, let's get out a minute,* and out he came and you asked him point-blank. And he said *I didn't know you'd be interested,* and you said *Hell, I'm not,* and he said, *Yes, you are. Look here, come along to the Saturday meeting, in the Gallowgate, 3 Pitcarles Wynd.* And afore you well kenned what it was you had done you'd promised to be there—oh, sod the whole business! (*GG* 80)

The use of "you" in this passage constitutes a form of diallage, because readers of differing political persuasions can without much difficulty imagine themselves drawn into political debate—connected—by the challenge his not discommendable obstinacy issues. For Ewan, being the protagonist of a novel, rather than a pile of stones, has studied us glout and gloss as tenaciously as we might hope to study him. He is both obdurate and flexible, hard and soft, as we discover during the weekend he spends in the Glen of Drumtochty with his girlfriend, Ellen—one of Chris's lodgers, a schoolteacher, and English—whose political commitment comes fatally into question. When they arrive at the inn where they will spend the night, Ewan immediately engages in gossip with the landlady.

> But as always with the working people everywhere, however she dreamed of justice for them, flamed in anger against their wrongs, something like a wall of glass came down cutting her off from their real beliefs, the meanings in tones and intonation, the secret that made them bearable as individuals. But Ewan had now the soap-box trick of pretending to be all things to all kinds of keelies—that was damn mean and wasn't true, there was no pretence, he WAS all things—sometimes, frighteningly, it seemed to her that he was the keelies, all of them, himself. (192)

Ellen has stopped at the point where Auden stops at the beginning of "Consider this and in our time." She gazes through a window, through a "wall of glass," at something she cannot touch. Ewan, by contrast, becomes all things to all men and women: the window that separates him from other people is made of flexible or at least moldable plastic. Ewan and Ellen have supper in the warm parlor.

> Sometimes the whoom in the lum would still, then roust and ring as though the storm going by beat a great bell in the low of the lift. And Ellen felt happy and content again, sleepy as a cat, a little bit like one: and something a moment touched through to Ewan, a hand from other days, other nights, queerly. He said *You're thinner, you were always slim, but plump in a way as well that time we climbed the Barmekin.* She shook her head, she was just the same, only horribly sleepy, was he coming now? (193)

The Scots terms (whoom, lum) announce a primitivist relapse in Ewan from optic to haptic. As the narrative idiom synthesizes itself, so something touches through Ewan, a hand from other days, prompting renewed concern for Ellen. The primitivism, however, does not last long. The next morning, Ewan finds out that Ellen has left the Communist Party, fearing for her job: he dumps her on the spot. His face, as he does so, is "a stone, a stone-mason's face, carved in a sliver of cold grey granite" (194). For Gibbon, then, as for MacDiarmid, the revolutionary has to be made of the sternest of stuffs, to behave as a stone would, if stones "behaved." But both knew that, just as stones do not "behave," so behavior rarely resembles a stone in its not discommendable obstinacy. Certainly, to speak of human behavior is to depend on words that more closely resemble plastic than they do stone. That is where synthetic English comes in. Gibbon has opposed adherence to adhesion as ferociously as MacDiarmid. But he, too, cannot bring himself obstinately to discommend adhesion: the moment touching through queerly from other days, other nights; or nostalgia for the present. In that respect, they are not altogether unlike Auden.[82]

Lucite

In this chapter and the last, I have sought to establish how the tension between nature and artifice built into a variety of semisynthetic substances became a powerful imaginative resource for writers and filmmakers. Techno-primitivism, restlessly turning from optic to haptic and back again to optic, characterized important tendencies in the literature and cinema of the period between the wars. It found, or made, the slack in an increasingly mediated "system." My contention is that it continues to perform this function more effectively than anything that still goes by the name of "Modernism" or "the postmodern." But I want also to acknowledge that the balance between nature and artifice altered significantly, in the production of plastics, toward the end of the period that concerns me, and with it, no doubt, the quality and extent of the imaginative spell they cast. The pace of the development of wholly synthetic resins picked up in dramatic fashion from the mid-1930s onward. Two final examples, one from MacDiarmid, will alert us to the onset of a transformation the specific consequences of which far exceed the scope of my argument.

On March 25, 1936, Naum Gabo, one of the pioneers of Soviet Constructivism, which had fused abstraction in art with technological purpose, and indeed with the politics of technology, first set foot in London, after years spent in Berlin, Paris, and elsewhere. Like his fellow émigrés Walter Gropius, Marcel Breuer, Naum Slutzky, and László Moholy-Nagy, he was rapidly absorbed into a London art world whose leading figures were Ben Nicholson, Barbara Hepworth, the architect Leslie Martin, and the critic Herbert Read. Read's book *Art and Industry* (1934), together with the presence of Gropius and others, revived interest in ideas of "functionalist" design that had been current across Europe during the 1920s. Gabo wrote a piece titled "Constructive Art" for the *Listener* in November 1936, and threw himself enthusiastically into the planning of *Circle*, an international review meant to expound and promote the Constructivist program of the 1920s, now outlawed in its countries of origin, Soviet Russia and Nazi Germany. Published in July 1937, *Circle* was more of a book than a review. Its expressed intention was to equate the new abstract act with science and technology, as an (impersonal, collective) exercise of reason that had the potential to provoke social and political change. What matters from our point of view is that it also placed considerable emphasis on "truth to materials." By working in and with substances both ancient and modern, the artist could reawaken a deep-rooted (that is, "primitive") awareness of existence, and, in particular, where sculpture and architecture were concerned, of space. In an essay in *Circle*, "Sculpture: Carving and Construction in Space," Gabo maintained that he and his colleagues were "realists" who did not neglect "any of those psychological emotions which belong to the basic group of our perceptions of the world."[83]

In London, Gabo became more closely involved in practical design projects than at any other time in his career. He designed advertising material
for Imperial Airways, as well as objects such as plastic coat-hangers and
bathroom fittings. Shortly after his arrival, Marcus Brumwell, director of
the Stuart Advertising Agency, introduced him to John Sisson, a chemist
working in the plastics division of Imperial Chemical Industries. Early in
1937, Sisson told Gabo about Perspex, the proprietary name for polymerized methyl methacrylate, a transparent plastic much lighter than glass and
not liable to splinter. Gabo returned home in a state of high excitement,
declaring "I have found my material!"[84] The material he had found was
entirely synthetic. Perspex had been marketed by ICI since 1935 but with
an intriguing, and ominous, restriction. A report on the British Industries
Fair held in February 1936 noted that the whole output to date had been
absorbed in the expansion of the Royal Air Force: specifically, in the manufacture of cockpit windows. "The material is less than half the weight of
glass, does not become brittle at low temperatures, and remains free from
discoloration by the ultra-violet light to which aircraft are much exposed in
the upper air."[85] Gabo, who from April 1937 had access to an oven in which
he could heat materials before bending them into shape, began to work
exclusively in plastic. As Martin Hammer and Christina Lodder observe,
the use of transparent materials enabled him to realize his ambition to
sculpt in or with space itself, because in visual terms they preserve rather
than interrupt the "spatial flow." Surface registers by way of reflections
only, while the edges "catch and refract the light, creating immaterial, luminous lines which appear to define configurations of pure space." Each of
these works constitutes a "crystallization of forces" rather than a "material
entity appealing imaginatively to the sense of touch."[86] Sculpture, perhaps,
for the information age.

Gabo could be said to have completed a task he had set himself twenty
years before, of expressing the dynamic interior of objects. But the forces
expressed by his London sculptures often crystallize, if not exactly as a
material entity appealing to the sense of touch, then as a difference in
translucency and texture solicitous of some form of haptic attention from
the viewer. Consider the superb *Construction in Space with Crystalline
Centre*, of 1938–1940.

Abstraction in art meets the science of crystallography. The work involves a strong contrast, as Hammer and Lodder put it, "between the recti-
linear, crystalline form apparently suspended at the centre of the construc-

Translucency. Naum Gabo, *Construction in Space with Crystalline Centre,*
1938–1940. Perspex and celluloid. Dimensions: $324 \times 470 \times 220$ mm. © Tate,
London, 2013 / The Work of Naum Gabo © Nina & Graham Williams.

tion, and the flowing, curvilinear planes which define its outer spatial
parameters." "The pure transparency of the material means that space appears to flow without interruption through the form."[87] But we need to
note that the contrast depends on a difference in translucency and texture
between the outer elements made of Perspex, and the inner element, understood from the side as a form in its own right, which consists of two
Perspex tetrahedrons wrapped around thinner, celluloid sheets that have a
faint bluish tint and black edges. Gabo's techno-primitivism is perhaps the
most subtle of all, because in provoking "psychological emotions" belonging to the "basic group of our perceptions of the world," it turns back from
the optic of an entirely artificial transparency to the haptic of a "nature"
already semisynthetic: natural merely by virtue of its relative instability,
brittleness, and discoloration. The "centre," it turns out, is far from "crystalline." Hesitating thus between Perspex and celluloid, *Construction in
Space* demonstrates both how hard it had become to stay techno-primitivist,

by the late 1930s, and how productive—how necessary—that attempt still remained (and, indeed, remains).

On July 6, 1937, E. I. DuPont de Nemours and Company patented a version of Perspex under the proprietary name of Lucite. An emphasis on light replaced an emphasis on seeing through, though to much the same effect. It was as Lucite that Hugh MacDiarmid got to know and reflect on polymerized methyl methacrylate in the process of researching his most ambitious attempt at a "poetry of fact," *In Memoriam James Joyce*, begun, it may be, as early as 1936, in the Shetland Islands, and finally published in book form in 1955.[88] In this poem-manifesto, MacDiarmid declares the need for an idiom in keeping both with the "new quantum mechanics" and with the "human nervous system," that is, with "human-natural-history fact." The prescription comes with an anti-primitivism clause. The new idiom should steer well clear of the "restriction to cruder animalistic patterns" that had hitherto reduced poetry to the status of astrology (*CP* 782–3). Understandably enough, Robert Crawford sees *In Memoriam James Joyce* as an important example of a literary cybernetics. MacDiarmid's aim in this poem, Crawford argues, is to combine lyricism with science, alerting us to

> The endless joys of *Scripta Mathematica*,
> Recalling that when young ferns unfold in springtime
> They are seen as logarithmic spirals,
> When light is reflected under a teacup
> A catacaustic curve is spotted,
> And so on
>> Through all creation's forms forever. (*CP* 803)

Crawford has chosen MacDiarmid at his most Poundian (we are not far from the *Pisan Cantos*). But in quoting this sentence, he rather oddly truncates it at "spotted," thus omitting the characteristically offhanded note of "And so on," and the (un-Poundian, perhaps) generality of the reference to "all creation's forms." He has omitted MacDiarmid's reassertion of poetry as poetry by means of a primitivizing return from optic to haptic.[89] For what happens as the sentence unfolds is that the impersonal passive constructions ("are seen as," "is spotted") appropriate to quantum mechanics and natural-historical fact yield to an acknowledgment of constraint appropriate to a man (as it were) on a raised beach, studying the structure of the universe glout and gloss. In particular, the pause after "And so on" is the pure product of speech rhythm. It enacts a certain sullenness concerning what one person could conceivably know, or say.

The optic from which MacDiarmid returns to a haptic "And so on" is a formidable one, if not quite on the scale of quantum mechanics. Like Gabo, he had found Perspex. The paragraph of which the sentence about *Scripta Mathematica* forms a part begins with him proposing a "calculus of ideas" such as a simple logarithmic progress "Translated into a delicate spiral of lucite" (*CP* 802). Lucite, a substance lodged among "Jekuthiel Ginsburg's paraphernalia" (802), has become for him one of the endless joys of *Scripta Mathematica*. Jekuthiel Ginsburg, a mathematician and historian of mathematics, founded *Scripta Mathematica*, a journal of the history and philosophy of mathematics, in 1932. He declared its policy in an editorial in the first issue. "*Scripta Mathematica*," he wrote, "is primarily designed to serve as a means of communication between scholars engaged in the study of mathematics as the raw material for a new knowledge."[90] It is a formulation that would no doubt have appealed to Gabo as well as to MacDiarmid. For such was the level of technicality in debate that their respective techno-primitivisms were required to engage with.

Coda

The aim of this chapter has been to track a fundamental change in the value attached to the artificial "film" of mechanisms and habits traditionally thought to shield a person from the true nature of the world she or he inhabits, from negative to positive. The Danish painter Knud Merrild, who spent a great deal of time with Lawrence in New Mexico in the winter of 1922–1923, reports him as grumbling that, far and wide though we travel in search of authenticity, "we never once go through the curious film which railroads, ships, motor cars, and hotels stretch over the surface of the whole earth." Warming in Modernist fashion to his theme, Lawrence apparently added that in our desire for experience, "we are like flies that crawl on the pure and transparent mucous-paper in which the world, like a bonbon, is wrapped so carefully that we can never get at it."[91] In very much the same spirit, William Gerhardie remarked of the protagonist of *Of Mortal Love* (1936) that if he "could have penetrated that film, that glass which, in the confusion that sleep has shed upon our world, separates us from each other and from ourselves as we are in the real world in which we move and have our being, all would have been different."[92] What I have tried to demonstrate is that as glass gave way to semisynthetic plastic as the membrane that separates us from the real world, and mucous-paper to cellophane in the wrapping of bonbons, so it became possible to enjoy rather than to deplore the experience of the technological mediation of experience. It also became possible to enjoy poetic language as semi-synthesis: techno-primitivism producing a mother tongue out of dictionaries. That is why the chapter requires a coda. For James Joyce's *Finnegans Wake*, although not a poem, would seem to share some of the preoccupations of the poetries of knowledge I have discussed. Because this text shows little or no interest in the state of Britain between the world wars, the coda will be a brief one.

There are now various approaches to *Finnegans Wake* that treat it not as a database: a text already primed for hypertextual, and indeed hypermedial, use.[93] Steven Connor draws on the distinction Lewis Mumford made in *Technics and Civilization* (1934) between "paleotechnics" and "neotechnics" to separate out phases in the delivery of the scientific promise of universal convertibility of forces. In the paleotechnic era that stretched from the late eighteenth century to the late nineteenth, the emphasis fell primarily on the thermodynamic conversion of energy into work. In the neotechnical era of the emergence of broadcast media, it fell primarily on electromagnetic conversion: a prosthetic enhancement of the senses whose outcomes are not so easily measurable in terms of work performed. Connor adds a third, digital era, dating roughly from the Second World War, in which any conceivable input of energy can be converted into information, with the emphasis now falling on the speed and multiplicity of the conversions themselves. *Finnegans Wake* seems to him to predict the digital era of universal convertibility.[94] My own preference is to situate it in relation to some of the emergent communication technologies of the first media age, notably television and radio. *Finnegans Wake* is, as Jane Lewty puts it, a "radio-imbued text."[95]

How does a communication technology imbue a text? In this case, by linguistic techno-primitivism. "In the beginning was the gest he jousstly says": like the linguist Marcel Jousse, one of whose lectures he attended in late 1926 or early 1927, Joyce thought that the origin of language lay in gesture.[96] He believed that by basing Wakese on gesture, or hieroglyphic, he could create a universal night-idiom to complement the universal day-idioms then being put forward in the guise of Esperanto, Volapuk, and Basic English.[97] Wakese, however, only leads back to the original or "primitive" in language after and as a result of as complete as possible an absorption of the technical vocabularies of the first media age. In a 1933 letter to the *Free Man,* MacDiarmid acknowledged that he had taken the lead from Joyce in a "synthetic use" of a language: that is, one drawing upon its "illimitable powers of word formation."[98] In the first media age, few areas of human endeavor tested those illimitable synthesizing powers quite as strenuously as the rapid development of complex communication technologies. The term "television," for example, runs together words derived from Greek and Latin, as Connor notes. There were plenty of other less successful devices that required naming: photophone, phonautograph, magnetophone, and so on.[99] The *Wake*'s "collideorscape" (*FW* 143) bristles with outlandish variants: teleframe, televox, telewisher, teilvision, velevision, dullaphone. Joyce sought to capture language's original gesture in and through palpable synthesis.

The technical vocabulary of wireless reception dominates *Finnegans Wake* II.3. HCE's obliging patrons appear to install in his Dublin pub a "tolvtubular high fidelity dialdialler, as modern as tomorrow afternoon and in appearance up to the minute": a piece of gear, we learn,

> equipped with supershielded umbrella antennas for distancegetting and connected by the magnetic links of a Bellini-Tosti coupling system with a vitaltone speaker, capable of capturing skybuddies, harbour craft emittences, key clickings, viaticum cleaners, due to woman formed mobile or man made static and bawling the whowle hamshack up a melegoturny marygoraumd, electrically filtered for allirish earths and ohmes. (*FW* 309–10)

Throughout the episode, snatches of broadcast interrupt the talk in the pub, as the reception wanders from one frequency to another, or dials are manipulated. The notebooks relating to it contain cryptic clusters of technical and semitechnical wireless vocabulary.

oscillation
howl
crystal speakers
refuse if seal broken
dull
atmospherics
tune strays[100]

Radio is clearly the topic here (we recall Sir Clifford Chatterley's struggle with the uneasy atmospherics of the Midlands). But what is interesting about the list is the way it mixes technical terms with the sort of phrases that would not be at all out of place in a catalog of luxury goods or a handbook of instructions. Other notebook pages show Joyce beginning to resynthesize technical vocabulary even as he absorbs it. For example, a page apparently dedicated to the difficulties of wireless reception includes the technical term "variometer"—a device used to tune a circuit by altering the relative position of coaxial coils—as well as the self-explanatory colloquial phrases "parasitic noise" and "mind dial." Interwoven are less easily identifiable coinages: "lettrodyne," "neutrozine," and "gambol coil."[101] I take these, speculatively, to constitute resynthesizings of technical terms used widely enough at the time in newspaper and magazine coverage of the problems of wandering reception and "parasitic noise," or in the advertisement of solutions to them: heterodyne, neutrodyne, gimbal coil. A coda such as this is not the moment at which to pursue research into the daytime sources from which Joyce gathered his night idiom. My main aim in embarking on it has been to lead the argument back from semi-synthesis in material substance via techno-primitivist literary practice to the question of media, which the next chapter explicitly resumes. The words at the *Wake* are thermoplastic: reheated, they have been made to flow into new shapes. Techno-primitivism, discerning the "verbivocovisual" gesture in terms invented the day before, gently applies the heat. As a result of its ministrations, the *Wake*'s words keep on becoming even after they have been fired at the bombardment screen.

⚜

FOUR

Talkativeness

THE FINAL TWO CHAPTERS of this book return from the technological mediation of experience in general to specific technologies of communication: radio, in Chapter 4; airplane and automobile, in Chapter 5. Here, I take up again the distinction between the representational and connective uses of media, enlisting broadcast radio on the side of telephony and cinema on the side of literature. This time, however, the emphasis is more directly political. The kinds of cool I described in Chapters 2 and 3 were on the whole individualizing and individualistic, whatever their overt political orientation. But cool was not the only way to resist, or to survive while slyly benefiting from, the mandates of mobile privatization. In order to understand fully how and why resistance might arise, we need to combine an argument concerning media with the customary view of the 1930s as a decade of vivid, and increasingly lethal, political adherences. To what extent was it possible to hold out against, or propose an alternative to, capitalist exploitation of the connective potential of broadcast radio, television, and telephony? I shall suggest that literature used the still relatively new experience of cinema to imagine a new representational sociability equal in intensity to, but more democratic and more militant than, the connective sociability encouraged by the steadily increasing popularity of new telecommunications technologies. The literary form I have chosen to concentrate on is the so-called "collective novel," epitome of the leftist ambition to reinterpret a world ripe for changing. The Popular Front moment of the early and mid-1930s could be said to have crystallized around a conviction that informal social solidarity might yet serve as the basis for formal political solidarity.

The difficulty lay in imagining a solidarity that would take shape within the limits of capitalism's media system, and yet open out beyond it. It is not surprising, then, that cool returns, even in texts of a Marxist tendency, as a habit not to be despised. Some of the texts I will discuss envisage an informal sociability that might under other circumstances have become the basis for formal political solidarity, but which even as it is qualifies as cool, and should be celebrated as such.

Suburbia

By the 1930s, sociability had become a political issue. During the decade, the landscape of Britain, and in particular that of the South of England, was altered fundamentally by the construction of vast numbers of semidetached villas, mostly in the form of "ribbon development" along arterial roads. As Ross McKibbin points out in his highly informative study of classes and cultures in England between the wars, the consequence of so much "physically disaggregated housing" was the erasure of traditional ideas of community. There was, McKibbin adds, a clear political dimension to the housing boom, which had been engineered by Conservative or Conservative-led governments. "The possession of property, the delights of a garden, and the demands and satisfactions of a small but healthy family provided, it was argued, the best kind of support for an individualist politics." The reconfiguration of middle England set the family home apart from shops, theaters, cinemas, and other places of entertainment, from pubs, clubs, and associations. "The social separation of men from work and the physical separation of men and women from collective life or informal sociability became, therefore, a fact of middle-class life—as it was later to become a fact of much working-class life."[1] Community could of course be reconstituted, even in suburbia. Reporting in April 1924 on "another successful year" for Slough Estates Limited, the chairman noted that "serious efforts" had been made to "set an example to other working neighbourhoods in bringing happiness, sociability, and 'something to do' into the lives of dwellers in the district."[2] The middle classes were good at setting an example. What distinguished them, McKibbin observes, was "their obvious propensity to join clubs and associations by way of formal membership and direct subscription."[3] But the basis for *casual* sociability, of the kind that throve in working-class districts where there was no ready distinction to be made between "neighbor" and "friend," remained uncertain. Did connective media fill the gaps in suburban community?

In "The Narrow Bridge of Art" (1927), Virginia Woolf envisaged a city of boxes, "each of which is inhabited by a different human being who puts locks on his doors and bolts on his windows to ensure some privacy, yet is linked to his fellows by wires which pass overhead, by waves of sound which pour through the roof and speak aloud to him of battles and murders and strikes and revolutions all over the world."[4] The wires passing overhead and the sound waves pouring through the roof might be thought to constitute the basis for a mediated casual sociability: one, furthermore, whose topics of conversation could include strikes and revolutions all over the world, as well as local murderousness. Between 1922 and 1939, the number of households in Britain holding a radio license increased dramatically.[5] Listening in was no longer a luxury pursuit requiring some technical expertise, as it had been in *Lady Chatterley's Lover.* Despite its mass appeal, however, radio became increasingly identified with suburbia. Already, in the mid-1920s, it was something to be held against the transformation of England. Shabby-genteel Mrs. Haye, in Henry Green's *Blindness* (1926), reckons that selling the family home could have dire consequences for her stepson, who has just lost his sight in an accident: "Sell Barwood!—No, and he would appreciate still having it when he grew older. To be blind in one of those poky little suburban villas, with a wireless set, and with aeroplanes going overhead, and motor bikes and gramophones. No."[6]

Suburbia boasts a rich array of horrors. But the wireless set and the gramophone, unlike the airplanes and motorbikes, which are someone else's business, have been brought inside. They are the way in which the occupants of the villas choose to be sociable. The experience of his *English Journey* (1934) led J. B. Priestley to conclude that there were now three distinct Englands: Old England (cathedrals, manor houses, inns, parsons, squires, highways and byways); industrial England (coal, iron, steel, cotton, railways, mills, warehouses); and suburbia. Returning to London at the end of his journey, Priestley found himself unmistakably in suburbia: "If the fog had lifted I knew that I should have seen this England all round me at that northern entrance to London, where the smooth wide road passes between miles of semi-detached bungalows, all with their little garages, their wireless sets, their periodicals about film stars, their swimming costumes and tennis rackets and dancing shoes." A further reflection indicates why it was that suburbia so appalled the likes of Mrs. Haye. "Notice," Priestley instructed, "how the very modern things, like the films and wireless and sixpenny stores, are absolutely democratic, making no distinction whatever between their patrons."[7] There were, however, and continue to be, different ways in which to be absolutely democratic. The wireless epitomized a democracy shaped by mobile privatization.

To begin with, telephony was not regarded as a suburban malaise (nor did it feature in Woolf's city of boxes). In Dorothy L. Sayers's *Murder Must Advertise* (1933), socialite and drug fiend Dian de Momerie suggests that Lord Peter Wimsey ring up Pamela Dean, her rival for his affections, only to correct herself: "she's not on the phone . . . how suburban not to be on the phone." Actually, Pamela *is* on the phone, and Wimsey's first action after leaving Dian's flat is to ring her up.[8] However, as the Telephone Development Association campaigns and the heavyweight articles in the *Times* amply demonstrate, wiring suburbia up became an urgent priority. There is some evidence to suggest that the new kind of talk soon caught on. In 1934, the GPO was able to report that its policy of cheap night trunk calls had generated a substantial increase country-wide in the number of calls made, and their duration. This outbreak of "loquacity" had almost brought the system to a halt.[9] There can be little doubt that telephony rapidly entered the suburban picture. What really needs explaining, however, is the role ascribed to broadcast radio in the development of a connective sociability.

Radio began as a method of point-to-point communication at a distance, and the fact that the messages sent could be received by people for whom they were not meant (its broadcast dimension) was initially seen not as an asset, but as a grave disadvantage.[10] Radio's subsequent appropriation during the 1920s by the embryonic British broadcasting industry embedded it in a national culture that both sustained and was sustained by its claim to inform, educate, and entertain.[11] That broadcast dimension had as much to do with the "place" radio found in the home as the design of the set. Radio was heard in an already socialized space, whether public or private, café or kitchen. The telephone, by contrast, always drew the user into a space apart, whether public or private, phone booth or bedroom. What is at issue here is the "centripetal power" with which it is possible to endow media, under particular circumstances, as a way to offset the centrifugal force of a mobile privatization significantly enhanced by the spread of telephony.[12] There is no shortage of testimony to the centripetal effect of the public service network created by the formation of the BBC in 1922. In Ruby Grierson and Ralph Bond's documentary *Today We Live* (1937), made for the National Council of Social Service, the broadcast heard in middle-class home and working-class café alike inspires the regeneration of both rural and urban communities. Whereas newspapers are read singly, George Buchanan remarked in September 1939, at a time when solidarity was in urgent demand, people generally listen to the radio in groups. "You can walk down a street and hear the same voice busy in every house. Thus radio news is community news: it is a united gesture of a society listening at the same time."[13] Telephony and broadcast radio might be thought to have constituted the basis for different kinds of virtual sociability, the one centrifugal in effect, the other centripetal.

But that is not quite how broadcast radio was understood. The terms the medium attracted during the period were likely to include "loudspeaker" and "blaring." To many commentators, radio was above all invasive: like telephony, it spoke directly in your ear; unlike telephony, it spoke into everyone's ear at the same time. It could be hard to tell the centripetal apart from the fascist, as Woolf understood so well. William Uricchio has described the experimental installation of gigantic loudspeakers in Berlin in 1930, as part of an attempt to cover first the city, then the country as a whole, with sound. The aim was to redefine the public sphere by enabling the voice of authority to own the attention of as many listeners as possible, in real time, individually, and yet en masse. The conjunction of loudspeaker, radio, and television technologies in the German electronics industry of the late 1920s and early 1930s produced the dream of media at once broadcast in scope and narrowcast in focus and intensity, a public-private sphere of simultaneous national event and simultaneous national presence.[14] Radio was made for, and eagerly adopted by, dictators, including, some would say, John Reith, director general of the BBC, often compared at the time to Mussolini.[15] Before the end of the decade, with broadcasting in America in mind, Theodor Adorno would speak of the "isolated listener" overwhelmed by the "might" of the "personal voice of an anonymous organization." The more deeply this radio voice penetrates into the listener's privacy, Adorno added,

> the more it appears to pour out of the cells of his most intimate life; the more he gets the impression that his own cupboard, his own phonograph, his own bedroom speaks to him in a personal way, devoid of the intermediary stages of the printed word; the more perfectly he is ready to accept wholesale whatever he hears. It is just this privacy which fosters the authority of the radio voice and helps to hide it by making it no longer appear to come from outside.[16]

In the 1930s, broadcast radio was still thought of as a kind of mass telephony. What both lacked, by this account, was the time and space for reflection made available by the "intermediary stages" of a representational medium like the printed book. Reading, however, was as unsociable an activity as listening in. Might it be possible to reconstitute, in direct opposition to broadcast radio, television, and telephony, a *representational* sociability based on (and valuing highly) the live performance of social, professional, and even political roles in public or semipublic space? Might literature at least alleviate its own privacy effect by discovering in cinema a way to represent face-to-face encounters of that kind? The live performer presents a role already perfected through practice, through rehearsal. The representation of such performances in a novel or a film could be thought to emphasize the extent to which any presentation is always already a re-presentation.

Of course, there was no universal pattern of use. According to McKibbin, the tendency in most working-class households was to turn the set on and leave it on, whereas middle-class listeners were more discriminating: they turned the set on for particular programs only.[17] That difference in the construction of audiences, and thus of ideas of sociability, led some commentators to imagine other kinds of talk than the connective, often by reference to working-class practice, and to invent or reinvent for those other kinds of talk the already socialized spaces, neither wholly public nor wholly private, that made them possible. In August 1936, Trystan Edwards waxed lyrical in the *Times* concerning the "little street" that slum dwellers

> are usually so loath to leave, either for the dormitory suburb in "open development" or for the block of tenements (the only alternatives now provided by the housing "expert"), [and which] represents for them a playground for their children, a place of friendly intercourse for grown-up people, an attractive club, which costs them nothing, immediately accessible from their front doors—it is, in fact, an integral part of their home. This concept of the street as the architectural expression of human sociability is a very valuable one.[18]

That Edwards's view of the street had a mythical dimension is confirmed by the fact that he was writing from his West End club, the Athenaeum. But he was by no means the only commentator who sought to define a space for expressions of sociability. In Patrick Hamilton's *The Midnight*

Bell (1930), for example, Bob's somewhat shaky telephone habit stands in stark contrast to the verbal command exercised by his coworker Ella over the space of the public bar. Consider the richness of the reproof she administers to Bob after she has seen him flirting with a couple of prostitutes.

> Ella, as she served him, was ironic and reserved.
> "I'm surprised at *you*, Bob," said Ella.
> "Surprised at me? What's up?"
> But she preferred mystery. "I'm surprised at *you*, Bob," she reaffirmed; and left him.[19]

Ironic and reserved, Ella says little, but conveys a great deal: or would do, if only Bob was paying attention. This is a representational sociability both in the sense that it involves role-playing that might or might not deepen into relationship, and in the sense that it lends itself to further representation (for example, in literature or film). The fiction of the early 1930s evinces a sharp curiosity about the attenuation through connective sociability of the sorts of face-to-face encounter fostered by semipublic spaces. Anthony Powell's first novel, *Afternoon Men* (1931), maps the eerily contentless camaraderie of a series of parties, gatherings, or occasions that take place in and around London over a relatively short period of time. It soon becomes clear that the only transactions that have any lasting significance or effect are those conducted in a kind of parallel universe, that is, by telephone. The point of meeting in person is to arrange to speak on the phone—to get the number of someone you fancy, or want to do business with.[20] The minimalist conversational style developed by the main protagonist is an acknowledgment of the futility of face-to-face encounter.

Both radio and telephone sought to own the listener's consciousness: to speak in private with such insistence that the authority of the voice speaking no longer appeared to come from outside. Literature, by contrast, wanted words with some drama to them, words that represent one person to another. In search of those words, it drew increasingly on film, the dominant mass medium of the age.

Multiple Media Awareness

It is worth noting that most if not all of those who live by the telephone in the novels discussed in Chapter 1 are also dedicated moviegoers. In Patrick

Hamilton's *Hangover Square,* George Harvey Bone, who has succeeded in pinning the elusive Netta down on the phone, celebrates with fish and chips, and a movie. He decides on the Plaza, "because he usually went there when he was up like this." Moviegoing is primed for emotion, for sensuousness, for experience. "He cried a little at the end of each film, came out over the super-soft carpet into the thronged electric-lit darkness of the winter's afternoon at a quarter to five, and took the tube to Earl's Court."[21] Hamilton quite explicitly contrasts the cinema's bias toward meaning with telephony's bias toward information. The moviegoer, like the star, has a role to play. Julia, in Jean Rhys's *After Leaving Mr Mackenzie,* is similarly an enthusiast for the representational media available both in London and in Paris: in her case, not just the cinema, but the Pathéphone Salon. "She went in, sat down on one of the swivel-chairs, bought several discs, and, without changing the register before her, set the thing in motion." Like Hamilton describing Bone's afternoon at the cinema, Rhys goes into detail. The telephones in the salon Julia has entered connect only to a recording device. "She felt the hardness of the receiver pressed up against her ear." The recording brings her, as *Say It in French, Escape from Yesterday,* and *Popeye* were successively to bring George Harvey Bone, to the brink of tears. "She put the receiver down hastily and looked up something else."[22] Julia could be said to have counted the cost of all that counting of costs: all those calculations as to how far another couple of pounds will get her. She, too, performs a private anguish in public. Representational media, it would seem, encourage a reflection on, and voicing of, desire. They appeal even, or especially, to exponents of telephone sex, by way of antidote.

It is hardly surprising that cinema's audiences and auditoria should have become a topic for the sort of realist fiction that claimed to document modern life in its everyday or lower-class aspects. J. B. Priestley's *Angel Pavement* (1930), for example, devotes a great deal of attention to the cinema habit of young Turgis, a clerk in the staid City firm of Twigg & Dersingham whose favorite Saturday night resort is the Sovereign Picture Theatre in London's West End. In chapter 4, Priestley prefaces a lengthy account of one such Saturday night out with a short treatise on the Picture Theatre understood as a "frontier outpost of the new age," all "steel and concrete and carpets and velvet-covered seats and pay-boxes." The feature is a talkie called *The Glad-Rag Way,* about a beautiful girl who goes to New York to dance in cabarets, and for a while forgets about her sweetheart, a poor but noble inventor, who lives in dismal lodgings, like Turgis, but, unlike Turgis, also contrives to have his hair exquisitely waved at regular intervals. The inventor has received a letter inviting him to New York for an interview. As the train roars across the screen, Turgis hears a voice say "'Scuse me" and feels a "dim feminine shape" squeeze past him and drop into the seat on his left. The new arrival's scent immediately associates her, sight unseen, with the prettiness of the girl who has gone to New York to dance in cabarets. "Turgis took in all that the film had to offer him, but now he was no longer lost in it; he was living intensively in the tiny darkened space between him and the girl." Elbows touch, and then legs. There is a kind of virtuosity to this fumble. Taking in what the film has to offer, but no longer lost in it, Turgis has made full use of the element of slack in the system created by the disparity between cinema's two times and two spaces. He has become himself. Rather, he has performed himself, briefly. The film's conclusion breaks the erotic circuit. When the lights go up, both participants understand immediately that whatever went on in the tiny darkened space between them has no future: "those two intimates were ghosts now."[23] There is a kind of sangfroid in that understanding.

In chapter 19 of *The Midnight Bell*, Bob takes Ella, who has fallen as deeply in love with him as he has with Jenny, one of the prostitutes she watched him serving, to the pictures to see her favorite actor, Richard Dix. Entering the auditorium, they immediately adopt the "blank, calm, inhuman stare of the picturegoer": less inclined to be tearful than George Harvey Bone, they prepare for sangfroid. In this case, however, the picturegoer's stare turns out to be all too human in its tendency to erect the fantastic "here and now" on the screen (which is in fact a "there and then") into a standard against which to measure the shortcomings of the circumstantial "here and now." The Richard Dix feature is followed by "a German film called *The Spy*." "'This is *your* type, ain't it, Bob?' said Ella at the appearance of the leading lady" (a "large-eyed, slim and shingled blonde"). Ella is cool, because she takes in what the film has to offer without becoming lost in it. She makes its representation of sexual type the topic of a debate that could conceivably (if only Bob had his wits about him) have real consequences. Bob, meanwhile, has made a new discovery, that "women were miraculous" (at least on the screen). You either had "it" or not, he decides. Ella emphatically does not (*TTS* 85–87). That, of course, is harsh on Ella, whose attractiveness resides in a rare combination of tact with force of personality, and whose preferred medium is face-to-face encounter in the semipublic spaces of pub or cinema. But the discovery does at least result in a degree of largesse, on Bob's part, toward Ella (tea in a little restaurant over the road rather than a Lyons or A.B.C.). And it does foster a degree of self-awareness. He knows that the miraculous creature on the screen is not for him. "In calm and loveliness she eclipsed even the little beauty to whom he had given a pound two nights ago" (86). But he does not know this enough, in the way that young Turgis knows it. If he could just have gone on knowing it, when he first calls Jenny the next day, he might not have fallen for telephony's promise, for the siren's music that owns him as soon as it has come into his ear.

To put it schematically, cinema, primarily a representational medium, operates from the side of desire, of technique, and of meaning; while telephony, primarily a connective medium, operates from the side of information, of protectiveness, of necessity reconstituted as technological system. Neither exists independently of the other.

There were, of course, other kinds of desire to represent, and other kinds of necessity; while the relationship between primarily representational and primarily connective media did not have to be conceived as rivalrous. Novelists who sought rather more assiduously than Priestley ever did to change the form of the novel remained as ambivalent as he was about the fantasies allegedly gripping the cinema's new audiences, and the encounters allegedly occurring in its new auditoria. In Storm Jameson's *Company Parade* (1934), Hervey Russell, a young woman from the North of England, finds work as an advertising copywriter in London in the years immediately after the First World War, as Jameson herself had done, and starts to publish novels. But it is another aspiring northern novelist, William Ridley, loosely modeled on Priestley, whom Jameson sends out onto the streets, on Armistice Day in 1921, "in search of his novel," then into a pub, and finally, to complete the anthropological tour of duty, to the cinema. The results of the survey are uniformly bleak. Ridley notices an obviously pregnant young woman, thin and shabby, in a telephone booth, and slips into the next one to listen.

> "You aren't coming?" Ridley heard. "What? Oh but you said. It's the fourth time you haven't." This was followed by a moment in which she laid her hand over her mouth and listened. "Jim, I want you so," she said. "Jim, you said you—" A start ran through her body and he felt certain that the listener at the other end had gone. It was so. She spoke again, listened, spoke once more, in the voice of a child, and gave it up.[24]

For those like the unfortunate young woman who have not mastered telephony's protocols, it can prove a bitter ordeal, a brutal demonstration of
necessity. On the phone, as on radio, it is possible to fail to own the listener's
attention. Technique's failure entails a failure of identity. Rhys's Julia would
at least have kept the man talking.

Ridley's visit to the pub yields, in Eliotic fashion, some stoical frankness
about sex on the part of two women who make no distinction between
want and need where men are concerned. The cinema, however, provides
a scene in stark contrast to the desolate, necessity-ridden phone booth.
There, want has been uncoupled altogether from need.

> It was full and he had to stand at one side, close to the screen. From here
> he could see the organist and the faces of the worshippers. Their eyes were
> turned slightly upward. They were adoring a half-clothed young woman
> reclined in a room of inexplicable splendour, where like Aholah in the
> scriptures she doted on her lovers. This finished better than anyone could
> have hoped. The organ then rose several feet into full view, luminous,
> changing from rose to green to blue, and afterwards sank again, to the de-
> light of the people. You don't see miracles every day, not to notice them.
> Ridley went out. (*CP* 286)

Ridley—Priestley with a curl added to his lip—notices that cinema's is a
double miracle. Rather, it becomes miraculous if, and only if, what happens here and now in the auditorium (elbows and legs touch, an organ
rises, changing from rose to green to blue) can be felt to supplement the
there and then that reappears on the screen. This all seems like more fun
than the average phone call, or an evening in an Eliotic pub. Ridley, however, is simply doing some impromptu social anthropology of the kind that
the Mass Observation movement was soon to make fashionable. The behavior he observes is that of a class, the working class. His proposed novel
seems rather less likely than *Angel Pavement* or *The Midnight Bell* to tell
us about the uses to which cinema's double miracle might be put.

In chapter 2 of *Company Parade,* Hervey Russell's fellow lodger Delia
Hunt goes to the movies. At this point, all we know about Delia is that she
is large and cheerful and has knocked about a bit, not least in Johannesburg in 1890. As the section describing the expedition opens, she goes into
a restaurant in Piccadilly Circus at seven in the evening. A brief conversation with the waiter, an old acquaintance, reveals that she had once eaten
there with her husband, in 1889, before they left for South Africa. In 1892,

she had left *him,* and come home. Now he has written to ask if she will have him back. She has to make up her mind by midnight. There is, it turns out, a purpose to this specification of dates. For the film she takes in to pass time until midnight makes a Proust of her. "The branches of a tree, moving with the movement of bright water, filled the screen. Involuntarily she remembered that great tree she had admired as a child." *That* great tree, utterly remote in time and space, has reappeared in or as *this* one, the one palpably in motion in front of her: a miracle she actually notices.

> Now the tree was gone, and a room, a parlour of the 'nineties, took its place. It was empty, then the door opened and a young woman came in. Delia was seized with a powerful and mysterious emotion. Half trembling, she murmured to herself: "She's going to light the gas." As the flame jetted up she pictured the blue spring raying into yellow. A dozen scenes from her past offered themselves rapidly one after another, and it seemed to her that the whole of her youth with its coarse vital ardours was released when she thought of a gas-lit room—it was the same room whether it existed in Brixton or Johannesburg. (*CP* 26)

It is Delia who does the picturing, now, not the film. Rather than recalling under external stimulus her past existence as past, she becomes again what she once was. Cinema's projection of the past as a passing present has brought her to her senses as effectively as Connie Chatterley's tennis shoes, light raincoat, and perfume by Coty. It has enabled her to strike a balance between desire and necessity, expectation and acquiescence. "A sudden contempt for her husband (she could only think of him as a young man) filled her, and at the same time, with a light shiver of pleasure, she thought that she could have him with her that night if she chose. I can do as I like, she thought" (26).

After the show, Delia walks back down Regent Street to the telephone booth in the underground station at Piccadilly Circus, reaching it at twenty minutes to twelve. Doing as she likes has come down to, and will only ever be realized as, a phone call to her not altogether appealing husband: connectivity's make-or-break. Yet I think it would be true to say that cinema has equipped her for this moment. The "powerful and mysterious emotion" to which the film she has just seen gave rise persists as a phenomenology.

> For another moment she stood watching the people hurrying this way and that past the telephone box, weaving another thread into the multi-coloured

fabric of London, so strong, and yet frailer than the trees which grow of themselves between its houses and one day will push them over. Her mind darted backwards and forwards along this fabric, as pliant to stretch itself in time as her fingers to close round the receiver. As soon as she touched it the present came about her with a rush. (*CP* 27)

Delia's darting backward and forward along London's "fabric" oddly resembles Lawrence's conceit of the telephonic almond trees, which I discussed in my Introduction. She, too, has found a way to represent connectivity to herself. If the present is to come about one with a rush, as the imminent telephone call demands, better that it should do so with a pliancy derived from reflection. Cinema has enabled Delia to introduce some give or slack into the relation between technique and technology, desire and necessity. She, too, is cool.

The Talkies

Cinema, in short, had become a medium for writers to think with, as well as about, and to think with *against* other media such as telephony and broadcast radio. But cinema itself no longer stood in direct opposition to telephony and broadcast radio. For one thing, the advances in microphony driven by the rapidly expanding requirements of the radio and phonograph industries had also eased the transition to sound in cinema. By 1934, the microphones used in broadcasting were so sensitive, R. H. Chamney remarked, "that the intelligibility is really marvelous."[25] In Hollywood, still further technical advances during the decade secured the complete ascendancy of intelligibility over naturalness as the primary criterion for the reproduction of sound in cinema.[26] The development of directional mikes and mobile booms made it possible to follow characters around the set, and to capture a high degree of direct sound.[27] Whatever the angle or distance of shot, close miking created, as engineers Harry F. Olson and Frank Massa put it in 1934, "a sonic 'centre of gravity' comparable to the 'centre of gravity' of the action."[28] I am going to argue that filmmakers, in Hollywood and elsewhere, went to considerable lengths to extend and refine the construction of the second of these centers of gravity in order to counteract the sway increasingly exercised, not always to benevolent effect, by the first. Their embedding of conversations of a particular kind in narrative space of a particular kind defined talkativeness as a social, moral, and political, rather than merely technological, value. But I need first to establish the nature and scope of the sway exercised by sound film's construction of a sonic center of gravity.

Synchronous sound was not just an additional feature, or supplement. As Charles O'Brien observes, it "wholly transformed the phenomenology of film."

> Although attempts to link motion pictures and phonographs dated from the late nineteenth century, the new sound films, with their powerful electronic amplification and, in the case of films with optical soundtracks, their lock-tight synchronization, impressed viewers as absolutely novel. Essential in this regard was the strong sense of the clarity and immediacy of actors' performances enabled by electronic sound recording and reproduction, with its vastly expanded frequency range.[29]

The ideas of clarity and immediacy compelling this transformation derived from radio and telephony. The rate of installation of sound reproduction systems peaked in 1929. While audiences flocked to the talkies, Donald Crafton notes, "their newspapers, fan magazines, scientific and other popular journals were running advertisements placed by a subsidiary of AT&T touting films as a product of the telephone. Meanwhile, the Radio Corporation of America challenged these claims. RCA sponsored advertisements on behalf of its movie-making subsidiary, RKO-Radio Pictures, to proclaim that the talkies were a form of radio."[30] Both claims were misleading. What matters, historically, is that they should have appeared plausible enough at the time for the film industry and its partners in developing sync sound to pitch film as a technological complement to radio, at least, if not telephony. As Paul Young observes, advertising for the rival processes (Warners' Vitaphone, Fox's Movietone, RCA's Photophone) "encouraged the public to consume sync sound films in terms of the technologies of recording and amplification that made telephony, phonography, and radio possible." Hollywood, Young continues, wrapped its experiments in talkativeness in the "aura" of radio. Sound films "borrowed forms and formats from the recording and radio industries." Such self-conscious hybridization "offered the notoriously fickle film audience a paradigm within which to understand and take pleasure in their favourite actors' newfound ability to speak and sing." Young uses the famous scene in *The Jazz Singer* (1927) in which Jack Robin (Al Jolson) flirts with his mother (Eugenie Besserer) before serenading her with "Blue Skies" to demonstrate how the film's "radiophilic discourse" had combined intimacy with the dramatization of exchange. "Staged in the Rabinowitz parlour, the mother-son reunion synthesizes the voyeuristic thrill of watching domestic scenes from one's theatre seat (as one did during silent narrative films) with the sense of being addressed directly by a radio announcer." Young's conclusion is that the early talkies were "a public medium that imagined itself as a private medium (broadcast radio) that imagined itself as a public medium (silent classical cinema)."[31] The terms I have been developing in this book suggest a slightly different formulation. The early talkies were a broadcast representational medium that imagined itself as a broadcast connective medium that still imagined itself as the narrowcast connective medium it had once been (that is, as a kind of telephony).

In a highly informative account of jazz-themed talkies up to and including *Blonde Venus* (1932) and *King Kong* (1933), Young characterizes the redevelopment of classical narrative as a struggle to purge sound cinema of the very "devil" of "radio fantasy" that had made it possible. Sound cinema reasserted the value of representation (two places at two times) over the value of connection (two places at one time). It allowed for reflection upon a reflection of the world. Or, as Young puts it, it offered the viewer a critical distance from which to "consider the consequences of the radio-jazz invasion." Hollywood made jazz (and, implicitly, radio) synonymous with a "sonic otherness," which once visualized—blond Venus Marlene Dietrich in a gorilla suit, Kong's Broadway debut—could be kept in check.[32] Here, I want to trace a parallel redevelopment of classical narrative, which aimed not so much to contain radio as to provide an alternative to it: a different kind of talk, and a different value for the act of conversation; a semipublic relative unintelligibility to set against a semiprivate relative intelligibility, an aura of meaning against an aura of information. It was by developing that different kind of talk that cinema was able to offer its audiences, at least for a brief moment in the early 1930s, a supplement to cool.

In order to provide an alternative to a newly empowered radio fantasy, cinema had first to reinvent a narrative space that was neither wholly public nor wholly private. It needed to reinvent a space in which both participants in a dialogue could be seen to be present to each other, to represent themselves to each other, physically, socially, morally, and politically—while remaining absent from the viewer, and so potentially a reflection to reflect upon.

Let us start from the technological fact that radio did dialogue differently from film. "In a broadcast dialogue," Rudolf Arnheim remarked in his 1936 book on radio, "only the person who is speaking exists acoustically."[33] Unlike film, which can frame and edit images in multiple ways, radio, as Young puts it, "cannot single people out unless they speak, nor can it induce listeners to attend to mute objects or other elements of setting. Thus, the radiophonic subject effectively owns the listener's attention for as long as she or he is speaking."[34] The political implications of such ownership in the loudspeaker culture of the 1930s are clear enough, as I have already indicated. Putting the dialogic back into dialogue, without any sacrifice of intelligibility, turned out to be a matter of space, or rather of the social coding of space.

The understanding of space I have in mind evolved during the transition, in the years immediately before the First World War, from a cinema of attractions to a cinema of narrative integration: the period of the establishment of the classical continuity system. It is certainly evident in some of the last and best of the four hundred or so films D. W. Griffith made for the Biograph company between 1908 and 1913, films that have long been regarded as a laboratory for the development and testing of methods or "patterns" by which actions spread across multiple spaces might be edited together in such a way as to generate and clarify narrative.[35] One such pattern was an organization of narrative space designed to figure or make intelligible the relation between the interior and exterior of a building.[36] That relation matters, in art as well as in life, because it is also, according to the "social logic" identified by Bill Hillier and Juliette Hanson in a wide range of architectural modes, the relation between a public and a private realm. The most important distinction that logic maintains, Hillier and Hanson argue, is between a "deep" space within a building attainable only by passage through other spaces, and thereby adapted for its owner's exclusive use, as sanctuary or shrine; and the "shallow" spaces (neutral, inclusive, open-ended) through which the visitor must pass in order to attain it.[37] A deep space, we might say, is one in which power and desire renew themselves, and each other, or are finally found out. The area of transit that social elites have traditionally interposed between that deep space and the public street gives rise, by contrast, to actions that are in some measure inessential, to behavior amounting to ceremony rather than to revelation. In sound cinema, shallow space fills up with activity providing the perfect excuse for conversation, and plenty of it.

In the office buildings of the period, the distinction between deep and shallow space was constructed socially and technologically. The boss occupied the inner office, the telephone on his (or very rarely her) desk providing a means of instantaneous, discreet communication, through the interface of an exchange hidden away in a basement or backroom, with other offices in the same building, or with other offices in other buildings. Telephony, impalpably connecting privacies, was widely understood to constitute and epitomize *system*. Tom Gunning has shown how throughout his career Fritz Lang used the telephone in his films not just as a way to tell stories, but as an emblem of the grip power exerts on system, and through system on time and space. In the tour de force opening sequence of *Dr. Mabuse the Gambler* (1922), for example, the telephone enables the master criminal to orchestrate a daring heist from his hidden lair.[38] But executive offices required for privacy's sake a barrier of some kind: a reception and filtering area telephonically connected, but also the scene of all sorts of comings and goings between public street and inner sanctum. The female clerical worker who controlled that domain became, as Lawrence Rainey has shown, "both the addressee and protagonist of plays, postcards, comic strips and cartoons, novels serialised in tabloid newspapers, conduct books, popular songs, poetry, and, above all, film."[39] Sound cinema created the bustling, talk-laden shallow space of the outer office as an alternative, or counterweight, even, to telephony's segregating enclosures. In that domain, the new class of information workers built its own petit bourgeois semipublic sphere, sometimes in alliance with disaffected members of other classes. And it did so by talking a lot. It was on that terrain that the wisecracking private eye and the lowlier half of the screwball couple first found a voice. Their wit constitutes in its pleasurable virtuosity (its bias toward meaning) a technique that both mimics and challenges the necessity constituted by the information management systems encompassing it. They know that they have to solicit an attention they can never own completely. But these feisty conversationalists are not merely the epitome of cool. During the Popular Front moment of the early and mid-1930s, their virtuosity counted as political.

Hollywood made ample narrative use of the outer office (there are, for example, countless scenes in which the protagonist charms or forces a way past some functionary in an outer office in order to take power by surprise in its lair). But I want now to examine in greater detail an equally prominent and in some ways more complex shallow space, the hotel lobby. Siegfried

Kracauer, writing in the mid-1920s, described the hotel lobby as a negative church, or depository of alienation.[40] I shall suggest, on the contrary, that it became in Hollywood films a way to imagine, if not exactly congregation or community, then at least some kind of temporary intra- and even inter-class alliance. The lobby I have in mind features in *Grand Hotel* (1932), based on a novel by the German writer Vicki Baum whose subtitle (very roughly: "a sensation novel with some depth to it") announces its engage-ment with modern experience.[41] Contemporary with *Blonde Venus* and *King Kong*, *Grand Hotel* devotes as much energy to combating the devil of telephony as these films do to negating the devil of jazz radio. But the film's aim is not containment, so much as the elaboration of an alternative under-standing that is also an alternative politics: the reinstitution of bustling, talk-laden space.

Grand Hotel, directed by Edmund Goulding for MGM, concerns the attempts of the charmingly bankrupt Baron von Geigern (John Barrymore) to steal some jewels belonging to Grusinskaya (Greta Garbo), a Russian ballet star in decline. She catches him red-handed in her bedroom, and they fall in love. Meanwhile, a stolidly brutal industrial magnate called Preysing (Wallace Beery) lies his way through negotiations concerning a merger with a rival firm, while attempting to bed his glamorous temp, Flaemmchen (Joan Crawford), and at the same time fob off an insurrec-tionary employee, Kringelein (Lionel Barrymore), who, discovering that he has not long to live, has resolved to blow his savings on a Berlin binge. There is also a porter, Senf (Jean Hersholt), whose wife is in labor during a large part of the action, and a choric doctor, Otternschlag (Lewis Stone), horribly disfigured during the war, who constantly awaits messages that are never delivered. It all ends badly for Preysing, who, finding the Baron in his room, shoots him dead, and by the same token for the Baron, and for Grusinskaya, who leaves the hotel at the end not knowing that the love of her life is no more, but well for Kringelein and Flaemmchen, who go off together to try out other grand hotels in other grand cities.

The film is a multi-star vehicle, and consideration of the way in which the story involving Joan Crawford develops alongside and to some extent displaces that involving Greta Garbo can tell us quite a lot about its repre-sentation of social hierarchy. All the action takes places within or immedi-ately outside the Grand Hotel, so the elaborate art deco set created by Cedric Gibbons, head of the art department at MGM since 1924, is itself, in its gleaming up-to-dateness, a star (though, unlike the film it sustains, it did not scoop an Oscar).[42] The "world" thus shown can be divided into the deep space of the bedrooms, where desire and power reveal themselves behind firmly closed doors, and a set of shallow spaces consisting of the lobby and adjacent facilities, the wide balconies on each floor (in effect an extension upward of the lobby), and the American Bar with its jazz band and copious supply of Louisiana slings. These shallow spaces have in effect been defined against deep space, against telephony.

The film begins with a high-angle pan across telephone operators in the hotel exchange.

The location of the exchange is never identified. No one enters or leaves it, thus establishing its relation to the building as a whole. The space it occupies can be read as a deep space. It constitutes the hidden heart of the system that connects one privacy to another, in the process subsuming the "social" as traditionally understood. The high-angle pan is followed by a series of shots of individuals making calls from booths off the lobby. Two only among the main protagonists do not appear in this series: Flaemmchen,

The telephone exchange as deep space. Frame grab from *Grand Hotel* (1932, MGM, dir. Edmund Goulding).

whose status as interloper is confirmed by her relatively late arrival on the scene, striding purposefully through the lobby; and Grusinskaya, who has sent her maid to convey the message, which she will soon revoke, that she does not intend to perform tonight. Operating by remote control even in the ambiguous zone of the booths off the lobby, Grusinskaya declares her allegiance to deep space. The talk during these frantic calls is uniformly of imminent crisis, of careers literally "on the line." Telephony is made once again to reveal its built-in bias toward information rather than meaning. Hereafter, in this film, it will be conducted not in the relative seclusion of a booth, but in the complete seclusion of a bedroom that may also function as an inner office.

The film immediately counteracts its own initial investment in deep space by gloriously unfolding the shallowness of a lobby crammed with performative bustle. The Baron seeks out a bellboy to take his dog for a walk. Initially held up when his dog is snagged by a well-wisher, he extricates himself for a lateral surge right to left across the lobby, with the camera following him every step of the way, as ready as he is to immerse itself in the incidental. Here is someone fully at home in shallow space. That he may soon not be at home anywhere else is indicated by his failure to tip the bellboy. Grusinskaya is also present in this scene, by her absence from it. At its beginning, we have it confirmed that she will not need her car this evening, because she is (allegedly) too ill to perform. By its end, the decision has been reversed, on her behalf, by her manager, who means to persuade her that she cannot let her fans down.

Shortly, we will see her take the decision to fulfill her commitments at the theater, in the deep space of her bedroom, in radiant close-up, and then sweep laterally across the shallow space of balcony and lobby and into her waiting car. The shallow space she regards merely as a troublesome hiatus between bedroom and street has been endowed with considerable narrative significance, immediately prior to her departure, by a scene set on the balcony outside her bedroom door, during which the Baron forges an impromptu alliance with the petit bourgeois aspirants, Kringelein and Flaemmchen, who have taken cautious possession of it. Flaemmchen and Von Geigern enter into conversation as they lean over the balcony rail looking down into the lobby, in shallow space. The encounter is at once casual, in that it never exceeds social and sexual ceremony, and profound, in that it raises quite explicitly the question of class difference, and of the hierarchy of entitlements that class difference has put in place. Soon, Kringelein joins them, as Preysing emerges from his suite to claim Flaemmchen for strenographic purposes.

It is a space already quite densely plotted, then, already meaningful, that Grusinskaya barely notices on her way to the lift that will take her down to the lobby. There is an odd moment when, having brusquely dismissed her maid, she halts in her majestic progress to help a little old lady into the lift. Consideration (being nice to dogs and little old ladies) is one of the things people get up to, or ought to get up to, in shallow space. Grusinskaya, however, has just exchanged admiring glances with the Baron, who loiters nearby. She could be putting the consideration on for his benefit. The scene is nicely ambiguous. Might Grusinskaya belong in shallow space, after all, or is she just slumming?

Let us compare this departure with a later one, which takes place after the plot's main hinge point, when Grusinskaya decides to fall in love with the Baron rather than report him to the police. This time she sets out for work in the afterglow of a romantic choice made once and for all. Folded into the scene is a further plot development, as the Baron's chauffeur and sinister accomplice puts pressure on him to deliver the money he owes. It might seem that generic convention, with its enduring reliance on vaguely Ruritanian imbroglios, is about to supersede the inquiry into the alternatives to system. Not a bit of it. For Kringelein and Flaemmchen feature in the scene, too, creatures of shallow space, and no less vivid for that, as they pursue their education in living. And we cannot help but notice the revolving door through which Grusinskaya purposefully exits. The revolving door was in fact a Victorian invention, patented by a Philadelphia engineer called Theophilus Van Kannel in August 1888, as James Buzzard points out in his admirable contribution to revolving door studies.[43] But it became and remained an emblem of modern American city life (even if this one is notionally in Berlin). When Man Ray moved to Manhattan, after a spell in small-town New Jersey, he inaugurated the new experimental phase in his career with *Revolving Doors* (1916–1917), a series of abstract collages hung on a stand, which spectators could turn at will. One section of John Dos Passos's novel *Manhattan Transfer* (1925) is entitled "Revolving Doors." In a rather more sober vein, Rayner Banham notes that the device was an important step toward the establishment of full control both over access to a building and to the atmospheric conditions inside it.[44] The revolving door was not merely modern: it helped to define shallow space. It does not separate the public from the private. Rather, it separates the public from the

semipublic: the anonymous street from the lobby of an office block or hotel, where neither intimacy nor complete mutual detachment prevails. The
revolving door requires not only courtesy, among those who use it, but active collaboration: all the parties involved must push at the same time, in
the same direction, and with the same amount of force. Its successful
operation enacts the regard—civic, functional, and kindly—that the occupants of shallow space ought ideally to display toward each other. In the
novel, the Baron first meets Kringelein when he extracts the permanently
flustered provincial bookkeeper from the revolving door, which he has
tried to enter in the wrong direction.[45] That is where Kringelein's education in living begins. It seems to me that Grusinskaya, by contrast, wants to
transcend the device, to convert it into a fully public stage, an arena, rather
than to collaborate with others in making it work. The counterpart to
Grusinskaya's attempt to transcend the revolving door is Preysing's igno-
minious exit, in handcuffs, at the end of the film through the subsidiary
door beside it, after his arrest for manslaughter. Revolving doors are hard
to use if you happen to be chained to someone else at the time. Neither
Preysing nor Grusinskaya is cut out for shallow space.

It would of course be foolish to claim a great deal for *Grand Hotel* as a
political statement. The alliance the bookkeeper, the stenographer, and
the renegade aristocrat form through casual yet profound encounters in
and around the lobby does not survive the onset of melodrama. But there
is a real inventiveness and gusto, a real spirit of defiance, to the ways in
which they claim squatters' rights over shallow space. I am thinking in
particular of a conversation between the Baron and Flaemmchen, as they
both lean over the balcony rail above the lobby, before Grusinskaya's first
appearance.

In its articulation of the pleasures consenting adults might expect
equally to take in each other's company, the scene anticipates screwball
comedy. After all, Frank Capra's *It Happened One Night* was only two
years away, in 1932. A petit bourgeois semipublic sphere regulated by the
exercise of curiosity, wit, pragmatism, and kindness holds no interest for
the industrial magnate intent on power in the boardroom and respectabil-
ity in the bedroom (except when it suits him) and the ancien régime star
dreaming of full houses and Russia under the czar. The film, I think, is
on the side of Kringelein and Flaemmchen, who at the end get a story to
themselves: an adventure, within strictly defined limits, in other lobbies in
other grand hotels in other cities. In terms of the politics of the studio,

Claiming squatters' rights over shallow space. Frame grab from *Grand Hotel* (1932, MGM, dir. Edmund Goulding).

Grand Hotel is definitely Crawford's film, rather than Garbo's. When in 1966 Manny Farber deplored the disappearance from Hollywood cinema of "those tiny, mysterious interactions between the actor and the scene that make up the memorable moments in any good film," moments of "peripheral distraction, bemusement, fretfulness, mere flickerings of skeptical interest," he had Crawford in mind, and in particular Crawford in *Grand Hotel*.[46] *Grand Hotel* shows what Hollywood could achieve, under the right circumstances, through the use of representational or narrative hierarchy both to evoke an existing awareness of the spatial hierarchies built into the lived environment and to provoke that awareness into critical reflection upon social hierarchy.

It is certainly my contention that Hollywood sustained this achievement, by and large, and with considerable variety of emphasis, throughout the studio era, though I cannot attempt to prove as much here. But I want to offer, as a further and final Hollywood example, a film that associates a hotel lobby with an outer office as sites encouraging curiosity, wit, and

pragmatism, if not always kindness. John Huston made the crime melodrama *The Maltese Falcon* for Warner Bros. in 1941. It was one of the films
whose exhibition in Paris in 1946 prompted the French discovery or invention of film noir.[47] In *The Maltese Falcon*, the office and the apartment
occupied by Sam Spade (Humphrey Bogart) each constitute a *double* space
incorporating inner and outer rooms. Huston uses the same rightward pan
to bring Spade's partner Miles Archer (Jerome Cowan) into the inner office
they share, during the initial encounter with Brigid O'Shaughnessy (Mary
Astor), as he does thereafter to bring successive sets of visitors—two po-
licemen, then Brigid and Joel Cairo (Peter Lorre)—through a vestibule
into the studio apartment in which Spade conducts both business and pleasure. In each case, the pan exerts a kind of force: it pulls the visitors into
deep space, past a briefly glimpsed shallow space (outer office, vestibule),
and then arrays them in the form of a tableau, a triptych with Spade always
at the center, for inspection from a viewpoint itself deeply embedded in
deep space. But the reiteration of the pan masks a significant difference:
the apartment vestibule is little more than a threshold, whereas the outer
office run by Spade's redoubtable amanuensis Effie Perine (Lee Patrick)
expands to fill narrative space.

The transition between a couple of brief, intriguing scenes that take
place roughly halfway through the film pairs this outer office with a lobby.
Spade goes to the Hotel Belvedere to interview Joel Cairo. The hotel detective tries to get personal and so muscle in on the plot by expressing his
sadness at the news of Miles Archer's death, but Spade will have none of it.
He is there not for consolation, but for banter and peacock display. He asserts himself by out-bantering both Cairo and his hapless bodyguard
(Elisha Cook Jr.). The triumph has no narrative function, but vividly establishes Spade's occupancy of a place or level in the world. He belongs in
shallow space. After advising Cairo to get some sleep, Spade returns to his
office, or strictly speaking to the outer office presided over by Effie Perine,
which we recognize in all its clutteredness and spatial complexity. Spade
will pass through, to the inner office, where Brigid O'Shaughnessy awaits
him, and the further disclosure of desire. But his primary allegiance, if
only he would acknowledge as much, has always been and will always be to
that outer office, which also serves as an outer bedroom, since Effie is in
fact the only woman in his life. He could have learned from the mistake
Bob makes, in Hamilton's *The Midnight Bell*. There is a certain pathos,
even, in the discrepancy between his loitering in the hotel lobby and his

scramble through the outer office to deluded entanglements with Brigid and telephony. These scenes nonetheless out him as a paid-up member of the petite bourgeoisie. Like Flaemmchen, in *Grand Hotel*, he is cool; like her, he has a class affiliation, and therefore potentially a politics.

Hollywood, for all its global preeminence, did not, of course, enjoy a monopoly over sound reproduction technologies, or over representations of shallow space. Such representations flourished even in French cinema, where the criterion for sound reproduction was fidelity to the original performance, as in phonography, rather than intelligibility, as in radio and telephony. To be sure, French cinema relied as heavily as Hollywood on the visibility of its star performers across media. "Rather than incarnate fictional characters," Charles O'Brien observes, "actors displayed public personas that had been cultivated outside the cinema, on the popular stage and also increasingly on radio and on 78-rpm disc." Phonography, however, unlike radio, or the popular stage, is a representational storage medium: two places at two times. A phonographic cinema did not have quite as virulent a telephone or radio devil to exorcise. "In the context of the French cinema's recording-orientated conception of film acting, the scene was thought of less as an assemblage of shots than as the recording of an extrafilmic performance; as a consequence, sound-film style in France diverged from that in the United States and in Germany, where a conception of the scene as construction rather than a recording held sway during the 1930s."[48] The technique of direct rather than post-synchronized sound perhaps took the edge off the need to construct a space and a way of talking *against* telephony, against connection, against the system. But construction there certainly was, even in films defiantly faithful to performance, to the sights and sounds of everyday phenomenal life, especially if politics were involved.

Jean Renoir's *Le Crime de Monsieur Lange* exemplifies the scope and verve of the Popular Front propaganda of the early 1930s: that rallying of democratic forces against fascism that led to the election of France's first left-wing government under the constitution of the Third Republic. It advocates collective action against the ruling classes, and cheekily extols the virtues of the work of popular art in an age of mechanical reproduction. In March 1935, shortly before the signing of the Franco-Soviet accord, Renoir had traveled to Moscow. In July, Paris saw a major Bastille Day mobilization against fascism. In August, the Seventh Congress of the Comintern began the repudiation of "Class against Class" doctrines that would engender

Popular Front movements throughout Europe. *Le Crime de Monsieur Lange* was released on January 24, 1936.[49]

Amedée Lange (René Lefèvre) is the author of cowboy stories whose wild popularity sustains the shaky print and publishing empire of the devious Batala (Jules Berry) and then, after Batala has taken himself off to avoid prosecution for debt, a cooperative involving workers, middle management, and the principal creditor's playboy heir. When Batala returns unrepentant, having survived a train crash, Lange guns him down, western-style, and then escapes with his lover Valentine Cardet (Florelle). Although often spoken of as a dramatization of conflict between capital and labor, the film in fact concerns itself primarily, as Alan Williams has pointed out, with a relatively narrow social spectrum. Batala owns and directs a small business, as does Valentine, whose laundry occupies rooms in the same building. Lange is petit bourgeois by dress, manner, and (as Batala's assistant) occupation.[50] It celebrates an insurrectionary petty bourgeoisie capable of forming an alliance with other classes against its own complicity with capitalism.

So complex was the set of *Le Crime de Monsieur Lange,* built in its entirety in the studios at Billancourt, and so clearly integral to the film's dramatic effect, that André Bazin felt moved to include a diagram in his discussion of the rigor of the camera movements that expose it to view.[51] Much of the action takes place in the interior of Batala's first-floor printing and publishing works, which consists of a long composing room with Batala's office at one end. The film makes an exact distinction between deep and shallow spaces.

When Batala arrives in the morning, he is accosted by his principal creditor's emissary, whom he at first invites up to his office, but then, after a confrontation on the stairs, fobs off with a bribe. Two lengthy high-angle panning shots, one from each end of the shop, conduct him in leisurely fashion across semipublic shallow space to the door of his office. Once inside the inner office, Batala starts the day by groping his secretary and current mistress, Edith, and then, as she leaves, Valentine, who has brought his laundry. The camera gazes from deep space into its further depths. The private office evidently doubles as bedroom. When Valentine in turn leaves, we look in the opposite direction, from deep space, out through the open door down the length of the composing shop's activity and casual friendliness, into shallow space. "What's going on?" Valentine inquires, easing herself back into popular culture's indiscriminate camaraderie. "Crisis and

Scandal . . ." It is in the office's deep space that Batala will do his dirty deals; and there, too, that he will seduce (or rape) Estelle, who works for Valentine, and whose consequent pregnancy can be regarded as yet another capitalist crisis and scandal requiring a collective or cooperative response.

Renoir's camera movements connect interior to exterior, and so extend the shallow space of the composing room out into the courtyard at the center of the tenement block that houses Batala's business, and Valentine's. That extended shallow space constitutes an inclusive petit bourgeois semipublic sphere. The political solidarity that will save Lange from the consequences of his crime—acquittal by an impromptu proletarian jury convened in an inn close to the Belgian border—has in effect been built upon the social solidarity it figures. Deep space, meanwhile, has been characterized by its reliance on telephony and broadcast radio, on the systems that connect one privacy to another. As Batala flirts with Valentine in the inner office, telephone and desk lamp frame the ex-lovers, before a reverse angle pulls the telephone into the foreground. Radio, too, belongs to system, and to system's subsumption of the social. It breaks anonymously in on a single anonymous listener in the tenement block, announcing (falsely) that Batala has been killed in a train accident. Cinema, by contrast, is associated with the cooperative at its most cooperative, when its bourgeois ally, the playboy Meunier fils, decides to bankroll an adaptation of Arizona Jim for the screen. When Batala returns from the dead to resume control of his company, Lange, behaving as though he were in a western, guns him down. That is the "crime" of which he will subsequently be acquitted by the proletarian jury. In establishing its petit bourgeois semipublic sphere (a certain kind of space for a certain kind of talk), Lange has carefully set representation against connectivity, a bias toward meaning against a bias toward information, relative unintelligibility against relative intelligibility.

It would be possible to find parallels in British cinema of the period, though the petit bourgeois semipublic sphere envisaged there tends for the most part to be technocratic in nature and function. A good example would be Michael Powell's The Love Test (1935), which I discussed in Chapter 3. The Love Test imagines a chemical laboratory as the solvent of class and gender hierarchy, in stark contrast with a row of cell-like offices showcasing senior management's formulaic behavior. But I want now to consider the construction of shallow space in fiction.

Collective Novels

Ross McKibbin has argued that the explanation for the burgeoning self-confidence of the middle classes in Britain during the period between the world wars lies in increased prosperity, and in the fact that the "new" middle class was not only more numerous but more broadly technical and scientific in experience and attitude. Not unreasonably, its members came to think of themselves as constituting the most modern of Britain's social classes. Because they were modern, and because many of them were employed either by central or by local government, they were on the whole less hostile than previous generations had been to the state and the working class. One aspect of this burgeoning self-confidence was the interest they took in a "literature of modernity," which could also be considered a "literature of public life." Novels like Winifred Holtby's *South Riding* (1936) and A. J. Cronin's *The Citadel* (1937), both as public spirited as they were soppy, became massive best sellers, and successful films. *The Citadel* was the more directly political. Its protagonist, Andrew Manson, begins his professional life as a company doctor in a mining town in South Wales, before gravitating to London, where he takes a job as a Home Office medical inspector, and then establishes a flourishing general practice (Cronin had done both), before disaster strikes. McKibbin points out that despite its "personal and sexual theme," *The Citadel* is "essentially a novel of public life, a critique of Britain's medical hierarchies and (in part) of private medicine itself." It celebrates the triumph against great odds of a group of innovative and socially conscious young professionals. But it has as little as *South Riding* to say about the transformation of both public and private life during the period by communication technologies.[52]

Cronin's politics, in *The Citadel,* and in his previous best seller, *The Stars Look Down* (1935), were progressive rather than radical. In what remains of this chapter, I want to propose that the most astute critique of the consequences of technological change in British fiction of the 1930s occurs in the work of writers who were politically on the left, and sometimes on the far left. It is a matter of record that those writers took a profound interest in the mass media as an instrument of capitalism.[53] What remains to be demonstrated is, first, the subtlety and scope of their exposure of the irreversible (classed and gendered) technological mediation of individual and collective experience; and second, the enduring validity of the resistance they were able to mount, from within that technological mediation, to its class and gender bias.

Legend has it that Cronin sent the manuscript of his first novel, *Hatter's Castle* (1931), to Victor Gollancz after his wife stuck a pin into a list of publishers. Gollancz continued to publish Cronin, because novels were both profitable and prestigious, while political nonfiction such as Mitchison's *Vienna Diary*, which held a much greater interest for him, were often neither.[54] In 1936, Gollancz founded the Left Book Club, as a contribution to the emergent Popular Front alliance of socially progressive and politically interventionist writers and readers against fascism. The key event in the emergence of a cultural Popular Front in Britain was the formation of a British Section of the Writers' International in February 1934. The section's organizers included some Communist Party members, notably Tom Wintringham; most of the others were at least contemplating membership. Launched later in 1934, *Left Review* became its official organ, and the main forum for Popular Front literary activity. It was thus already thriving by the time the Comintern renounced "Class against Class" doctrines at its Seventh Congress in August 1935. "Our main work as revolutionaries," Wintringham had announced in March 1935, "is to get a 'united front' for common action *among all those who are not revolutionaries*" but who nonetheless "feel the need to defend culture and literature against the effects of modern capitalism, against Fascism, war from the air, the throttling of free discussion. Here is the key to our future work."[55] The most important initiative launched from the other—fellow-traveling—end of the Popular Front was John Lehmann's *New Writing*. If *Left Review* was a monthly responsive to political developments, *New Writing* would be a literary quarterly receptive to work too lengthy or too experimental for *Left Review* or indeed other existing periodicals. It is more than twenty years now since Andy Croft demonstrated that these initiatives were to prove, for all their manifest deficiencies, a fertile ground for working-class writers, and for writing about the working classes.[56] Recent research by Christopher Hilliard, which draws extensively on archival resources, has shown how the Popular Front moment "made literary collaboration across the divide between classes, and between the metropolis and the industrial provinces, seem desirable and urgent."[57] One of the most notable forms developed as a result of this surge of interest in working-class conditions and experience was the so-called collective novel.

Discussion of what counts as a collective novel has often come down, quite literally, to a counting of heads. Storm Jameson spoke of *Company Parade* as a book "crowded with men, women, and a child or two."[58] Her *Mirror of Darkness* trilogy—*Company Parade, Love in Winter* (1935), and

None Turn Back (1936)—follows the more or less equally weighted lives of twenty or so different individuals, mostly in London, in the years from 1919 to 1926. Others posted rather more ambitious totals. George Buchanan's *Entanglement* (1938) could claim 40 plus, Naomi Mitchison's *We Have Been Warned* (1935) 80 plus, Winifred Holtby's *South Riding* 150 plus, and so on. The idea, of course, was that these lives should indeed be understood as thoroughly entangled with one another. It is sometimes said that either a class or a city—most often London, but sometimes Birmingham—is their "collective protagonist."[59]

Various attempts have been made to characterize the collective novel more fully by defining its methods. Hilliard has established conclusively that the basis for literary collaboration between the classes during the Popular Front moment was the belief that writing was a profession, rather than an adjunct to militancy, and that aesthetic considerations should weigh equally with political in its pursuit. Working-class writers like Sommerfield, James Hanley, and James Barke were fully aware of the rich tradition of experiment in contemporary literature in English.[60] Joyce and Woolf had set the bar high, when it came to the rendering of collective protagonists. John Dos Passos, author of the urban epic *Manhattan Transfer* (1925) and the all-encompassing *USA Trilogy—The 42nd Parallel* (1930), *1919* (1932), and *The Big Money* (1936)—enjoyed quite a high profile in Popular Front circles. The *Daily Worker* of May 9, 1936, gave up most of a page to one of his "Camera Eye" texts, reprinted from the American *Esquire,* together with elaborate instructions as to how it should be read.

> First, do not insist upon making consecutive sense of every phrase and sentence as you go along. The effect is as cumulative as that of music or painting.
>
> Second, remember that this is the verbal equivalent of the inclusive technique of photography, registering apparently irrelevant and even distracting details for the sake of achieving a complete atmospheric approximation of reality.[61]

The difficulty that remained for literature, as Storm Jameson put it in a symposium in *Fact* in July 1937, was "of expressing, in such a way that they are at once seen to be intimately connected, the relations between things (men, acts) widely separated in space or in the social complex." For her, the solution lay in the montage techniques of experimental documentary or "newsreel" films such as Walter Ruttmann's *Berlin: Symphony of a*

Great City (1927) and Dziga Vertov's *Man with a Movie Camera* (1929).[62] Critics of the collective novel have agreed that this was indeed its chosen method.[63]

Informative though they are, these descriptions have little to tell us about what seems to me one of the collective novel's primary aims, and its greatest achievement: exposure of and resistance to the class and gender bias of the technological mediation of experience. The Popular Front moment made it possible to understand connectivity as political through and through, as an instrument of power. Rex Warner's political fable *The Professor* (1938) is the story of an eminent classicist propelled into the chancellorship of a failing mid-European state about to be overrun from within and without by militant fascism. In the opening chapter, immediately prior to his assumption of office, the Professor lectures to a packed hall on the merits of the Greek polis, which for him clearly constitutes a public realm spatially conceived: "an enclosure, a safety zone, or outpost against what to the Greeks (and in a very real sense their view was correct) was actually the barbarism of others who were outside this on the whole liberal organization." Once in power, the Professor resolves to broadcast to the nation, in defense of democracy. He will live the 1930s dream of media at once broadcast in scope and narrowcast in focus and intensity, reconstituting electronically an enclosure or safety zone of simultaneous national event and simultaneous national presence.

> As the clocks were striking eleven it seemed, even from the upper room in the Chancellory, as though a hush had fallen upon the city. From the windows one might have seen the whole street packed with faces, still eagerly upturned in expectation, although now their attention was directed not so much to the windows themselves as to the black protuberances of loudspeakers which had been placed at regular intervals on balconies along the front of the building. In other streets, too, the sight would have been the same, while in hundreds of thousands of homes families were gathering around radio sets in large or small rooms, staring at the instruments, whether home-made or expensively manufactured, as though those arrangements of wood, glass, and wire were oracles, gods, or idols.

The Professor, furthermore, "was exceptionally well equipped as a radio orator." There can be little doubt that, in addressing the citizens of the republic at once individually and en masse, he will "both convince and reassure." But the strength of a broadcast medium is also its weakness. It can be cut off at its source. The Chief of Police has seized the radio station and is in the process of proclaiming himself chancellor in the Professor's place. The Professor's eager adoption of radio's infinitely enlarged polis has turned out to be a pact made with the devil. He pays for his gullibility by enduring a radical contraction both of physical space and of the social and political solidarities space allows. The only refuge he can find from the fascist gangs is in a house owned by the father of his one remaining loyalist. "The Professor was sitting in a space so small as to suggest that what now did duty for a sitting-room must have been designed in the first place as a closet or cupboard."[64] A couple of Kafkaesque chapters ensue, during which people squeeze themselves into this cupboard in order to engage in farcical debate, and are somehow extruded from it. Resisting such contractions, the collective novel sought in informal social solidarity (a certain kind of talk in a certain kind of space) a basis for formal political solidarity.

My argument so far has been that technological advances in cinema created an opportunity to imagine a particular kind of talk as a moral and political value, and to incorporate it into a social logic of space: an understanding of coexistence, of cross-class cooperation, of community, even. The semipublic space in which that kind of talk took place was not an expression of nostalgia for a lost paradise of face-to-face civic encounter, but rather the dialectical product of the extreme claims made on behalf both of a narrowcast medium (telephony) and of a broadcast medium reconfigured as narrowcast (radio). Cinema absorbed connectivity, but only as the basis for a representation of its (de-privatized) antidote. I want briefly to establish the implications of this dialectic for the collective novel by isolating two emphases in the film criticism of Graham Greene, whose interest in cinema was more extensive than that of any other writer of the period.

Greene reviewed film regularly for the *Spectator* from 1935 to 1940. He did not regard cinema as anything other than a mass medium. "The Cinema," he wrote in 1937, "has got to appeal to millions; we have got to accept its popularity as a virtue, not turn away from it as a vice."[65] Greene's firm conviction that sound was essential to cinema made him especially sensitive to its radio aura. Bernard Bergonzi and Laura Marcus have both pointed out that he made vivid (and vividly antipathetic) use of the idea of the "crooner" in his 1938 novel *Brighton Rock*.[66] The crooner, whispering in the audience's ears, was an invention of radio. The new electrical microphones amplified the voice to such an extent that singers did not need to project their voices in order to be heard. Crooning repurposed a broadcast medium as (virtually) narrowcast. It helped to create and maintain the illusion that each listener might enjoy an "unmediated and personal" relationship with the broadcaster, that she or he was being separately sung to. Since radio was most often listened to in the home, the result was a new (albeit consensual) invasion of privacy.[67] By reproducing that seductive murmur, cinema imitated radio at its most telephonic.[68] Greene thought these imitations deplorable. Reviewing *Rose of the Rancho* in the *Spectator* on March 6, 1936, he took aim at the sickliness of its music, and at an actor called John Boles. "I find Mr Boles, his air of confident carnality, the lick of black shiny hair across the plump white waste of face, peculiarly unsympathetic; and never more so than in this film as he directs his lick, his large assured eyes, towards Miss Swarthout and croons."[69] In *Brighton Rock*, Pinkie, a young man at once enthralled and revolted by life in general, finds a focus for his ambivalence in the crooner who performs in the dance hall to which he has taken his girlfriend, Rosie.

> A spotlight picked out a patch of floor, a crooner in a dinner jacket, a microphone on a long black musical stand. He held it tenderly as if it were a woman, swinging it gently this way and that, wooing it with his lips while from the loudspeaker under the gallery his whisper reverberated hoarsely over the hall, like a dictator announcing victory, like the official news following a long censorship. "It gets you," the Boy said, "it gets you," surrendering himself to the huge brazen suggestion.

At once broadcast and narrowcast, brazen and suggestive, crooning acknowledges no distinction between the private and public spheres. It "gets you" one by one, en masse. By 1938, there were dictators whispering hoarsely from loudspeakers and wireless sets all over Europe. It had been Hollywood's surrender to the aura of crooning that first alerted Greene to connectivity's threat. A later episode in *Brighton Rock*, when Pinkie takes Rosie to see a romantic film, makes it clear that he had not forgotten Mr. John Boles. "The actor with a lick of black hair across a white waste of face said, 'You're mine. All mine.'"[70]

The antidote to crooning would involve, as we have already seen, the construction of a narrative space that belonged neither to the public nor to the private sphere, and the exercise within it of an informal social solidarity. Greene sought the antidote out in such unpromising locations as *The Petrified Forest* (1936), a film now remembered solely for its part in launching

Humphrey Bogart's career as a tough guy. In this adaptation of a play by Robert E. Sherwood, the *Times* noted, Leslie Howard "plays the extremely talkative hero who, suffering from the discouragement of his creative impulse, commits suicide that a pretty girl with the gift of an artist may be free to develop her genius." And he is not the only one. Most of the characters gathered in a remote service station in the Arizona desert feel the autobiographical impulse, "and once the notorious 'killer' and his confederates have 'drawn a bead' on the company the temptation to review the past and state grievances against life becomes irresistible."[71] Greene thought the film's "opening movement," in which the disparate group assembles in the service station diner, "very promising." The Hollywood diner is a classic shallow space. Here, it provides a more productive arena for the airing of grievances than the secluded rooftop on which the talkative hero denounces the modern world for the benefit of the pretty girl with the gift of an artist (Bette Davis), a monologue framed by a swath of telephone wires, connectivity's non-ideographic ideograph.

It is true, as Greene was quick to point out, that the use the film makes of this arena is scarcely dynamic. Talk so heavily laden with "stale abstractions" seems unlikely to promote social solidarity. "But life itself, which crept in during the opening scene, embarrassed perhaps at hearing itself so explicitly discussed, crept out again, leaving us only with the symbols, the too pasteboard desert, the stunted cardboard studio trees."[72] Even so, the glimpse of "life" initially afforded by the idea of the diner as shallow space was something Greene could appreciate. When he came across something comparable in other films, he tended to recall *The Petrified Forest*, despite its manifest faults. *Winterset* (1936), for example, like *The Petrified Forest*, was a "romantic play" mixing poetry with gunmen, which nonetheless boasted a productive shallow space, an arena for informal sociability, in the shape of a "bleak rain-drenched square under the arches of Brooklyn Bridge."[73] *Idiot's Delight* (1938), on the other hand, resembled *The Petrified Forest* rather too closely in its "moral pretentiousness" and a "kind of cellophaned intellectuality." Greene's vote went to a British thriller *They Drive by Night* (1939), directed by Arthur Woods, from a novel by James Curtis. What he liked about it was its ability to get a "realistic twist out of every situation." The situations that stuck in his mind were the shallow spaces favored by an itinerant "low-life" cast of truck drivers and prostitutes: pub, café, dance hall, service station.[74] Curtis was one of several London writers who specialized in getting a realistic twist out of such situations.

The collective novel in Britain drew more extensively on cinema than it did on Joyce and Woolf; and it drew on cinema not so much for montage technique as for the stylized representation of a space for sociability, a space neither wholly private nor wholly public. It may indeed have drawn specifically on *Grand Hotel*. Dot Allan had probably seen the film, or read the novel, before she wrote *Hunger March* (1934). Set in Depression-hit Glasgow on the day of a demonstration that culminates in a rally in George Square, *Hunger March* is for the most part concerned with the views of a variety of middle- and lower-middle-class protagonists as they observe and respond to the spectacle of militant poverty. In chapter 2, a journalist arrives at the fictional equivalent of the square's North British Railway Hotel to interview a celebrated diva, Adèle Elberstein, whose sense of desolation will prove a match for Grusinskaya's. "But behind all the fantastic posturing, the foolish, exaggerated gestures, there lay the artiste." The Railway Hotel is more provincial than grand, but it does give rise to a mildly Kracauer-esque vision of the lobby as negative church. The assistant manager, Miss Smithers, acts as chorus. "Hotels, as she knew from experience, tended to bring out the worst side in human nature. She wondered frequently if it was because a hotel with its keys, its numbered doors, was so akin in its way to a prison."[75] The motif of hotel guests blockaded in a hotel was to be taken up by Henry Green in *Party Going* (1939).

Green, in fact, had established in *Living* (1929) a more telling precedent for the collective novel than *Ulysses* or *Mrs Dalloway*. Green's father was a wealthy Birmingham landowner and industrialist. After Eton and Oxford, which he left in 1926 without taking a degree, he returned to Birmingham to engage in the family business, at first on the shop floor, and then as managing director, experiences he drew on substantially in *Living*. Green was during this period at once "more interested than most of his friends in crossing social boundaries," as Jeremy Treglown points out, and "deeply entrenched" in his own genteel background.[76]

Living is a novel sensitive to the subtle distinctions not only between and within a variety of classed and gendered behaviors and ways of speaking, but also between and within a range of industrial and domestic spaces, including the picture palace as an arena for the sorts of informal sociability that can determine the outcome of sentimental and other educations. The choice Lily Gates makes between almost reliable Jim Dale and almost adventurous Bert Jones is an exploration of the limits of the freedom available to a young working-class woman in Britain in the 1920s. Valentine

Cunningham pauses in the middle of a withering survey of the withering contempt many intellectuals felt at the time for the movies to note that *Living* "does not disapprove of Lily's cinema-inspired visions of emigration, nor the tawdry touches of beauty that movies intrude into her existence."[77] I would put it more strongly than that. Lily's courtship of and by her two admirers is conducted for the most part within and by means of the semipublic sphere of the "cinema": the building, the institution, the images on the screen. Lily, palpably lured by the images on the screen, but not yet ready to surrender to them, as Pinkie surrenders to the dictatorial crooner in *Brighton Rock*, exercises the sort of command over her niche in the auditorium that Ella the barmaid had exercised over her niche in the saloon bar, in Hamilton's *The Midnight Bell*.[78] Cinema's constitutive disjunction (two places at two times) enables her to reflect upon a reflection of the world.

For there is a cardinal opposition, in this novel, not between fantasy and fact within cinema, but between cinema as a medium and radio as a medium. Lily keeps house for Mr. Craigan, a foundry worker and a friend of her feckless father. Craigan's first act in the novel is to forbid Lily to get a job, as she would like to do. " 'None o' the womenfolk go to work from the house I inhabit' he said" (*L* 215). Lily's sentimental education by cinema is also an education in the alternatives to domestic servitude. Like all tyrants, Craigan must render himself oblivious to any claims his subjects might address to him. "Lily Gates was saying half smiling to Jim Dale it gave her the creeps Mr Craigan always sitting at home of an evening. He listened to the wireless every night of the week except Mondays" (242). Connectivity liberates Craigan from circumstance, from awareness of the representations Lily has made on her own behalf. On Sundays, he spends "all the morning listening to preachers in foreign countries, why when you didn't know the language she couldn't see what was in it, and the afternoon and evening the same, right till he went to his room, she said" (242). These broadcasts in a foreign language can have no meaning for him. Like another failing tyrant, Sir Clifford in *Lady Chatterley's Lover*, he wants connection for connection's sake. As radio's grip on Mr. Craigan lessens, so does his on Lily. By the end of the novel, after a failed elopement, he is even offering her sixpence to go to the movies. "She said what alone, and to leave him! He said she'd better go, she was in too much he said. So that night she went" (377). The left-wing fiction of the 1930s developed further this association between radio and the exercise of authority, on one hand, and cinema and the reconstruction of a working-class or petit bourgeois semi-public sphere, on the other.

In November 1930, Harold Heslop, a young unemployed Durham miner, attended the Second Plenum of the International Union of Revolutionary Writers, in Kharkov, in the Soviet Union. When called upon to describe the state of "proletarian art" in Britain, he could only apologize for its backwardness. Heslop had already had one novel published in the Soviet Union, in 1925, and another, the semiautobiographical *The Gates of a Strange Field*, in Britain in 1929. In 1932, the first issue of the Moscow-based *International Literature* carried a fierce critique of the alleged petit bourgeois individualism of these texts, and the more recent *Journey Beyond* (1930), a novel about unemployment. *Last Cage Down*, published in 1935, just as Popular Front policies were gaining ground in Britain and the Soviet Union, responds to that critique by insisting on the paramount importance of Marxist-Leninist doctrine and discipline. Its protagonist, James Cameron, is secretary of the union lodge at a Durham coalfield, and a charismatic leader of Old Testament dimensions. His vanity leads him to turn the struggle between labor and capital into a personal vendetta against the company agent, John Tate. As the novel concludes, he has effectively been replaced as miners' leader by his colleague and rival, the Communist Joe Frost. By 1935, the figure of Joe Frost seemed to the *Daily Worker* and the *Left Review* like a throwback to "Class against Class" doctrines.[79]

I want to argue, however, that it was precisely this polemical honing on Heslop's part that sharpened the novel's Popular Front theme: the attention it gave to informal social solidarity as the basis for formal political solidarity. For it could have been very reactionary indeed, allying theoretical Marxism with paeans to the "glory in the toil of a miner." Our introduction to Cameron is an introduction to a traditional classed and gendered discourse of form and content, nature and culture. The miner, we are told, must "make this dead coal speak, speak with the many tongues of coal, weep as a woman weeps when she mourns."[80] Later in the novel, Cameron and the vastly experienced Bill Wardle perform "miracles of heroism" in rescuing the victims of a fall. "Often the tunnel was in imminent danger of collapse, and often by sheer magnificence of behaviour, of skilled mining technique, they averted the danger" (251). By this account, what is wrong with the mining industry under capitalism is that it has been "Fordized" (229), to the detriment of heroism and artisanal technique. "They were turning out coal like they turned out cars"—or, as Heslop cannot resist adding, like Bloomsbury produces novels and plays (229–30).

But that is by no means the whole story. For the social and cultural world in which the mine exists, and in which the discourse concerning its future takes shape, is a world penetrated throughout by communication technologies. Cinema informs Cameron's initial confrontation with Tate.

> Cameron leaned back in order to get his breath. "Is that so?" he sneered.
>
> "Yes, that is so, Mr Cameron," said Tate. "And please do not introduce the slang of the talkie in this office. Now, let us proceed . . ." (*LCD* 29)

Cameron, the artisan, the Old Testament prophet, has thoroughly absorbed, and even relishes, the slang of the talkie, which he has every intention of introducing into management's inner sanctuary. When the miners' lodge meets to discuss the terms Tate has set for ending a strike, his mental response to the fierce criticism of his leadership delivered by Joe Frost again derives from, and moreover has as its subject, the talkativeness of the talkies. "Go on, Frost, shoot your mouth off, as the pictures say. Pour it all out. It doesn't worry me" (85). Cameron's addiction to talkie slang should not be understood as the stigma of petit bourgeois individualism. On the contrary, it embeds him further, as no amount of "sheer magnificence of behaviour" could do, in his community. In the coalfield town, movie idiom and movie gestures have become the discursive medium in which social exchanges are often conducted. Cameron's lover, Betsy, as down to earth as they come, nonetheless seems to his mother, Elsa, to have caught the habit, shrugging her shoulders "like an American girl Elsa had seen on the films" (146). More significantly still, that idiom informs even the fiercest of political debates among militant factions: "'we're posh now we've got the talkies, aren't we?' he asked" (289). For the novel does rather more than resist its own residual nostalgia for a lost paradise of face-to-face civic and artisanal encounter. It imagines talkativeness mediated by one or other of two competing media technologies.

The political value of technologically mediated talkativeness is by no means self-evident. Rather, it emerges dialectically in relation to the increasing presence and authority in working-class communities of the social medium of radio. On the whole, broadcasting attracted ambivalence, at best, among left-wing commentators in Britain.[81] Cecil Day-Lewis, writing as Nicholas Blake, was forthright enough. His detective, Nigel Strangeways, rages against the "ubiquitous bawling of the loudspeaker."[82] We need to look closely at the terms in which the prevailing ambivalence was framed. Arthur Calder-Marshall, for example, began by expressing unstinted admiration for radio in its connective function. "It has linked the countries of the earth together: and both aided travel from one country to another and made it less necessary by the almost instant transmission of messages." Although Calder-Marshall's main interest lay in the medium's conversion to broadcasting, and the consequent establishment of a "vast new social activity," he clearly conceived its propaganda effect, as broadcasting, in terms of that original connective or narrowcast function. "Radio-bibbing," or connection for connection's sake, had become a national habit, he claimed. "Housewives cook and make the beds and dust to music: and not to music only. They have got now to be oblivious to subject. Music or talking, it is all the same." Fiction was to dispute the gendering of such an account, but not the idea that radio was often at its most effective ideologically when it meant least: when the voice that owns the listener's attention seems no longer to come from outside, and is therefore no longer to be argued with. Calder-Marshall thought that the live broadcasting of state occasions had similarly drained them of meaning. "The material world has given place to the ethereal." Television, furthermore, would most likely repeat the dose. Calder-Marshall reported that the BBC's head of television saw the future of the medium as lying "not so much in films, which he calls 'canned television' just as gramophone records are canned sound, as in direct, personally viewed programmes."[83] He was not far wrong. Television today functions both as a representational and as a connective medium; but connectivity is what it sells the hardest.

In *Last Cage Down*, the talkified James Cameron rages against the "fatuous balderdash" of "Children's Hour" emerging scratchily from a loudspeaker in Betsy's kitchen: "but as he was not so learned in the programmes of the British Broadcasting Corporation he could not ask for the alternative, which in all probability would be a jazz band, blaring and 'putting in the obscene dirt' of muted trumpets and trombones and so forth" (*LCD* 194). But Cameron's hostility is not necessarily Heslop's. For the novel introduces Joe Frost, Cameron's rival for leadership of the miners, as a recent convert to radio. "Franton miners could not understand Joe Frost at all. He was one of that new breed of men, who read diligently, who owned a radio, and who was not greatly interested in the footling vaudeville programmes of the BBC" (*LCD* 42). Bertolt Brecht had characterized radio as a medium that by negative example seems to know "how to let the listener speak as well as hear, how to bring him into a relationship rather than isolating him."[84] Frost's selective listening in informs his role in the community, and in the novel, as a theorist of revolution. "He taught the young men the theories of Marx" (42). The rivalry between Frost and Cameron is a rivalry between connective and representational understandings of the basis of political action.

The novel's crucial scene involves a contest between those understandings. That the standoff takes place in shallow space might indicate where its allegiance, if not that of its author, actually lies. Frost decides to reach out to Cameron, as the latter spirals into self-destruction, by confronting him on his own territory, the pub where he customarily drinks, and where Betsy works as a barmaid. Frost wants to persuade Cameron to abandon his vendetta against Tate. But he does so, in the first instance, by exemplifying the more measured approach to politics he himself can be thought to take. His opening gambit is to explain that he has recently "taken to music," and bought a radio.

> Cameron nodded. "Just like the silly devil you are," he said affably. "Going and buying a wireless set . . ."
>
> "It's interesting," returned Joe calmly. "Besides, I don't go raking all over the earth just to see how many stations I can get. Of course, I tune in on the German stations, now and then."
>
> "I see," said Cameron. "You've got a licence, then?"
>
> Joe nodded. "That chap Goebbels is always bawling on some German radio," he went on. "It's a wonder somebody doesn't ram a loudspeaker down his throat . . . him and his . . . Fuehrer."
>
> "And who the hell's that?"
>
> "Hitler, of course." (*LCD* 106)

Frost engages Cameron's interest in music in order to demonstrate the value of a conscious and discriminating use of a connective medium, first, to provide a better standard of entertainment, and second, to establish a broad national and international context for political action. Before long, he is talking revolution (110). Cameron, however, refuses to be drawn: that is, he refuses to be drawn out of the time and place that is a pub in a mining town, out of the ways in which he has chosen to represent himself. His affability, fueled by drink, becomes a tough-guy hysteria. "The saloon bar, sensing drama, watched the enactment of the scene in silence" (109). Cameron starts to behave as though he were in a western. "'I could drill a hole through you with this fist, Joe,' he said" (109). It is, of course, a dialogue of the deaf: an excess of radio-inspired theory confronting an excess of cinema-inspired practice. But the ground has moved beneath this standoff. By seeking Cameron out in his own territory, Frost has admitted that informal sociability can provide the basis for a formal politics. The scene is in its way a Popular Front moment.

Police surveillance of political activity is a constant feature of 1930s mining novels. For example, the first chapter of Lewis Jones's *We Live* (1939) introduces a pair of constables listening at a keyhole while those inside discuss the prospects of a lockout. A few pages later, the constables are summoned to report what they have heard to the inspector and "another, uniformed individual."[85] In the collective novel in general, systems for the management of information were rendered palpable, socially and politically, if not always physically, by their use against working-class movements. John Sommerfield's remarkable *May Day* (1936) devotes particular attention to the abuse of connective technology for such purposes. Sommerfield left school at age fifteen to work as a newspaper runner, then as a carpenter, and merchant seaman. He joined the Communist Party and wrote for *Left Review, New Writing,* and the *Daily Worker,* where he had a column. He served in a machine-gun unit in the International Brigade during the Spanish Civil War: *Volunteer in Spain* (1937) was one of the first eyewitness accounts in English. *May Day* attracted a good deal of attention, and praise, if not massive sales. "Unlike most novels of today," Philip Henderson wrote in *The Novel Today: A Study in Contemporary Attitudes* (1936), "Sommerfield's is alive with hope and a sense of direction."[86] Looking back, in the "Author's Note" for the 1984 edition, Sommerfield himself described it as "Communist romanticism."[87]

Henderson, however, was right to suppose that there was a method to Sommerfield's romanticism. *May Day,* he observed, "makes a synthesis of the apparently chaotic life of London by relating its many-sidedness to the unifying principle of the class struggle." In his view, the novel's great virtue was that it presented this struggle "in terms of men and women with whose personal lives we can sympathize, while still seeing them in their true social perspective."[88] But how does Sommerfield establish that "social perspective" on sympathetic individual lives? Not by montage technique, that is for sure. And not by the spider's web of spider's-web metaphors (*MD* 87, 160, 190) that again and again asserts an underlying principle it cannot define. Rather, Sommerfield makes a distinction: between media uses, between spaces, between kinds of talk. That distinction provides perspective.

Telephony, connecting privacy to privacy, depends upon occlusion: in the house, in the factory, in the office complex. The novel's action centers on events at Langfier's Carbon Works, where the workers, provoked by a terrible industrial accident, vote to go on strike and join the May Day demonstration. A couple of days before the demonstration, Langton, chief engineer at Langfier's, takes a shortcut back to his office through the factory's business entrance, a hall equipped with a glass case full of samples where a few commercial salesmen sit around ogling the secretaries. As he passes through the hall, Langton overhears the end of a conversation, which Sommerfield splits across two narrative sections.

> He heard the telephone operator saying, "No, madam. He left this morning and hasn't been back since."
>
> ❀ ❀ ❀ ❀ ❀
>
> "Well, I really don't know what can have happened to him," sighed Lady Langfier in her irritatingly placid voice as she put down the 'phone. And she turned to Henry McGinnis, the chauffeur. (*MD* 83)

The break between sections exposes telephony as system connecting two privacies, that of the home and that of the inner office, via an operating system. The break is also a blank: the gap in information where meaning ought to be. Lady Langfier has learned that her husband is not at work. What this might mean, she does not know, or pretends not to know. In fact, Langfier's absence from the factory is symptomatic. He is one of many enfeebled or failing patriarchs in these novels—closest, perhaps, to Mr. Dupret Senior, in *Living*—and has been trying to sell his stake in the Carbon Works to Amalgamated Industrial Enterprises. He has lost his grip on telephony, among other things.

Sommerfield re-embeds the idea of connectivity not just in deep space, but in social, cultural, and political attitude. He was by no means the first novelist to understand telecommunication as both instrument and emblem of the systems by which power is exercised. In William Gerhardie's *Doom*, first published as *Jazz and Jasper* in 1927, tyro author Frank Dickin spends a good deal of time in the office of a volcanic newspaper magnate, Lord Ottercove. Ottercove appears to have immediate access by telephone, at virtually any time of day or night, to the members of a political and financial élite. "Frank had a feeling that he was at the centre of all things, in the very signal-box from which all the wires were pulled and the signals flashed the wide world over."[89] Sommerfield stepped the analysis up a level. The politics of telecommunication are rendered explicit at the very end of the novel, when the May Day contingents converge on Hyde Park. "The top of the Marble Arch is a nerve centre for electric messages. Here sound voices from police cars and aeroplanes and 'phone boxes. The police chiefs stand like officers on the bridge of a battleship going into action." For obvious reasons, Sommerfield cannot introduce into this particular deep space a passerby who might by chance catch the final words of momentous conversations. He must rely on metaphor instead. But the metaphor has been earned by the exposure of connectivity's inner workings (as much attitude as technology) in scenes like Langton's alert passage through the entrance hall. For there is indeed a war going on: class war. The chief of police, breathing "aristocratic militarism," wishes that he was back in India so that he could call out a company of guards with fixed bayonets (MD 238).

The working class can deploy only the most makeshift of electronic or mock-electronic countermeasures. "The ranks of the marchers conducted the news of the strike like wire conducting an electric message" (MD 233).[90] Far better, Sommerfield proposes, to attempt to reestablish the informal social solidarity—a certain kind of space, neither wholly public nor wholly private, for a certain kind of talk—that might become the basis for formal political solidarity. Vernacular London novels like James Curtis's *They Drive by Night* and Gerald Kersh's *Night and the City* (both 1938) were to contrive a Hollywood-inflected, bohemian semipublic sphere out of pubs, cafés, tea shops, nightclubs, and dance halls. In *May Day*, James Seton, seaman, Communist, and Spanish Civil War veteran, like Sommerfield himself, whose return to London inaugurates the narrative, takes refuge in a dingy café in central London during a shower of rain. "Behind the counter a billowing shapeless woman wrapped in a dirty white overall sat thinking about a film she had seen last night." The presence of this woman, sunk in a gendered daze, somehow frees Sommerfield to describe a scene of utter (blissful) homosocial banality, the sort of scene that, had it been in a British film, Greene would surely have lit on rapturously: "Two lorry-drivers were talking about motor engines. A small cabinet-maker with a gingery waxed moustache and a bowler hat was reading the leading article in the *Daily Herald*. At the next table a young mechanic in a clean, faded boiler-suit was talking to two unemployed youths (in rakish peak caps, knotted white scarves, etc.) about dog racing." Seton takes the *Daily*

Worker out of his pocket. "A snuffly loud-speaker uttered waltz tunes" (163). He begins to feel a bit sleepy. And yet, inside this minimal sociability becalmed between cinema daze and radio daze, for no apparent reason, debate stirs. "Absently he spooned sugar into his tea and stirred it. He began to be aware of a changed atmosphere behind him. He turned around and looked. The cabinet-maker had put down his *Herald,* the unemployed and the mechanic had stopped their conversation and were leaning forward towards the lorry drivers, who were letting off" (164). They are letting off about the next war. Soon the others join in. Can war be stopped? Only by militant strike action, James maintains. "It's fine, he was thinking, it's grand the way everyone is arguing and talking about politics and war and everything now, so different to what it was when I was last home. The workers are waking up . . ." (165). The scene is all Communist romanticism, of course; far more so, at any rate, than the confrontation between James Cameron and Joe Frost in *Last Cage Down.* But it, too, reconstitutes, as a certain kind of talk in a certain kind of space, the informal social solidarity out of which formal political solidarity might conceivably grow. The dingy café is every bit as much of a Popular Front semipublic sphere as the yard in *Le Crime de Monsieur Lange.*

Technological Mediation

The spaces I have examined in this chapter are a mixture of the relatively old (café, pub) and the relatively new (outer office, hotel lobby). In each case, however, the sociability they nurture has been defined against the media systems that penetrate and surround them. That sociability comes after, and as a result of, technological mediation, not before it. I shall conclude the chapter as I began it, by remarking on the degree of hostility felt in Popular Front circles to radio understood as a connective medium. In Allan's *Hunger March,* for example, Joe Humphry, a young unemployed man, assaults a bystander who appears to be mocking the marchers, and escapes from the center of Glasgow into the suburbs, by bus, and then on foot. Entering a village, he passes a "large white villa from which the blare of a wireless band was issuing." The music is like an assault: "followed by a blast of crazy negro music, he turned up a steep lane which ran at right angles with the village, and which he hoped would take him past it by devious ways." The assault, however, is as aggressive in its insinuations as it is in its volume. "The crooner's voice, cleaving the darkness, had conjured up for him the same sort of pictures as the shipping companies' posters of Canada invariably did—pictures of contented labourers working under blue skies, of vast yellow fields of corn swooning in the sun . . . The sun! It warmed you to think of it on a night like this."[91] Joe's criminal act has excluded him from the actual community of the hunger march and its supporters. Even more painful, though, is his exclusion as a vagrant from the virtual community created by suburban wireless crooning.

A more complicated case is that of Kevin Rede, in George Buchanan's *Entanglement* (1938). *Entanglement* takes a broad view, from the captain of industry and his disenchanted wife (her favorite toy is a *white* telephone) down through air ace, civil servant, and suburban couple to the exquarryman who has fought in Spain and now works as a trades union organizer and peace activist. Although clumsily written, it is the most subtle as well as the most assiduous of all collective novels in its detailing of the technological mediation of experience. Fascism and the prospect of world war shadow the stately progress of the narrative. Born a couple of generations earlier, Kevin Rede, its focal protagonist, would have been a Wellsian technocrat of the "new Machiavelli" type destined not just to dream about but in a small measure to implement the reform of society, until undone by a woman.[92] As it is, his brilliant career peters out in captivity by cool.

At the beginning of the novel, Kevin, who has been trained as an engineer, works in a shop selling radio and gramophone equipment. He is a believer in virtual community, telling one of his customers that "a machine has come into being which makes it possible for the whole world to live together in—how shall I say?—a shared present."[93] Before long, his social contacts land him a job working for Charles Manwick, head of the aeronautics division of a large engineering firm, whose confidence he quickly gains. His new gospel of "scientific management" comes with a different notion of community attached. "His was now a more *social* existence: he was working in association with a greater number of people than at the shop" (*E* 254–55). However, the principles of scientific management have a hard time overcoming the envious rivalry of his colleagues, and Manwick's suspicion of his politically motivated idealism. Never fully at home in the deep spaces where boardroom, club-land, or dinner-party intimacies form, Kevin finds it harder and harder to create an alternative "shared present" that might serve as the basis for political thought, if not political action. For Buchanan, as for Jameson, the most transformative of all the new media, the telephone, offers no more than the spectacle of mobile privatization. In each of the phone booths in Piccadilly underground station, Kevin sees "a man or a woman, bent slightly forward, talking into the instrument to invisible people elsewhere, to lovers, business men, anxious husbands or wives, or perhaps embezzlers and confidence tricksters" (184). He feels that, locked separately into an array of virtual communions, they are all nonetheless in some sense more substantial than he is. "He was, as it were, a shadow moving among solids." What Kevin has paused to observe is meta-connectivity: communication by telephone as commentary on communication by underground railway or other means of transport. He understands that both systems, connecting one privacy to another, have in effect erased the sociable, and the social. Data flows are the new solids, among which flesh and blood moves as though a shadow. Equally mobile, equally private, are the occupants of the mass-transit systems that complement and reinforce connective media. Commuting to work by tube, he is forced into close physical contact with complete strangers. "Often in the city this happened: you found yourself a member of a group in a bus, Tube, at a shop counter. Perhaps you all shared a joke. Then the group broke up and vanished" (275). Like *Hunger March*, unlike *May Day*, *Entanglement* cannot imagine an informal social solidarity that might serve as the basis for formal political solidarity.

In the end, what saves Kevin is a woman in a "heavy waterproof coat" whom he literally bumps into during the demonstration of a new kind of parachute (*E* 294). Almost immediately, his attitude to his work changes. The tenuousness of his position no longer worries him. "It must always, for him, be like this—that is, if he remained true to his proper movement, not in the sense of seeking stability but in ever breaking his stability in order to keep closer to the movement of life" (304). The key to this change of attitude is that his new muse, Rona Maxwell Smith, secretary to a Tory MP, is *cool*. "She was all shrewdness and repressed tenderness, determined to avoid emotional entanglements" (309). At last, an explanation for the novel's title! Cool objects not to strong feeling, but to inappropriate feeling, or to feeling inappropriately expressed. Kevin and Rhona fall passionately in love with each other, to the extent of a couple of pages of sub-Lawrentian sex (349–50). And of course they go to the cinema; in this case, to see a suitably thought-provoking March of Time news film about the decline of the great English estates (365). *Chatterley* territory, again. Like Connie and Mellors, like Ursula Brangwen and Rupert Birkin, in *Women in Love*, they become increasingly detached from concerns about professional and social position. For them, however, there will be no alternative to the "organized fate" of the city's inhabitants (388). They will continue to exploit the slack in a system they have given up any hope of changing. The best they can hope for is that "black-out of the mind" that can best be understood as a "projection of the fear of their own blotting-out" (388). This is, after all, 1938. At the end of the day, *Entanglement* is not so much a collective novel as a bildungsroman for the information age.

Would there be any point in regarding *Finnegans Wake*, a text fully conversant with the idiom of new media like radio and television, as a collective novel of a very odd sort? Its cast of characters is smaller than that typically recruited by collective novels, and by Joyce himself in *Ulysses*, but large enough, all the same, to require the author to devise in his working notes and explanatory correspondence a system of sigla, so that he could keep track of who was doing what to whom at a given moment. The published version includes a footnote referring to the "Doodles family" by their respective marks.[94] Beyond the family—father (HCE), mother (ALP), two sons (Shem and Shaun), and a daughter (Issy)—there are two domestic servants to be reckoned with, as well as a charwoman, four minatory old men, and twelve customers in the pub Earwicker runs in Chapelizod. Of course, these characters are not "characters" so much as discursive transformations of an identifying siglum, which is roughly speaking what one might say of the personnel thronging texts like *May Day* and *Entanglement*.

The episode in *Finnegans Wake* that most closely resembles the British collective novel, in preoccupation if not in method, is the one in which radio and television feature most prominently: II.3. The opening of the *Wake* drops us, as Margot Norris has remarked, "without map, clock, compass, glossary, or footnotes, into an unknown verbal country, and the voice of the tour guide, alas, speaks their language rather than ours."[95] By the time we reach II.3, however, it has all started to look a bit more familiar, at any rate to judge by the confident tone of the commentaries. "The tale begins in an atmosphere of drunken camaraderie, in the pub owned by HCE. The radio is blaring, and the raucous behavior of the pub's patrons stops just short of a brawl."[96] So much for that "unknown verbal country." It is not just that the setting and props are identifiable, but that we know how the scene came to be arranged as it is. "The customers have given Earwicker a radio, but insist that it be in the bar and that they call the stations."[97] It could be a novel by Patrick Hamilton. These reconstructions of the scene, while

surely assuming too much, are not wholly far-fetched. The pursuit of sociability in places like pubs, in opposition (or indifference) to the messages
broadcast by connective media, was a topic not unknown in the fiction of
the period. In II.3, the radio breaks into the story of the Norwegian captain and the tailor Kersse in the cadences of the police bulletin—"Rowdiose
wodhalooing. Theirs is one lessonless message for good and truesirs"—and
the "Welter focussed," or weather forecast (FW 324). Later, two vaudev-
illians called Butt and Taff relay, apparently by television broadcast, the
story of Irishman Buckley's long-range shooting of a Russian general during the Crimean War. Radio and television constitute the mediatic world-
system: all the news about everything, from anywhere, all the time.

But news of what, in this case?[98] If the twelve customers are indeed as
raucous as they are assumed to be, it does not seem likely that their informal social solidarity will become the basis for formal political solidarity.
However, Richard Robertson has shown that Joyce, still revising the story
of Buckley and the Russian general as late as May 1938, freighted the telling of it with allusions to current political and military maneuvers only too
likely to eventuate in world war. The Crimea, like Ireland the site of an old
story about an old conflict, stands in for all those central and eastern European territories now, in 1938, under threat of annexation by the Nazi or
Soviet empires.[99] Could this Crimean tale be intended to provoke the sort
of debate about militant or physical-force Irish nationalism that erupts in
the pub scene in "Cyclops," in Ulysses?[100] Irishman Buckley does after all
shoot Russia in general (that is, empire) when he shoots the Russian general. There might be scope for further historical inquiry into what exactly
it is that, as the episode begins, "was now or never in Etheria Deserta,
as in Grander Suburbia, with Finnfannfawners, ruric or cospolite, for
much or moment indispute" (FW 309).[101] Irish identity—rural, suburban,
cosmopolitan—would seem to be the (or a) short answer. The provocation
to debate in any case emanates, as it increasingly did throughout Europe in
the 1930s, from Etheria Deserta: from loudspeakers blaring ever more
ominously, if not always to reliable effect. In 1938, during the Munich crisis, Henry Green and his wife, who were on holiday in Cork, asked if they
could listen to a political broadcast from London on the only wireless set in
the hotel. The manager refused, because the broadcast clashed with a box-
ing match involving the Irish heavyweight Jack Doyle. Later, Green joined
the crowd around the wireless set. The avid listeners heard what they
thought was wild applause from the arena. But for whom? The answer

came in the form of a hearty rendition of "Deutschland über Alles." The set had been tuned by mistake to a Nazi rally in Berlin.[102] Green could have been in the pub in Chapelizod. So, for that matter, might Louis MacNeice, touring the West of Ireland in August 1939 with his friend Ernst Stahl, ever more anxious about the imminence of war. "Ernst and I got in the car to drive to Dublin, stopping at pubs to hear the latest broadcast."[103]

❃❘❃

FIVE

Transit Writing

THE AIM OF THIS CHAPTER is to revive a venerable but recently over-looked idea in media theory, and to extend it by reference to British fiction in the interwar period. The idea is that of transport as telecommunications medium. For centuries, the term "communication" referred equally to the movement of people and goods and to the movement of information. The second meaning gradually displaced the first.[1] The development this change of emphasis records is the supersession of travel by transit as a key modern experience: something to write home about. I began, in Chapter 1, with the telephone as the medium that changed the game: the world's first fully functioning real-time interactive telecommunications technology. I shall conclude by discussing the fundamental transformation that took place during the first media age in attitudes to mechanized transport.

Transit

So when did it all start? Transit originally meant the action or fact of pass-ing across or through. A second meaning took shape around the beginning of the nineteenth century: the passage or carriage of persons or goods from one place to another. Transit was now not just a passing across or through, but the process or system by which passage across or through had been or-ganized. By the beginning of the twentieth century, the term had come to be associated strongly, in industrial societies, at least, with public passen-ger transport. Significant travel was now for the few, significant tourism for the many, and significant transit for practically everyone, as a means of communication with places of work and leisure alike. "And the trains carry us about," Louis MacNeice sourly observed; it is only during a "tiny portion of our lives" that we are *not* in them.[2] "Or, if not in trains," Valentine Cunningham adds, with reference to the literature of the 1930s more generally, "at least in transit in some other mode of long-distance transport."[3]

One context for an understanding of these changes would have to be the view that the invention of mechanical vehicles marked modernity's arrival on the world scene. That was certainly a view promoted vigorously during the first three decades of the twentieth century, as Enda Duffy has shown.[4] Traditional societies, we are often told, could only ever expand as far and as fast as the locomotive power of human or animal legs would permit: with mechanical transport, the sky is the limit. According to this theory, as one commentator notes, modernity originated in the "mechanical ability to speed movement up," which undid the "pre-modern stability of the relationship between time and space."[5] The theory's key concept is that of time-space compression: the conversion of spatial distance into temporal durations of ever shorter span with a view to the efficient and profitable exchange of goods, capital, labor, information, ideas, and identities. Time-space compression overlaid one kind of communication so closely on another that it has become hard to separate them. It converted transport systems into communications media: most notably, in the period between the world wars, the automobile and the airplane. Speed allied to directness and versatility meant that these two modes became during the period a primary mechanism for the principle of connectivity. Increasingly, speed mattered only in so far as it could be thought to improve connection.

On September 5, 1926, Captain Leonard S. Plugge, a London Underground Railways engineer, reached Paris on completion of a tour of Europe in a twelve-cylinder motorcar equipped with a wireless receiving set, frame aerial, and loudspeaker. Throughout his journey, Plugge had been able to "listen-in" while traveling at fifty miles an hour. "At Bucharest and other places in the Balkans crowds gathered round the car to listen to the chiming of Big Ben and the music of the Savoy bands." The car was also fitted with a less powerful transmitting set. Plugge was reported as claiming that it would not be long before "motor tourists" were able to hold conversations by wireless while on the road.[6] Transport could now be understood as an enhancement of connectivity. It was about staying in touch while getting from one place to another. But Plugge also understood that there was time to be filled, a lot of it, between departure and arrival—or at least between conversations by wireless. Whiling away the hours spent in transit had become the new priority (a priority scarcely less urgent today than it was then).

For we need to acknowledge that time-space compression is also *expansive*. Mechanical speed meant it became possible to travel farther faster. But traveling farther faster has often involved traveling for longer. It has meant more people (in fact, almost everyone) spending a greater proportion of their lives in transit than ever before in human history. However fast you are traveling, transit always seems like a slow business. "The whole system of railroad traveling," John Ruskin had complained in a commentary on station design in *The Seven Lamps of Architecture* (1854),

> is addressed to people who, being in a hurry, are therefore, for the time being, miserable. No-one would travel in that manner who could help it—who had time to go leisurely over hills and between hedges, instead of through tunnels and between banks: at least those who would, have no sense of beauty as that we need consult it at the station. The railroad is in all its relations a matter of earnest business, to be got through as soon as possible. It transmutes a man from a traveller into a living parcel. For the time he has parted with the nobler characteristics of his humanity for the sake of a planetary power of locomotion. Do not ask him to admire anything. You might as well ask the wind. Carry him safely, dismiss him soon: he will thank you for nothing else.[7]

The purpose of mass-transit systems is to connect. The more closely the traveler resembles a "living parcel," an object to be laid in a rack rather than a subject prone to look out of windows, the more efficiently she or he will be conveyed from one place to another, and with the least possible attendant misery. To put it in the yet starker terms appropriate to twentieth-century mass-transit systems, the more closely he or she resembles a message transmitted from one place to another, the better.

It has become customary for cultural histories of modernity to incorporate transport understood as a representational medium: a mechanism or apparatus for the production of views. There is, for example, no shortage of studies of the train as both product and emblem of capitalist technological modernization, transforming by the superb intentness of its velocity the ways in which time and space are experienced. Current theories of the effect of this particular modern mechanism were framed in the 1970s, in work by Wolfgang Schivelbusch and Michel de Certeau. They were framed exclusively from the mechanism's point of view: that is, from the point of view of representation and its limits. According to Schivelbusch, the passenger looking out through the window of the train sees a world "filtered through the machine ensemble."[8] According to de Certeau, such a point of view creates an "imperative of separation which obliges one to pay for an abstract ocular domination of space by leaving behind any proper place, by losing one's footing."[9] Capitalist technological modernization in the shape of the train produces and is produced by a specific cognitive order, which Schivelbusch terms "panoramic."[10] This perceptual-locomotive apparatus is said to have created the basis for the subsequent "construction" of the cinema spectator.[11] By contrast, Ruskin's insistence that the passenger should not be asked to "admire anything" opens up a dimension of modern travel about which cultural historians have had little to say. The cultural historian looks out of the window, in order to write a book about representation and its limits. The passenger does not.

Henri Lefebvre, in his reflections on everyday life, provides some useful categories for the experience of temporality induced by transit.

> Time-tables, when comparatively analysed, reveal new phenomena: if the hours of the days, weeks, months, and years are classed in three categories, *pledged time* (professional work), *free time* (leisure) and *constrained time* (the various demands other than work such as transport, official formalities, etc.), it will become apparent that constrained time increases at a greater rate than leisure time. Constrained time is part of everyday life and tends to define it by the sum of its constraints.[12]

For Lefebvre, transit is by no means the only activity productive of constrained time. But the double sense of constraint—as obligation, as physical cramping—surely fits our experience of being ferried about in planes, trains, ships, and automobiles.

So how was the experience of transit, of being communicated, of time under constraint, to be understood? To some extent, by pretending that the type of constraint on offer, while doubtless constraining, need not be unpleasantly so—particularly if you could afford to travel first class. In Britain, the four major railway companies did their best through sustained advertising campaigns to convince potential customers that trains were not only faster than automobiles, and more direct, but also safer, and more comfortable. Their propaganda in effect established two distinct axes along which the train's superiority could be measured. Speed operates, as it were, along a vertical axis, compressing the time spent between departure and arrival into a blur; while comfort operates along the horizontal. In advertisements, passengers lounge at their ease in first-class accommodation serenely undistorted by the physical stress of rapid advance, with a crystal-clear window to gaze out of should they opt for "abstract ocular domination." "Civilized velocity" was the impression the advertising campaigns meant to create, as Colin Divall has shown; to that end they portrayed the first-class compartment as a quasi-domestic space in which men and women would feel equally at home.[13] In fact, the railway compartment more closely resembled a semipublic "shallow" space like the outer office or the hotel lobby than it did a domestic drawing room. It was routinely represented as such in the railway thrillers that became a staple of 1930s narrative cinema, and which begin by assembling a selection of disparate class or national "types" in the compartment's shallow space. Needless to say, the sociability thus enforced is more likely to lead to romance or murder, or both, than it is to political debate. Even so, what is striking about these films is the extent to which they, too, depend on a contrast between the vertical axis of speed (ensuring communication) and the horizontal axis of comfort (ensuring sociability). In Josef von Sternberg's *Shanghai Express* (1932), for example, the train bound for Shanghai carries spies carrying information; at every halt, a spy hops off in order to speed things up even further by sending a telegram. The vehicle has in effect been converted into a connective medium the function of which is to get messages through as securely as possible. One of these reaches Shanghai Lily (Marlene Dietrich). Lily has been reunited for the duration of the journey, at least, with the love of her life, Captain Donald Harvey (Clive Brook), an army surgeon with an upper lip so stiff it might have been cast in concrete, who had left her five years before, thinking she had been unfaithful to him. The telegram turns out to be from a more recent (and clearly less worthwhile) admirer, stating that he awaits her arrival in Shanghai eagerly. This message, too, converting vehicle into connective medium, has created an anticipatory virtual co-presence. It is significant that Lily receives her telegram while she and the captain, both at a low ebb, talk gloomily on the observation platform at the very rear of the train. At this point, the camera tracks behind the train, complicit with the axis of communication's hypervelocity. Somehow, the train has to be made to go slowly enough, has to be halted often enough, for Lily and Captain Harvey to realize that they are made for each other. Fortunately, the director is on their side. From the outset, von Sternberg often shoots transversely, across the breadth of the carriage, bringing into play the layered social logic of space: semipublic luxury compartment, public corridor, the world beyond seen through a window.

The gramophone, a representational storage medium, anchors the compartment's shallow space against mere communication, steadying it sufficiently for talkativeness to occur, and, eventually, to take effect. Something roughly comparable happens in perhaps the most celebrated express thriller of them all, Alfred Hitchcock's *The Lady Vanishes* (1938). Iris (Margaret Lockwood) and Gilbert (Michael Redgrave) have lunch in the diner. She is almost ready to accept that Miss Froy (May Whitty), the lady she thought she had met, and who has since vanished, was a hallucination. Complicit now with the axis of velocity, she tells the crestfallen Gilbert that she is looking forward to their arrival in London, where she is to be married. Hitchcock then shoots transversely across the carriage to reveal the word **FROY** outlined in the steam on the window.

The social logic of space. Frame grab from *Shanghai Express* (1932, Paramount Pictures, prod. Adolph Zukor, dir. Josef von Sternberg).

The transverse look produces meaning. Frame grab from *The Lady Vanishes* (1938, Gainsborough Pictures, prod. Edward Black, dir. Alfred Hitchcock).

The transverse look by which cinema reasserts itself as a representational medium has produced meaning. It slows the train's progress down long enough for Iris and Gilbert to realize that they are made for each other. That slowness remains opposed not just to the conspiracy to hustle Miss Froy off the train, but to the progress of the message she carries, which, as pure information, has been transcoded into a tune. Gilbert, reporting at the Foreign Office, driven to distraction by Iris's acceptance of his marriage proposal, forgets the tune. Fortunately, Miss Froy herself is at the piano next door.

There is a general recognition, in these instances from the popular arts of advertisement and cinema, that while communication's progress can be slowed down, it cannot, and indeed should not, be brought to a halt. Messages have to be conveyed, transit systems ought to operate as seamlessly as possible. For Ruskin, as for Captain Plugge, to while away the time in transit was not to hold it up, but somehow to endure its vacancy. We can, perhaps, feel the first faint tremor of Samuel Beckett's appearance on the scene. Beckett was to define a way to endure transit, to understand it, even to relish it, grimly, in "Ding-Dong," one of the stories or "bottled climates" that made up *More Pricks than Kicks* (1934). The protagonist, Belacqua Shua, a student of Dante at Trinity College, exists in a kind of "moving pause," or permanent nervous breakdown. He likes to exercise his temperament by taking it for walks in the Dublin streets.

> Not the least charm of this pure blank movement, this "gress" or "gression," was its aptness to receive, with or without the approval of the subject, in all their integrity the faint inscriptions of the outer world. Exempt from destination, it had not to shun the unforeseen nor turn aside from the agreeable odds and ends of vaudeville that are liable to crop up. This sensitiveness was not the least charm of this roaming that began by being blank, not the least charm of this pure act the alacrity with which it welcomed defilement. But very nearly the least.[14]

"Gress," not progress; "gression," not progression (or, indeed, regression, or even digression). For Beckett, writing itself took the form of gression. As Steven Connor points out, Beckett could be said to have participated in the programs of miniaturization that constitute a modern or postmodern sublime, and which have as their culmination the nano-engineered processor based on a single molecule. And yet in his writing, miniaturization is not accompanied by lightness or speed. Beckett, Connor says, is in fact "perhaps the most important inaugurator of a mode of aesthetic defection from speed." The slow going is both subject and method.[15] In general, transit involves progress that *feels like gress*. Transit writing, which is the subject of this chapter, elicits the gress from a progress measured by the reconfiguration of transport systems as telecommunications media. Its only "alacrity" lies in the welcome it gives to "defilement." Transit writing tells us what mobile privatization feels like at its most acute, its most fundamental, its most transformative. If *Shanghai Express* and *The Lady Vanishes* are anything to go by, its triumphs are likely to involve the exploitation for personal benefit of slack in the system. They should probably be filed under cool.

Travel Writing

There seems to be general agreement that the period between the world wars (a period after exploration, but before mass tourism) should be regarded as travel writing's belle époque.[16] Combining broad popular appeal with renewed imaginative scope and intensity, travel writing could claim to have articulated as fully as any other literary form some of the age's most urgent preoccupations.[17] More recently, the emphasis has fallen on the genre's implication in literary Modernism understood as a "metropolitan art of diaspora." Charles Burdett and Derek Duncan state the case starkly (perhaps too starkly) when they argue that Modernism's provocative "formal alterity" was "the consequence of travel and of the unpredictable fusions and fragmentations that occur when cultures are forced into unusual proximity."[18]

Travel writing was, and remains, a representational literature. The travel writer re-presents what she or he can be taken to have witnessed, in the past, and somewhere else, the further away the better, in the reassuring guise of a text. As the scope and diversity of these encounters increased during the 1920s and 1930s, the argument goes, so the very basis of representation itself came into question. Who was looking at whom? Was there anything at all present there and then, in the first, faraway place, to be re-presented: apart from the (often melancholic) desire to represent? There is certainly a case to be made along these lines. What remains unclear is the extent to which travel writing as a representational literature, Modernist or not, ever came to terms with the principle of connectivity informing globalization. Transit understood as the movement of messages, as well as people, goods, and capital, constituted both an internal (generic) limit to travel writing's attempts to re-present, to bring presence back from afar, and an external (historical) limit to literary Modernism's attempts to comprehend the scale of social and economic change.

Space, clearly, is at issue in any definition of travel writing's contribution to a metropolitan art of diaspora. Andrew Thacker's reading of one of the best-known travel books of the period, Graham Greene's *Journey without Maps* (1936), usefully extends and complicates the influential distinction drawn by Michel de Certeau between place (the domain of the map) and space (the domain of the tour). The narrative of Greene's Liberian adventure establishes a "discourse of spatial movement," as Thacker puts it, which could be said to exceed and to unsettle the "cartographic image" accompanying it. Invoking Henri Lefebvre, Thacker rightly concludes that to understand how the dialectic of place and space functions in travel writing in general, we must first address the "social production of spatiality."[19]

There is, however, in *Journey without Maps,* as there is in many other travel books of the period, an episode, or interval, that appears to exist outside the dialectic of place and space, of map and tour. In order for travel to begin, transit had first to end. The journey with maps Greene undertook *on the way to* his journey without maps had four distinct stages: by the 6.5 Express from Euston Station to Liverpool; by cargo ship from Liverpool to Freetown, in Sierra Leone; by slow train from Water Street Station, in Freetown, to the railhead at Pendembu; and by truck from Pendembu to the government rest house at Kailahun, on the Liberian border. To begin with, it was all a bit discouraging. Dinner on the 6.5 from Euston, for example, consisted of "little pieces of damp white fish." But the subsequent journey by cargo ship from Liverpool to Freetown does seem to have assumed a distinct shape in Greene's mind. It became an episode in its own right, requiring several pages of description. Those pages develop a preoccupation with sameness as intense, in its way, as the preoccupation with difference that will supersede it once the border has been reached. They tell us little or nothing of the ship itself as either space or place. Instead, we learn about the contents of the library.

> One reads strange books in a ship, books one would never dream of reading at home: like Lady Eleanor Smith's *Tzigane,* and the novels of Warwick Deeping and W. B. Maxwell: a lot of books, written without truth, without compulsion, one dull word following another, books to read while you wait for the bus, while you strap-hang, in between the Boss's dictations, while you eat your A.B.C. lunch; a whole industry founded on a want of leisure and a want of happiness.

The contempt Green expresses for pulp fiction is familiar enough. What interests me in it is its catalog of satisfactory sites for the consumption of trash: bus stop, underground train, outer office, tea room. These sites are not really sites at all. They are, instead, areas in which waiting takes place. To experience transit is to experience duration. The novels of Warwick Deeping and W. B. Maxwell, Greene adds, are just "ways of filling up time."[20] Reading *Journey without Maps,* we wait for transit to end, at the Liberian border, and travel to begin; for experience to supersede analysis, for space to distract us from time. But that hiatus is no mere interval. It has its own shape, as an episode. Representation of what Greene witnessed during it requires a kind of writing that is not exactly travel writing. The cargo ship conveying him from Liverpool to Freetown may have compressed time in general: that is, the time previously taken, before the age of mechanical transport, to get from one place to the other. But in doing so it expanded time in particular, *his* time. It created for him a time to while away: an interval or episode he did not so much represent, in *Journey without Maps*, as fill, stuff with odds and ends.

Transit was what the travel writer, en route to representation, to a discourse of spatial movement exceeding cartography, did not write about. But she or he could scarcely fail to notice it, as travel's increasingly pervasive negation. Representing what the new, doubly communicative mass transit systems actually *did* would require something other than either a map or a tour. Indeed, it might require something other than representation, as customarily understood. I want now to explore the premonitions of an (information) superhighway that flicker briefly in two justly celebrated travel books of the period, D. H. Lawrence's *Twilight in Italy* (1916) and Robert Byron's *The Road to Oxiana* (1937). In both cases, the superhighway is understood to negate travel, and to block or interrupt travel writing, but not necessarily to destructive effect.

Lawrence left England for the first time in May 1912, and at once assumed the mantle of the travel writer, recording his impressions of life abroad for the benefit of an audience at home. The essays of this period, many of them included in *Twilight in Italy*, were, as Paul Eggert observes,

> part of his continuously evolving meditation on culture, English as well as foreign, during that period of intense and remarkable development which saw him finish *Sons and Lovers*, write or fundamentally revise the stories of *The Prussian Officer* volume, finish (but declare he must write again) the "Study of Thomas Hardy" and "The Crown" (published in part in 1915), bring to completion *The Rainbow* and turn, two months after finishing the proofs of *Twilight*, to his first full version of the novel which would become *Women in Love*.[21]

Lawrence and Frieda Weekley lived for just under seven months, from September 18, 1912, to April 3, 1913, in Villa di Gargnano, by Lake Garda in Northern Italy. The resulting series of sketches, "By the Lago di Garda," was first published in the *English Review* in September 1913, and then, after substantial revision, in *Twilight in Italy*. I want to discuss the first sketch in the series, "The Spinner and the Monks," as an example, in its final version, both of the process by which Lawrence became a travel writer of a particular, philosophical kind, and of what that process left out, or, rather, left in, but curiously unattended, curiously inaccessible to philosophy.

Entranced by the sight and sound of the Church of San Tommasso, which stands above the village of Gargnano, Lawrence had resolved to climb up to it by way of a purgatorial "broken staircase" evidently in general use as a latrine. He emerges suddenly, "as by a miracle," clean into a liminal space, a "world of fierce abstraction." "It was all clear, overwhelming sunshine, a platform hung in the light" (*TI* 104). Liminality, in High Romantic tradition, is where we confront (for there is shock, even hostility) the other who is also the same: that is, a version of ourselves as we might have been. William Wordsworth, encountering on the lonely moor an old man gathering leeches from a pond, body bent double from the effort, felt himself admonished as though in a dream.[22] Lawrence turns from the view out across the Lago di Garda to discover, on the other side of the terrace, an old woman spinning. "She was like a fragment of earth, she was a living stone of the terrace, sun-bleached. She took no notice of me, who was hesitating looking down at the earth beneath. She stood back under the sun-bleached solid wall, like a stone rolled down and stayed in a crevice" (105). As Lawrence revised the sketch, the spinner became for him the embodiment of pure being, of unself-consciousness; of blood rather than spirit, of the Flesh, as opposed to the Word. A philosophical travel literature steeped in High Romantic mythography has converted impression and anecdote into meaning. Too much meaning, indeed. Made to feel wholly inadequate in his Hamlet-like participial reverie ("hesitating looking down") by the spinner's fleshliness, Lawrence escapes farther up the hill. Reaching the top, sitting in the "warm stillness of the transcendent afternoon" (110), he looks out again across the lake, and then down into the garden of the monastery above San Tommasso. He sees two monks pacing backward and forward, locked in inaudible conversation. This time, his philosophy saves him. He decides that the monks are even more Hamlet-like than he is. "Neither the blood nor the spirit spoke in them, only the law, the abstraction of the average" (112). Lawrence's position on the hill, above and beyond both liminal spaces, both worlds of "fierce abstraction," enables him to look down upon and condescend to these distinctly average specimens. Narrative, as well as philosophy, or instead of philosophy, has restored the balance between self and other. That is how travel writing works.

But that is not quite all there is to this sketch. Something else happens in it, between flight from the spinner and condescension to the monks. Arrival at the summit of the hill produces new sounds before it produces new sights. Here is how the new sounds reach Lawrence in the first, *English Review* version of the sketch.

> A mule driver "Hued!" to his mules on the *Strada Vecchia*. High up on the *Strada Nuova*—a beautiful wide highway, newly made, that does not *quite* reach the frontier yet—I heard the crack of an oxen whip, and the faint clank of a wagon. (*TI* 56)

This passage, too, Lawrence expanded substantially when revising the text for book publication. The expansion, however, has nothing at all to do with the philosophy of blood and spirit. It is entirely rhetorical.

> A mule driver "Hued!" to his mules on the Strada Vecchia. High up, on the Strada Nuova, the beautiful, new, military high-road, which winds with beautiful curves up the mountain-side, crossing the same stream several times in clear-leaping bridges, travelling cut out of sheer slope high above the lake, winding beautifully and gracefully forward to the Austrian frontier, where it ends: high up on the lovely swinging road, in the strong evening sunshine, I saw a bullock wagon moving like a vision, though the clanking of the wagon and the crack of the bullock whip resounded close in my ears. (110)

The sentence concerning the Strada Nuova now has a luxurious double movement, rather than a single movement interrupted by a parenthesis. Not only does the revised version dwell rather surprisingly on the beauty of the road's newness, which we cannot help but contrast with the spinner's dour archaism; it also attributes to this engineering feat and landscape feature an extraordinary power of movement, an elegant *locomotion*. The road "travelling cut out of sheer slope" has been reconfigured as a transit system, as the carriage of persons and goods from one place to another. To be sure, the bullock wagon moves at something less than the speed of light. But the vision encompassing it is a vision of a different kind of fierce abstraction. Is not that how a channel of communication "moves," as it were, traveling cut out of sheer slope (of one kind or another)?

One would not, of course, expect Lawrence to remain unambivalent concerning this new kind of fierce abstraction. The final essay in *Twilight in Italy*, "The Return Journey," rages, with an appetite fed by the spectacle of war, against mechanization. It returns, among other things, to the new Italian roads, now understood as an object of terror, as new settlements arise in their wake, "swarming with a sort of verminous life, really verminous, purely destructive" (*IT* 223). According to Lawrence, these new Italian roads have destroyed the "social organism" as effectively as war itself. "So that it seems we should be left, at last, with a great system of roads and railways and industries, and a world of utter chaos seething upon these fabrications: as if we had created a steel framework, and the whole body of society were crumbling and rotting in between" (224). Lawrence's rage reveals as clearly as his earlier appreciation that he had grasped the principle animating the great system of roads and railways and industries: the principle of connectivity.

Robert Byron, old Etonian, urbane, witty, and politically astute, seems about as far from Lawrence as it is possible to get. Byron's passion was for Islamic architecture, and his masterpiece, *The Road to Oxiana*, describes a journey from Italy through Palestine and Syria to Iran, and then on to Afghanistan and finally down into India. Fragmentary in form, and often cryptic, it has, as Helen Carr notes, a "modernist timbre."[23] Its most radical insight, I would suggest, has nothing to do with Modernism, and concerns transit rather than travel. It arises more or less as an afterthought, as Byron returns to "civilization" by way of the Khyber Pass. "As passes go, the Khyber is invitingly mild. It is this which makes it the theatre of such stupendous works." The works include two roads and a railway.

> Roads and railway are embanked on shelves of hewn stone linking mountain to mountain; iron viaducts carry them across the valleys and each other. Sheaves of telephone wires fastened to metal posts by gleaming white insulators, red and green signals jewelled in the torrid haze . . . all complete the evidence of the neat grey blockhouses perched on every ledge and peak: that if the English must be bothered to defend India, it shall be with a minimum of personal inconvenience.

Here are military roads to match Lawrence's Strada Nuova. These roads travel all the more effectively cut out of sheer slope because they are accompanied by telephone wires. They constitute channels of communication in both senses of the term. What Byron has borne witness to is the principle of connectivity. By the time of his journey, the sheaf of telephone wires had long since become in photography and film, as we saw in the Introduction, a perverse signage or non-ideographic ideograph: not so much a condensation of meaning as a gesture at the excess of bits and bytes that is data flow. Byron, it is worth noting, was enough of a travel writer to conclude *The Road to Oxiana*, as Greene had begun *Journey without Maps*, with a sour reflection on the ordeal of transit by boat. "None the less it is an appalling penalty: a fortnight blotted out of one's life at great expense."[24]

Transit writing constitutes travel writing's internal (generic) limit: the point at which it ceases to be itself. Byron's first travel book, *Europe in the Looking-Glass: Reflections of a Motor Drive from Grimsby to Athens* (1926), attributes a somewhat uncertain role to the "large touring Sunbeam" that conveyed him and his companions across Europe. On one hand, this mobile platform made representation, and therefore travel writing, possible. On the other, it left its occupants with a good deal of constrained time on their hands. "Motoring down the plain of Lombardy is not interesting," Byron remarks at one point. Later, leaving Rome, the travelers enter a world topologically rather than topographically ordered. "The road was bad, but improved when it ceased to be the Appian Way. It became unswervingly straight and quite flat for thirty miles, along the side of a completely straight canal and beneath a completely straight range of mountains. The utter straightness of everything began to affect our nerves. We became giddy with rectitude."[25] Giddy with rectitude: such is the experience of transit, and a feeling the travel writer cannot tolerate; or at least not for long. Byron subsequently traveled the road to Oxiana by car, truck, and on occasion bus. He had a good deal to say, in one way or another, about mechanized transport. Or, rather, he had a good deal to say about vehicles breaking down, or upended by rough terrain. For it is only when the vehicle has shuddered to a halt that travel writing can begin, either in on-the-spot observation, or as a record of the encounters shuddering to a halt has brought about. One such halt, in the mountains north of Herat, engenders near-Transylvanian speculation as to whether it would be wiser to proceed on foot to a nearby village, allegedly the haunt of brigands, or stay in the car. "Christopher replied that it was nonsense to suppose the wolves would be deterred by headlights or the engine running, and that if we stayed in the car, they would raven their way through the side curtains and pick our bones clean." In the event, the worst that happens is a torrential downpour.[26] But the tale is the point. This is travel writing. Travel writing does not do transit.

The Motorcar

Of all modern forms of transport, the motorcar is the one most intriguingly poised between individual will and collective necessity, freedom and con-

straint, luxury and function, platform and container, private realm and public realm, and, if we are thinking of it as a medium, the representational
and the connective. The period between the wars saw a rapid increase in
the availability and use of motor vehicles. In Great Britain in 1914, roughly
one person in 232 owned a car; by 1922, it was one person in 78; by 1938,
one person in 24. The middle classes had come to rely on motor transport.
Furthermore, by 1933 the annual number of passenger journeys by bus
and tram exceeded 9,450 million; approximately half of these can be attributed to the rapid development of motor-bus routes during the 1920s.[27]

Evidence for the ease with which the motorcar, at least, could be understood as a representational medium—as a platform for the production and
potential storage of individually selected "views"—lies in the popularity of
"motoring pastoral." "Between 1918 and 1939 open-air leisure in Britain
took on a new scale and scope," David Matless observes in his highly informative account of the assiduous Englishing of English landscape during
this period. The increase in car ownership "reflected falling prices and a
trend to smaller vehicles, allowed the car to establish a middle-class right
of way on the road. With the bus and charabanc facilitating working-class
movement, rural leisure became restyled around the petrol engine, and a
motoring pastoral developed, in terms of both the object and style of movement." The English landscape came to be conceived as a public or semipublic space for the cultivation of good citizenship. "While a landscaped
citizenship is set up as potentially open to all and nationally inclusive, it
depends for its self-definition on a vulgar other, an anti-citizen whose conduct, if not open to re-education, makes exclusion necessary." To adapt the
terms I developed in Chapter 4, landscape could be seen as shallow space:
as a bourgeois semipublic sphere productive, as long as its protocols were
duly observed, of sociability. Hence, perhaps, the urgency of the debates
about road safety and speed. After the First World War, the Automobile
Association transformed itself from anti-speed-trap vigilante into a respectable club providing tour guidance. AA handbooks invariably opened
with an appeal for courtesy. Aesthetic appreciation, or departure from the
main highways in search of the picturesque, became an important element
in the definition of landscape as selectively sociable shallow space. Landscaped citizenship, Matless argues, was thought to require both appropriate conduct and a measure of aesthetic awareness.[28]

Motoring pastoral flourished in forms at once popular and complex: for
example, the Shell County Guides published from the late 1930s under the

editorship of John Betjeman and John Piper.[29] Discussing Shell posters, Patrick Wright notes that during this period the countryside took its shape "around the passage of the motor car."[30] And not just for day-trippers and tourists. Steve Ellis has drawn a connection between the "stripped classicism" of T. S. Eliot's *Four Quartets* and the response of commentators such as Cyril Connolly to the England the posters portray.[31] H. V. Morton's *In Search of England* (1927), in its twenty-sixth edition by 1939, had provided motoring pastoral's catalyst. Morton is forever to be found "bowling" down narrow lanes into villages, though he has to dismount in order to complete his quest by interviewing the locals. *In Search of England* has been rather too easily dismissed as a nostalgic identification of true Englishness with village life.[32] As Matless points out, Morton consciously plays the role of questing knight or pilgrim. His England is theatrical, replete with signs of itself.[33] It is worth adding that he was fully aware of the spread of networks whose communicational scope overshadowed the news he was able to bring back by means of his mobile viewing platform. Never more so than when he finds himself listening to the radio, in a farmhouse in a village in Cornwall, in a room with pictures of Queen Victoria and Lord Kitchener on the wall.

> "He's a beauty, he is!" said the old man, pointing with his pipe stem to the valve set. "Durin' that bit of a strike you had up in Lonnun we could heaar 'zactly all that wor passing as clear as I can see you, sor."
>
> "Aye," said the old lady, "we liked that Mr Baldwin, for he wor as plain as if he wor in this room, but Mr Churchill hemmed and hawed till you felt like wishing to get up behind him and give 'un a shove."
>
> They all laughed.

But the real thrill is the dance band at the Savoy. "Into my ears, across miles of emptiness, came the sound of the Savoy. The door opened, and a cat walked in. I could hear people in London putting down their liqueur glasses, a tinkle of coffee cups, and a buzz of talk beneath the rhythmic thrumming of the dance band." The interpolated cat serves economically to establish connectivity's maxim: two places at one time. The experience appears to have a rather more powerful effect on Morton than it does on the ancient farmer and his family.

> I listened to a tango from the Strand and became sunk in a deep weariness.
> I said good-night, and the old man took up my headphones. As I walked

down the little path I turned and saw, framed in the yellow window, the new picture of rural England: old heads bent over the wireless set in the light of a paraffin lamp. London coming to them out of space: Queen Victoria and Lord Kitchener watching with a certain stern amazement.[34]

The new picture was to persist, as we saw in Chapter 3, in Auden's "Consider this and in our time," as the Sport Hotel's efficient band relays feeling to farmers and their dogs in fenland kitchens.

For the most part, the representation of travel by car in the literature of the period has been understood as a testing of the limits of subjectivity, and of representation itself. Sara Danius has described the development by Marcel Proust and other turn-of-the-century writers of a "syntax of velocity."[35] Among British writers, E. M. Forster was perhaps the least sanguine concerning what these new perspectives might reveal. For Margaret Schlegel, in *Howards End* (1910), the journey from London to Wales proves the reverse of syntactic. "She looked at the scenery. It heaved and merged like porridge. Presently it congealed. They had arrived."[36] In *Howards End*, and later in *A Passage to India*, motoring is a dangerous business associated with accident, interruption, and trauma. Leonard and Virginia Woolf, by contrast, who purchased a secondhand Singer for £275 in July 1927, became staunch advocates. "This is a great opening up in our lives," Virginia noted in her diary. "One may go to Bodiam, to Arundel, explore the Chichester downs, expand that curious thing, the map of the world in ones mind."[37] The metaphor suggests travel writing, and it is clear that for Woolf the motorcar did constitute a mechanism or apparatus for the production of views. "What I like, or one of the things I like, about motoring is the sense it gives one of lighting accidentally, like a voyager who touches another planet with the tip of his shoe, upon scenes which would have gone on, have always gone on, will go on, unrecorded, save for this chance glimpse."[38] The scenes were often enough inflected by pastoral. "Now & again one comes across something consciously preserved like the Wren house at Groomsbridge. One stops the motor & looks. So do other motorists."[39] On the whole, though, Woolf has been considered as a Modernist exponent of a syntax of velocity.[40] In *Orlando* (1928), for example, the "process of motoring fast" is said to resemble the "chopping up small of identity which precedes unconsciousness and perhaps death itself."[41] Equally striking, however, is her awareness of the ways in which time-space compression actually expands the time spent in transit, if not the space. Returning through France from a continental tour in May 1935, she resolved not to set foot in a car again for as long as possible.

> The pane of glass that is pressed firm over the mind in these travels—there I am vitreated on my seat—cant read talk or write—only look at the end-less avenues—plane trees poplars—rain, rain—old man with a cart—ask the mileage—look at map light a cigarette & turn over the old problems—chiefly the same, because I cant start a new one till the cage doors are opened—all this makes the last 2 days as intolerable as the first two are rapturous.[42]

It is a powerful protest against motoring (or at least the experience of tran-sit motoring entails), the implications of which have rather too easily been eclipsed by talk of a Modernist syntax of velocity.

The propaganda for speed nonetheless intensified. Aldous Huxley thought being driven in a car at a speed above seventy-two miles per hour the only original sensation he had ever had (LSD still lay in the future).[43] Such exuberance has led to some ambitious claims. According to Enda Duffy, for example, "speed itself" became "the very narrative heft of much modernist artistic production."[44] The experience of speed certainly fea-tures in the literature of the period, and more broadly in the culture at large, as a chopping up small not just of identity, but of representation. However, from the late 1920s onward, that experience became associated increasingly either with a social and political ancien régime, or with an avant-garde aesthetic that had had its day. Huxley was behind the times in thinking speed the next new sensation. Connectivity was the next new sensation: the sound of the Savoy coming into one's ears across miles of emptiness. By contrast, the tour Connie Chatterley takes through the Not-tinghamshire mining country (in a chauffeur-driven limousine, of course) simply provides further evidence of the terminal decline of the social and political order to which she still owes allegiance. "Connie, belonging to the leisure classes, had clung to the remnants of the old England." The tour lands her at the gates, not of Mellors's cottage in the woods, but of a neighboring estate; that is, in the past, rather than the future. "There was a gap in the continuity of consciousness, almost American: but industrial, really. What next?"[45] However mobile the platform, the view it delivered was not likely to fill the gap in the continuity of consciousness. As we saw in Chapter 2, Connie's deliverance will not take the form of motoring (anti-)pastoral.

It was too late, as well, for the syntax of velocity. So Edward Upward concluded, at any rate, in *Journey to the Border* (1938), which incorporates one of the most complex motoring episodes in the literature of the period. Upward joined the Communist Party early. For him, Samuel Hynes observes, "Party membership seems to have been a mode of salvation in a desperate time, and he embraced it like a religion."[46] The "English Kafka," coauthor in 1928 with Christopher Isherwood of the fantastic "The Railway Accident," argued in his 1937 essay "Sketch for a Marxist Interpretation of Literature" that no book written at the present time would succeed unless it fully acknowledged capitalism's decay and the inevitability of revolution. Proust, Joyce, and Lawrence had failed. There was no place for the sort of fantasy—for "The Railway Accident," in short—that implies "a retreat from the real world into the world of imagination." A note to the essay states that Upward "is at present writing a novel in which he hopes to deal more adequately and more concretely with some of the problems he has raised in this essay."[47]

That novel was *Journey to the Border.* It concerns a day in the life of a young man employed, as Upward himself had once been, as "a tutor in an ordinary country house."[48] The tutor longs for a "bogus ceremony of purification" that would "wash off all the dismal servilities of the past three months" (*JTTB* 12) and so restore his integrity. In the event, he merely confirms his lowly status by failing to decline his employer's invitation to spend the day at the races. Here, a ceremony of some kind does in fact take place. A series of carnivalesque temptations and affronts tests his grip on himself—that is, his status as middle-class servant to the middle classes—to the limit. By the end of the day, he has resolved to commit himself to the revolutionary workers' movement.

The novel's tripartite structure maps the three phases of a traditional rite of passage of the sort ubiquitous in the late-Romantic writing of the interwar period: separation from a fixed point in the social order; apartness, in some marginal or threshold milieu, during which the "ritual subject," stripped of status and possessions, remembers what it is to be merely human; and reentry, thus made over, at a different point in the social order.[49] The first section describes the journey to the racetrack, by car; the third, the journey away from it, on foot. During the second, the tutor, very much the ritual subject, undergoes a ceremony of purification. Various siren voices propose false solutions to his dilemma. A jeering mountebank humiliates him. The racetrack laid out on a plateau or "tableland" constitutes the marginal or threshold milieu in which ceremonies of purification customarily occur. Upward may well have in mind the milieu evoked in Auden's "Spain 1937": that "tableland scored by rivers" on which "Our fever's menacing shapes are precise and alive."[50] In both cases, the purification to be undergone was political, primarily. Upward, however, unlike Auden, took a dim view of tablelands and the ceremonies they might be thought to sustain. The racetrack engenders fantasy; no more so than during the two car rides the tutor takes during the event, one with an attractive young woman who preaches socialism to dockers, the other with a colonial mining engineer who turns out to be a prominent blackshirt (*JTTB* 59–71). Both encounters prompt fantasies of travel as an instant escape from servitude. The tutor asks the young woman to elope with him: "Now. Just as we are. With no preparations. Without even a toothbrush. Clear of all impedimenta" (60). His next idea is to show his admiration for the engineer as "the real traveller, the pioneer, the genuine man of action" by emigrating to South Africa (69). But he has little difficulty in acknowledging the implausibility of these aspirations. To put it another way, one form of expression the rite of passage will not provoke in him is travel writing. For Upward, rites of passage are feeble stuff, mere exercises in convention. There is no journey, in *Journey to the Border*, and no border, either. But there is transit. There is a journey (by car) to the "journey"; and a journey (on foot) away from it. Transit provokes a transit writing of some political consequence.

The politics of *Journey to the Border*, at once so overt, so inconclusive, and so hostile to fantasy of any kind, conventional or not, have always seemed problematic. Hynes, discussing it in the context of three other political parables published in 1938—Stephen Spender's *Trial of a Judge*, Auden and Isherwood's *On the Frontier*, and Rex Warner's *The Professor*—can only conclude that it falls short as Marxist critique, because the failure represented is an individual rather than a social failure. So what sort of text might *Journey to the Border* be? "We could say that it is a study of neurotic epistemology; or that it is a kind of confession, the convert exposing his past fantastic sins; or that it is a parable of modern madness, and of the neurotic function of political conversions."[51] The most helpful of these suggestions concerns the study of neurotic epistemology. For the text does indeed incorporate such an inquiry, conducted with calculating gusto by the protagonist himself, into himself.

The tutor travels to the racetrack by car, in the company of his employer, Mr. Parkin, Mr. Parkin's son, Donald, a neighboring plutocrat, Mr. Mac-

Creath, and a well-provisioned hamper. The tutor sits in the front, next to the chauffeur, Stokes, "rigid as an idol at the steering-wheel." For this is a *social* technology, an arrangement of functions, vantage points, and privileges. The chauffeur rigid at the steering wheel is held in place by hierarchy. "At a sharp bend in the road a wall of dark fir-trees made a temporary mirror of the windscreen, showed him pug-nosed, hemisphere-eyed, faintly grinning with mumbo-jumbo insolence. He *was* an idol. The Parkins depended on him, thought him infallible" (*JTTB* 27). The vehicle, its windscreen a temporary mirror, *represents* hierarchy in operation. The task the tutor sets himself during the journey is to force it to represent something else. He proposes to alter his own attitude to his subservience by developing a new cognitive technique. "He would change his so-called surroundings, he would not only think and feel differently, he would see and touch and hear differently, as he wanted to, happily" (32). The motor-car becomes the laboratory in which he will conduct experiments in the phenomenology of perception.

> The landscape, seen through the windows of the car, had lengthened and broadened, become a tremendous panorama. It was like an infra-red photograph. The tutor had the impression that he could see at least fifty miles. And not only had details at a great distance become extraordinarily clear but colours also had become far more vivid. Emerald green and earth-red and ink-black and sea-blue. White insulators on telegraph poles and new copper wires gleamed along the coast road. Behind the town rose a wooden brewery tower and farther up the coast double-wheeled pit gear. A moving coal-conveyor crawled with rattling buckets to the top of a power station. (32)

And so on. What is at issue, here, is the sort of view, and the sort of representation, made possible not by neurosis, but by a particular social and mechanical apparatus. The landscape seen through the car windows is like a landscape seen in panorama, or photographically. And the vividness thus yielded, of telegraph pole and pit gear, is not unlike the vividness of an Auden poem. It is a vividness the tutor cannot sustain. His subsequent "experiment with hearing" fails, too. For a moment, he captures with unprecedented clarity the very sound of a conversation between Parkin and MacCreath. Again, the apparatus has ensured the clarity. Such a sound could only ever be *over*heard, by someone in the position of servant or companion, not expected to participate. The experiments may have failed to free the tutor from dependence. But they have laid bare its structure. Rather, they have laid bare the ways in which a particular technology both structures and is structured by class ideology. They have explored the limits of a representational medium from within. To my mind, the one truly estranging detail in the tutor's vision, as it had been in Robert Byron's survey of the Khyber Pass, is the gleam of the telegraph wires: a non-ideographic ideograph.

In the novel's third and final section, the tutor walks away from the marquee in which some of his most disturbing encounters have taken place toward the far end of the racetrack. The section ends with his refusal of a lift back with the Parkins. "He would walk into the town. It was not more than five miles away, and he would arrive there within an hour and a half. He would visit the newsagent's shop outside which he had once seen a poster advertising a meeting of the Internationalist Workers' Movement. He would ask the newsagent to put him in touch with the local secretary of the Movement" (135). Not in itself constituting a new political direction taken by the tutor, this walk nonetheless negates the collusion with transport as a representational medium (a way of seeing and hearing more intensely) that had at first drawn him in, appearing to alleviate the servility it in fact reinforced. The novel's third section answers its first, engaging purposefully in the long-term politics of the ownership and use of social technologies. In contrast, the short-term political fixes of one kind or another that unfold allegorically during its second section exert relatively little purchase. The fever's menacing shapes are not as precise and alive in it as they had been in Spain according to Auden. What *is* precise and alive, however, precise enough and alive enough to drive Upward into exile from literature, is an understanding of the nature and scope of the slow going required to loosen capitalism's hold on speed: a going so slow that it ceases to represent altogether.

One way of going very slowly indeed, of course, was to crash. No vehicle was invulnerable, in the complex traffic systems taking shape across Britain in the 1930s, as the increasing outcry about road casualties testified. Furthermore, the limits of representation could be seen as clearly from the outside as from the inside. Absorbed in his phenomenological experiments, the tutor has failed to notice a near-collision, when a steamroller emerges suddenly from a hidden side road. "But Stokes, who had no visions, had already slowed down. He changed gear, preparing to drive on again" (*JTTB* 36). A rather more apocalyptic curtailment of the enabling powers of speed occurs in *A London Story* (1935), by George Buchanan, whose *Entangle-ment* I discussed in Chapter 4.

A London Story concerns two brothers, John and Nicholas Coombe, who both work at Drancers, a fancy London emporium owned and run by the tyrannical, lecherous Lord Flowerfield. The mildly bohemian Nicholas loses his job, and, finding that he cannot endure unemployment, resolves to create for himself a rite of passage.

> He desired to reflect and meditate and gradually gather mental strength to make the act of will required for beginning again his life which was broken across—smashed—by sheer accumulated misunderstanding and folly. In some quiet spot, far out, he could surely decide on the course of his renewal, and then he would re-enter the city, a changed person, and set to—to do what? He would consider.[52]

What better way to seek out liminality than to rent a car? A familiar, mildly cinematographic discourse unfolds. "Strangely enough, no sooner had he gathered speed, and shelves of houses begun to reel past, and the rush of air to cool his face and hands, than his mind was quickened" (*LS* 175). However, Buchanan's indulgence in the cult of speed, as a testing of the limitations of representation, proves short-lived. Nicholas's car veers off the road at an unexpectedly sharp bend, and he finds himself pinned beneath the wreckage. The accident puts him in a ward full of "battered creatures," the "victims of collisions in streets and roads, all mutilated by the motor-cars of the careless" (185). The cult of speed has ended in motoring Arma-geddon. What interests Buchanan about these battered creatures is not the pathos of mutilation, but the evidence their battering provides of the need for system *in general:* for the expenditure of data rather than of energy.

Redemption arrives in the predictable shape of the love of a good woman. But the accident appears to be more than the culmination of the moral, physical, and emotional damage capitalism has done to a sensitive soul. Nicholas's experience of transit at its most intense—in that unrepre-sentable degree zero of slow going that is accident—has reprogrammed him. Alienation simply ceases.

> He knew that nothing separated him any longer from society: he *was* soci-ety, he *was* life. Accordingly all that former seeming complexity had van-ished, all those intricate links, associations and relations were not difficult, not matters to awaken timidity, and to appear onerous. With no separation,

he had no gulfs to bridge. He would move in a world of signed documents, filed correspondence, of dossiers and passports, of contracts, agreements and undertakings as simply as his forbears moved in a world of complex forests, the worrying presence of dangerous beasts and snakes, and the occasional violence of other men. (*LS* 196)

The gress in Nicholas's progress amounts to acknowledgment of a supervening virtual reality. Transit's interruption has made him over as the sort of signed document that at least ensures further transit. "He was what is called 'integrated'—that is to say, the main ingredients of his life were easily recognizable to outsiders. He was the subject of a series of simple and satisfactory labels such as can be written down in a passport—married, occupation so and so, etc." (255). In future, he will travel as information, as a message sent rather than a parcel posted.

Buchanan did not conceive of transport itself as a connective medium, as the route taken by information. Wyndham Lewis did. *The Revenge for Love* (1937) includes the most elaborate description of a car journey in the literature of the period: an analysis, we could say, of transport as at once representation's limit and the catalyst for a new and spectacular conjunction of system, accident, damage, and data. The plot has to do with the smuggling of arms into Spain before the outbreak of Civil War. At its climax, Victor Stamp, a talentless Australian artist who has been tricked into acting as a decoy for the smugglers, and his lover Margot Savage, who risks her life to alert him to the springing of the trap, escape from the Spanish police in a high-powered motorcar. Margot, it turns out, has risked her life in vain. Victor's passport, integrating him by its simple and satisfactory labels into a system of all-encompassing state surveillance, proves their death warrant.

The novel had been completed by January 1936, but owing to Lewis's by now obligatory disputes with publishers did not appear until May 1937, a year after war had broken out. As Paul Edwards points out, the timing of its publication, together with the short shrift it gives to middle-class bohemian fellow-traveling, has tended to obscure its "metaphysical dimensions." It is not, in fact, a political novel. It is not *Homage to Catalonia* with better jokes. Edwards approaches it as a further expression of the concern with the Absolute articulated in *Time and Western Man* (1927) and then again in the conclusion to *Men without Art* (1934), a book of essays examining the effects of moral, political, and religious belief on contemporary literature.[53] In *Men without Art*, Lewis claimed that laughter is a human being's most "'god-like' attribute." Laughter occurs when our "reason" makes us aware of the absurdity of our condition from a "god-like" point of view: a "dangerous, philosophic, 'god-like' prerogative—that wild nihilism that is a function of reason and of which . . . laughter is the characteristic expression." Laughter establishes that life is a game, "in the sense that no value can attach to it *for itself*, but only in so far as it is well-played or badly played."[54] The challenge for Lewis was to incorporate that point of view into a novel: that is, a text generically predisposed to attach value to life.

Lewis's enigmatic title, usually sidestepped in commentary, addresses the dilemma directly. *The Revenge for Love* is a novel (by no means the first, or the last) about a man and a woman who love each other uncompromisingly. They play that game well, to heroic effect. But what sort of revenge should we expect to be exacted upon them, for playing it well? And by whom? What sort of text would *The Revenge for Love* have to be in order to establish the "god-like" point of view from which the value that love attaches to life could be understood as requiring for its authentication an act of revenge carried out by a third party with no discernible stake in the matter? The question may be metaphysical. The answer Lewis was to provide, however, draws vividly on an understanding of the ways in which technology had changed the world. If there is a god in this text, its name is information.

Lewis creates his metaphysical dimension, as he had done since *Enemy of the Stars* (1914), by starkly opposing an embodiment of mind to an embodiment of matter. The first of *The Revenge for Love*'s seven parts describes the failure of the British, working-class, Communist agitator Percy Hardcaster to escape from a prison in Spain. Lewis deploys the style of unforgiving external observation he had perfected in the Breton and Spanish stories of *The Wild Body* (1927) to pin down all the men assembled in this prison, convict and guard alike, as examples of automatism in thought, speech, and gesture. The style itself is a Modernist machismo, its semi-automated explosions of metaphor matching blow for blow each stance taken or insult flung. Lewis deliberately repeats himself. For example, the description of the visual and verbal missiles launched by one of the Spanish prisoners, in chapter 3 of *The Revenge for Love*, closely resembles that of the various violent provocations that constitute the innkeeper Bestre in *The Wild Body*.[55] Bestre's gift for antagonism is said to derive from his Spanish ancestry.[56] Lewis had long regarded masculinity as a performance.

A man, he had said in his 1926 polemic *The Art of Being Ruled,* is made, not born. "He has to be propped up into that position with some ingenuity, and is always likely to collapse."[57] The business of all the men assembled in the Spanish prison is to perform masculinity, even, or especially, in politics. Percy Hardcaster justifies his communism to himself by performing it to the limits of rigor. "Bluff stood in the same relation to the revolutionary expressionism as does sangfroid to the pugnacity of the duellist" (*RL* 53). Percy is cool. And so is Lewis. He justifies his satire by performing it to the limits of rigor. His Modernism, too, is a bluff. Energies conspire. Victim and assailant richly deserve each another. By 1937, Modernism's commitment to vital energies could only ever be the subject of a nostalgic performance.

Lewis, however, unlike Percy, knows that the game is up (masculinity's game, satire's game, Modernism's game). There is a woman in the Spanish prison: Josefa, the "young peasant" (*RL* 14) who delivers Percy's plan of escape in the false bottom of a basket of food. Josefa, present for much of the episode, does not speak a single word. Lewis does not confront her directly in style, or through style. Instead, he permits the casual misogyny of convict and guard alike to reduce her to automatism (to biology, to Nature). When she bursts into tears, one of the guards announces that she must be having her period (31). What she knows, but they do not, however, is that the message she brings Percy has been intercepted. The escape will undoubtedly fail. Josefa's tears express (they do not perform) a radical pessimism. She is uncool. Her lack of cool alerts us to the dangerous complacency of the varieties of bluff that surround her, including that of satire itself. The novel will have to divest itself of sangfroid in order to attain, and perhaps even to exceed, the knowledge incorporated in tears. In its first part, the men energetically perform a "strict male canon" (17): chapter 3 even encompasses a small riot. The woman, by contrast, communicates data. As such, she is vulnerable to interception. Her communicativeness brings into play a state apparatus otherwise indifferent to, because so much more powerful than, the prisoners engaged in carnivalesque riot. Her face strikes the chief civil guard, Don Alvaro, as an "unimportant puzzle, that taxed his recording machinery, like a question of mislaid fingerprints" (15). The puzzle gains in importance when found to constitute a channel of communication into the prison. Don Alvaro will use his knowledge of the contents of the message Josefa carries to entrap Percy and his accomplice. Her tears, in turn, convey a knowledge of the vulnerability of human energies to data exchange.

Part 2 is entitled "Victor Stamp," but immediately and emphatically introduces a second woman, Victor's partner, Margot, who starts the day purposefully while he slumbers on, a Molly Bloom to her Leopold. This second woman also knows something. Within a couple of pages, she has voiced the novel's title, attributing the "ill-luck" that has consistently dogged Victor to her love for him. "It was because *she* was there that no pleasant thing ever happened. It was *the revenge for love!* This, on the part of fate, was the revenge for love. There was no way out, unless she could kill love" (*RL* 70). Fate is the Absolute, the "point of view" from which the absurdity of any attempt to attach meaning and value to life becomes manifest. Whether Margot understands that point of view any better than her Spanish counterpart, Josefa, remains at this stage open to doubt. She is a different kind of performer: a petit-bourgeois aspirant who, born poor, has "taught herself English," evolving a "composite speech of her own" flavored with "American talkie echoes" (71). A self-synthesizer, she would feel pretty much at home in *Grand Hotel*, or a novel by Jean Rhys. But for the time being all she can do under the burden of what she knows is, like Josefa, to burst into tears (78–79).

What happens thereafter is unexpected, to say the least, in a text by Wyndham Lewis. *The Revenge for Love* has a cellular structure, each of its seven parts constituting a more or less self-contained onslaught on a figure or figures representative of a moral flaw of some kind. The spirit of Lewis's earlier satire, *The Apes of God* (1930), certainly lives on. Furthermore, at least one of these parts acquires, in Modernist fashion, a style of its own. In part 3 each appearance of boisterous Jack Cruze, an accountant who subsidizes fake artists in order to seduce their wives, provokes the narrative voice not just into boisterousness of its own, but into a self-exhibition strikingly at odds with the strict impersonality it otherwise consistently maintains. However, a further development has already begun to take shape, beneath, or through, this militant, Modernist cellularity. Margot acquires a bildungsroman of her own.

In part 4, at a party thrown by fellow-traveling communist Sean O'Hara to celebrate Percy Hardcaster's return from Spain, Margot takes food to Victor, as Josefa had once taken food to Percy, and in doing so stumbles across a conspiracy that involves the forging of Victor's signature. She understands immediately that she and Victor are engaged in a "battle of wills" with O'Hara and his accomplices, "to decide who should possess most *reality*—just as men fought each other for money, or fought each other for food" (*RL* 177). The battle of wills is a battle of representations, then; or, to adopt the terms I have been developing in this book, a battle fought by means of representational media. "They could only browbeat you like a gramophone, or impose on you like the projections on the screen of the cinema" (178). Which side in the dispute over reality will make the best propaganda film? It is not that Margot remains immune to satire. Far from it. Lewis pursued his vendetta with Bloomsbury by allowing her to worship at the feet of Virginia Woolf. It is, rather, that she is at the same time a character in a novel: a genre, as I have said, predisposed to attribute meaning and value to life. Next up for her is a rite of passage.

The conspiracy against Victor involves dispatching him to the South of France to smuggle guns into Spain, accompanied by Margot. Spain had always been for Lewis the most metaphysical of regions. The early Breton sketches eventually collected after much revision as *The Wild Body* include one or two forays across the border. Ker-Orr, the "Soldier of Humour" who emerged during revision as their narrator and chief protagonist, opens proceedings with the claim that "Spain is an overflow of sombreness." He will soon find himself "cast by fate" for an "essentially spanish comedy," which begins in the border town of Bayonne.[58] *Men without Art* returns to the theme. There, Lewis compares satire's relish for the grotesque to the lack of compunction shown by the Spanish toward dwarfs: an attitude vastly preferable, in his view, to hypocritical "Anglo-Saxon" pity or concealed disgust. "They feel perhaps that God has made them a present of these hideous oddities to be their sport: and the dwarf feels that too." So Spaniard and satirist alike understand the grotesque as no more than an extreme case of the absurdity that defines human existence in general. "There is no reason at all why we should not burst out laughing at a foetus, for instance. We should after all only be laughing at *ourselves!*—at ourselves early in our mortal career."[59] Spain, it would seem, was for Lewis satire's laboratory.

But *The Revenge for Love* is a novel. At the beginning of part 7, Victor and Margot, awaiting orders in a small town on the border, decide to spend the day in Spain, as tourists. Before long, they are accosted by a dwarf, who malevolently selects Margot "to be his dramatic mother" (*RL* 296). As Edwards points out, the context for this performance is the discussion of satire in *Men without Art*.[60] Satire is on the dwarf's side. So is Victor, who, with an artist's "passion for the grotesque," sketches him, laughing heartily (299). Poor Margot bursts into tears (298). What is most interesting about this episode is that Lewis should go out of his way to create for her tears, as he had earlier done for Josefa's, an audience of men—and some ostentatiously masculinized women scratching their moustaches and beards (301). Again, the misogyny that greets Margot and Josefa is an expression and indictment not only of male bluff, but of satire itself, which so delights in bluff. Weeping, as she is more or less bound to in a novel, Margot knows something about the absurdity of existence that Lewis's Modernism does not know. Victor's laughter makes her sick (299). That moral and physical nausea hardens into knowledge: a "grimace," as Victor recognizes, or as Lewis recognizes on his behalf, "deeply grafted, and directed outward at nothing in particular—or at the nothingness which is all that is there, unless you conjure things up for yourself, and furnish this white screen with your private pictures" (301–2). Margot has got to where satire is, by some means other than satire. Unlike the satirist, she does indeed conjure meaning and value up for herself. Unlike the men (of both sexes) who surround her, she cannot simply regard the dwarf as a spectacle: to her, he is a human being for whom she is in some small measure responsible, and who has responsibilities toward her, which he has singularly flouted. Responsibility is what she knows, that satire does not, about absurd existence. And it is no mere metaphysical knowledge. Responsible above all for Victor, in his statuesque beauty as much of a man-child as the dwarf, she has already noticed on his behalf the unusual interest taken in his passport details by the civil guard at the frontier (294). Now, after the dwarf has finally taken himself off, she notices that they are being shadowed by a pair of dubious characters (305–7). She has probably read enough thrillers to know that these men are police spies. The "fate" exposed at this point, as about to take its revenge for love, is the apparatus or system of state surveillance.

Margot has one further novel-like ordeal to undergo before she can take full responsibility for Victor. Her recuperation from the dwarf takes the form of a day in the mountains accompanied by John Ruskin's essay on heroic (submissive) femininity, "Queens' Gardens." Her reverie is sharply interrupted by a vision of "the figures of herself and Victor stopped at the frontier by the military police, as if in a diorama" (*RL* 313). This representation, or private picture projected onto the white screen, reveals to her the extent of her responsibility for his exposure to state surveillance. Transformed from "hermit-girl" to "amazon" (316), she descends the mountain and well-nigh goose-steps up the village street to the Hotel Internationale, where Victor, Percy Hardcaster, and the socialist hotel-keeper contemplate a letter bearing Victor's forged signature. As she asks the hard questions Victor is too manly to ask, Percy, unsettled by her determination to get at the truth, retreats into misogyny, as he had done before, in the Spanish prison, when Josefa burst into tears (322). Margot, however, is not crying. Instead, she adopts once again the "grimace" first provoked by the dwarf, a look that Victor grasps as entirely "rational" (320). Margot *knows*. And we might note that, goose steps notwithstanding, her sudden appearance in the middle of this male chorus has given an "impression of magical inter-loping" (318). Margot belongs rather more to the communication of data than she does to the communication of people and goods. Before the epi-sode concludes, the hotel-keeper's baby boy has vomited all over her, in yet another denial to this amazon of properly dramatic motherhood, yet an-other premonitory revenge for love (325).

Victor's gun-running expedition across the border to Figueras occupies two chapters in the novel's final section. Margot, realizing that his London confederates propose to use him as a decoy, and have to that end forged his signature on an incriminating document, follows him by train. She recon-noiters the trap set for him in Figueras, and, behaving exactly like the heroine of a thriller, manages (somehow) to intercept him on the road, much to his astonishment. "She must have chartered an aeroplane! For how had she done it, if not by air? Or she must have arrived like the Egyp-tian symbol of the psyche" (*RL* 349). This second magical interloping takes the form of data flow. "He perceived that Margot was the bearer of news" (311). The message Margot bears is that Victor himself, as the mere physi-cal counterpart of data inscribed in documents, is a message sent by some-one else to the Spanish police, a message long since received at a passport office on the frontier and now in wide circulation. This is the moment of an energetic man's maximum exposure to the (superior) force of information, embodied in a woman. The agent of the revenge for love is not fate, then, but the knowledge Margot has earned, which Victor is too willful, or too stupid, to earn. Her knowledge is a knowledge of abstract systems of data flow: of surveillance, of forged documents; of the sorts of things that might happen to a person with the surname of "Stamp." The agent of the revenge for love is information.

Lewis's description of Margot's point of view on their subsequent high-speed dash to the border, in the course of which they run over a civil guard, has become a locus classicus for attempts to characterize "Modern-ist" style.[61] In truth, it offers a fairly orthodox account of the motorcar as representational medium, and of speed as a challenge to representation: "Meanwhile trees, rocks, and telegraph-poles stood up dizzily before her and crashed down behind. They were held up stiffly in front of her astonished eyes, then snatched savagely out of the picture. Like a card-world clacked cinematographically through its static permutations by the ill-bred fingers of a powerful conjurer, everything stood upon end and then fell flat" (*RL* 353–54). As in *Journey to the Border*, the cinematographic testing of the limits of representation throws up a non-ideographic ideograph: a glimpse of telegraph poles that acknowledges the futility of all merely mechanical prostheses. These poles, perhaps, carry the very wires along which the news of Victor's arrival in Spain with a carload of contraband guns has already flashed. Margot understands that the impact of machine on body, when their car subsequently strikes a civil guard who tries to halt them in their tracks, is less, in the larger moral and political scheme, than the impact of a message that, now beyond recall, explodes across the system, triggering alerts at one point in it after another. "They in their car were like a cork, tossed in some turgid medium" (363). The car is a message, the roadblock manned by civil guards its channel. The *OED* cites Lewis's sentence as an example of an older sense of the term "medium"— "any substance considered with regard to its properties as a vehicle of light or sound"—which we might nonetheless regard as descriptive of technological innovation. Lewis was one of the first to imagine transport as a connective rather than a representational medium. For Margot, uniquely, perhaps, in the fiction of the period, is not representation's creature. Through her, and despite her, information has taken its revenge not just on energy, on the "crude speeding passion" (354) of a man in a motorcar, but on satire's complicity with—Modernism's complicity with—that semiautomated performance.

One other aspect of *The Revenge for Love* deserves brief mention: the frequent comparison of Victor Stamp to Clark Gable, at that time Hollywood's prime sample of alpha-maleness. Lewis pays particular attention to the hydraulics of Victor's Clark Gable smile, "one side of his face all sardonic half-mirth, the scalp muscles ploughing up the forehead to make it all go careworn, so as to embitter the one-sided smile down below still more" (*RL* 90). This smile, the product of a representational medium, is a gift to Lewis's decayed-Modernist ambition to represent behavior from the outside, as a painter would, or a filmmaker. It reappears sporadically (e.g., 301, 319, 335), more often than not in counterpoint to Margot's emergence as a figure of knowledge and moral responsibility. Indeed, it is still there at the very end of the tale, as Victor contemplates the cargo the car is carrying in its false bottom: not guns, at all, as he had fondly imagined, but a nondescript pile of bricks (373). The Clark Gable smile's sardonic half-mirth is about as close as the he-man gets to reflexivity.

The film this episode most reminds me of is 1934's smash hit *It Happened One Night,* directed by Frank Capra, in which Gable is cast as a commentary on his own machismo. *It Happened One Night* is a transit film. The screwball protagonists, down-on-his-luck journalist Peter Warne (Gable) and spoilt heiress Ellen Andrews (Claudette Colbert), make their way by bus and stolen jalopy from Miami to New York City. From the outset, transport is to be understood as a communications medium. Boarding the bus in Miami, Warne finds his seat occupied by a mound of newspapers, which he summarily dispatches through a window. Thereafter, messages continually arrive in the shape of newspaper headlines, some of them planted by Ellen's wealthy father. Warne in turn sends various messages to his editor concerning Ellen and her whereabouts. "You're just a headline to me," he tells her, though he does not really mean it. Ellen's father, who wishes to locate her, with the help of her fortune-seeking husband, "King" Westley (Jameson Thomas), and then to annul the marriage, has at his disposal an altogether different order of transport as medium. He twice overtakes the truant couple while they are en route, initially by means of a private airplane that doubles as communications hub, and then by means of a motorcade with full police escort.

In both scenes, Andrews continually urges greater speed. Westley, we might note, who proposes to arrive in an autogyro at the formal ceremony that he hopes will confirm his marriage to Ellen, belongs to a series of 1930s aviator-idiots culminating in André Jurieux, in Jean Renoir's *La règle du jeu* (1939).

Peter and Ellen, by contrast, must go slowly enough to fall in love. They must while away enough time to elicit the gress in progress. They must erect obstacles, most notably the "wall" made of a blanket that divides their shared bedrooms; or establish a Belacqua-like "moving pause." The talk is always rapid-fire, in screwball comedies, but its function is to retard and impede, to prevent the protagonists from throwing themselves away on someone else. In *It Happened One Night,* the process of transit, under most circumstances dedicated to the reduction or pampering of obstinacy, instead brings it out. Thus, Peter has a startling moment of he-man mulish-

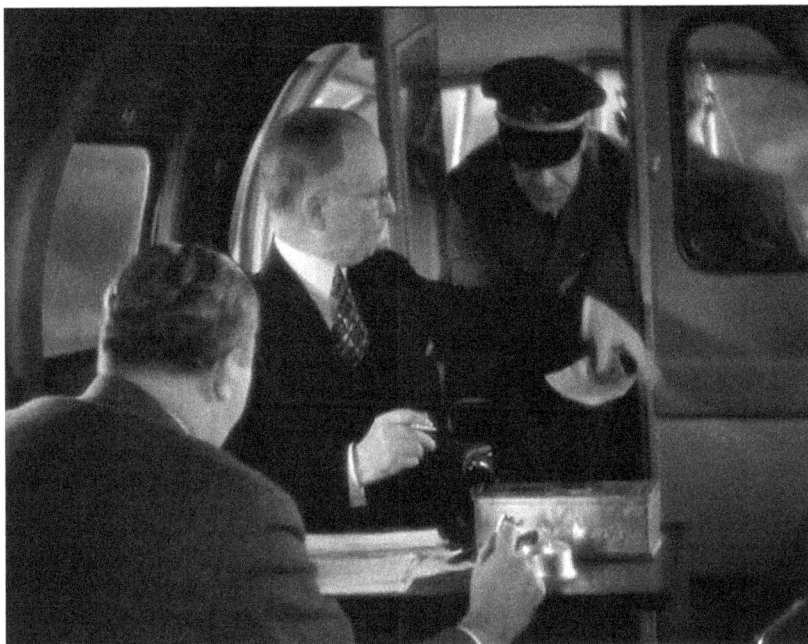

The private aircraft as communications hub. Frame grab from
It Happened One Night (1934, Columbia Pictures, prod. Harry Cohn,
dir. Frank Capra).

ness, when he brutally rejects Ellen's open avowal of her feelings for him.
This looks like a mistake; and it would be, too, if obstinacy were not love's
only reliable measure. The mulishness is in fact a declaration of sorts. It
indicates that he will slow down enough, as Mr. Andrews speeds by, to fall
in love: that is, to stop Ellen becoming no more than a message transmitted
from wealthy father to wealthy husband. In a comedy, you can do that.

Victor Stamp, of course, is overtaken and intercepted not by the agents
of a corrupt political system, but by the woman who loves him. Her magical interloping nonetheless provokes in him, too, an oddly reflexive mulishness. The news she brings, that the house for which he is heading has been
surrounded by the police, strikes Victor as in itself a vicious betrayal. "In
his eyes there was almost a glare: it was *she* after all who had betrayed *him*.
This was revenge, or had that appearance. It was the revenge of love, if that
was love" (351). Victor, he-man style, has shot the messenger. The mulishness, so entirely in character, and yet at the same time a revelation—

concerning love, and the revenge love might appear to take on its object—affords rare insight into the state of a mind rarely capable of insight. In his previous novel, *Snooty Baronet* (1932), Lewis had explored at some length the obstinacy love requires, if it is to be love, or stay love. The narrator's lover Val not only sticks by her man through thick and thin, but, like Margot, grasps the extent of the conspiracy into which he has been drawn far more readily than he does himself. The knowledge earns her instant, temporary rejection. Rejecting her, Snooty admits that she has told the truth because she loves him, and that it is better to be loved than not to be loved. His obstinacy, equaling hers, albeit perversely, is a declaration of love, the only one he is ever likely to make.[62] Victor arrives at a comparable glimmer of awareness. He feels doubly thwarted: in the truth Margot has told, and in the difficulty she herself constitutes when it comes to acting upon the knowledge he now has of his predicament. "He had certainly been trapped. For something that called for action had just been brutally announced to him. And here was a notable obstacle to action. It was the obstacle itself that had delivered the news!" (351). "Obstacle" and "obstinacy" share a common root. Both involve standing against or in the way of something. Victor has been trapped in obstinacy, by obstinacy. Or call it love. It is love's obstinacy, its determination to attribute meaning and value to life, which invites revenge. Margot's confirmation that Victor is no more than message, for all his bravado, or more precisely *in* his bravado, because of his bravado, is fate's revenge on them for having loved each other. Rather, it is the revenge on him *of* the love she bears him, for loving and being loved by her. This is as close as the he-man will get to reflexivity; at least until the sight of crates full of bricks extracts from him a last Clark Gable grin. Unlike *It Happened One Night, The Revenge for Love* is a tragedy. To compare novel and film, however, is to begin to understand that transport's reconfiguration as communications medium between the world wars provided an extraordinarily rich and various imaginative resource, for ex-Modernist and Hollywood mythmaker alike.

In *The Revenge for Love,* Lewis had acknowledged transit's new reality by a generic displacement that subordinates the conventions of the satirical Vorticist word-picture to the conventions of the novel, or indeed, ultimately, the conventions of a very particular kind of novel. One of the things Margot knows is that she is in a spy thriller: the kind of novel in which information can be guaranteed to give energy a good run for its money. In that respect, though scarcely in any other, *The Revenge for Love* could be

compared to Stevie Smith's *Over the Frontier* (1938). Sent to a Baltic resort to recover from a disastrous love affair, the protagonist finds herself
caught up in and utterly transformed by a quasi-Ruritanian adventure involving espionage and romance in just about equal portions. In this case,
the system that transports her from one genre to another is the telephone.

> As I round the corner to come in through the doorway into the lounge
> there is the telephone in its kiosk and in the kiosk telephoning is Colonel
> Peck, but he is speaking German, but this does not at first convey very
> much to me as I stand to listen. I stand to listen because his voice, this Col-
> onel Peck voice, is suddenly become so incisive, so very un-absentminded,
> so very unlike the vagueness of Colonel Peck, that I am amazed and so in
> my great surprise at this uncharacteristic voice that is so completely foreign
> to the picture we have built up on the very most circumstantial of evidence,
> the picture of this distracted Colonel Peck, I must stand and listen.[63]

Stand and listen is what she will increasingly learn to do, in her new guise
as spymaster (gender difference being one of several boundaries crossed in
the process). Like Buchanan's *A London Story*, like *The Revenge for Love*,
Over the Frontier should perhaps be regarded as a bildungsroman for the
information age. Of the writers I have discussed in this chapter, Lewis
came closest to writing transit itself: the reconfiguration of transport as
medium. But circumstances arose often enough, in the fiction of the period, that required some reflection at least on what transit was, and how it
might be written. In what remains of the chapter, I want to suggest that
the status it assumed more widely in the literature of the period was
paratextual.

Customs Sheds

The First World War had necessitated, on a scale never seen before, both
mass transit and systems for the licensing and regulation of mass transit.
Boundaries between nations became legal entities.[64] For some, such as the
heroine of Rose Macaulay's *Crewe Train* (1926), frontiers still exuded romance. "Not all the nagging *douanes* and impatient queues of passengers
could spoil it. Say frontier, frontier, frontier, ten times, and the word unlike
most words so treated, still retains a meaning. Love, hate, friendship, virtue, vice, God—these become as sounding brass and tinkling cymbals, but
frontiers remain."[65] Impossible to avoid, increasingly hard to ignore, the

douane's nagging acquired a kind of glamour of its own, especially among those desperate for copy. By 1930, Evelyn Waugh was declining to follow the example of the professional travel writer who finds "a peculiar relish in discomfort. Bed bugs, frightful food, inefficient ships and trains, hostile customs, police and passport officers, consuls who will not cash cheques, excesses of heat and cold, night club champagne and even imprisonment are his peculiar delights."[66] Such, too, was the peculiar relish of the spy novelist. The protagonists of Eric Ambler's *The Dark Frontier* (1936), in rivalrous pursuit of the formula of an atom bomb recently tested in the East European republic of Ixania, run into a spot of bother on the frontier.

> Groom, protesting with studied ill-humour, was made to open his two huge suitcases and submit them to the pummellings and proddings of one of the soldiers. It was Carruthers' turn next.
>
> Following Groom's example, he complained vigorously in English, French and German. The official took no notice and ordered him curtly to unlock his suitcase. With a tremendous show of bad grace, Carruthers obeyed. The official undertook the examination himself, removing singly every article in it and keeping up a running fire of unintelligible comment as he did so.[67]

The camera found in Carruthers's suitcase is duly confiscated. Groom, however, has a substitute concealed on his person. Such foresight convinces Carruthers of his opponent's caliber.

The *OED* dates from 1921 the use of the term "customs" to designate the area at a seaport, airport, or border control where goods, luggage, and other items are examined. Customs is a constrained space that supplements—that is, at once adds to and exposes—the constraint built into transit. Like the telephone apparatus held in the hand, it constitutes an interface between consciousness and system, storage and communication, the representational and the connective. George Buchanan's *Entanglement* (1938) finds the apt metaphor for a telephone conversation between Charles Manwick, head of the aviation division of a large engineering firm, and Lord Flowerfield, head of Drancer's department store. Manwick enters his office to find that "the telephone was ringing, with Flowerfield's voice as its cargo."[68] The customs inspection, like the transponder in the telephone apparatus, is the point at which message reveals itself as cargo: a materialization provoking thought about immateriality.

As the European plot thickened, in the years after 1920, so the ceremonies of inspection became, if not more threatening, in most cases, then more obtrusively ceremonial. On May 9, 1935, Virginia Woolf endured an anxious wait on the Dutch-German border, while Leonard went in to negotiate, with a novel by Lawrence for company.

> Sitting in the sun outside the German Customs. A car with the swastika on the back window has just past through the barrier into Germany. L. is in the customs. I am nibbling at Aaron's Rod. Ought I to go in & see what is happening? A fine dry windy morning. The Dutch Customs took 10 seconds. This has taken 10 minutes already. The windows are barred. Here they came out & the grim man laughed at Mitz. But L. said that when a peasant came in & stood with his hat on, the man said This office is like a church & made him move it. Heil Hitler said the little thin boy opening his bag, perhaps with an apple in it, at the barrier. We become obsequious—delighted that is when the officers smile at Mitz—the first stoop in our back.[69]

In this case, of course, the obtrusiveness of the ceremony does amount to a threat. The barred windows, the grim man's laugh, the bullying of the peasant, the response all this prompts even in those not directly threatened: in the 1930s, transit was political. To put it differently, fascism's theatrical policing of borders prompted the thought that the experience of transit had always been political, had always been an enactment of the meaning and value of communication in modern societies. In Graham Greene's *Stamboul Train* (1932), the Jewish businessman Myatt feels only intense relief at escaping from the customs shed at Ostend into the enveloping smoke of the railway terminus. "He forgot that his suede shoes were ruined, that the customs officer had been impertinent over two pairs of silk pyjamas. From the man's rudeness and his contempt, the syllables '*Juif, Juif,*' he crept into the shade of those great tents."[70] The episode, we might note, occurs at the very beginning of the novel. For the shape taken by transit writing in the 1930s was often that of a position occupied, or a stance held, on the threshold of the text.

The most celebrated customs inspection in the fiction of the period occurs in chapter 2 of Waugh's *Vile Bodies* (1930). Preceded by an epic account of a bad channel crossing—" 'Too, too sick-making,' said Miss Runcible, with one of her rare flashes of accuracy"—it can scarcely be said to stand on the threshold of the text.[71] In fact, it generates the entire plot. Confiscation of the typescript of his precocious memoirs, destined for a London publisher, ensures that Adam Fenwick-Symes will spend most of the rest of the novel in vain pursuit of the money he needs to marry the

expensive Nina Blount. And the customs inspection has a further central-
ity. It illuminates the novel's enigmatic title. It lays bare the "vileness" of
vile bodies (that is, their existence as base matter). The customs officers
sift through Adam's books in an inner office stacked with "contraband
pornography and strange instruments," while from next door come "the
shrieks and yells of poor Miss Runcible, who had been mistaken for a well-
known jewel smuggler, and was being stripped to the skin by two terrific
wardresses."

> Miss Runcible came through the office, working hard with lip-stick and
> compact.
>   "Adam, darling, I never saw you on the boat," she said. "My dear, I can't
> *tell* you the *things* that have been happening to me in there. The way they
> looked . . . too, too shaming. Positively surgical, my dear, and *such* wicked
> old women, just like *Dowagers,* my dear. As soon as I get to London I shall
> ring up every Cabinet Minister and *all* the newspapers and give them all
> the most shy-making details." (*VB* 20)

This skirmish has to be understood as a violation. Waugh had first written
"The places they looked in," which he then amended to "The way they
delved," before finally settling on the weaker, though still suggestive, "The
way they looked . . ." The inspection has clearly involved an obscene prob-
ing of bodily cavities. Agatha Runcible works hard to restore her pride not
only with lipstick and compact, but by telephone. The chapter concludes
with a glimpse of newspaper headlines concerning a peer's daughter's Dover ordeal (29). As we have already seen, this is a novel entranced by, and
ready to adapt itself to, telecommunications technology. Agatha's Dover
ordeal vividly defines the interface between consciousness and system that
it has been my aim to establish as an important new topic in the literature
of the period. She does more than anyone else in the novel to put the gress
back into progress, not least by crashing spectacularly out of a motor race
(152–53). Her story, too, is a bildungsroman for the information age.
Waugh's ambivalence about that story found remarkable expression in a
piece he wrote for the *Daily Mail* denouncing her as "crazy," "dissolute,"
and "sordid"—and nonetheless the novel's true "heroine."[72]

More interesting, from a formal point of view, is the customs inspection
that occupies the first couple of pages of Kate O'Brien's *Mary Lavelle*
(1936). "The trunk of a 'Miss' going over the Pyrenees, is no great matter,"
the book opens. The Miss in question is a young Irishwoman traveling to

Spain, in 1922, to take up a post as a governess. She will remain generic (though the book's title has already named her) throughout the ordeal, which takes place in a timeless, or frequently recurring, present. One might expect to find on the tray of the trunk belonging to such a person two hats, two evening dresses, and a frilly afternoon frock.

> When the tray is lifted the owner of the trunk, still anxiously at authority's disposition, yet hopes for a lessening of scrutiny. The officials are free to examine her face-powder, her lavender water, her talc. Clean handkerchiefs, darned stockings, new stockings. Petrol-smelling gloves. Frilly blouses, woollen jumpers. The silver brushes mother gave her on her sixteenth birthday. A workbox, a little manicure set. Nothing to be ashamed of. But chemises, too, and nightdresses. The owner of the trunk grows fidgety as official hands plunge deep among these necessities until they reach her wrapped-up shoes, her handful of books, her odds and ends of parting presents. The trunk is shut then and the chalk squiggle imposed upon it. The girl and her equipment for the decent life may enter Spain.

No Agatha Runcible, then. But O'Brien, like Waugh, grasps with some relish the obscenity of official hands plunging deep among chemises and nightdresses. Neither the customs officials nor the owner of the trunk imagine that anything of any significance has occurred. "Nevertheless, the strap-fastening and chalk-squiggling are gestures of fate, and she is afoot now, befriended by her trunk, on the errand of keeping alive."[73] The strap-fastening and chalk-squiggling have released this particular Miss from generic surveillance into singularity, and, by the same token, into narrative. For the episode of the customs inspection takes the form of a separately paginated "Prologue." Stood on the threshold of the text, aware of the imminence of narrative, but not anticipating it, the prologue explicitly asks us to consider what it might take for the generic Miss with the chemises and nightdresses to become known as Mary Lavelle.

We should not be surprised, perhaps. One of the most famous introductory sketches in all literature, preceding Hawthorne's *The Scarlet Letter* (1850), is titled "The Custom-House." Both sketches are paratexts. As such, they are to be numbered among the various liminal devices that mediate a book to its readers: title, subtitle, foreword, dedication, epigraph, preface, and so on. As J. Hillis Miller has observed, the prefix "para" denotes "something inside a domestic economy and at the same time outside it, something simultaneously this side of a boundary-line, threshold, or margin, and also beyond it, equivalent in status and also secondary or subsidiary, submissive as of guest to host, slave to master."[74] Drawing on Miller, Gerard Genette describes the function and scope of a wide range of devices that mediate a text's interiority.[75] The prologue to *Mary Lavelle* surely counts as a paratext as Miller and Genette describe it; so, rather more equivocally, might the opening chapter of *Vile Bodies* or *Stamboul Train*. In other narratives, however, customs inspections take place when proceedings are already well under way. We need also to consider episodes that behave like paratext, without in any way advertising themselves as such.

Equally suggestive is Jacques Derrida's commentary, after Kant, on the idea of the parergon (for example, the frame of a picture) as a supplement to representation.

> A parergon comes against, beside, and in addition to the *ergon,* the work done [*fait*], the fact [*le fait*], the work, but it does not fall to one side, it touches and cooperates within the operation, from a certain outside. Neither simply outside nor simply inside. Like an accessory that one is obliged to welcome on the border, on board [*au bord, à bord*]. It is first of all on (the) bo(a)rd(er) [*Il est d'abord l'à-bord*].

Derrida's metaphors glance directly at my claim for the customs inspection as that event which, always taking place on the border, and sometimes on board, or if not on board then between the end of one journey and the beginning of another, provokes the gress or moving pause that is transit writing. There are two further emphases in his account that have some bearing on the liminal devices that concern me. The parergon, he argues, is always likely to deteriorate into the "perversion" of mere adornment: an interminable performance of the "attraction of sensory matter." I have noted the varying degrees of relish with which Waugh and O'Brien dwell on official borderline delving into bodily and other cavities. But there is something oddly unobtrusive—sheepish, even—about this relish. Here, too, Derrida can help. He notes that, on account of its liminal status, the parergon cannot obtrude in one direction without at the same time vanishing in another. The parergon stands out alternately both from the work of art it frames, and from the milieu that frames the work of art, like a figure on a ground. But in standing out from the work of art, it merges with milieu; and in standing out from milieu, it merges with the work of art. "There is always a form on a ground, but the *parergon* is a form which has as its traditional determination not that it stands out but that it disappears, buries itself, effaces itself, melts away at the moment it deploys its greatest energy."[76] Standing out from the story yet to commence, the prologue to *Mary Lavelle* merges into all the questions ever asked about narrative art; standing out from the circumstances in which the novel was written and published, it merges with the story of an Irish governess in Spain. The form the parergon takes is that of camouflage: a tactic not unknown to persons passing through customs, especially in certain kinds of fiction.

In Ambler's *Uncommon Danger* (1937), Kenton, a British journalist severely down on his luck, takes the train from Nuremberg to Linz, in Austria. A fellow passenger, a Jew who claims to be on the run from the Nazis, offers him garlic sausage, and then bribes him to carry some papers through German customs: which he does, the envelope with the papers in it lodged down a sock, German banknotes in a shoe.[77] *Uncommon Danger* boasts a prologue; but this is not it. For the undertaking impulsively given while in transit has already enmeshed Kenton in conspiracy. It *is*, already, the plot. William Bradshaw, the narrator of Christopher Isherwood's *Mr Norris Changes Trains* (1935), seems to have read a lot of books of that kind. The "flurried gestures" made by the man he has asked for a light, in the train to Berlin, the man who will turn out to be Arthur Norris, suggest various possibilities. "For all they conveyed, he might equally have been going to undress, to draw a revolver, or merely to make sure that I hadn't stolen his money."[78]

I have already shown that the durable, intermittent relationship that develops between Bradshaw and the man with the baffling gestures is a *mediated* relationship, telephonic-telepathic in its essence. Nothing meaningful—nothing revelatory—arises out of the (often trivial, or false) information the two men regularly exchange, usually by telephone. This, too, is a bildungsroman for the information age. Rather than testing his own innocence against Norris's apparently hard-earned experience, as the bildungsroman requires, Bradshaw discovers in his patron and mentor an innocence equivalent to his own. The episode in the train unsettles our expectation (that is, Bradshaw's expectation) that the exposure of data concerning the performance of social-symbolic identity will prove less problematic than the exposure of objects that point indexically to desire's hidden truth. Its main event is arrival at the Dutch-German border, or, rather, the varying degrees of anxiety this arrival provokes in Arthur Norris. Asked to show his passport, Norris suffers a minor nervous breakdown. Bradshaw observes that it could have been a lot worse, since innocent people are forever being mistaken (like Agatha Runcible) for famous jewel thieves and strip-searched on the spot. That, however, is a prospect Norris views with equanimity. His troubles have to do with data, with the social-symbolic. The exposure of indexicality by delving into luggage or bodily cavities holds no terrors for him. "The customs examination, when it came, seemed positively to give Norris pleasure." He makes a joke of a bottle of Coty perfume which, he assures the official in fluent German, is for personal use only (*BN* 10–11). Norris's desires will prove to be the most obvious, and least decisive, thing about him. Camouflage is in this instance both the parergon's subject and its method. Standing out from the story yet to commence, it merges into the conventions of spy fiction. Standing out from the conventions of spy fiction, it merges into the story yet to commence by insisting that the "affectionate protectiveness" Norris already inspires in Bradshaw will "colour" all their future dealings (10). Isherwood's novel, which begins in transit writing, continues happily to deceive. Just about the only thing Mr. Norris definitely does not do in it is to change trains.

Elizabeth Bowen: "In Transit *Consciously*"

Elizabeth Bowen, as we have seen, admitted to endowing her protagonists with an enthusiasm for transport. "Zestfully they take ship or board planes: few of them even are *blasés* about railways. Motor-cars magnetise them particularly." Someone had apparently once remarked that her characters are "almost perpetually in transit." "I agree," she went on, "Bowen characters are in transit *consciously*."[79] Bowen characters do not just find themselves taking ship, plane, train, or motorcar; they expect their vehicle of choice to enable them to express themselves in ways they could not otherwise have done, as it conveys them from one place to another. To be in transit consciously is also, in novels such as *To the North* (1933) and *The House in Paris* (1935), to be in telecommunication consciously. Transit writing sustains and is sustained by an attention to connectivity in general.

To what purpose? It is worth recalling at this point Maud Ellmann's argument that in *To the North* and *The House in Paris* the "transport of messages via post, telephone, and telegraph, combined with the transport of persons via motorways, shipping routes, and flight paths, has the effect of alienating speech and motion from the human will." "Extending into every area of private life," Ellmann adds, "these networks override the boundaries that separate one person from another, creating mysterious and uncontrollable relations of dependency."[80] She has understood better than any other critic how and why Bowen became the laureate of mobile privatization: the writer of her time most profoundly alert to the fundamental changes wrought in individual and collective experience by the spread of communications networks. It is not altogether clear, however, that Bowen regarded alienation or dependency as the inevitable consequence of routine, all-encompassing transport. I have already described the technocratic community happily created by Cecilia Summers, in *To the North,* as a foretaste of telephony's Facebook effect. I want now to examine the (ambiguously) enabling consequences of transit by train, plane, and ship, as envisaged in that novel and in *The House in Paris.* What was at issue, when it came to network effects, was not so much the human will's absolute alienation from speech and motion as its resurgence by means of the new forms of speech (that is, behavior in general) encouraged by new forms of motion. Emotion was in its most literal sense Bowen's topic.

The opening chapter of *To the North* lasts as long as the train journey from Milan to Boulogne during which Cecilia picks up, or is picked up by, the mock-Byronic Markie Linkwater. Desire is the old emotion most frequently made new by transit writing: made new as the opposite of *flânerie,* or cruising. To "cruise" is to travel about at random with a very specific aim in mind: business, plunder, pleasure, or casual sex. Transit can only ever be undertaken with a very specific aim in mind: getting from A to B. And yet its constrained time and space generates on occasion, and apparently at random, a startling lack of constraint. Cruising is unpredictable in form, predictable in content. Transit, by contrast, always takes the same form, while its content arises unpredictably. The desire Cecilia and Markie feel for each other—pure product of transit—is peculiar indeed.

Cecilia's boredom propels her to the dining car in time for that first service, which, "with its suggestion of the immoderate, does not commend itself to the English." Already, she is ahead of herself, or of (English) convention. "She watched fellow-passengers shoot through the door and stagger unhappily her way between the tables, not knowing where to settle. The train at this point rocks with particular fury." Bowen has gone out of her way to specify the constraints of time and space that create the occasion. We might note the mildly paratextual effect of the brief incursion of the present tense. The train rocking with particular fury is not just the train Cecilia has caught, but any train passing this point on the line. The genre it rocks in is transit writing, not narrative fiction. The paratext, however, creates an opportunity. "She was not, however, unwilling to dine in company. Looking up once more, she met the eyes of a young man who, balancing stockily, paused to survey the car. A gleam of interest and half-recognition, mutually flattering, passed between them. They retracted the glance, glanced again: the train lurched, the young man shot into the place opposite Cecilia."[81] The colon in the final sentence of this immaculate paragraph is a suspension creating suspense; or, rather, it feints at suspense. For the logic of circumstance has by now gained such impetus that the train is bound to lurch, and the young man shoot, at once compelled and willing, into the place opposite Cecilia. What will come of this encounter? Markie and Cecilia agree to meet again in London. He makes sure that she is in the telephone book. At the end of the chapter, Bowen, admitting that neither has a "nice character," and that mistrust has underlain the whole "interlude," nonetheless blames such shortcomings on the constraints of time and space specific to transit (*TTN* 10). She thus identifies the chapter as a whole as parergic. It is, in fact, a feint on her part, an act of camouflage. We assume that a story will be generated out of the encounter. But it is Emmeline Summers, not her sister-in-law Cecilia, who embroils herself fatally with Markie. Cecilia's relationship with him remains, to adapt a phrase from *The House in Paris* to which I will return, "on the plane of potential rather than merely likely behaviour."[82]

Like the parergon, as Derrida defines it, the episode on the Milan-Boulogne express might be expected to stand out from the "plane" of merely potential behavior—all that Cecilia and Markie could have become had they not met—while merging into the plot it has given rise to: the likelihood that Cecilia and Markie will meet again in London, as indeed they do. For Bowen, plotting was a felt necessity, rather than a matter of choice. "The particular plot is something the novelist is driven to. It is what is left after the whittling-away of alternatives." What is to be told could not be told in any other manner.[83] The opening of *To the North* establishes a necessity that will turn out not to have been felt at all. Cecilia's friendship with Markie gets rapidly whittled away. Viewed retrospectively, the episode on the Milan-Boulogne express stands out from what is to follow, merging instead into the kinds of "likely behaviour" represented in comparable episodes in texts such as *Mr Norris Changes Trains* and *Mary Lavelle*. That Cecilia "belongs" in transit writing rather than in a novel is confirmed both by her technocratic command of the new social medium of telephony and by her relative exclusion from the climax of the action.

What about Emmeline? Markie's switch of interest from Cecilia to Emmeline has the immediate narrative effect of associating her with transit. Shortly after the intimate dinner during which he first shows himself interested, she retreats in some confusion to the Gloucestershire home of her cousin and confidante, Lady Georgina Waters. Among the guests is a recently disengaged young man who, as the party breaks up, claims the privilege of driving her back to London. For Emmeline, however, transit is transit is transit. She firmly keeps a lid on its unpredictable content. "Skirting the rotten ribs of the White City, Tim asked her *when* they might meet: she was uncertain" (*TTN* 64). Bowen cordons this episode off in a separate section at the end of an otherwise seamless chapter. Emmeline has been linked parergically with Markie, unlike the hapless Tim a virtuoso of constrained time. For their affair does indeed crystallize—if that is the right term for something itself so uncertain—in transit, during an airline flight from Croydon to Paris. It is a business trip, but Emmeline has brought Markie along for the ride. As the Imperial Airways advertisements for the Croydon–Paris service suggest, there were various ways of whiling away the time spent in the air.

Whiling away the time. Imperial Airways advertisement, 1934. Illustrated London News Ltd. / Mary Evans Picture Library.

This time, Emmeline does not defend herself against transit's unpredictable content.

Emmeline is an experienced traveler, while Markie has never flown before. Her response to the experience of flight remains, however, the more enthusiastic. To Emmeline, some "quite new plan of life, forgotten between flight and flight," once more reveals itself. "No noise, no glass, no upholstery boxed her up from the extraordinary . . ." (*TTN* 136). Markie, by contrast, finds nothing to admire in the view from the window. He does not wish to represent it to himself, to reflect on it. For him, all forms of transit constitute an exercise in the manipulation, rather than the overcoming, of constraint. He improvises, as an antidote to the cabin's deafening hum, and an exploitation of the opportunity it uniquely affords, a makeshift code of communication. He and Emmeline exchange notes scribbled in the margins of her copy of the *Tatler.*

> Markie, smiling, crumpled one leaf and tore out another. The manner of this correspondence began to appeal to him: deliberation unknown in speaking, boldness quite unrebuked by its own vibrations and, free of that veil of uncertainty and oblivion that falls on the posted letter, the repercussions upon her of all he said. The indiscretions of letter-writing, the intimacies of speech were at once his.

Markie and Emmeline have begun to behave telegraphically. Their jotted notes, dependent on abbreviation, offer a distant foretaste of the text message: *"There are those 2 Serbs"* (137). This improvised code of communication, at once speech and writing, enables them to get to know each other, to entertain each other, to love each other, even, though it is hard to tell exactly. Having declared themselves, as they otherwise would not have done, they break off the exchange. There follows "a pause in which both felt something gained or lost, though neither, perhaps, knew which" (138–39). Have they perhaps located Belacqua's "moving pause," his unit of gress? This is a relationship made in the image of constrained time. It could only ever have come about in transit. Markie and Emmeline have not so much fallen in love, we could say, as fallen in connectivity.

Emmeline, however, is not cut out for transit, or for transit writing. Her unwillingness or inability to remain within the moving pause created by transport as a communications medium casts her back into the novel as novel. She literally drives herself—and Markie—to distraction along, or rather off, the Great North Road. This final, fatal journey begins as transit (she had agreed to give him a lift to King's Cross) and ends as travel. "An immense idea of departure—expresses getting steam up and crashing from termini, liners clearing the docks, the shadows of planes rising, caravans winding out into the first dip of the desert—possessed her spirit, now launched like the long arrow." Indeed, the Great North Road's unfolding recalls that earlier glimpse of a "quite new plan of life" on the plane to Paris.

> Blind with new light she was like somebody suddenly not blind, or, after a miracle, somebody moving perplexed by the absence of pain. Like earth shrinking and sinking, irrelevant, under the rising wings of a plane, love with its unseen plan, its constrictions and urgencies, dropped to a depth below Emmeline, who now looked down unmoved at the shadowy map of her pain. (*TTN* 244)

Poor Markie, creature of transit writing, gets no say at all in the novelistic *Liebestod* Emmeline now stages for his benefit, and at his expense. Before he can grab the wheel, the little car, "strung on speed," has left the road (245).

In theory, transit requires the suspension—for a period of time, between one place and another—of relatively purposeful, relatively unconstrained behavior. To be more precise, the purpose of the constraint it imposes is clear: to get from one place to another as rapidly as possible. But that purpose will itself have to be suspended, by all those in transit who are not members of the crew. If we do not all fasten our seatbelts when instructed and switch off our portable electrical appliances, thus putting ourselves under radical constraint, the plane will never take off. That necessary suspension or constraint of purpose may produce its own opposite: a purposefulness without purpose, hostile to constraint, ready for action. Markie Linkwater, staggering between the tables as the train rocks furiously, understands that Cecilia has signaled him to join her. Who knows what may yet transpire? In Siegfried Kracauer's melancholic view, such fleeting erotic exchanges are all that threads the mutual estrangement at once brought about and expressed by the institution of the hotel lobby. "Remnants of individuals slip into the nirvana of relaxation, faces disappear behind newspapers, and the artificial continuous light illuminates nothing but mannequins. It is the coming and going of unfamiliar people who have become empty forms because they have lost their password, and who now file by as ungraspable flat ghosts." For Kracauer, the hotel lobby is a kind of transit lounge. He might well have included Isherwood's Mr. Norris or Lewis's Victor Stamp among the empty forms that, having lost the password, now file by as ungraspable ghosts. He did also believe, however, that the hotel lobby offered, if not a perspective on or an escape from the everyday, then at least a "groundless distance" from which it could be understood and rendered *aesthetically.* "The person sitting around idly is overcome by a disinterested satisfaction in the contemplation of a world creating itself, whose purposiveness is felt without being associated with any representation of a purpose." According to Kracauer, the genre best adapted to contemplate that ghostly "world creating itself" was detective fiction.[84] We have already seen in this chapter how the conventions of the spy thriller might be thought to provide that "groundless distance" from which the coming and going of unfamiliar people could be understood and rendered aesthetically. We have also seen, however, that a contemplation of those moments during which transit's suspension is itself suspended— for example, at the customs post on the frontier—can result not just in the thriller's felt purposiveness, but in something like the "representation of a purpose." Suspension suspended hints at meaning. Transit writing suspends itself parergically, at once inside and outside narrative. The greatest transit writing—*The Revenge for Love, The House in Paris,* or Henry Green's *Party Going* (1939)—asks how meaning can be made out of the meaningless pauses or suspensions that make up so much of the everyday; or, rather, how meaning *is* made, whether we want it to be or not. They do so by folding parergon back into ergon.

The House in Paris begins and ends parergically in, or with, the moving pauses of transit. In the first chapter, a taxi conveys young Henrietta Mountjoy and her companion for the day, Miss Naomi Fisher, from the Gare du Nord to the house owned by Naomi's bedridden mother; in the last, another taxi conveys her, in the evening of the same day, this time in the company of Ray Forrestier and his potential foster child, Leopold, from the Fisher house to the Gare de Lyon. Each short journey either completes or precedes a longer one by train. At the edges of the novel, transit brackets transit. These double brackets frame the narrative. Henrietta is the ultimate Ruskinian parcel. Her widowed English father has in effect put her in the post to his mother-in-law, Mrs. Arbuthnot, currently residing in Menton. It is her destiny to be picked up and put down again, stowed away in compartments, signed for on delivery; indeed, she has a harder time of it than her own trunk, which has been registered straight through to Menton. She could also be regarded as an e-passenger, a message sent down the wires from one point in the system to another. Neither of the women who have been hired to accompany her on her train journeys are known to her, or to Miss Fisher, whom she herself has never met. As a result, all parties to the delivery are obliged to sport cerise cockades as an identifying mark. Even that does not prove sufficient. "For the lady in whose charge Henrietta had made the journey from London, Miss Fisher's cockade, however, had not been enough; she had insisted on seeing Mrs Arbuthnot's letter which Miss Fisher said she had in her bag" (*HiP* 17). The message sent from London (Henrietta) is cleared for onward transmission by its concordance with the message sent from Menton (Mrs. Arbuthnot's letter). Bowen understood that transport had become a telecommunications medium.

Between Henrietta's arrival at the Gare du Nord and her departure from the Gare de Lyon, suspension is itself suspended. She is still in transit, still constrained: her efforts to see a bit of Paris come to nothing. But the moving pause has ceased to move. It might be truer to say that it has been brought to a halt; that an obstacle has been placed in its path. The obstacle takes the form of young Leopold, Karen Michaelis's son, who has been sent by train (put in the post) from Spezia, where his foster parents live, to the house in Paris, where he is to meet her for the first time. That Leopold's presence in the house and in Henrietta's consciousness will not remain neutral rapidly becomes apparent. Almost his first act is an inadvertent customs inspection. He picks up Henrietta's dispatch case and shakes it so vigorously that its contents spill out across the floor, exposed in all their pitiful objecthood: two apples, a cake of soap, an ebony-backed hairbrush, a *Strand Magazine,* the *Malheurs de Sophie,* and a sponge bag that drops with a "dull thud" (*HiP* 35). The unmovingness of this pause will provoke reflection. It will cut into the flow of information in such a way as to create meaning. Leopold is soon at it again. Noticing that Miss Fisher had left her handbag behind when she took Henrietta upstairs to see her mother, he at once ransacks it for information concerning himself. There are three envelopes in the bag, all addressed to Miss Fisher, two of which contain letters. The act of interception converts data into meaning. The first letter, from his foster mother, reveals what other people know about him, which far exceeds what he knows about himself, and which colors what they think and feel about him. He, in turn, feels mortified. The second letter, from Mrs. Arbuthnot, concerns Henrietta, and is to that extent reassuringly dull. But it, too, proves thoroughly revealing, to us, if not to Leopold. The warmth of its tone makes it clear that remote and eminently respectable Mrs. Arbuthnot has a crush on Miss Fisher, and fond memories of the time they have spent together (42–44). Such are the secrets that a customs inspection brings to light. The third envelope, however, is the acute disappointment. Addressed in a hand that Leopold recognizes as his mother's, it contains no letter. All he can do is to know it, provisionally, as information. He presses it to his forehead, seeking by telegraphic-telepathic mimesis to reconstitute the original letter, the original act of transmission (45). Leopold's interceptions, like those of the customs inspector, have created the possibility of meaning. But he has not yet become enough of an obstacle, either to himself or to other people, to realize it.

The unmoving pause, during which Henrietta, Leopold, and the Fishers await developments, occupies the novel's first and third sections, each titled "The Present." It is itself suspended for the duration of the novel's lengthy middle section ("The Past") by an account of Karen's affair with Max Ebhart, at that time Naomi's fiancé, of which Leopold is the product. That account supplies, as it were, the content of the letter missing from the envelope addressed in Karen's hand. It supplies, "on the plane of potential rather than merely likely behaviour" (67), the explanation of his origin and circumstances Karen might have given Leopold, had she shown up at the house in Paris.

The account begins in transit: in the realm of information rather than of meaning. Karen, seeking some respite from the pressures of her engagement to Ray Forrestier, arrives by boat in Cork to visit her Aunt Violet. The visit proves rather too much of an unmoving pause. Disconcerted by the blanketing "calm" (79) of her aunt's house, and even more so by the "unmoved stillness and sadness" (83) with which her aunt regards her own less than remarkable life, Karen finds consolation, but little more than that, in solitary walks and expeditions to the post box. As if to reinscribe her as a creature of transit, Bowen devotes several pages to a description of the otherwise inconsequential meal she shares with a woman known only as Yellow Hat on the ferry back to Fishguard (90–95). Yellow Hat, it might be noted, drops into the chair opposite Karen with something of the aplomb Markie Linkwater had shown in taking his chance on the Milan-Boulogne express, in *To the North;* her connection to Karen, like his to Cecilia, owes a good deal to the irregular movement of their respective vehicles. Journeys by boat bracket Karen's visit to Aunt Violet, just as they will bracket the two primary occasions of her affair with Max. Karen and Max fall as much in connectivity as in love.

To put it another way, the difference between adults and children, in Bowen's novels, is that adults are in transit *consciously*. They make meaning out of the occasions uniquely afforded by existence in or as a moving pause, a suspension. Max and Karen discover and declare their feelings for each other when he is in London with Naomi. Four weeks later, he invokes transit's extraterritoriality by ringing her up and inviting her to lunch in Boulogne. The brief phone conversation, as laconic as any of those examined in Chapter 1, makes a Cecilia of her (132–33). As a result of this meeting, Max subsequently crosses over to Folkestone, and they spend the night together in a hotel in Hythe. It is in the pause between the third and fourth crossings, between Max's going over and coming back, that meaning arises. "Having done as she knew she must she did not think there would be a child: all the same, the idea of you, Leopold, began to be present with her" (151–52). The abrupt lapse into direct address, outing the implied author, establishes "The Past" as parergon to the ergon of "The Present": as an introduction to Leopold, and his encounter with Henrietta. Or is it the other way round, since the two halves of "The Present" bracket "The Past"? It would be more accurate to say that each narrative both frames and is framed by its counterpart. As A. S. Byatt puts it in her illuminating introduction to the Vintage Classics edition, "the woman, Karen, and the man, Max, are continuations of the children Leopold and Henrietta, although they are also means to the re-definition, the restatement, of the child Leopold, in the light of our knowledge of them" (*HiP* 12).

The man and woman are in transit *consciously*. The redefinition or restatement they bring about requires a knowledge of transit produced in and by transit. Karen and Max, meeting in Folkestone, take a taxi to Hythe. One indication that something is in the wind is a brusque manifesto for semi-synthesis: one of the ways in which the first media age sought to distinguish itself, as I have already shown at length in this book. Confronted by "broken weather," Max buys himself a mackintosh in Folkestone. "The mackintosh, with its new rubbery smell, slid about during the drive out, showing its check lining and the chain inside the collar to hang it up by" (149). Connie Chatterley and Mellors they are not; but the taxi is in fact conveying them into techno-primitivism. Theirs, however, is a techno-primitivism produced in and by transit. Karen feels, for the first time, that she is alone with Max.

Till today, they had not, when alone, ever been two; always either three or one. Now, what they did was cut off from any other thing, their silence related to them only. Tamarisks flying past the rainy windows were some dream—not your own, but a dream you have heard described. Not what they both say—the sea, the bare hill, the railway arch, trees, villas—but the sense of *not* seeing these stamped their drive for her. (150)

In transit, the view from the window holds no interest. Like Woolf, Karen and Max have been "vitreated" on their seats. Unlike Cecilia and Markie, they do not text each other. But their silence constitutes a knowledge of just how far they have come. That knowledge made in transit's moving pause will make the meaning that is Leopold, in the unmoving pause of a night in a hotel in Hythe. The next day, they go for a walk in the suburbs. Max, it is true, does not dance naked in the rain wearing nothing but his mackintosh. But their separation from the world is almost as emphatic as that of Connie and Mellors. "Karen, walking by Max, felt more isolated with him, more cut off from her own country than if they had been in Peru" (157).

The episode functions as a meta-parergon. It alerts us to its own capacity to frame other comparable episodes. So, when Ray Forrestier escorts Henrietta to the Gare de Lyon in a taxi, with Leopold in tow, we expect it to be raining, and we expect Henrietta and Leopold to behave a bit like Karen and Max. Henrietta, still unreconciled to transit, looks out of the window with "heartbroken animation." "What a party to miss!" Leopold, by contrast, looking neither to left nor right, appears to her to be "holding off Paris almost violently" (232). Although by no means silent, and escorted by an adult, they, too, are in a sense alone together for the first time. The meaning produced by that knowledge finally arises on the platform at the Gare de Lyon, after Ray has completed the exchange of signals with Henrietta's companion on the next stage of her journey ("I am Miss Fisher, virtually"). Henrietta converts information into meaning by offering her cockade to Leopold as a gift.

"You said you liked the colour," said Henrietta, hurriedly, to Leopold.
  "Yes, I like it; it reminds me of you." (236–37)

Not love, exactly, perhaps: but an exchange, nonetheless, arising out of the exchange of information, of something more than information. The children can be seen to have restated *themselves* as adult. There is enough gress in this transit, enough obstacle, for meaning to arise out of it that would not otherwise have arisen, as Henrietta and Leopold represent their feelings about each other to each other. They do not yet need to be cool. But they are certainly capable of it.

After Modernism

Elleke Boehmer has drawn some highly instructive parallels between the "networked" political and literary commentaries of ca. 1900 and those of our own postcolonial (or post-postcolonial) moment. Boehmer describes an "incremental" globalization, already under way by 1900, which we have not yet got to the end of. At the beginning of the twentieth century, she points out, the "world" of the British Empire "was wired as never before—at that time by telegraph cables, and, more metaphorically, by railway networks and steamship travel. Moreover, British and colonial subjects at the time imagined themselves in this way, as interconnected, cross-cabled, while many of their activities and aspirations were informed by the existence of cross-empire networks." Within these networks, as Boehmer's chosen examples richly demonstrate, stretched "intertextual webs" of metaphor and image that gave rise not only to the consolidation of network, but to varieties of critique. Indeed, she boldly proposes that the "Edwardian imperialist collage text" *Scouting for Boys* (1908) anticipated T. S. Eliot's *The Waste Land* in its fragmentariness.[85] More recently, she has made the case for a "networked" colonial Modernism (Mulk Raj Anand, Katherine Mansfield, Claude McKay, William Plomer, Jean Rhys, and others) shaped in the "crucible" of "outsider colonial experience."[86] While I agree entirely with her emphasis on incremental globalization, I believe that the "increment" constituted by the rapid and widespread development during the late 1920s of telephony and radio, in particular, rendered Modernism's diagnostic fragmentariness obsolete. Other techniques supervened, as an acknowledgment of, and resistance to, information overload.

John Ruskin did not consider going by railroad as travel at all: "it is merely 'being sent' to a place, and very little different from becoming a parcel; the next step to it would of course be telegraphic transport."[87] By the end of the First World War, it was by no means uncommon to speak of "communication through space by means of wireless telegraphy and telephony and aircraft."[88] This chapter has been about the experience of transit, which today even more than in the 1930s is that not just of being sent to a place, but of being communicated telegraphically or, rather, to follow the main drift of my argument concerning the first media age, telephonically. We are no longer even parcels; we are packages of data. Airlines and governments signal us from departure to arrival by means of passenger tracking and e-Borders systems. The steady expansion of the intricacy and reach of electronic media since the mid-nineteenth century has immeasurably enhanced the capacity of transport networks to communicate in both senses of the term. While we are on the move, we reconfigure ourselves as messages, which send and receive messages. In the process, we create new techno-social spaces and protocols. In 2012, the Czech car manufacturer Skoda brought the developments I have described in Chapter 5 to a culmination of some kind when it marketed its latest model, the Citigo, as a "communication tool" replete with apps. The purpose of this social medium posing as a vehicle was, the advertisements proclaimed, "to meet your friends in real life." The real-life meeting has become an adjunct to virtual sociability. If we are to survive all this being-communicated, we will need some of the sangfroid with which Bowen endows Henrietta and Leopold.

Conclusion

THIS BOOK HAD TWO AIMS. The first was to demonstrate the extent to which an awareness of the proliferation of new media and new material substances increasingly suffused British society and culture in the years between 1927 and 1939. Rumors to the contrary notwithstanding, many of the writers who came into their own during that period looked outward from these islands, and forward into a future in which information would flow further and faster than energy. Their work continues to remind us that communications technology is an attitude before it is a machine or a set of codes. I have argued that the two most consequential manifestations of the historically specific technological attitude that took shape in British society and culture in the late 1920s were the telephone and the emergent global transit system reconfigured as a connective rather than a representational medium. My second aim was to characterize a literary meta-attitude: the attitude taken in literature to the attitude exemplified by the proliferation of connective uses of media. Awareness of the profound differences in principle between the use of media primarily to represent and the use of media primarily to connect fed into a new understanding of the technological mediation of experience in general. The meta-attitude thus provoked in literature was a prototype of what we would now call cool. Writers represented the slack in the connective systems that had begun to put in place a new global order by developing versions of techno-primitivism, or by imagining an informal sociability that could under other circumstances have become the basis for formal political solidarity, or, sometimes, just by going slow (the detour through parergon). This performative

slackness cannot simply be regarded as late Modernist. It is far more interesting than that. In conclusion, I want to indicate, first, that much else of
interest remains to be investigated along similar lines; and second, that,
taken together, these lines of inquiry may yet lead further than we might
expect into our own era of digitalization and "convergence culture."[1] *Lady
Chatterley's Lover, Living,* "Consider this and in our time," *The Midnight
Bell, To the North,* "On a Raised Beach," *Company Parade, A House in
Paris, May Day, The Revenge for Love, Journey to the Border, The Years,
Finnegans Wake:* these are survivor's guides we still need.

Illusion and Reality (1937), by Christopher Caudwell, the most brilliant
English-speaking literary Marxist of the period, includes a stalwart defense of something like techno-primitivism as a blueprint for a revolutionary literature. A book about poetry, though scarcely about poets or poems,
despite its awareness of I. A. Richards's *Principles of Literary Criticism*
(1924) and William Empson's *Seven Types of Ambiguity* (1930), *Illusion
and Reality* was still in press when Caudwell left Britain to fight in Spain,
where he was killed in February 1937. Its epigraph, from Friedrich Engels—
"Freedom is the recognition of necessity"—reveals the extent to which
the Marxism of the period made explicit a philosophical frame of reference for understandings of cool that I have for the most part left implicit.
For Caudwell, art and science, although bourgeois accomplishments
through and through, remain valuable this side of the revolution in so far
as they exploit the slack in the capitalist system. "Art is the expression of
man's freedom in the world of feeling, just as science is the expression of
man's freedom in the world of sensory perception, because both are conscious of the necessities of their worlds and can change them—art the
world of feeling or inner reality, science the world of phenomena or outer
reality." Following Marx and Engels, Caudwell proposed a materialism
that, countering the scientific reduction of matter to an "empty wave-
system," would once again surround the world of sensory perception with a
"sensuous poetic glamour." "Poetry restores life and value to matter, and
puts back the genotype into the world from which it was banished." The
primitivism infusing this approach has been roundly condemned. But it is,
I would argue, a *techno*-primitivism. Caudwell concludes that, like culture
and society as a whole, "poetry has moved away from concrete living by the
development of its technique." However, the fetishization of technique
need not make of poetry a luxury item for a "few chosen spirits," as long as
we recall that poetic technique belongs to the body's rhythms, understood

in and through imitation, and to that original prosthesis or tool, the words spoken by one person to another. So the movement forward from bourgeois culture will at the same time require a movement back to the "social solidarity of primitive communism," but one that gathers up whatever else has happened in the (long) interim, including "freedom, individuation and consciousness." "This change in the technique of poetry is a reflection of the way art returns into the life from which it has flown away, bringing back with it all the development produced by the cleavage." In almost Brechtian fashion, Caudwell argued that cleavage's most striking product in his own time had been the development of new media. Broadcasting, for example, would give to poetry a "new collective appearance" by ensuring that the "individuality of the actor" no longer conflicted with the "poetic instant." "It seems also (though this is bare conjecture) that the film, because it realises the highest possibilities of the bourgeois stage in a more collective, more richly powerful and more flexible form, will only come into its own in communism."[2] Caudwell's primitive communism was a primitive communism to be created after, and as the result of, bourgeois technology, bourgeois art, and bourgeois science. In the long interim, which was where he still found himself as he embarked for Spain, techno-primitivism's sensuous poetic glamour would have to do. As I pointed out in my Introduction, theories of cool often take an ethnographic turn.

Of course, Caudwell did not advocate cool. He understood that by the end of his life Lawrence had settled for freedom in spite of, rather than through, "social relations," but mistook the nature and function of the primitivism motivating texts like *Lady Chatterley's Lover* and *Sketches of Etruscan Places*.[3] The collective novel should perhaps have appealed to him by its coaxing of informal social solidarity into formal political solidarity. But, although he did commend the "collectiveness" of the novel as a literary form, he seems to have shown no interest in any of the writers I discussed in Chapter 4.[4] *Illusion and Reality* makes a powerful case in theory for the capacity of bourgeois art and science to exploit slack in the capitalist system, as a way to transform both themselves and it. However, its failure to provide specific examples of a forward-looking literature is matched by its failure to take adequate account of the extent to which, as I argue consistently in this book, new media had become a force for mobile privatization.

It would certainly be possible to expand that argument further, to take in, for example, the genre of detective fiction, which I have barely touched on. As is well known, detective fiction enjoyed huge popular and critical success during the period between the wars. On the whole, the genre's success, then and since, has been attributed to its social and literary conservatism. What these stories conserve, by tone as well as narrative outcome, is the first of J. B. Priestley's three Englands: the "Old England" of cathedrals, manor houses, inns, parsons, squires, highways and byways. Inward and backward looking, they dramatize acts of detection the purpose of which is to restore order to ways of life disrupted by modernity. "O Poirot, deliver us," intones Auden's *The Orators*.[5] And the many and various Poirots put forward by the fiction of the period did just that, Valentine Cunningham adds: they supplied meaning and value to the anxious inhabitants of "an otherwise absurd, murderously contingent universe."[6] But if contingency really was what modern murder had become, then a fiction substantially devoted to modern murder would surely have to sample contingency before delivering us from it. That, too, I shall argue, the Poirots did.

Poirot's creator, Agatha Christie, has long been regarded as the chronicler and champion of a version of Old England. But that does not seem right. In her groundbreaking, contrarian study of Christie as a "popular modernist," Alison Light identifies in the most celebrated whodunits of the era an attitude akin to cool. "In Christie's world," Light argues, "nothing is sacred. Crime makes not for tragedy, nor even for the shudders of melodrama, but oddly and startlingly, for a laugh." The brightness of tone evident in her first collection of stories, *Poirot Investigates* (1925), distinguishes it as writing for and about a younger generation. Outlasting the Jazz Age, Christie's brightness of tone evolved into a method, a way to conceive a new "England." In this new England, melodrama, or sensationalism, was simply "bad form": uncool, and ineptly crafted. Poirot himself, though scarcely youthful, endured in novel after novel: cosmopolitan, suavely Modernist in taste, a knowing travesty of Old English masculinity. The attitude he exemplified became a creed. "Whodunits," Light observes,

> belong to those "designs for living" which became available across the social classes between the wars, those new and modern productions of English social life which "theatricalized" it. Like film and radio and cut-price fashion, the whodunit offered a representation of English behaviour and character which could be copied by anyone who took the trouble to learn the right lines or surround themselves with the right props.

In its sampling of a murderously contingent universe, detective fiction spoke primarily not to Cunningham's anxious Poirot-cultists, but to "a readership reconciled to the present, unfrightened by change, and confidently domestic."[7] We remember Ross McKibbin's argument that a "new" middle class not only more numerous but more broadly technical and scientific in outlook had begun to express its self-confidence by taking an interest in a "literature of modernity."[8] The whodunits of the period should be understood as at once propaganda for and a survivor's guide to the technological mediation of experience.

It is very much to the point, as Light notes, that of the twenty-four books Christie published during the 1930s, her most prolific decade, a majority should involve the experience of travel. In these stories, the journey itself, the mere tricky business of getting from one place to another, "offers the best metaphor for the disruptive process inaugurated by a murder and for the founding of a society of strangers who come together as its result." Of course, this particular literature of modernity, unlike that which concerns McKibbin, was not a literature of public life. The informal social solidarity somewhat unreliably fostered by the corpse-strewn Orient Expresses of the era did not constitute the basis for formal political solidarity. Instead, being under suspicion became a courtship ritual. For Christie, as Light puts it, murder is a marriage bureau.[9] In detective fiction, as in thrillers and screwball comedy, time-space compression proves expansive. Mechanized transport slows lives down long enough for mutual attraction to take root. For Christie, it happened one night, *all the time.*

Under the right circumstances, detective fiction assumed the aura of transit writing. Those circumstances were no more and no less than air travel. Of course, airplanes added a welcome dash of dernier cri to the whodunit, while any writer worth his or her salt would relish the chance to insert corpses plausibly into spaces as inhospitable to lethal assault as a cockpit or a luxury compartment. Mass transit, however, like the telephone, changed the game. Furthermore, one of the era's most fundamental discoveries, as we saw in Chapter 5, was of transport as medium. Transit understood not just as a passing across or through, but as the process or system by which passage across or through had been organized, did its bit to change the detection game. Poirot is a sleuth for the information age. Or at least he is in *Death in the Clouds* (1935), which concerns a corpse found slumped in a seat in first-class accommodation on the midday service from Le Bourget to Croydon. The terms I developed in Chapter 5 for the customs inspection as transit writing's mise en abîme may help us to grasp this change of approach. We will need to bear in mind, as well, that national borders were no longer exclusively terrestrial. The proliferation of air forces during the First World War had put the question of what constituted "airspace" firmly on the agenda. It was widely understood that new government agencies would be required for "aerial police" and "aerial customs." "Marking out routes with aerial ports and aerodromes, lights, and pilotage" might furthermore lead to the establishment of official bodies with duties roughly corresponding to Trinity House in maritime matters.[10]

Poirot, it turns out, is traveling on that fateful midday service from Le Bourget to Croydon. Noting the favorable treatment accorded to him by the police, a fellow passenger remarks that he must be a "customs spy." Already installed in Croydon aerodrome, it also turns out, and ready to take charge of the investigation, is Poirot's old acquaintance Inspector Japp. The inspector has been after "rather a big bug in the smuggling line." From the outset, then, both official and unofficial sleuthing is to be understood in this case as a form of customs inspection. What that might entail soon becomes apparent when Poirot very firmly insists that the police should make an "exact list" of all the passengers' possessions. It is a sensitive matter, of course. As Inspector Japp points out, one or two of the better-connected among them might well "cut up rough," like Agatha Runcible in *Vile Bodies,* to the extent, even, of getting a question put in the House of Commons about police brutality. But Poirot knows that the Le Bourget to Croydon flight has communicated data as well as persons and goods, that the persons and goods *are* data. His job is to hold up the flow of information so that meaning emerges from it. "You do like making things difficult, don't you?" Japp remarks. Precisely. The detective no longer interprets. Like a customs official, he halts information in its tracks, holds it up to view, re-materializes it. The novel's crucial chapter displays the police's "exact list" of possessions for the benefit not just of Poirot and Japp, but of the reader. Absorbing that information at leisure, at our own tempo, we can at least attempt to figure out who done it. Interpretation begins here, on the basis of the temporarily halted dataflow. Japp, too much of a customs official, perhaps, or too Edwardian, deduces an incriminating lack of "moral restraint" from the fact that one of the passengers has smuggled cocaine. Poirot, more modern, cooler, bides his time. His aim is not to suspend transit understood as a mechanism for the production of places as nodes within networks of wealth and power so much as to exploit the slack in it created by a bit of police brutality. His own deductions will rest on evidence generated by the global electronic connectivity that everywhere reinforces that mechanism. There is nothing more romantic in the modern world, he claims, than the transatlantic telephone and the telegraphed photograph.[11]

In 1930s detective fiction, the airplane brings with it an emphasis on connectivity, and on the exploitation of slack in the system as the best or indeed only way to bring criminals to justice. Light includes Margery Allingham's Albert Campion among the New Model detectives, men whose character traits are likely to include "a narcissistic delicacy, inane giggling, and even laziness."[12] In *The Fashion in Shrouds* (1938), Campion finds himself on the spot when Sir Raymond Ramillies is found dead in the cockpit of the plane that is to convey him to Ulangi, on the West Coast of Africa, of which he is the governor. It is the New Model detective's exemplary dilemma. "A dead man in a gilded aeroplane in the midst of a crowd, with a broadcast imminent, an African flight about to begin, and in authority a Cabinet minister who does not wish to be convinced that anything unpleasant has occurred, is a responsibility which absorbs all one's attention." What absorbs Campion's attention with increasing urgency is *system:* a "machinery" or "organized flavour" or "unostentatious organization" that incorporates both a conspiracy to commit murder and a conspiracy to ignore it. Information flows so rapidly through and across this system, and in so many directions simultaneously, that it is no longer possible to tell the conspiracies apart. Campion's job, as the "only disinterested agent" around, is to halt the flow. Not for nothing has he witnessed Ramillies's last act on earth, an "obvious" attempt to smuggle a particularly elaborate rifle out of the country. Campion, like Poirot, delivers. But Allingham goes a good deal further than Christie in establishing the technological dimension of the system within which her protagonist is obliged to operate, and which he must turn to his advantage. Chapter 19 of *The Fashion in Shrouds*, dramatically enhancing Waugh's experiment in *Vile Bodies*, consists of thirty-eight phone calls made by a wide variety of characters, simultaneous or consecutive, successful and unsuccessful, without contextualization or commentary. These conversations and non-conversations (the intent to communicate counts as communication) neither advance the plot significantly nor yield significant meaning. What they do instead is enact, and so represent, the flow of information through and across a system.[13] By the standards of the detective fiction of this or any other period, the chapter is a startling tour de force, as subtle and as far-reaching in its representation of connectivity as any other text I have discussed in this book. It proves that the genre did indeed slip occasionally into transit writing.

In terms of background, temperament, and intellectual ambition, Christopher St. John Sprigg was about as remote from Christie and Allingham as it is possible to get. His seven detective novels, unlike theirs, have long since dropped out of print, and out of view. A journalist by trade, he ran an aeronautics publishing company with his brother. Aeronautics, in fact, was something of a passion. His most expansive book on the subject, *British Airways*, first published in March 1934, offers an insider's view of the process I describe in my Introduction: the reconfiguration of empire as an integrated space of flows, from the mid-1920s onward, by means of the establishment of worldwide air routes and telecommunications networks. "Already the story of Imperial Airways is impressive. In its tenth year, ending March 31st 1933, its air liners flew 2,030,993 miles on regular air routes, and carried 60,966 passengers. The letters carried amounted to 8,300,075." For Sprigg, too, the Air Mail was at once agent and emblem of connectivity. With absolute consistency, he put the emphasis on system: the grid of routes, the navigational aids, the teams of support staff. Air routes were to him what the radio had been to Lawrence: a system to which there is no outside. Before long, he predicted in concluding his book, no two places in the world would be "much more than a day's flying apart."[14] *British Airways* was reprinted in December 1934. By that time, Sprigg had discovered Marxism. The following year, he wrote the first draft of a manuscript that was eventually to be published as *Illusion and Reality* after his death on the battlefield in Spain, under the pseudonym of Christopher Caudwell. In the conclusion to *that* book, from which I have already quoted at some length, he took strong exception to detective novels as opium for the masses, like jazz and religion.[15] But the best of his detective novels drew extensively on the aeronautical passion displayed in his propaganda for Imperial Airways to delve rather more deeply into the intricacies of mobile privatization than his literary theory had done.

Death of an Airman (1934) concerns a racket in which cocaine is smuggled from France into Britain in bundles of newspapers. We learn that newspaper delivery by airplane is a popular advertising stunt. "The idea is to have a few copies available in a foreign country early on the day of issue. It impresses readers travelling abroad with the circulation of the paper and its general up-to-dateness, and they talk about it when they get home." The smugglers simply conceal packets of cocaine in copies of *La Gazette Quotidienne* distributed by air throughout Britain. The criminal mastermind gleefully explains that the "genius in the scheme was, of course, the use of air transport, so that the drug was in the hands of the consumer before the end of the day on which it left the centre." Under such a scheme, he adds, none of the couriers need know that they are shipping anything other than newsprint. Its genius lay in the seamless integration of legal and illegal flows (of goods, of data). The murder of the one courier who did become suspicious creates a new flow of information around and over the site of an accident that may not have been an accident. The detective's job, in these circumstances, is to halt the flow of information long enough for its different strands to be disentangled. So it is that Sprigg, like Christie, puts a detective investigating the murder in harness with another already investigating the distribution of drugs. They begin to get at the truth about murder by interrupting the flow of information that determines how the drugs are distributed. It is worth noting that for Sprigg, as for Christie, murder is a marriage bureau. In this case, the premarital pair of suspects—an Australian bishop and his flying instructor—behave on occasion as though they were in *It Happened One Night*.[16] When there is no longer any outside to system, cool is the best you can hope for. Caudwell would not have settled for that; Sprigg does.

Just as there are other genres of fiction that merit consideration, so there are other media, and other forms of transport. I have already discussed in passing the association of telephony with the London underground system in Storm Jameson's *Company Parade* and George Buchanan's *Entanglement*. One could add Rose Macaulay's *Keeping Up Appearances*, in which suburbanite Mrs. Arthur, visiting London for the sales, rings her husband and offspring from telephone booths in a succession of tube stations: Knightsbridge, Piccadilly Circus, Bond Street, Sloane Square, each associated with a separate swath of purchases.[17] Indeed, the London underground loomed large in the literature of the period.[18] Notorious at least since George Gissing's *The Odd Women* (1893) and Henry James's *The Wings of the Dove* (1902) as an opportunity for sexual encounter, it became in the early 1930s a site for displays of both cool and uncool.

Alfred Hitchcock's *Rich and Strange* (1931) includes a quietly compelling scene set on a tube train packed with office-weary commuters. The heavens open as the dim and sluggish hero leaves work, and he soon finds himself in the subway next to a blond in a beret and a white raincoat, who appears (inexplicably, one might think) to cruise him. He manages to ignore her completely. His antics amuse her, evidently, but there is a hint of pleasurable speculation in her glance, too, an assessment, perhaps, of what he might yet amount to. And that is it. She departs from the film as abruptly as she entered, taking with her pretty much all that is rich and strange about it. For, although it was retitled *East of Shanghai* for U.S. distribution, and does indeed include scenes of seduction in exotic places during the regenerative world tour undertaken by the hero and his wife, it is by Hitchcock's standards relentlessly dull. Its only tremor of sexual magnetism is the glance almost invisibly thrown in transit in the opening scene.

In *The Waves* (1931), Virginia Woolf identified use of the underground with the two protagonists out of six who could be said to cultivate sexual promiscuity, Neville and Jinny. Neville's brief reflections on the underground as underworld are portentously Eliotic. For him, it is little more than a theme-park ride equipped with special effects left over from *The Waste Land* (a "hollow wind" roars across "desert boulders"). "The descent into the Tube was like death," he intones, sounding now like the Eliot of "Burnt Norton" (1935), who gloomily contemplates the "strained time-ridden faces / Distracted from distraction by distraction": "Men and bits of paper, whirled by the cold wind / That blows before and after time."[19] Neville, however, likes to "push out into the heterogeneous crowd." He likes to be "buffeted." His underground journey prompts thoughts about love's duration, and durability, that might not otherwise have been prompted.[20]

Jinny's long rumination in and about Piccadilly Circus station proves yet more specific, since it concerns the consequences of the fundamental re-design and refurbishment the station had undergone in 1928.[21] A crucial part of that overhaul had been the introduction of two flights of escalators leading down to the platforms. Escalators began as a Coney Island novelty ride in the 1890s, but soon proliferated in factories and department stores. When they came into operation at Earls Court station, in October 1911, the London Electric Railway found a man with a wooden leg to demonstrate how safe they were (passengers tempted to inquire how the wooden leg had come about in the first place took the lift instead). Earls Court soon became a destination for joyriders. Something of this uncertainty of status and function clung to the escalator even after it had long been established as the underground system's most distinctive portal, and a fixture in the stores. The first set Charlie Chaplin installed in the Lone Star Studio in Hollywood in March 1916 was a department store complete with moving stairway. Escalator mayhem propels *The Floorwalker*, one of his sharpest comedies of the period. Jinny, however, takes heart from the expressiveness encouraged, in and through constraint, by time spent on an escalator.

As I noted in Chapter 3, she declares her "adhesion" to the pulsating, opportunity-laden world the underground station constitutes, coolly resynthesizing herself as she rises up again to the surface.[22]

Such adhesion became, if by no means commonplace, then recognizable. The first section of Louis MacNeice's *Autumn Journal* (1939) concludes with MacNeice arriving by train at Waterloo Station, and entering the underground:

> And so to London and down the ever-moving
>   Stairs
> Where a warm wind blows the bodies of men together
> And blows apart their complexes and cares.[23]

The poem tips over travel's edge into transit, into suspension and constraint. The outcome of the speaker's impending conversion into a mere parcel or message remains at this point uncertain. Complexes and cares ought indeed to be blown away. But blown *apart?* It was not just the commute that impended, of course, in the autumn of 1938. Still, *Autumn Journal* as a whole suggests that MacNeice, too, like Bowen and Lewis, was learning to slow down. If so, his warm wind serves as a reproof to Eliot's cold one.

My contention has been that the world changed, just a little, in 1927. It certainly changed again in 1939. The most immediate effect of the outbreak of war was abruptly to reverse some of the key developments I have been tracing. "Mobile privatization" does not really cut it as a Churchillian battle cry. For example, when war broke out, the General Post Office moved swiftly to *discourage* people from using the telephone.

The system's full capacity was required for civil defense and other military functions. It would continue to serve as a social medium, of course, but was no longer advertised in those terms. Posters reconfigured connectivity's dominant non-ideographic ideograph, the swath of wires, by introducing the figure of the stalwart repairman.

The addition of meaning could scarcely be more explicit. The repairman's vital work becomes a metaphor for dedicated effort in general. Its vitality is a *human* vitality. The battered soles of the repairman's boots, no less than his muscular pose, speak of sweat, at the very least, and possibly blood, too. Meaning, we could say, has been reclaimed from information. The new emphasis was necessary, because warfare rationed the supply of connectivity, among much else. Another key connective technology significantly affected by the outbreak of war was television. The BBC's television

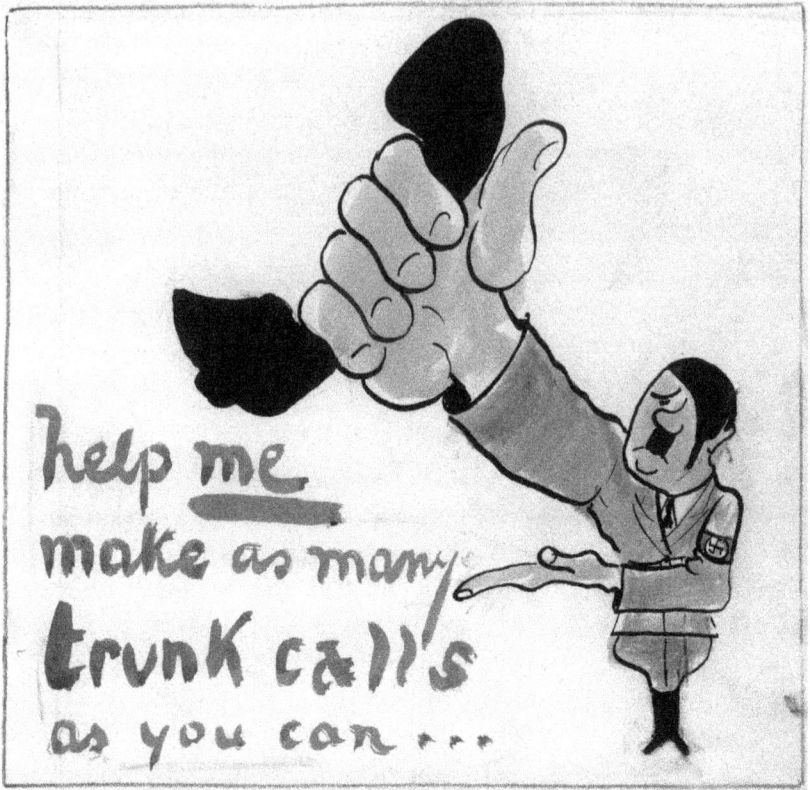

"Help *me*. Make as many trunk calls as you can." Draft version of GPO poster. Courtesy of BT Heritage. Post 109/601.

service was suspended on September 1, 1939, because of fear that the transmissions might guide enemy bombers to the center of London.

For obvious reasons, the duress of conflict put a premium upon meaning. The propaganda war against Nazi Germany invoked a largely pretechno-logical and even preindustrial Britain as the source of values worth dying for. Think of the difference in tone between two Michael Powell films made ten years apart. In *The Love Test* (1935), as we saw in Chapter 3, experiments conducted on celluloid in the laboratory had made it possible to conceive the resynthesizing of heterosexual romance, and a good deal else besides. In *I Know Where I'm Going* (1945), by contrast, the generic plastic that sheathes both the dress in which the heroine is due to marry

"He is doing vital war work . . . and so are you." GPO poster. Courtesy of BT Heritage. Post 109/596.

the chairman of Consolidated Chemical Industries, and the dream images of death-in-life it prompts in her, must be rejected, along with the hapless chairman, in favor of a rough embrace by a tweedy Scottish feudalism set to ceilidh and ancestral curses. This is primitivism without any techno- in it at all. And there was a further reason for the volte-face. It was not just that the national war effort had revalued tweedy Scottish feudalism. It was that the rapid proliferation of new and wholly synthetic materials from the mid-1930s onward, and during wartime in particular, had altered fundamentally the delicate balance struck in semi-synthetics like cellophane and cellulose acetate between nature and culture, in effect normalizing chemical creation ex nihilo. The duress of conflict accelerated the developments I described in Chapters 2 and 3 to the point that they became something else altogether. The "age of plastic" had begun in earnest. Some way other than techno-primitivism would have to be found to exploit the slack in the system. MacNeice, returning to London from New York in 1940, saw in the gas mask with which he had been issued the "paradox of technology." "It begins with sheer creative imagination and it ends—at least that is how it

looks in 1940—in a brute and random necessity, negation of human freedom."[24] Little chance, then, for Lady Chatterleys to dance in the rain in
their rubber tennis shoes. Apart from anything else, the Japanese army
was about to invade Malaya. It would not have made sense to try to extend
my argument beyond 1939.

The histories that my own account of literature in the first media age has
been shadowing tend to draw the line, or a line, at around the middle of the
century. For some, the key event was the arrival, in the immediate after-
math of war, of information theory, or, rather, as Michel Serres has put it,
of a "new organon," which would reconcile an account of thermodynamic
process with an account of the ways in which communication takes place.[25]
According to Bruce Clarke, this new organon constituted a threshold in
the development of modern techno-science.[26] Introducing the essays collected in *From Energy to Information*, Clarke and Linda Henderson draw
out the cultural consequences of energy's demise as an organizing concept.
By the 1960s, they propose, a "distinct shift towards *information* as the
prime stimulus for art and other forms of creative expression" was under
way. "Visual and literary representations of energy and entropy were to be
superseded by a range of data-scapes, by artistic installations and comput-
erized video screens that wired energy technology directly into the display
of images and texts."[27] For Alan Liu, in his history of cool, a threshold was
reached in the 1950s with the computerization of the workplace. Drawing
on a wealth of evidence, Liu describes the development of the information
economy from an emphasis on "automating" (1880s–1940s)—information
applied to the control of matter—to an emphasis on "informating" (1950s–
1980s), or information applied to the control of information, with today's
networks being something else again.[28] The shape of a modern information-
processing society had become apparent in rough outline, James Beniger
concludes, by the end of the Second World War.[29] I have consistently
sought to distinguish the literary meta-attitude I have defined in this book
from Modernism. Whether that meta-attitude survived the full onset of an
information-processing society—and, if so, whether its postwar versions
require to be distinguished from what has loosely come to be known as
the "postmodern"—are questions which lie beyond its scope. In my view, the
"postmodern" is about as uncool as it gets. But the sober point to be made
is that we should not expect too much continuity.

For example, and speaking rather more narrowly, there can be little
doubt that television's displacement of cinema as the dominant mass me-

dium during the 1950s fundamentally altered the media ecology I have described in this book. Such an alteration had consequences for literature that are only just beginning to be understood. For example, the theory and practice of radio informing Samuel Beckett's work for that medium originated in the 1930s, but underwent a series of significant modifications during and after the Second World War.[30] Media ecologies evolve, often by small-scale but nonetheless decisive changes of emphasis. Julian Murphet has shown persuasively that the theory and practice of analog monochrome television, a medium itself on the cusp of decline by the mid-1960s, informed not just the play Beckett wrote for it at the time, *Eh Joe*, but his writing in general. That medium requires the instantaneous synchronization of two distinct signals, image (television) and sound (radio). Beckett understood this "radical disjunction" to exemplify the entire media landscape of the postwar era, in which "a semi-autonomous Voice could be said to have floated free from all anchors of embodiment."[31] The media ecology within which Beckett's thinking about face and voice came to fruition was a postwar ecology dominated by television.

All that said, however, I have found it hard at times to resist the temptation to draw parallels between the ways the new media of the 1920s and 1930s sometimes appeared to people at the time and the way the new media of our own era sometimes appear to us. Between 1927 and 1939, the telephone was marketed as a social medium not all that dissimilar, in scope and function, to Facebook. There was a moment when television could have become more like Skype than the news and entertainment behemoth of the second half of the twentieth century. If Markie Linkwater, in Bowen's *To the North*, had brought his smartphone with him on the flight to Paris, he would surely have texted Emmeline that *"There are those 2 Serbs."*[32] And so on. What all these examples point to is the emergence of connectivity as the principle that would henceforth shape the technological mediation of experience in general: that is, the ways in which human beings engage with the world and each other not only when speaking on the telephone, or gazing at a screen, alone or in company, but when on the move. The very idea of representation came under challenge, from the 1920s onward. The threat (which we might alternatively regard as an opportunity) has never been greater than it is now. The literature of the interwar period may not be continuous with that of our own. But it remains exemplary.

What will happen to representation, if a digitally enhanced connectivity ever establishes itself as the dominant principle in media use? It is a question we might want to ask about the sixty hours or so of video uploaded to You-Tube every minute. If a story is a representation of a sequence of events from which meaning can be deduced, then YouTube is a narrative medium. But that is not quite all there is to it, as rapidly becomes apparent if you view the first-ever YouTube video, uploaded at 8:27 p.m. on Saturday, April 23, 2005, by cofounder Jawed Karim. It lasts nineteen seconds, and it is called, with unerring accuracy, "Me at the Zoo." Jawed stands in front of the elephant cage in San Diego. The gist of the tale he has to tell is that elephants have really, really long trunks. "And that's cool," he adds. Weighty pause. "And that's pretty much all there is to say." And then he is gone. The cool belongs to Jawed, of course, rather than to the elephants, who have had to take their trunks pretty much as they find them. But what is his cool about? Clearly, he is not one to make a big deal out of an inaugural event like the emergence of a new social medium. Event there is, nonetheless. For Jawed is not just standing anywhere. He is standing in a particular place at a particular time, and he wants to tell us about it. There could have been, and perhaps there ought to have been, a representation—shocking, poignant, slapstick, whatever—of elephants in a zoo. But there will not be. Not this time. For the nineteen seconds of video, while it looks like the beginning of a story, is in fact something else altogether. What greets us is not a fictional world that has some bearing, direct or indirect, on the world we ourselves inhabit. It is a piece of information: henceforth YouTube exists. Jawed has sent us a message—"Me at San Diego Zoo on YouTube"—to which the only appropriate response would be another message: "Me, too, at [enter location here] Zoo on YouTube." Many have since responded, in one way or another.[33]

Jawed's amiable performance conceals a fundamental disagreement concerning the best use of a medium like YouTube. A message is the "business" we entrust to a channel of communication, human, mechanical, or electronic. Mission is a closely related term. When we say that we are going to send someone a message, we do not mean that we are going to tell him or her a story. Stories, it is customary to say, do not have a message. They do not amount to a mission statement; or if they do, they fail as stories. By not telling a tale, when it looks as though he ought to, Jawed declares that You-Tube will be a messaging rather than a narrative medium. His video is thus a representation—the images and sounds captured in San Diego Zoo in 2005 made present once again as we watch and listen in hundreds of thousands of different places in 2012 and thereafter—which denies its own status as representation. It would rather be a message instantly provoking other messages. He might just as easily have phoned it in.

This is not a book about YouTube. My claim, rather, is that the questions YouTube ought to provoke were first raised, in Britain at least, during the period between the world wars, and that the answers then given to them, in some forms of literature, may yet serve us well.

Notes

Introduction

1. Ralph Waldo Emerson, *Society and Solitude, Collected Works,* vol. 7, ed. Douglas Emory Wilson and Ronald A. Bosco (Cambridge, MA: Belknap Press of Harvard University Press, 2007), 81.
2. William Uricchio, "Historicizing Media in Transition," in *Rethinking Media Change: The Aesthetics of Transition,* ed. David Thorburn and Henry Jenkins (Cambridge, MA: MIT Press, 2004), 23–38, p. 24.
3. Lisa Gitelman, *Always Already New: Media, History, and the Data of Culture* (Cambridge, MA: MIT Press, 2006), 7. I am also indebted to Carolyn Marvin, *When Old Technologies Were New: Thinking about Electric Communication in the Late 19th Century* (New York: Oxford University Press, 1988); and Jonathan Sterne, *The Audible Past: Cultural Origins of Sound Reproduction* (Durham, NC: Duke University Press, 2006).
4. Uricchio, "Historicizing Media," 26.
5. Ann L. Ardis and Patrick Collier, eds., *Transatlantic Print Culture, 1880–1940: Emerging Media, Emerging Modernisms* (Basingstoke: Palgrave Macmillan, 2008).
6. Garrett Stewart, *Between Film and Screen: Modernism's Photo Synthesis* (Chicago: University of Chicago Press, 1999); Sara Danius, *The Senses of Modernism: Technology, Perception, and Aesthetics* (Ithaca, NY: Cornell University Press, 2002); David Trotter, *Cinema and Modernism* (Oxford: Wiley-Blackwell, 2007); Laura Marcus, *The Tenth Muse: Writing about Cinema in the Modernist Period* (Oxford: Oxford University Press, 2010); Andrew Shail, *Cinema and the Origins of Literary Modernism* (London: Routledge, 2012).

7. Todd Avery, *Radio Modernism: Literature, Ethics, and the BBC, 1922–1938* (Aldershot: Ashgate, 2006); Debra Rae Cohen, Michael Coyle, and Jane Lewty, eds., *Broadcasting Modernism* (Gainesville: University Press of Florida, 2009).

8. Tim Armstrong, *Modernism* (Cambridge: Polity Press, 2005), 109–14; Melba Cuddy-Keane, "Virginia Woolf, Sound Technologies, and the New Aurality," in *Virginia Woolf in the Age of Mechanical Reproduction*, ed. Pamela L. Caughie (New York: Garland, 2000), 69–96; Ivan Kreilkamp, "A Voice without a Body: The Phonographic Logic of *Heart of Darkness*," *Victorian Studies* 40, no. 2 (1997): 211–43; John M. Picker, *Victorian Soundscapes* (Oxford: Oxford University Press, 2003), 110–45; Juan A. Suárez, *Pop Modernism: Noise and the Reinvention of Everyday Life* (Urbana: University of Illinois Press, 2007), 119–40.

9. John Brooks, *Telephone: The First Hundred Years* (New York: Harper & Row, 1976); Ithiel de Sola Pool, ed., *The Social Impact of the Telephone* (Cambridge, MA: MIT Press, 1977); Claude S. Fischer, *America Calling: A Social History of the Telephone to 1940* (Berkeley: University of California Press, 1992). For a cogent revisionist approach, see Robert MacDougall, "Long Lines: AT&T's Long-Distance Network as an Organizational and Political Strategy," *Business History Review* 80 (2006): 297–327; and Richard R. John, *Network Nation: Inventing American Telecommunications* (Cambridge, MA: Harvard University Press, 2010).

10. Donald Crafton, *The Talkies: American Cinema's Transition to Sound, 1926–1931* (Berkeley: University of California Press, 1997), 34. See also Paul Starr, *The Creation of the Media: Political Origins of Modern Communications* (New York: Basic Books, 2004), ch. 6.

11. Roland Marchand, *Creating the Corporate Soul: The Rise of Public Relations and Corporate Strategy in American Big Business* (Berkeley: University of California Press, 1998), ch. 3.

12. Facts from "A History of the British Post Office," http://web.online.co.uk /freshwater/bpo.htm.

13. F. G. C. Baldwin, *The History of the Telephone in the United Kingdom* (London: Chapman & Hall, 1925), 615–18.

14. Asa Briggs and Peter Burke, *A Social History of the Media: From Gutenberg to the Internet* (Cambridge: Polity Press, 2002), 152.

15. Raymond Williams, *Television: Ideology and Cultural Form*, 2nd ed. (London: Routledge, 1990), 26.

16. Avital Ronell, *The Telephone Book: Technology—Schizophrenia—Electric Speech* (Lincoln: University of Nebraska Press, 1989); Jacques Derrida, "*Ulysses* Gramophone: Hear say yes in Joyce," in *Acts of Literature*, trans. Tina Kendall, ed. Derek Attridge (New York: Routledge, 1992), 253–309,

pp. 266, 269; Laurence A. Rickels, *Aberrations of Mourning: Writing on German Crypts* (Detroit: Wayne State University Press, 1988), 279–93.

17. Eileen Bowser, "Le coup de téléphone dans le primitif du cinéma," in *Les premiers ans du cinéma français,* ed. Pierre Guibbert (Perpignan: Institute Jean Vigo, 1985), 218–24; Tom Gunning, "Heard over the Phone: *The Lonely Villa* and the de Lorde Tradition of the Terrors of Technology," *Screen* 32, no. 2 (1991): 184–96; Jan Olsson, "Framing Silent Calls: Coming to Cinematographic Terms with Telephony," in *Allegories of Communication: Intermedial Concerns from Cinema to the Digital,* ed. John Fullerton and Jan Olsson (Rome: John Libbey Publishing, 2004), 157–92.

18. Richard Menke, *Telegraphic Realism: Victorian Fiction and Other Information Systems* (Stanford, CA: Stanford University Press, 2008), 10–11, 3. Mark Goble, starting where Menke leaves off, with Henry James, has taken this story up in compelling fashion. For Goble, American literary Modernism's desire for communication provoked an avid interest in, precisely, photography, cinema, the telephone, and the gramophone. The writers he investigates, from James through Gertrude Stein, William Carlos Williams, F. Scott Fitzgerald, and James Weldon Johnson to George Oppen and James Agee, "manifest a shared commitment to the more sensuous and visceral experiences of other mediums that communicate somehow outside the competence of verbal expression": *Beautiful Circuits: Modernism and the Mediated Life* (New York: Columbia University Press, 2010), 16.

19. Donald Crafton, "Mindshare: Telephone and Radio Compete for the Talkies," in Fullerton and Olsson, *Allegories of Communication,* 141–56, pp. 150–51.

20. "Television," *Times* of London (henceforth *Times*), October 1, 1929, 26.

21. Richard Overy, *The Morbid Age: Britain and the Crisis of Civilization, 1919–1939* (London: Allen Lane, 2009), 375–76.

22. Julian Murphet, *Multimedia Modernism: Literature and the Anglo-American Avant-Garde* (Cambridge: Cambridge University Press, 2009), 15.

23. Henry Jenkins, *Convergence Culture: Where Old and New Media Collide* (New York: NYU Press, 2006), 2.

24. Jay David Bolter and Richard Grusin, *Remediation: Understanding New Media* (Cambridge, MA: MIT Press, 2000).

25. Murphet, *Multimedia Modernism,* 15. Fredric Jameson has discussed in rather more general terms the process by which, in the 1960s, the traditional fine arts came to consciousness of themselves as "various media within a mediatic system." *Postmodernism or the Cultural Logic of Late Capitalism* (Durham, NC: Duke University Press, 1991), 162.

26. For an illuminating account of the uses cinema has made of its "extra dimension of volume and temporality," see Dudley Andrew, *What Cinema Is! Bazin's Quest and Its Charge* (Oxford: Wiley-Blackwell, 2010).

27. For some instructive cheerleading, see Lee Sproull and Sara Keisler, *Connections: New Ways of Working in the Networked Organization* (Cambridge, MA: MIT Press, 1991), with regard to business practice; and, with regard to leisure activities, and the imagination in general, Alan Kirby, *Digimodernism: How New Technologies Dismantle the Postmodern and Reconfigure Our Culture* (New York: Continuum, 2009). It is not of direct relevance, but worth noting all the same, that from the early 1990s Jean-Luc Godard's meditations on media have had as their focus a distinction between projection (cinema) and transmission (television). For a lucid account of these meditations, see Daniel Morgan, *Late Godard and the Possibilities of Cinema* (Berkeley: University of California Press, 2012), ch. 5.

28. Gitelman, *Always Already New*, 4.

29. David Rodowick, *The Virtual Life of Film* (Cambridge, MA: Harvard University Press, 2007), 135–37. Rodowick enters productively into dialogue with two other important discussions of the virtual life of images: Stanley Cavell, "The Fact of Television," in *Cavell on Film*, ed. William Rothman (Albany: SUNY Press, 2005), 59–85; and Lev Manovich, *The Language of New Media* (Cambridge, MA: MIT Press, 2001).

30. Rodowick, *Virtual Life of Film*, 139.

31. "The House of the Future," *Illustrated London News*, February 18, 1928, 258–59.

32. "Practical Television Is Here!" *Times*, August 4, 1928, 4.

33. "Television for All," *Times*, June 22, 1928, 23.

34. Trotter, *Cinema and Modernism*, 173–74; Marcus, *Tenth Muse*, 80–86; Tom Gunning, " 'The Very Thing': Rudyard Kipling's 'Mrs Bathurst,' " in *Reading the Cinematograph: The Cinema in British Short Fiction, 1896–1912*, ed. Andrew Shail (Exeter: University of Exeter Press, 2010), 116–28; Alex Goody, *Technology, Literature, and Culture* (Cambridge: Polity Press, 2011), 52–53.

35. "Television for All," 23.

36. Gertie de S. Wentworth-James, *The Television Girl: A Novel* (London: Hurst and Blackett, 1928), 12–13, 66.

37. James Joyce, *Finnegans Wake* (London: Faber and Faber, 1968), 52, 349. Henceforth *FW*.

38. Donald F. Theall, "Beyond the Orality/Literacy Dichotomy: James Joyce and the Pre-History of Cyberspace," in *Hypermedia Joyce*, ed. David Vichnar and Louis Armand (Prague: Litteraria Pragensia Books, 2010), 17–34, p. 17.

39. "The Technique of Television: A New Scientific 'Miracle' Enabling Fireside 'Telescanners' to See Distant Events," *Illustrated London News*, February 23, 1935, 306–7.

40. William Uricchio, "Storage, Simultaneity, and the Media Technologies of Modernity," in Fullerton and Olsson, *Allegories of Communication*, 123–38, pp. 125, 132.

41. David Bordwell, Janet Staiger, and Kristin Thompson, *The Classical Hollywood Cinema: Film Style and Modes of Production to 1960* (London: Routledge, 1985); Charlie Keil, *Early American Cinema in Transition: Story, Style, and Filmmaking, 1907–1913* (Madison: University of Wisconsin Press, 2001); Charlie Keil and Shelley Stamp, eds., *American Cinema's Transitional Era: Audiences, Institutions, Practices* (Berkeley: University of California Press, 2004). See also Paul Young's admirable study of the ways in which American cinema has "represented the consumption of newer media, and specifically media that differ from film in terms of their liveness—the simultaneity of the transmitted event or text with its reception—and their situatedness in the private sphere": *The Cinema Dreams Its Rivals: Media Fantasy Films from Radio to the Internet* (Minneapolis: University of Minnesota Press, 2006), xiii.

42. David Harvey, *The New Imperialism* (Oxford: Oxford University Press, 2003), 98. See also Harvey, *The Limits to Capital* (Oxford: Blackwell, 1982), and *The Condition of Postmodernity* (Oxford: Blackwell, 1989), pt. 3.

43. Barney Warf, *Time-Space Compression: Historical Geographies* (London: Routledge, 2008), 9.

44. Gwen Urey, "Telecommunications and Global Capitalism," in *Telecommunications Politics: Ownership and Control of the Information Highway in Developing Countries,* ed. Bella Mody, Johannes M. Bauer, and Joseph D. Straubhaar (Mahwah, NJ: Lawrence Erlbaum Associates, 1995), 53–83. For a comprehensive account of the history of these developments, see Peter J. Hugill, *Global Communications since 1844: Geopolitics and Technology* (Baltimore: Johns Hopkins University Press, 1999).

45. Daniel R. Headrick, *The Invisible Weapon: Telecommunications and International Politics, 1851–1945* (Oxford: Oxford University Press, 1991), 93–98. In his very useful survey of recent research into the role of mass media in promoting imperial "connections" and "networks," Simon J. Potter draws attention to the constraints brought about by technological change, as well as to the opportunities it afforded: "Webs, Networks, and Systems: Globalization and the Mass Media in Nineteenth- and Twentieth-Century British Empire," *Journal of British Studies* 46, no. 3 (2007): 621–46.

46. This paragraph relies heavily on Daniel R. Headrick, "Shortwave Radio and Its Impact on International Telecommunications between the Wars," *History and Technology* 11 (1994): 21–32.

47. "Empire Air Routes," *Times,* February 3, 1920, 6.

48. "Imperial Communications," *Times,* July 7, 1921, 11.

49. Michael North, *Reading 1922: A Return to the Scene of the Modern* (New York: Oxford University Press, 1999), 126. For Northcliffe's personal reflections on the state of the empire, see *My Journey Round the World (16 July 1921–26 February 1922),* ed. Cecil Harmsworth and St. John Harmsworth (Philadelphia: J. B. Lippincott, 1923).

50. "From London to the Cape by Air," *Times,* February 4, 1920, 9.

51. "Aviation and the Empire," *Times,* May 22, 1925, 13.

52. Michael Heffernan, "The Cartography of the Fourth Estate: Mapping the New Imperialism in British and French Newspapers, 1875–1925," in *The Imperial Map: Cartography and the Mastery of Empire,* ed. James R. Akerman (Chicago: University of Chicago Press, 2009), 261–99, p. 293.

53. "The Imperial Conference," *Times,* October 29, 1926, 9.

54. Gordon Pirie, *Air Empire: British Imperial Civil Aviation, 1919–1939* (Manchester: Manchester University Press, 2009).

55. Martin Stollery, *Alternative Empires: European Modernist Cinemas and Cultures of Imperialism* (Exeter: University of Exeter Press, 2000), pp. 167–68. Michael North describes Carter's exploits as "the first truly modern media event": *Reading 1922,* 19.

56. Warf, *Time-Space Compression,* 148.

57. Dorthe Gert Simonsen, "Accelerating Modernity: Time-Space Compression in the Wake of the Aeroplane," *Journal of Transport History* 26, no. 2 (2005): 98–117, p. 100. For widely differing but equally informative accounts of the consequences of such acceleration for national sovereignty and national identity, see Gillian Beer, "The Island and the Aeroplane: The Case of Virginia Woolf," in *Nation and Narration,* ed. Homi Bhabha (London: Routledge, 1990), 265–90; and David L. Butler, "Technogeopolitics and the Struggle for Control of World Air Routes, 1910–1928," *Political Geography* 20 (2001): 635–58.

58. "Empire Wireless Chain," *Times,* April 7, 1921, 9.

59. Headrick, "Shortwave Radio," 24–25. See also Hugill, *Global Communications,* ch. 5; and Aitor Anduaga, *Wireless and Empire: Geopolitics, Radio Industry, and Ionosphere in the British Empire, 1918–1939* (Oxford: Oxford University Press, 2009), 63–72.

60. For a detailed account, see Dwayne R. Winseck and Robert M. Pike, *Communication and Empire: Media, Markets, and Globalization, 1860–1930* (Durham, NC: Duke University Press, 2007), 306–29.

61. Headrick, "Shortwave Radio," 27. See also Hugill, *Global Communications since 1844,* 118–19, 128–34.

62. Lee Grieveson, "The Cinema and the (Common) Wealth of Nations," in *Empire and Film,* ed. Grieveson and Colin MacCabe (Houndmills: Palgrave, 2011), 73–113.

63. For a broader discussion of the representation of connectivity in films about colonial Ceylon, see my "Representing Connection: A Multimedia Approach to Colonial Film, 1918–39," in Grieveson and MacCabe, *Empire and Film,* 151–65.

64. Popular fiction and popular film both balked at the prospect, instead reworking mid- to late-nineteenth-century preoccupations with the "embourgeoisement" of empire. On film, see Priya Jaikumar, *The End of Empire: A Politics of Transition in Britain and India* (Durham, NC: Duke University Press, 2006); and Julie Codell, "Domesticating Empire in the 1930s: Metropole, Colony, Family," in Grieveson and MacCabe, *Empire and Film,* 189–203.

65. E. M. Forster, "Notes on the English Character," in *Abinger Harvest* (London: Edward Arnold, 1936), 3–14, p. 14.

66. E. M. Forster, *A Passage to India* (Harmondsworth: Penguin Books, 2005), 265–66, 277.

67. E. M. Forster, *Howards End* (Harmondsworth: Penguin Books, 1961), 27.

68. Introduction to Bruce Clarke and Linda Dalrymple Henderson, eds., *From Energy to Information: Representation in Science and Technology, Art, and Literature* (Stanford, CA: Stanford University Press, 2002), 1–15, pp. 2–3.

69. Ezra Pound, "The Serious Artist," in *Literary Essays,* ed. T. S. Eliot (London: Faber and Faber, 1954), 41–57, p. 49.

70. Ezra Pound, *The Spirit of Romance,* rev. ed. (London: Peter Owen, 1952), 97.

71. Tim Armstrong, *Modernism, Technology, and the Body: A Cultural Study* (Cambridge: Cambridge University Press, 1998), 19. Armstrong has proved indefatigable in demonstrating Modernism's saturation in electrical energies. See also his *Modernism: A Cultural History* (Cambridge: Polity Press, 2005), 115–22; and Bruce Clarke, *Dora Marsden and Early Modernism: Gender, Individualism, Science* (Ann Arbor: University of Michigan Press, 1996).

72. Sir Philip Sidney, *An Apology for Poetry,* ed. R. W. Maslen, 3rd ed. (Manchester: Manchester University Press, 2002), 113.

73. Ernest Fenellosa, *The Chinese Written Character as a Medium for Poetry* (San Francisco: City Lights Books, 1969), 12. For an important elaboration of and commentary on this claim, see Ian F. A. Bell, "The Real and the Ethereal: Modernist Energies in Eliot and Pound," in *From Energy to Information,* 114–25.

74. Christopher Bush, *Ideographic Modernism: China, Writing, Media* (Oxford: Oxford University Press, 2010), 39, 58. Photography, Michael North notes, became not just a medium, but "a kind of modern writing." "It was the context, simultaneously technical, social, and aesthetic, within which both writers and artists in the avant-garde worked out their ideas about representation." *Camera Works* (Oxford: Oxford University Press, 2004), 3, 16.

75. Jean Toomer, *Cane*, ed. Rudolph P. Byrd and Henry Louis Gates Jr. (New York: W. W. Norton, 2011), 55.

76. Michael North, *The Dialect of Modernism: Race, Language and Twentieth-Century Literature* (Oxford: Oxford University Press, 1994), 170–71. See Richard Aldington, "The Art of Poetry," *Dial* 69 (1920): 170. Toomer is not mentioned by Mark Goble, but "Her Lips Are Copper Wire" would provide a good test of his thesis that in Modernist writing the "carnality of desire" is understood as "largely the aftereffect of a medium's materiality": *Beautiful Circuits,* 20. Toomer seems rather to want to inject into telecommunication a carnal desire it is felt to lack. I describe Modernism as a doctrine of energy for energy's sake, rather than art for art's sake, or medium for medium's sake, in "Modernism Reloaded: The Fiction of Katherine Mansfield," forthcoming in *Affirmations* 1, no. 1 (2013).

77. Karen Jackson Ford, *Split-Gut Song: Jean Toomer and the Poetics of Modernity* (Tuscaloosa: University of Alabama Press, 2005), 83.

78. James R. Beniger, *The Control Revolution: Technological and Economic Origins of the Information Society* (Cambridge, MA: Harvard University Press, 1986). Beniger's examples are corporate and North American. We need also to acknowledge that the state played its part, as well as private enterprise, and that different states played their parts differently: Jon Agar, *The Government Machine: A Revolutionary History of the Computer* (Cambridge, MA: MIT Press, 2003). In both cases, however, Agar points out, the "conversion to systematic management preceded the widespread introduction of office machinery" (p. 144). On the British cultural response, see also W. Boyd Rayward, "The March of the Modern and the Reconstitution of the World's Knowledge Apparatus: H. G. Wells, Encyclopaedism and the World Brain," in *European Modernism and the Information Society: Informing the Present, Understanding the Past*, ed. W. Boyd Rayward (Aldershot: Aldgate, 2008), 223–39. There was, of course, information, and systematic information gathering, long before there was an information society or age: Daniel R. Headrick, *When Information Came of Age: Technologies of Knowledge in the Age of Reason and Revolution, 1700–1850* (Oxford: Oxford University Press,

2000); Toni Weller, *The Victorians and Information* (Saarbrücken: VDM Verlag, 2009).

79. There is a vast sociological literature on the topic. I rely here on a range of historical studies: Barbara Ehrenreich, *Fear of Falling: The Inner Life of the Middle Class* (New York: HarperCollins, 1989); Jürgen Kocka, *White Collar Workers in America, 1890–1940: A Social-Political History in International Perspective*, trans. Maura Kealey (London: Sage, 1980); Shoshana Zuboff, *In the Age of the Smart Machine: The Future of Work and Power* (New York: Basic Books, 1988).

80. Gitelman, *Always Already New*, 68. See Friedrich A. Kittler, *Discourse Networks, 1800/1900*, trans. Michael Metteer with Chris Cullens (Stanford, CA: Stanford University Press, 1990).

81. Sproull and Kiesler, *Connections*, 7. See also S. H. Aronson, "The Sociology of the Telephone," *International Journal of Comparative Sociology* 12 (1971): 153–67.

82. Katherine Hayles, "Escape and Constraint: Three Fictions Dream of Moving from Energy to Information," in *From Energy to Information*, 235–54, pp. 235–36.

83. Ibid., 241.

84. The allusion is to studies that have established a certain shrinking or inward turn—an "Anglocentric revival"—as the focus for an understanding of British "late" Modernism: for example, Jed Esty, *A Shrinking Island: Modernism and National Culture in England* (Princeton, NJ: Princeton University Press, 2004).

85. Rebecca L. Walkowitz, *Cosmopolitan Style: Modernism beyond the Nation* (New York: Columbia University Press, 2006).

86. Graham Greene, *England Made Me* (Harmondsworth: Penguin Books, 1970), 11.

87. Le Corbusier, *Aircraft* (London: Studio, 1935), 15–16.

88. Greene, *England Made Me*, 161–62.

89. Bruce Robbins, *Upward Mobility and the Common Good: Toward a Literary History of the Welfare State* (Princeton, NJ: Princeton University Press, 2007).

90. Tyrus Miller, *Late Modernism: Politics, Fiction, and the Arts between the World Wars* (Berkeley: University of California Press, 1999); Marina Mackay, *Modernism and World War II* (Cambridge: Cambridge University Press, 2007); Kristin Bluemel, ed., *Intermodernism: Literary Culture in Mid-Twentieth-Century Britain* (Edinburgh: Edinburgh University Press, 2009); Leo Mellor, *Reading the Ruins: Modernism, Bombsites and British Culture* (Cambridge: Cambridge University Press, 2011).

91. D. H. Lawrence, *Women in Love,* ed. David Farmer, Lindeth Vasey, and John Worthen (Cambridge: Cambridge University Press, 1987), 314.

92. D. H. Lawrence, "Bare Almond-Trees," in *Complete Poems*, ed. Vivian de Sola Pinto and Warren Roberts, 2 vols. (London: Heinemann, 1964), 1:300–301, p. 301.

93. Walter Benjamin, "Some Motifs in Baudelaire," in *Illuminations*, ed. Hannah Arendt, trans. Harry Zohn (London: Fontana, 1970), 157–202, p. 176.

94. Aldous Huxley, *Brave New World* (London: Flamingo, 1994), 115. See Laura Frost, "Huxley's Feelies: The Cinema of Sensation in *Brave New World*," *Twentieth Century Literature* 52, no. 4 (2006): 443–73. Chapters 3 and 4 of Mark Goble's *Beautiful Circuits* offer a persuasive account of phonographic and photographic recording projects that sought to "restore more direct, immediate forms of contact—between writers and readers, past and present, African-American and Anglo-American—even as they pursue increasingly involved commitments to the materiality and purely sensuous aspects of their mediums": *Beautiful Circuits*, 21. It is significant that these projects did not take shape, and perhaps could not have taken shape, before the 1930s. To Goble, they are Modernist. I would describe them as versions of techno-primitivism.

95. Dick Pountain and David Robins, *Cool Rules: Anatomy of an Attitude* (London: Reaktion Books, 2000), 19, 122.

96. Lewis MacAdams, *Birth of the Cool: Beat, Bebop and the American Avant-Garde* (London: Scribner, 2002). Also relevant is Helmut Lethen's description of a Weimar Germany in which the cultivation of artifice (and the distance thus established) could be seen as a way to resist the excesses of communitarian ideology: *Cool Conduct: The Culture of Distance in Weimar Germany,* trans. Don Reneau (Berkeley: University of California Press, 2002). The emotional temperature Lethen defines is in fact closer to cold than it is to cool. I discuss some of the same maneuvers under the heading of "anti-pathos" in *The Making of the Reader: Language and Subjectivity in Modern American, English and Irish Poetry* (Houndmills: Macmillan, 1984), 70–81.

97. Pountain and Robins, *Cool Rules,* 161.

98. Alan Liu, *The Laws of Cool: Knowledge Work and the Culture of Information* (Chicago: University of Chicago Press, 2004), 289–300.

99. Pountain and Robins draw on the work of the art historian Robert Farris Thompson, who translated the concept of *itutu,* fundamental to the animistic religions of the Yoruba and Ibo civilizations of West Africa, as "cool": *Cool Rules,* 35–39.

100. T. S. Eliot, "Last Words," *Criterion* 18 (1939): 271.

101. Wyndham Lewis, *Blasting and Bombardiering* (London: Calder and Boyars, 1967), 339, 340.

ONE Telephony

1. "More Telephoning," *Times,* July 14, 1932, 13.
2. James W. Carey, "A Cultural Approach to Communication," in *Communication as Culture: Essays on Media and Society* (Boston: Unwin Hyman, 1989), 13–36, pp. 15, 18. For an incisive restatement of the cultural approach, which also draws on Williams, see William Uricchio, "Historicizing Media in Transition," in *Rethinking Media Change: The Aesthetics of Transition,* ed. David Thorburn and Henry Jenkins (Cambridge, MA: MIT Press, 2003), 23–38.
3. Roger Silverstone and Leslie Haddon, "Design and the Domestication of Information and Communication Technologies: Technical Change and Everyday Life," in *Communication by Design: The Politics of Information and Communication Technologies,* ed. Robin Mansell and Roger Silverstone (Oxford: Oxford University Press, 1996), 44–74, pp. 47, 62.
4. Lisa Gitelman, *Always Already New: Media, History, and the Data of Culture* (Cambridge, MA: MIT Press, 2006), 7. For a subtle examination of the concept of protocol in the context of the Internet, see Alexander R. Galloway, *Protocol: How Control Exists after Decentralization* (Cambridge, MA: MIT Press, 2004).
5. Silverstone and Haddon, "Design," 60, 64.
6. Gitelman, *Always Already New,* 4.
7. Raymond Williams, *Television: Ideology and Cultural Form,* 2nd ed. (London: Routledge, 1990), 26.
8. Naomi Mitchison, *Vienna Diary* (London: Victor Gollancz, 1934), 9, 37.
9. Jonathan Sterne, *The Audible Past: Cultural Origins of Sound Reproduction* (Durham, NC: Duke University Press, 2003), 2, 22, 31–34.
10. W. H. Martin and C. H. G. Gray, "Master Reference System for Telephone Transmission," *Bell System Technical Journal* 8 (1929): 536–59, p. 536.
11. R. H. Chamney, "Features of the Essential Factors in Telephone Transmission," *Post Office Electrical Engineers' Journal* 26, no. 4 (1934): 301–3, p. 301. Henceforth *POEEJ.* Elaborate tests were devised for measuring intelligibility: John Collard, "The Accurate Measurement of Articulation," *POEEJ* 23, no. 1 (1930): 25–35; W. West, "Telephone Transmission Testing by Subjective Methods," *POEEJ* 31, no. 4 (1939), 286–92.
12. Colonel Sir Thomas Purves, "Telegraphy and Telephony," *Times,* September 21, 1931, xv; and, by way of slight variation, "Telephony and Telegraphy," *Times,* November 1, 1932, x.

13. Virginia Woolf, letter to Janet Case, July 24, 1927, in *Collected Letters,* ed. Nigel Nicolson, 6 vols. (London: Hogarth Press, 1975–1980), 3:403.

14. David Lodge, "Dialogue in the Modern Novel," in *After Bakhtin: Essays on Fiction and Criticism* (London: Routledge, 1990), 75–86, p. 81.

15. Henry Green, "A Novelist to His Readers: 1," in *Surviving: The Uncollected Writings of Henry Green,* ed. Matthew Yorke (London: Chatto & Windus, 1992), 136–42, pp. 137, 140.

16. Elizabeth Bowen, "Truth and Fiction," in *Afterthought: Pieces about Writing* (London: Longmans, 1962), 114–43, pp. 129, 133, 143.

17. Elizabeth Bowen, "Notes on Writing a Novel," in *Pictures and Conversations* (London: Allen Lane, 1975), 169–93, pp. 180–81.

18. Richard Aldington, *Death of a Hero* (Ottawa: Golden Dog Press, 1998), 283–84.

19. Wyndham Lewis, *The Ideal Giant,* in *Collected Poems and Plays,* ed. Alan Munton (Manchester: Carcanet, 1979), 123–39.

20. Ford Madox Ford, *Parade's End* (Harmondsworth: Penguin Books, 1982), 503–14; Dorothy Richardson, *Pilgrimage,* 4 vols. (London: Virago, 1979), 2:45. Philip Horne points out that Ford's handling of the episode owes a debt to Proust: "Absent-Mindedness: Ford on the Phone," in *Ford Madox Ford's Modernity,* ed. Robert Hampson and Max Saunders (Amsterdam: Rodopi, 2003), 17–34, p. 30. The failed telephone call might nonetheless be thought to complicate Bryony Randall's perceptive account of the temporal and spatial "axes" that define Miriam's working life: *Modernism, Daily Time and Everyday Life* (Cambridge: Cambridge University Press, 2007), 80–84.

21. Avital Ronell speaks of the telephone's "disconnecting force": *The Telephone Book: Technology—Schizophrenia—Electric Speech* (Lincoln: University of Nebraska Press, 1989), 9.

22. Sara Danius, *The Senses of Modernism: Technology, Perception, and Aesthetics* (Ithaca, NY: Cornell University Press, 2002), 12.

23. "The London-Paris Telephone Open Today," *Daily News,* April 1, 1891, 2.

24. "Telephone Usage," *Times,* October 3, 1924, 9.

25. Memorandum to Postmaster General, December 9, 1924, British Telecom (henceforth BT) Archives, POST 33/1874.

26. The role of the telephone operator, the focus of illuminating speculative and sociohistorical scholarship, was of little or no interest to the writers who will concern me here. See Brenda Maddox, "Women and the Switchboard," in *The Social Impact of the Telephone,* ed. Ithiel de Sola Pinto (Cambridge, MA: MIT Press, 1977), 262–80; Kenneth Lipartito, "When Women Were Switches: Technology, Work, and Gender in the Telephone Industry, 1890–1920," *American Historical Review* 99, no. 4, 1994, 1075–1111; Venus Green, "Goodbye Central: Automation and the

Decline of 'Personal Service' in the Bell System, 1878–1921," *Technology and Culture* 36, no. 4, 1995, 912–49; and Bernhard Siegert, "Switchboards and Sex: The Nut(t) Case," in *Inscribing Science: Scientific Texts and the Materiality of Communication,* ed. Timothy Lenoir (Stanford, CA: Stanford University Press, 1998), 78–90.

27. H. E. Powell-Jones, script for radio broadcast, June 1925, BT Archives, POST 33/1874.

28. *Times,* July 13, 1926, 9; July 13, 1926, 8.

29. Roland Marchand, *Creating the Corporate Soul: The Rise of Public Relations and Corporate Strategy in American Big Business* (Berkeley: University of California Press, 1998), 58–69.

30. Letter from H. E. Powell-Jones to R. A. Dalzell, January 20, 1925, and synopsis of cartoon film, BT Archives, POST 33/1874. The film may or may not have been made. It does not appear to have survived.

31. Memoranda, letter from G. E. P. Murray to the Secretary of the Treasury, and list of slogans, BT Archives, POST 33/3225B.

32. BT Archives, POST 84/8.

33. "More Telephoning," *Times,* July 14, 1932, 13.

34. Marchand, *Creating the Corporate Soul,* 73, 84–85.

35. "The Hand-Microphone," *Post Office Telephone Sales Bulletin* 4, no. 4 (1938): 54–55. Henceforth *POTSB.*

36. The BT Archives contain drawings and correspondence relating to a wide variety of proposed telephone attachments: POST 30/3629. But see also, for some contrary phenomenological reflections, Kenneth Haltman, "Reaching Out to Touch Someone? Reflections on a 1923 Candlestick Telephone," *Technology in Society* 12 (1990): 333–54.

37. *POEEJ* 25, no. 1 (1932): 81; *Daily Mail,* March 31, 1932, 6.

38. "Post Office Pavilion at the Empire Exhibition, Bellahouston Park," *POEEJ* 31, no. 2 (1938): 85–92, p. 85.

39. Loren M. Berry, "Helpful Hints for Selling Service," *POTSB* 1, no. 1 (1935): 4–6, p. 4. Berry was an American sales guru.

40. *POEEJ* 18, no. 3 (1925): 225; vol. 23, no. 3 (1930): 210; vol. 28, no. 3 (1935): 204; vol. 33, no. 2 (1940): 59; vol. 29, no. 4 (1937): 337; and vol. 31, no. 1 (1938): 63.

41. E. Dunnill, "Advertising and Atmosphere," *POTSB* 2, no. 1, January 1936, 8. For earlier American anxieties on this score, see Robert MacDougall, "The Wire Devils: Pulp Thrillers, the Telephone, and Action at a Distance in the Wiring of a Nation," *American Quarterly* 58, no. 3 (2006): 715–41.

42. Roland Barthes, "Introduction to the Structural Analysis of Narratives," in *Image—Music—Text,* ed. and trans. Stephen Heath (London: Fontana, 1977), 79–124, pp. 93–95.

43. George Orwell, *Complete Novels* (Harmondsworth: Penguin Books, 1983), 729–30.

44. John Grierson, "Perspectives of Salesmanship," *POTSB* 2, no. 4 (1936): 57–58.

45. Their conversations are therefore not an example, as John Mepham puts it, of "how the city is represented as throwing together strangers who cannot understand one another": "London as Auditorium: Public Spaces and Disconnected Talk in Works by Ford Madox Ford, Patrick Hamilton, and Virginia Woolf," in *London in Literature: Visionary Mappings of the Metropolis,* ed. Susana Onega and John A. Stotesbury (Heidelberg: C. Winter, 2002), 83–106, p. 101.

46. Patrick Hamilton, *Twenty Thousand Streets under the Sky: A London Trilogy* (London: Hogarth Press, 1987), 50, 79, 82–83. Henceforth *TTS.*

47. Patrick Hamilton, *Hangover Square* (Harmondsworth: Penguin, 2001), 60–66. Henceforth *HS.* See my "Phoning It In," in *The Uses of Phobia: Essays on Literature and Film* (Oxford: Wiley-Blackwell, 2010), 140–55, pp. 148–49; and Jeremy Noel-Tod, "The Wanderings of Bloom and Bone: *Ulysses, Hangover Square* and the Art of Gratuity," *Critical Engagements* 1, no. 1 (2007): 236–46, p. 239.

48. Evelyn Waugh, *Vile Bodies* (Harmondsworth: Penguin, 2000), 166–67. Henceforth *VB.*

49. Bronwen E. Thomas has admirably elucidated the chapter's subtleties: "'It's Good to Talk': An Analysis of a Telephone Conversation from Evelyn Waugh's *Vile Bodies*," *Language and Literature* 6, no. 2 (1997): 105–19.

50. Jean Rhys, *After Leaving Mr Mackenzie* (Harmondsworth: Penguin Books, 2000), 56. Henceforth *ALMM.*

51. Rosamond Lehmann, *The Weather in the Streets* (London: Virago, 1981), 145–46. Henceforth *WS.*

52. Randall Craig, "The Early Fiction of William Gerhardie," *NOVEL: A Forum on Fiction* 15, no. 3 (1982): 240–56.

53. William Gerhardie, *Of Mortal Love* (London: Macdonald, 1970), 136, 176. Randall Craig compares *The Polyglots* with *Black Mischief* in "Evelyn Waugh and William Gerhardie," *Journal of Modern Literature* 16, no. 4 (1990): 597–614.

54. Christopher Isherwood, *The Berlin Novels* (London: Vintage, 1999), 7. Henceforth *BN.*

55. The (slight) exception is chapter 7, which withholds the telephone call for a couple of pages.

56. Samuel Beckett, *The Unnamable,* translated by the author, in *Three Novels* (London: Picador, 1979), 272. See *Mercier and Camier,* translated by the author (London: John Calder, 1974).

57. Fredric Jameson, *Fables of Aggression: Wyndham Lewis, the Modernist as Fascist* (Berkeley: University of California Press, 1979), 59.

58. Samuel Beckett, *Murphy* (London: Calder & Boyars, 1969), 9.

59. Valentine Cunningham, *British Writers of the Thirties* (Oxford: Oxford University Press, 1988), 281.

60. Rose Macaulay, *Keeping Up Appearances* (Leipzig: Tauchnitz, 1928), 260, 273.

61. Walter Allen, *Blind Man's Ditch* (London: Michael Joseph, 1939), 53.

62. Elizabeth Bowen, "Places," in *Pictures and Conversations*, 34–57, pp. 41–42.

63. Maud Ellmann, *Elizabeth Bowen: The Shadow across the Page* (Edinburgh: Edinburgh University Press, 2003), 97, 110–12, 109. In *To the North*, Vike Martina Plock adds, "clothes literally connect people," as decisions about what to wear help to create or maintain social networks: "Sartorial Connections: Fashion, Clothes, and Character in Elizabeth Bowen's *To the North*," *Modernism/Modernity* 19, no. 2 (2012): 287–302.

64. Correspondence between H. E. Powell-Jones and F. H. S. Grant, BT Archives, POST 33/2964.

65. *Facilities for Telephones in New Buildings: For the Use of Architects, Surveyors, Engineers and Builders* (London: GPO, 1931), 6. There is abundant correspondence concerning this book in the BT Archives at POST 33/2964.

66. Letter from D. G. Freestone, July 26, 1934, BT Archives, POST 33/2964.

67. *Facilities for Telephones in New Buildings,* 65.

68. Editorial, *Post Office Telephone Sales Bulletin* 2, no. 10 (1936): 145. See also E. W. C. Rawes, "Where to Put the Telephone," in the same issue, 148–49.

69. Elizabeth Bowen, *To the North* (London: Vintage, 1999), 195, 105. Henceforth *TTN*.

70. *Times,* April 12, 1921, 10; June 5, 1930, 9; December 11, 1930, 22; September 21, 1931, xv; May 3, 1935, xxv; February 2, 1932, 16.

71. Virginia Woolf, *Diary,* ed. Anne Olivier Bell and Andrew McNeillie, 5 vols. (New York: Harcourt Brace Jovanovich, 1977–1984), 3:145.

72. Virginia Woolf, "The Leaning Tower," in *Collected Essays,* ed. Leonard Woolf, 4 vols. (London: Hogarth Press, 1966), 2:162–81, pp. 164, 175.

73. Woolf, *Diary,* 5:306.

74. Virginia Woolf, letter of April 7, 1937, to Stephen Spender, in *Collected Letters,* 6:115–16. Jed Esty notes the novel's "missing dimension of group ritual and public symbolism" and turns instead to *Between the Acts* (1941): *A Shrinking Island: Modernism and National Culture in England* (Princeton, NJ: Princeton University Press, 2004), 52–53, 85. Marina MacKay concentrates exclusively on *Between the Acts* in delineating

Woolf's "pastoral patria": *Modernism and World War II* (Cambridge: Cambridge University Press, 2007), ch. 1.

75. Woolf, *Diary*, 3:187. Ellipsis added.

76. Virginia Woolf, *The Years*, ed. Anna Snaith (Cambridge: Cambridge University Press, 2012), 276, 278. Henceforth Y. Laura Marcus has written perceptively about the relations between sight and sound that structure the novel: *The Tenth Muse: Writing about Cinema in the Modernist Period* (Oxford: Oxford University Press, 2007), 157–71.

77. Walter Benjamin, "On Some Motifs in Baudelaire," in *Illuminations*, ed. Hannah Arendt, trans. Harry Zohn (London: Fontana, 1970), 157–202, p. 177.

78. Ibid., 176.

79. When she began to think about the text that became *The Years*, Woolf noted that she could now "take liberties with the representational form" that she did not dare take in her earlier realist novel, *Night and Day* (1919): *Diary*, 4:142.

TWO Techno-Primitivism

1. Tim Armstrong, *Modernism: A Cultural History* (Cambridge: Polity Press, 2005), 140. See also Elazar Barkan and Ronald Bush, eds., *Prehistories of the Future: The Primitivist Project and the Culture of Modernism* (Stanford, CA: Stanford University Press, 1995).

2. Edward Said, *Culture and Imperialism* (New York: Alfred A. Knopf, 1993), 108.

3. John Marx, *The Modernist Novel and the Decline of Empire* (Cambridge: Cambridge University Press, 2005), 122–66, esp. pp. 122–23.

4. For the association of homosexuality with the primitive, in literature and psychiatry alike, see Hugh Stevens, *"The Plumed Serpent* and the Erotics of Primitive Masculinity," in *Modernist Sexualities*, ed. Stevens and Caroline Howlett (Manchester: Manchester University Press, 2000), 219–38; and Robin Hackett, *Sapphic Primitivism: Productions of Race, Class, and Sexuality in Key Works of Modern Fiction* (New Brunswick, NJ: Rutgers University Press, 2004), ch. 2.

5. Laura Doyle and Laura Winkiel, "Introduction: The Global Horizons of Modernism," in *Geomodernisms: Race, Modernism, Modernity*, ed. Doyle and Winkiel (Bloomington: Indiana University Press, 2005), 1–14, p. 1.

6. Joseph Conrad, *The Secret Agent*, ed. John Lyon (Oxford: Oxford University Press, 2004), 61.

7. James Joyce, *Ulysses*, ed. Jeri Johnson (Oxford: Oxford University Press, 1993), 253.

8. Rubber has only ever been of interest to Joyce scholars when abstracted into the form and function of a contraceptive device. James F. Carens, "Some Points on Poyntz and Related Matters," *James Joyce Quarterly* 16 (1979): 344–46; Zack Bowen, "Joyce's Prophylactic Paralysis: Exposure in *Dubliners*," *James Joyce Quarterly* 19, no. 3 (1982): 257–73; Mary Lowe-Evans, *Crimes against Fecundity: Joyce and Population Control* (Syracuse, NY: Syracuse University Press, 1989); Thomas Jackson Rice, "Condoms, Conrad, and Joyce," in *Cannibal Joyce* (Gainesville: University Press of Florida, 2008), 89–105.

9. Valerie Steele, *Fetish: Fashion, Sex and Power* (New York: Oxford University Press, 1996).

10. Linda Ruth Williams, *Sex in the Head: Visions of Femininity and Film in D. H. Lawrence* (Detroit: Wayne State University Press, 1993), ch. 4; David Ayers, *English Literature of the 1920s* (Edinburgh: Edinburgh University Press, 1999), 166–87; Allison Pease, *Modernism, Mass Culture, and the Aesthetics of Obscenity* (Cambridge: Cambridge University Press, 2000), 136–64; Gerald Doherty, *Oriental Lawrence: The Quest for the Secrets of Sex* (New York: Peter Lang, 2001); Ginette Katz-Roy, "Deconstructing Myth in *Lady Chatterley's Lover*," in *D. H. Lawrence: New Worlds*, ed. Keith Cushman (London: Associated University Presses, 2003), 258–69.

11. Andrzej Gasiorek, "War, 'Primitivism,' and the Future of 'the West': Reflections on D. H. Lawrence and Wyndham Lewis," in *Modernism and Colonialism: British and Irish Literature, 1899–1939*, ed. Richard Begam and Michael Valdez Moses (Durham, NC: Duke University Press, 2007), 91–110, p. 95.

12. D. H. Lawrence, *Letters*, vol. 5, ed. James T. Boulton and Lindeth Vasey (Cambridge: Cambridge University Press, 1989), 517.

13. Ayers, *English Literature*, 169.

14. Katie Gramich, "Stripping Off the 'Civilized Body': Lawrence's *nostalgie de la boue* in *Lady Chatterley's Lover*," in *Writing the Body in D. H. Lawrence: Essays on Language, Representation, and Sexuality*, ed. Paul Poplawski (Westport, CT: Greenwood Press, 2001), 149–61, pp. 149–50.

15. Jed Esty, *A Shrinking Island: Modernism and National Culture in England* (Princeton, NJ: Princeton University Press, 2004), 48.

16. Lawrence, *Letters*, 5:495.

17. Frieda Lawrence, foreword to *The First Lady Chatterley* (New York: Dial Press, 1944), v–xiii, p. vii.

18. David Ellis, *D. H. Lawrence: Dying Game, 1922–1930* (Cambridge: Cambridge University Press, 1998), 393.

19. Derek Britton, *Lady Chatterley: The Making of a Novel* (London: Unwin Hyman, 1988), 250.

20. D. H. Lawrence, *Lady Chatterley's Lover*, ed. Michael Squires (Harmondsworth: Penguin Books, 2006), 119. Henceforth *LCL*.

21. D. H. Lawrence, "John Galsworthy," in *Study of Thomas Hardy and Other Essays*, ed. Bruce Steele (Cambridge: Cambridge University Press, 1985), 209–20, p. 214.

22. D. H. Lawrence, "Preface to *Cavalleria Rusticana*, by Giovanni Verga," in *Phoenix: The Posthumous Papers of D. H. Lawrence*, ed. Edward D. McDonald (New York: Viking Press, 1936), 240–54, p. 248.

23. The main exponent of this kind of sprezzatura was W. B. Yeats. See Corinna Salvadori, *Yeats and Castiglione, Poet and Courtier* (Dublin: A. Figgis, 1965).

24. D. H. Lawrence, *Complete Short Novels* (Harmondsworth: Penguin Books, 1982), 535, 538.

25. Austin Coates, *The Commerce in Rubber: The First 150 Years* (Oxford: Oxford University Press, 1987), 15; and Henry Hobhouse, *Seeds of Wealth: Four Plants That Made Men Rich* (Basingstoke: Macmillan, 2003), ch. 3.

26. Thomas Hancock, *Personal Narrative of the Origin and Progress of the Caoutchouc or India-Rubber Manufacture in England* (London: Longman, 1857), 104–5. See also Philip Schidrowitz, *Rubber* (London: Methuen, 1911), 3–4; Hobhouse, *Seeds*, 128–29; and Charles Slack, *Noble Obsession: Charles Goodyear, Thomas Hancock, and the Race to Unlock the Greatest Industrial Secret of the 19th Century* (New York: Texere Publishing, 2002).

27. Susan Mossman, "Perspectives on the History and Technology of Plastics," in *Early Plastics: Perspectives, 1850–1950*, ed. Susan Mossman (London: Leicester University Press, 1997), 15–71, p. 27.

28. Adela Pinch, "Rubber Bands and Old Ladies," in *In Near Ruins: Cultural Theory at the End of the Century*, ed. Nicholas B. Dirks (Minneapolis: University of Minnesota Press, 1998), 147–71.

29. John Lethaby, "A Rubberless World," in *Rubber Romances and Slave Stories* (London: Walter Scott Publishing, 1910), 44–51, pp. 46–47.

30. Schidrowitz, *Rubber*, 24–31; Michael Edward Stanfield, *Red Rubber, Bleeding Trees: Violence, Slavery, and Empire in Northwest Amazonia, 1850–1933* (Albuquerque: University of New Mexico Press, 1998). For a concise summary, see Zephyr Frank and Aldo Musacchio, "The International Natural Rubber Market, 1870–1930," in *EH.Net Encyclopedia*, ed. Robert Whaples, http://eh.net/encyclopedia/article/frank.international.rubber.market.

31. E. D. Morel, *Red Rubber: The Story of the Rubber Slave Trade on the Congo* (London: T. Fisher Unwin, 1906).

32. E. M. Forster, *Howards End* (Harmondsworth: Penguin Books, 1961), 183.

33. Harvey S. Firestone, *The Romance and Drama of the Rubber Industry* (Akron, OH: Firestone Tire and Rubber Co., 1932), 41.

34. For detailed discussion of these developments, see Schidrowitz, *Rubber,* ch. 5; J. H. Drabble, *Rubber in Malaya, 1876–1922: The Genesis of the Industry* (Kuala Lumpur: Oxford University Press, 1973), ch. 3; and Colin Barlow, *The Natural Rubber Industry: Its Development, Technology, and Economy in Malaysia* (Kuala Lumpur: Oxford University Press, 1978), ch. 2.

35. The association's *Minute Books* for the period 1907–1944 are held in the Guildhall Library: Ms 24863. Henceforth *MB.* For a record of an initial meeting held on June 24, 1907, see *MB,* 1:1–9.

36. Figures from Drabble, *Rubber in Malaya,* 220.

37. Ibid., 192–99.

38. *MB,* 9:115.

39. Ibid., 12:181–86.

40. Drabble, *Rubber in Malaya,* 75, 77–78; and Barlow, *Natural Rubber Industry,* 167–69.

41. *MB,* 10:23–24.

42. Ibid., 10:56.

43. Ibid., 10:123, 148.

44. Ibid., 11:94–95.

45. Ibid., 12:181–86.

46. Ibid., 13:140.

47. Ibid., 13:25.

48. Display advertisement, *Times,* June 4, 1924, 7. *Plus ça change.* In 2012, Clarks promoted their Desert Weaver shoe for women on the basis that it "cushions the foot on a leather-lined, foam-padded footbed and an extra-thick genuine plantation crepe outsole. Trek the world in the women's Desert Weaver, the perfect shoe for your own journeys."

49. *MB,* 13:110–12.

50. Ibid., 13:137.

51. Display advertisement, *Times,* April 12, 1923, 18.

52. "Company Meetings," *Times,* April 5, 1924, 19.

53. *MB,* 16:144.

54. Ibid., 17:110.

55. Ibid., 12:110, 18:185.

56. Ibid., 17:19–20.

57. Ibid., 15:20.

58. Ibid., 16:13–14, 47–48.

59. Ibid., 15:146.

60. D. H. Lawrence, *The First and Second Lady Chatterley Novels,* ed. Dieter Mehl and Christa Jansohn (Cambridge: Cambridge University Press, 1999), 200.

61. D. H. Lawrence, "Cypresses," in *Complete Poems,* ed. Vivian de Sola Pinto and Warren Roberts, 2 vols. (London: Heinemann, 1964), 1:296–98, p. 296.

62. D. H. Lawrence, *Sketches of Etruscan Places and Other Italian Sketches,* ed. Simonetta de Filippis (Cambridge: Cambridge University Press, 1992), 48, 50, 265.

63. D. H. Lawrence, "The Novel," in *Study of Thomas Hardy,* 177–90, p. 182.

64. Britton, *Making,* 247.

65. The relevant severities have been assembled in *Late Essays and Articles,* ed. James T. Boulton (Cambridge: Cambridge University Press, 2004).

66. Michael Arlen, *The Green Hat: A Romance for a Few People* (London: W. Collins, 1924), 1, 7.

67. J. A. Mangan and Roberta J. Park, eds., *From Fair Sex to Feminism: Sport and the Socialization of Women in the Industrial and Post-Industrial Eras* (London: Frank Cass, 1987); Mike Huggins and Jack Williams, *Sport and the English, 1918–1939* (London: Routledge, 2006).

68. Arlen, *Green Hat,* 7.

69. D. H. Lawrence, *The Lost Girl,* ed. John Worthen (Cambridge: Cambridge University Press, 1981), 211, 212, 215.

70. Elizabeth Dejeans, *The Tiger's Coat* (Indianapolis: Bobbs-Merrill, 1920), 73, 83–84.

71. Lawrence, *Letters,* 5:186.

72. Display advertisement, *Times,* April 27, 1926, 10.

73. Arlen, *Green Hat,* 9.

74. F. Scott Fitzgerald, *The Great Gatsby,* ed. Ruth Prigozy (Oxford: Oxford University Press, 1998), 59.

75. I discuss this scene in "Modernist *Toilette:* Degas, Woolf, Lawrence," in *The Uses of Phobia: Essays on Literature and Film* (Oxford: Wiley-Blackwell, 2010), 77–96, pp. 94–96.

76. Selfridges display advertisement, *Times,* January 30, 1928, p. 16.

77. H. D. [Hilda Doolittle], *Bid Me to Live* (London: Virago, 1984), 143–47. Henceforth *BMTL.*

78. Suzette Henke, *Shattered Subjects: Trauma and Testimony in Women's Life Writing* (Bloomington: Indiana University Press, 2000), 43–49.

79. Trauma is generally held to constitute the novel's method as well as its topic. For an informative account of the scene of Rafe's departure in these terms, see Bryony Randall, *Modernism, Daily Time and Everyday Life* (Cambridge: Cambridge University Press, 2007), 130–32.

80. Sarah Chinn, "'Something Primitive and Age-Old as Nature Herself': Lesbian Sexuality and the Permission of the Exotic," in *Palatable Poison: Critical Perspectives on "The Well of Loneliness,"* ed. Laura Doan and Jay Prosser (New York: Columbia University Press, 2001), 300–315, pp. 301–2, 313.

81. Radclyffe Hall, *The Well of Loneliness* (London: Virago, 1982), 260.

82. C. W. Cunnington and P. Cunnington, *Handbook of English Costumes in the Nineteenth Century* (London: Faber and Faber, 1970), 142; Brent Shannon, *The Cut of His Coat: Men, Dress, and Consumer Culture in Britain, 1860–1914* (Athens: Ohio University Press, 2006), 67.

83. G. K. Chesterton, "The Romantic in the Rain," in *A Miscellany of Men* (London: Methuen, 1912), 190–95, pp. 192–93.

84. Katherine Mansfield, "Something Childish but Very Natural," in *Short Stories* (New York: Ecco Press, 1983), 164–83, p. 164.

85. H. G. Wells, "Jimmy Goggles the God," in *Complete Short Stories*, ed. John Hammond (London: Phoenix Press, 1998), 477–86, p. 478.

86. Mary Schenk Woolman, *Clothing: Choice, Care, Cost* (New York: J. B. Lippincott, 1920), 89.

87. Virginia Woolf, *Mrs Dalloway* (Harmondsworth: Penguin Books, 1992), 12.

88. George Orwell, *Complete Novels* (Harmondsworth: Penguin Books, 2000), 434, 443, 566.

89. A point I make at greater length in "Lesbians before Lesbianism: Sexual Identity in Early Twentieth-Century British Fiction," in *Borderlines: Genders and Identities in War and Peace, 1870–1930*, ed. Billie Melman (London: Routledge, 1998), 193–211.

90. William Plomer, *The Case Is Altered* (London: Hogarth Press, 1932), 33–35.

91. Wyndham Lewis, *The Apes of God* (Harmondsworth: Penguin Books, 1965), 11–18; Charles Dickens, *Dombey and Son* (Harmondsworth: Penguin Books, 1985), 362.

92. Plomer, *Case Is Altered*, 102.

93. James Joyce, *Finnegans Wake* (London: Faber and Faber, 1964), 35.

94. For example, "The Short-Wave Radio Stations," *Times*, November 7, 1927, 22; "Indoor Aerials," *Times*, November 14, 1927, 20; "Radio Reception," *Times*, November 24, 1927, 25.

95. Henry Cantril and Gordon W. Allport, *The Psychology of Radio* (New York: Harper, 1935), 4, 19, 21.

96. Lawrence, *Letters*, 5:424.

97. "Broadcasting," *Times*, February 10, 1926, 23.

98. *Word-Lore: The "Folk" Magazine* 1, no. 1 (1926), inside front cover.

99. Lawrence's view of the bohemian community in Taos, New Mexico, as reported by Knud Merrild, *A Poet and Two Painters* (London: George Routledge, 1938), 13.

100. Lawrence, *First and Second Lady Chatterley Novels*, 333.

THREE Thermoplastic

1. D. H. Lawrence, *Lady Chatterley's Lover*, ed. Michael Squires (Harmondsworth: Penguin Books, 2006), 159–60, 194.

2. George Orwell, *The Road to Wigan Pier* (Harmondsworth: Penguin Books, 1989), 20.

3. Ibid., 18.

4. Jeffrey Meikle, *American Plastic: A Cultural History* (New Brunswick, NJ: Rutgers University Press, 1995). See also Robert Friedel, *Pioneer Plastic: The Making and Selling of Celluloid* (Madison: University of Wisconsin Press, 1983); and Susan Mossman, ed., *Early Plastics: Perspectives, 1850–1950* (London: Leicester University Press, 1997).

5. Judith Brown, *Glamour in Six Dimensions: Modernism and the Radiance of Form* (Ithaca, NY: Cornell University Press, 2009), 145–72. See also Rachel Bowlby, *Carried Away: The Invention of Modern Shopping* (London: Faber and Faber, 2000), 100–103.

6. Brown, *Glamour*, 152.

7. Penny Sparke, ed., *The Plastics Age: From Modernity to Post-Modernity* (London: Victoria & Albert Museum, 1990).

8. For an informative brief account of the opera in question, Virgil Thompson and Gertrude Stein's *Four Saints in Three Acts* (1934), see Brown, *Glamour*, 155–58. The Cole Porter song is "You're the Top," from the 1934 musical *Anything Goes*.

9. Elizabeth Shove, Matthew Watson, Martin Hand, and Jack Ingram, *The Design of Everyday Life* (Oxford: Berg, 2007). See also Pauline G. Beery's engaging *Stuff: The Story of Materials in the Service of Man* (New York: D. Appleton, 1930).

10. See, for example, Marc Manganaro, "Mind, Myth, and Culture: Eliot and Anthropology," in *A Companion to T. S. Eliot*, ed. David E. Chinitz (Oxford: Wiley-Blackwell, 2009), 79–90; and, more generally, Elazar Barkan and Ronald Bush, eds., *Prehistories of the Future: The Primitivist Project and the Culture of Modernism* (Stanford, CA: Stanford University Press, 1995).

11. Virginia Woolf, *The Waves*, ed. Gillian Beer (Oxford: Oxford University Press, 1992), 162.

12. Isobel Armstrong, *Victorian Glassworlds: Glass Culture and the Imagination, 1830–1880* (Oxford: Oxford University Press, 2008), 1, 3, 13.

13. Thomas J. Misa, *Leonardo to the Internet: Technology and Culture from the Renaissance to the Present* (Baltimore: Johns Hopkins University Press, 2004), ch. 6, "Materials of Modernism 1900–1950."

14. Walter Gropius, *The New Architecture and the Bauhaus*, trans. P. Morton Strand (London: Faber and Faber, 1937), 19–29.

15. Armstrong, *Victorian Glassworlds*, 11.

16. Anne Friedberg, *Window Shopping: Cinema and the Postmodern* (Berkeley: University of California Press, 1993), 160.

17. Franz Schultze, *Mies van der Rohe: A Critical Biography* (Chicago: University of Chicago Press, 1985), 103.

18. Hannes Meyer, "Project for the Palace of the League of Nations, Geneva, 1926–7," in *Buildings, Projects, and Writings* (London: Alec Tiranti, 1965), 24–37, p. 25.

19. Walter Benjamin, "The Destructive Character," in *Selected Writings*, ed. Michael W. Jennings, Howard Eiland, and Gary Smith, trans. Rodney Livingstone and others, 4 vols. (Cambridge, MA: Harvard University Press, 1996–2003), 2:541–42, p. 541.

20. Benjamin, "Experience and Poverty," ibid., 2:731–36, pp. 733–34.

21. Klaus Vogel, "The Transparent Man—Some Comments on the History of a Symbol," in *Manifesting Medicine: Bodies and Machines*, ed. Robert Bud, Bernard Finn, and Helmuth Trischler (Amsterdam: Harwood Academic Publishers, 1999), 31–61.

22. Wallace Stevens, "Asides on the Oboe," in *Collected Poems* (London: Faber and Faber, 1955), 250–51.

23. Allyson Booth, *Postcards from the Trenches: Negotiating the Space between Modernism and the First World War* (Oxford: Oxford University Press, 1996), ch. 7.

24. D. H. Lawrence, *Women in Love*, ed. David Farmer, Lindeth Vasey, and John Worthen (Cambridge: Cambridge University Press, 1987), 477.

25. Rod Mengham, "Broken Glass," in *The Fiction of the 1940s: Stories of Survival*, ed. Mengham and N. H. Reeve (Basingstoke: Palgrave, 2001), 124–33.

26. Dawn Ades, Neil Cox, and David Hopkins, *Duchamp* (London: Thames & Hudson, 1999), 94.

27. Mark Prendergast, *For God, Country, and Coca-Cola: The Definitive History of the World's Most Popular Soft Drink* (London: Orion, 2000), 103.

28. For a different but not incompatible view of that pathos of young men in Woolf's fiction, see Lisa Fluet, "Hit-Man Modernism," in *Bad Modernisms*, ed. Douglas Mao and Rebecca L. Walkowitz (Durham, NC: Duke University Press, 2006), 269–97, pp. 284–88.

29. Virginia Woolf, *Jacob's Room,* ed. Kate Flint (Oxford: Oxford University Press, 1992), 129, 57–58.

30. H. G. Wells, *Marriage* (London: Hogarth Press, 1986), 249.

31. John T. Brady, "The Inventions of the Future," *Popular Mechanics* 49, no. 4 (1928): 536–42, p. 541.

32. Advertisement for Armourplate glass, *Times,* May 28, 1936, 15.

33. Robert Friedel, *Pioneer Plastic: The Making and Selling of Celluloid* (Madison: University of Wisconsin Press, 1983), 111.

34. Samuel Beckett, *Murphy* (London: Calder & Boyars, 1969), 53 .

35. "Inflammable Buttons," *Times,* March 7, 1892, 4.

36. For example, "Big Fire at Cardiff," *Times,* January 30, 1917, 5.

37. Display advertisement, *Times,* December 20, 1912, 8.

38. H. V. Potter, "New Plastic Materials," *Times,* November 1, 1932, xxiv.

39. Louis MacNeice, *Collected Poems,* ed. Peter McDonald (London: Faber and Faber, 2007), 22.

40. Vogel, "Transparent Man," 41–43.

41. Steve Chibnall, *Quota Quickies: The Birth of the British "B" Film* (London: BFI Publishing, 2007), 223–26.

42. "The Queen at Olympia," *Times,* February 22, 1935, 11.

43. W. H. Auden, *The English Auden: Poems, Essays and Dramatic Writings, 1927–1939,* ed. Edward Mendelson (London: Faber and Faber, 1977), 46. Henceforth *EA.*

44. Rod Mengham, "The Thirties: Politics, Authority, Perspective," in *The Cambridge History of Twentieth-Century English Literature,* ed. Laura Marcus and Peter Nicholls (Cambridge: Cambridge University Press, 2004), 359–78, p. 363.

45. Michael O'Neill, "The Thirties Poetry of W. H. Auden," in *The Cambridge Companion to Twentieth-Century English Poetry,* ed. Neil Corcoran (Cambridge: Cambridge University Press, 2007), 105–16, p. 105.

46. Robert Crawford, "Modernist Cybernetics and the Poetry of Knowledge," in *The Modern Poet: Poetry, Academia, and Knowledge since the 1750s* (Oxford: Oxford University Press, 2001), 170–222.

47. Ibid., 188, 190, 199.

48. Peter Firchow, "Private Faces in Public Places: Auden's *The Orators,*" *PMLA* 92 (1977): 253–72.

49. Douglas Mao, "A Shaman in Common: Lewis, Auden, and the Queerness of Liberalism," in Mao and Walkowitz, *Bad Modernisms,* 206–37, pp. 227–28.

50. Lawrence, *Lady Chatterley's Lover,* 122.

51. I define the Audenesque in these terms in *The Making of the Reader: Language and Subjectivity in Modern American, English and Irish Poetry* (Houndmills: Macmillan, 1984), 113–23.

52. Stephen Spender, *The Destructive Element: A Study of Modern Writers and Beliefs* (London: Jonathan Cape, 1935), 270.

53. T. S. Eliot, *The Waste Land,* in *Complete Poems and Plays* (London: Faber and Faber, 1969), 59–80, pp. 62, 69.

54. Spender, *Destructive Element,* 270.

55. Edward Mendelson, *Early Auden* (London: Faber and Faber, 1981), 319.

56. Graham Greene, *England Made Me* (Harmondsworth: Penguin Books, 1970), 34–35, 138.

57. Margery Palmer McCullough, "Scottish Modernism," in *The Oxford Handbook of Modernisms,* ed. Peter Brooker, Andrzej Gasiorek, Deborah Longworth, and Andrew Thacker (Oxford: Oxford University Press, 2010), 765–81, pp. 765–66.

58. Robert Crawford, "MacDiarmid in Montrose," in *Locations of Literary Modernism: Region and Nation in British and American Modernist Poetry,* ed. Alex Davis and Lee Jenkins (Cambridge: Cambridge University Press, 2000), 33–56.

59. Nancy Gish, "MacDiarmid Reading *The Waste Land:* The Politics of Quotation," in *Hugh MacDiarmid: Man and Poet,* ed. Nancy Gish (Edinburgh: Edinburgh University Press, 1992), 207–29, p. 207.

60. Crawford, "MacDiarmid in Montrose," 33.

61. Ian Duncan, "'Upon the Thistle They're Impaled': Hugh MacDiarmid's Modernist Nationalism," in *Modernism and Colonialism: British and Irish Literature, 1899–1939,* ed. Richard Begam and Michael Valdez Moses (Durham, NC: Duke University Press, 2007), 246–66, p. 246.

62. Alan Riach, *Hugh MacDiarmid's Epic Poetry* (Edinburgh: Edinburgh University Press, 1991), 14. Riach offers an informative account of this evolution, ibid., 1–23.

63. Crawford, *Modern Poet,* 205–6, 212, 216–17, 210, 207.

64. Hugh MacDiarmid, "Charles Doughty and the Need for Heroic Poetry," in *Selected Essays* (London: Jonathan Cape, 1969), 75–85, p. 75.

65. Quoted in Herbert F. Tucker, *Epic: Britain's Heroic Muse, 1790–1910* (Oxford: Oxford University Press, 2008), 573. Tucker provides a scintillating brief account of Doughty's "scarification of ordinary English" (571–83).

66. MacDiarmid, "Charles Doughty," 75, 85.

67. Hugh MacDiarmid, "MacDiarmid at Large," BBC Third Programme, March 1960, quoted in W. N. Herbert, *To Circumjack MacDiarmid: The Poetry and Prose of Hugh MacDiarmid* (Oxford: Clarendon Press, 1992), 137.

68. Duncan, "'Upon the Thistle,'" 254, 258.

69. Hugh MacDiarmid, *Lucky Poet: A Self-Study in Literature and Political Ideas* (Manchester: Carcanet Press, 1994), 110.

70. Hugh MacDiarmid, *Letters,* ed. Alan Bold (London: Hamish Hamilton, 1984), 591.

71. Roderick Watson, "Landscapes of the Mind and Word: MacDiarmid's Journey to the Raised Beach and Beyond," in Gish, *Hugh MacDiarmid: Man and Poet,* 231–51, p. 243.

72. Hugh MacDiarmid, *Complete Poems,* 2 vols., ed. Michael Grieve and W. R. Aitken (Manchester: Carcanet Press, 1994), 422–33, p. 427. Henceforth *CP.*

73. F. R. Leavis, *New Bearings in English Poetry: A Study of the Contemporary Situation* (Harmondsworth: Penguin Books, 1967), 165, 168.

74. Riach notes and comments on the borrowing in *Hugh MacDiarmid's Epic Poetry,* 171–72.

75. Scott Lyall, *Hugh MacDiarmid's Poetry and Politics of Place: Imagining a Scottish Republic* (Edinburgh: Edinburgh University Press, 2006), 121. See James R. Nicolson, *Shetland* (Newton Abbott: David & Charles, 1972), 19.

76. Percy Bysshe Shelley, "Mont Blanc: Lines Written in the Vale of Chamouni," in *Poetical Works,* ed. Thomas Hutchinson and G. M. Matthews (Oxford: Oxford University Press, 1970), 532–35, p. 534.

77. Riegl developed his theory of haptic looking in *Problems of Style: Foundations for a History of Ornament,* first published in 1893; trans. Evelyn Kain (Princeton, NJ: Princeton University Press, 1993); and *Late Roman Art Industry,* first published in 1901, trans. Rolph Winkes (Rome: Giorgio Bretschneider Editore, 1985). He explained his choice of terminology in an essay of 1902, "Late Roman or Oriental?," trans. Peter Wortsman, in *German Essays on Art History,* ed. Gert Schiff (New York: Continuum, 1988), 173–90. Abbie Garrington writes informatively about the "haptic sense" in the literature of the period, without mentioning MacDiarmid, in "Touching Texts: The Haptic Sense in Modernist Literature," *Literature Compass* 7, no. 9 (2010), 810–23. See also David Trotter, *Cinema and Modernism* (Oxford: Wiley-Blackwell, 2007), 28–29.

78. Catherine Kerrigan, *Whaur Extremes Meet: The Poetry of Hugh MacDiarmid, 1920–1934* (Edinburgh: Mercat Press, 1983), 197. For a succinct account of some of the texts plundered in the poem, see Michael H. Whitworth, "Three Prose Sources for Hugh MacDiarmid's 'On a Raised Beach,'" *Notes & Queries* 252, no. 2 (2007): 175–77.

79. John Milton, *Paradise Lost,* ed. Alastair Fowler (London: Longman, 1986), 369, 356, 358–59: book 7, lines 216–17, 2–4, 23–31.

80. They collaborated most momentously on a collection of poems, stories, essays, and sketches, *Scottish Scene: Or, the Intelligent Man's Guide to Albyn* (London: Hutchinson, 1934).

81. Lewis Grassic Gibbon, *Grey Granite,* in *A Scots Quair,* ed. Tom Crawford (Edinburgh: Canongate, 1995), 117. Henceforth *GG.*

82. We should not, of course, ignore the remaining differences between MacDiarmid and Auden, which Lyall has examined succinctly: *Hugh MacDiarmid's Poetry and Politics of Place,* 143–46.

83. Quoted in Martin Hammer and Christina Lodder, *Constructing Modernity: The Art and Career of Naum Gabo* (New Haven, CT: Yale University Press, 2000), 243. I have relied heavily on their invaluable account of Gabo's London years: ibid., 231–67.

84. Ibid., 234, 251.

85. "Foreign Buyers at the Fair," *Times*, February 27, 1936, 9.

86. Hammer and Lodder, *Constructing Modernity*, 250.

87. Ibid., 262.

88. Riach provides the most thorough and informative discussion of the poem to date, including the circumstances of its composition: *Hugh MacDiarmid's Epic Poetry*, 59–157.

89. Crawford, *Modern Poet*, 215.

90. Jekuthiel Ginsburg, "Editorial," *Scripta Mathematica* 1, no. 1 (1932): 1.

91. Knud Merrild, *A Poet and Two Painters* (London: George Routledge, 1938), 15–16.

92. William Gerhardie, *Of Mortal Love* (London: Macdonald, 1970), 94.

93. For example, Louis Armand, *Techne: James Joyce, Hypertext and Technology* (Prague: Charles University Press, 2003).

94. Steven Connor, *James Joyce* (Plymouth: Northcote House Publishers, 1996), 94.

95. Jane Lewty, "What They Had Heard Said Written," in *Broadcasting Modernisms*, ed. Lewty, Debra Rae Cohen, and Michael Coyle (Gainesville: University Press of Florida, 2009), 199–220, p. 206. See also James A. Connor, "Radio Free Joyce: *Wake* Language and the Experience of Radio," in *Sound States: Innovative Poetics and Acoustical Technologies*, ed. Adelaide Morris (Chapel Hill: University of North Carolina Press, 1997), 17–31.

96. James Joyce, *Finnegans Wake* (London: Faber and Faber, 1964), 468. Henceforth *FW*.

97. Susan Shaw Sailer, "Universalizing Languages: *Finnegans Wake* Meets Basic English," *James Joyce Quarterly* 36, no. 4 (1999): 853–68.

98. MacDiarmid, *Letters*, 771.

99. Connor, *James Joyce*, 95.

100. James Joyce, *Finnegans Wake: A Facsimile of Buffalo Notebooks VI.C.1,2,3,4,5,7*, ed. Danis Rose (New York: Garland Publishing, 1978), VI.C.4–262.

101. Ibid., VI.C.7–128.

FOUR　Talkativeness

1. Ross McKibbin, *Classes and Cultures: England, 1918–1951* (Oxford: Oxford University Press, 1998), 75, 77–78, 81.

2. "Slough Estates Limited," *Times,* April 24, 1936, 24.

3. McKibbin, *Classes and Cultures,* 87–90.

4. Virginia Woolf, "The Narrow Bridge of Art," in *Collected Essays,* ed. Leonard Woolf, 4 vols. (London: Chatto & Windus, 1966–1967), 2:218–29, p. 222.

5. Richard Overy, *The Morbid Age: Britain and the Crisis of Civilization, 1919–1939* (London: Allen Lane, 2009), 375–76. See also Mark Pegg, *Broadcasting and Society, 1918–1939* (London: Croom Helm, 1983), 7.

6. Henry Green, *Blindness* (London: Harvill, 1993), 60–61.

7. J. B. Priestley, *English Journey* (Chicago: University of Chicago Press, 1984), 297–301. Simon Dentith uses this passage as the starting point for a highly informative essay, "Thirties Poetry and the Landscape of Suburbia," in *Rewriting the Thirties: Modernism and After,* ed. Keith Williams and Stephen Matthews (London: Longman, 1997), 108–23.

8. Dorothy L. Sayers, *Murder Must Advertise* (London: Hodder & Stoughton, 1969), 98, 127.

9. "Success of New Policy," *Times,* October 3, 1934, 9.

10. Asa Briggs and Peter Burke, *A Social History of the Media: From Gutenberg to the Internet* (Cambridge: Polity Press, 2002), 154.

11. See Pegg, *Broadcasting and Society;* and for a more sweeping account, Paddy Scannell and David Cardiff, *A Social History of British Broadcasting: Serving the Nation, 1923–1939* (Oxford: Blackwell, 1991); and Scannell, *Radio, Television and Modern Life* (Oxford: Blackwell, 1996).

12. I take these terms from Michael Geisler's description of developments in media theory in Germany: "From Building Blocks to Radical Construction: West German Media Theory since 1984," *New German Critique* 78 (1999): 75–107, pp. 98–100.

13. George Buchanan, "News Bulletins," *Spectator,* September 15, 1939, 376. A good deal of attention has rightly been paid to the part regular broadcasts by writers such as Eliot, Forster, and Woolf played in that gesture of unity. See in particular Todd Avery, *Radio Modernism: Literature, Ethics, and the BBC, 1922–1938* (Aldershot: Ashgate, 2006).

14. William Uricchio, "Storage, Simultaneity, and the Media Technologies of Modernity," in *Allegories of Communication: Intermedial Concerns from Cinema to the Digital,* ed. John Fullerton and Jan Olsson (Rome: John Libbey Publishing, 2004), 123–38, pp. 133–34.

15. Debra Rae Cohen, "Annexing the Oracular Voice: Form, Ideology, and the BBC," in *Broadcasting Modernism,* ed. Debra Rae Cohen, Michael Coyle, and Jane Lewty (Gainesville: University Press of Florida, 2009), 142–57.

16. Theodor Adorno, *Current of Music: Elements of a Radio Theory,* ed. Robert Hullot-Kentor (Frankfurt am Main: Suhrkamp, 2006), 114. See

David Jenemann, "Flying Solo: The Charms of the Radio Body," in Cohen, Coyle, and Lewty, *Broadcasting Modernism*, 89–103.

17. McKibbin, *Classes and Cultures*, 458.

18. Trystan Edwards, "Architecture and Slum-Dwellers," *Times*, August 12, 1936, 15.

19. Patrick Hamilton, *Twenty Thousand Streets under the Sky: A London Trilogy* (London: Hogarth Press, 1987), 34.

20. Anthony Powell, *Afternoon Men* (London: Fontana Books, 1971), 87, 89, 95.

21. Hamilton, *Hangover Square* (Harmondsworth: Penguin, 2001), 66–67.

22. Jean Rhys, *After Leaving Mr Mackenzie* (Harmondsworth: Penguin, 2000), 134.

23. J. B. Priestley, *Angel Pavement* (London: Everyman, 1937), 137. 140–41.

24. Storm Jameson, *Company Parade* (London: Virago, 1982), 285. Henceforth *CP*.

25. R. H. Chamney, "Features of the Essential Factors in Telephone Transmission," *Post Office Electrical Engineers' Journal* 26, no. 4 (1934): 301–3, p. 301.

26. For an exemplary account of this development, see James Lastra, *Sound Technology and the American Cinema: Perception, Representation, Modernity* (New York: Columbia University Press, 2000).

27. Donald Crafton, *The Talkies: American Cinema's Transition to Sound, 1926–1931* (Berkeley: University of California Press, 1997), 238–44.

28. Harry F. Olson and Frank Massa, "On the Realistic Reproduction of Sound with Particular Reference to Sound Motion Pictures," *Journal of the Society of Motion Picture Engineers* 23, no. 2 (1934): 71; quoted by Lastra, *Sound Technology and the American Cinema*, 193.

29. Charles O'Brien, *Cinema's Conversion to Sound: Technology and Film Style in France and the U.S.* (Bloomington: Indiana University Press, 2005), 3.

30. Donald Crafton, "Mindshare: Telephone and Radio Compete for the Talkies," in *Allegories of Communication: Intermedial Concerns from Cinema to the Digital*, ed. John Fullerton and Jan Olsson (Rome: John Libbey Publishing, 2004), 123–56, p. 123. See also Crafton, *Talkies*, 34–38.

31. Paul Young, *The Cinema Dreams Its Rivals: Media Fantasy Films from Radio to the Internet* (Minneapolis: University of Minnesota Press, 2006), 88–91, 94. For a discussion of film as radio and film as phonography at this time, see Rick Altman, "Introduction: Sound/History," in *Sound Theory/Sound Practice*, ed. Rick Altman (New York: Routledge, 1992), 113–25.

32. Ibid., 98.

33. Rudolf Arnheim, *Radio: An Art of Sound,* trans. Margaret Ludwig and Herbert Read (London: Faber and Faber, 1936), 158.

34. Young, *Cinema Dreams,* 80.

35. The authoritative account is Tom Gunning, *D. W. Griffith and the Origins of American Narrative Film: The Early Years at Biograph* (Urbana: University of Illinois Press, 1991).

36. For a full account of the development of this pattern, see my "The Space Beside: Lateral Exposition, Gender, and Urban Narrative Space in D. W. Griffith's Biograph Films," in *Cities in Transition: The Moving Image and the Modern Metropolis,* ed. Andrew Webber and Emma Wilson (London: Wallflower Press, 2008), 40–55.

37. Bill Hillier and Julienne Hanson, *The Social Logic of Space* (Cambridge: Cambridge University Press, 1984).

38. Tom Gunning, "Fritz Lang Calling: The Telephone and the Circuits of Modernity," in Fullerton and Olsson, *Allegories of Communication,* 19–37, pp. 21–24.

39. Lawrence Rainey, "Office Politics: *Skyscraper* (1931) and *Skyscraper Souls* (1932)," *Critical Quarterly* 49, no. 4 (2007): 77–88, p. 77. See also his "Fables of Modernity: The Typist in Germany and France," *Modernism/Modernity* 11, no. 2 (2004): 333–40; and "From the Fallen Woman to the Fallen Typist," *English Literature in Transition, 1880–1920* 52, no. 3 (2009): 273–97.

40. Siegfried Kracauer, "The Hotel Lobby," in *The Mass Ornament: Weimar Essays,* ed. and trans. Thomas Y. Levin (Cambridge, MA: Harvard University Press, 1995), 173–85, pp. 175–77.

41. On Baum, see Linda J. King, "The Image of Fame: Vicki Baum in Weimar Germany," *German Quarterly* 58, no. 3 (1985): 375–93; and Andrea Capovilla, *Entwürfe weiblicher Identität in der Moderne: Milena Jelenská, Vicki Baum, Gina Kaus, Alice Rühle-Gerstel* (Oldenburg: Igel Verlag, 2004).

42. Donald Albrecht, *Designing Dreams: Modern Architecture in the Movies* (London: Thames & Hudson, 1986), 138–42; Beverly Heisner, *Hollywood Art: Art Direction in the Days of the Great Studios* (Jefferson, NC: McFarland, 1990), 77–79; Christina Wilson, "Cedric Gibbons: Architect of Hollywood's Golden Age," in *Architecture and Film,* ed. Mark Lamster (New York: Princeton Architectural Press, 2000), 101–15.

43. James Buzzard, "Perpetual Revolution," *Modernism/Modernity* 8, no. 4 (2001): 559–81.

44. Rayner Banham, *The Architecture of the Well-Tempered Environment* (Chicago: University of Chicago Press, 1969), 73–74.

45. Vicki Baum, *Grand Hotel,* trans. Basil Creighton (London: Geoffrey Bles, 1930), 54.

46. Manny Farber, *Negative Space: Manny Farber on the Movies* (New York: Da Capo Press, 1998), 145, 152. Mark Goble has written illuminatingly about the telephone calls made in *Grand Hotel* as "the very symbol of all that is modern because they symbolize nothing in particular, a telling background noise that consumes as much meaning as it transmits." His focus is primarily on Garbo's last significant scene in the film, during which Grusinskaya picks up the phone and asks to be connected to Von Geigern, not knowing that he is already dead: *Beautiful Circuits: Modernism and the Mediated Life* (New York: Columbia University Press, 2010), 114, 130–32. In my view, Grusinskaya's monologue constitutes the last gasp of an ancien régime, rather than a demonstration of "all that is modern." What is new, in the film, is the talkativeness of its petit bourgeois insurrectionaries.

47. The genealogy of metropolitan spatial representations in the film noir cycle has recently received welcome attention: Edward Dimendberg, *Film Noir and the Spaces of Modernity* (Cambridge, MA: Harvard University Press, 2004).

48. O'Brien, *Cinema's Conversion to Sound*, 56–57.

49. The most thorough account of the politics of Renoir's films remains Christopher Faulkner, *The Social Cinema of Jean Renoir* (Princeton, NJ: Princeton University Press, 1986). Faulkner's concern is to expose the limitations of Popular Front attitudes.

50. Alan Williams, "*Le Crime de Monsieur Lange,*" in *The Cinema of France,* ed. Phil Powrie (London: Wallflower Press, 2006), 31–39, p. 37.

51. André Bazin, *Jean Renoir,* trans. W. W. Halsey and William H. Simon (London: W. H. Allen, 1974), 44.

52. McKibbin, *Classes and Cultures,* 68, 484–86. See also Joseph McAleer, *Popular Reading and Publishing in Britain, 1914–1950* (Oxford: Oxford University Press, 1992).

53. Keith Williams's shrewd and wide-ranging *British Writers and the Media, 1930–1945* (Houndmills: Macmillan, 1996) remains an authoritative account. Williams discusses the mass media as subject matter and formal influence in the literature of the period, and the involvement of writers in film and broadcasting.

54. Ruth Dudley Edwards, *Victor Gollancz: A Biography* (London: Gollancz, 1987), 177.

55. Tom Wintringham, contribution to "Controversy," *Left Review* 1, no. 6 (1935): 221–25, p. 225.

56. Andy Croft, *Red Letter Days: British Fiction in the 1930s* (London: Lawrence & Wishart, 1990). Croft has continued to publish widely on the topic. See *Comrade Heart: A Life of Randall Swingler* (Manchester:

Manchester University Press, 2003); "Authors Take Sides: Writers and the Communist Party, 1920–1956," in *Opening the Books: Essays on the Social and Cultural History of British Communism,* ed. Geoff Andrews, Nina Fishman, and Kevin Morgan (London: Pluto Press, 1995), 83–101; and, as editor, *A Weapon in the Struggle: The Cultural History of the Communist Party in Britain* (London: Pluto, 1998). Further important contributions include H. Gustav Klaus, "Socialist Fiction in the 1930s: Some Preliminary Observations," in *The 1930s: A Challenge to Orthodoxy,* ed. John Lucas (Hassocks: Harvester, 1978); Jeremy Hawthorn, ed., *The British Working-Class Novel in the Twentieth Century* (London: Edward Arnold, 1984); and Pamela Fox, *Class Fictions: Shame and Resistance in the British Working-Class Novel* (Durham, NC: Duke University Press, 1994).

57. Christopher Hilliard, "Producers by Hand and by Brain: Working-Class Writers and Left-Wing Publishers in 1930s Britain," *Journal of Modern History* 78, no. 1 (2006): 37–64, p. 64. On another important publishing initiative launched during that moment, see N. Joicey, "A Paperback Guide to Progress: Penguin Books, 1935–c. 1951," *Twentieth Century British History* 4, no. 1 (1993): 25–56. It was at exactly this moment that the Union of Soviet Writers intensified its search for publication outlets in Britain. See Ian Patterson, "The Translation of Soviet Literature: John Rodker and PresLit," forthcoming in *Russia in Britain, 1880–1940: From Melodrama to Modernism,* ed. Rebecca Beasley and Philip Bullock (Oxford: Oxford University Press, 2013).

58. Storm Jameson, *Journey from the North,* 2 vols. (London: Virago, 1984), 1:328.

59. Croft, *Red Letters,* 256. The collective novel also found favor in Scandinavia. See Scott de Francesco, *Scandinavian Cultural Radicalism: Literary Commitment and the Collective Novel* (New York: Peter Lang, 1990).

60. Hilliard, "Producers by Hand," 61–64. Valentine Cunningham takes Barke's *Major Operation: A Novel* (1936) as his main example in "The Age of Anxiety and Influence: Or, Tradition and the Thirties Talents," in *Rewriting the Thirties,* 5–22. See also John Fordham, *James Hanley: Modernism and the Working Class* (Cardiff: University of Wales Press, 2002).

61. *Daily Worker,* May 9, 1936, 4.

62. Jameson, "Documents," *Fact* 4 (1937): 9–18, p. 18.

63. Stuart Laing, "Presenting 'Things as They Are': John Sommerfield's *May Day* and Mass Observation," in *Class, Culture and Social Change: A New View of the 1930s,* ed. Frank Gloversmith (Brighton: Harvester, 1980), 142–60; Williams, *British Writers,* 128–39; Cunningham, "Age of Anxiety and Influence"; Laura Marcus, *The Tenth Muse: Writing about Cinema in the Modernist Period* (Oxford: Oxford University Press, 2007), 92.

64. Rex Warner, *The Professor: A Novel* (Harmondsworth: Penguin Books, 1945), 11, 107–8, 119. We perhaps should not forget Norman Hunter's Professor Branestawm, who, in a children's book first published in 1933, comically miscalculates his first (and no doubt last) BBC broadcast: *The Incredible Adventures of Professor Branestawm* (London: Red Fox, 2008), 151–62.

65. Graham Greene, "Subjects and Stories," in *The Graham Greene Film Reader: Mornings in the Dark,* ed. David Parkinson (Manchester: Carcanet, 1993), 409–18, p. 414.

66. Bernard Bergonzi, *Reading the Thirties: Texts and Contexts* (London: Macmillan, 1978), 120–22; Marcus, *Tenth Muse,* 429–30.

67. Timothy D. Taylor, "Music and the Rise of Radio in Twenties America: Technological Imperialism, Socialization, and the Transformation of Intimacy," in *Wired for Sound: Engineering and Technologies in Sonic Cultures,* ed. Paul D. Greene and Thomas Porcello (Middletown, CT: Wesleyan University Press, 2005), 245–68, p. 261.

68. See Allison McCracken, "Real Men Don't Sing Ballads: The Radio Crooner in Hollywood, 1929–1933," in *Soundtrack Available: Essays on Film and Popular Culture,* ed. Pamela Robertson Wojcik and Arthur Knight (Durham, NC: Duke University Press, 2001), 105–33.

69. Greene, *Graham Green Film Reader,* 80.

70. Graham Greene, *Brighton Rock* (London: Vintage, 2004), 52, 195–96.

71. "New Films in London," *Times,* July 20, 1936, 10. On the whole, the talkativeness was not frowned on: "Criticisms of the Latest Films," *Picturegoer Weekly* 1 (August 1936): 24–27, p. 24; "What—and What Not—to See," *Film Weekly,* July 18, 1936, 31.

72. Greene, *Graham Greene Film Reader,* 122–24.

73. Ibid., 189.

74. Ibid., 283–85.

75. Dot Allan, *Makeshift and Hunger March,* ed. Moira Burgess (Glasgow: Association for Scottish Literary Studies, 2010), 281, 226.

76. Jeremy Treglown, *Romancing: The Life and Work of Henry Green* (London: Faber and Faber, 2000), 109.

77. Valentine Cunningham, *British Writers of the Thirties* (Oxford: Oxford University Press, 1988), 285.

78. Henry Green, *Living,* in *Loving, Living, Party Going* (London: Vintage, 2005), 216–17, 224–25, 244, 282, 301, 311, 320–21, 379. Henceforth *L. Living* is in itself sufficient to refute Genevieve Abravanel's claim that the advent of the talkies further intensified British literary culture's hostility to the "bad democracy of cinema": *Americanizing Britain: The Rise of Modernism in the Age of the Entertainment Empire* (New York: Oxford University Press, 2012), 94. Further counterexamples will follow.

79. Croft, *Red Letters,* 63–65, 84–85.

80. Harold Heslop, *Last Cage Down* (London: Lawrence & Wishart, 1984), 3. Henceforth *LCD.*

81. Williams, *British Writers,* 61–70.

82. Nicholas Blake, *Thou Shell of Death* (Boulder, CO: Rue Morgue Press, 2009), 36. First published in 1936.

83. Arthur Calder-Marshall, *The Changing Scene* (London: Chapman & Hall, 1937), 84–86, 102, 104.

84. Bertolt Brecht, "The Radio as an Apparatus of Communication," in *Brecht on Theatre,* trans. John Willett (New York: Hill & Wang, 1964), 51–53, p. 52. First published in 1932.

85. Lewis Jones, *We Live: The Story of a Welsh Mining Valley* (London: Lawrence & Wishart, 1978), 3–4.

86. Philip Henderson, *The Novel Today: A Study in Contemporary Attitudes* (London: John Lane, 1936), 271.

87. John Sommerfield, *May Day* (London: London Books, 2010), 243. Henceforth *MD.*

88. Henderson, *Novel Today,* 271.

89. William Gerhardie, *Doom* (London: Prion Books, 2001), 40.

90. In Jones's *We Live,* news of a mining accident passes "from mouth to mouth as quickly as a telephone message" (18).

91. Allan, *Hunger March,* 351.

92. It is hard to believe that Buchanan had not read Wells's *The New Machiavelli* (1911), which records Richard Remington's rise from shabby-genteel surroundings to parliamentary eminence as an advocate of technocratic efficiency, until his career is halted by an affair. He ends up designing destroyers for use in the next war.

93. George Buchanan, *Entanglement* (London: Constable, 1938), 1. Henceforth *E.*

94. James Joyce, *Finnegans Wake* (London: Faber and Faber, 1964), 299. Henceforth *FW.*

95. Margot Norris, "*Finnegans Wake,*" in *The Cambridge Companion to James Joyce,* ed. Derek Attridge (Cambridge: Cambridge University Press, 1990), 161–84, p. 161.

96. A. Nicholas Fargnoli and Michael Patrick Gillespie, *Critical Companion to James Joyce* (New York: Infobase Publishing, 2006), 121.

97. John P. Anderson, *Finnegans Wake: The Cure of the Kabbalah* (Boca Raton, FL: Universal-Publishers, 2012), 64.

98. The "broadcast" is often cited, without reference to its content, by scholars keen to demonstrate the acuity with which *Finnegans Wake* anticipates future developments in media and hypermedia: for example, Donald F.

Theall, "Beyond the Orality/Literacy Dichotomy: James Joyce and the Pre-history of Cyberspace," in *Hypermedia Joyce*, ed. David Vichnar and Louis Armand (Prague: Litteraria Pragensia Books, 2010), 17–34, pp. 25–26.

99. Richard Robertson, "Buckley in a General Russia: *Finnegans Wake* and Political Space," in *Joyce in Trieste: An Album of Risky Readings*, ed. Sebastian D. G. Knowles, Geert Lernout, and John McCourt (Gainesville: University Press of Florida, 2007), 170–87.

100. Emer Nolan has argued influentially that the styles in "Cyclops" are at times closer to the citizen's militant nationalist invective than has generally been assumed, and that Joyce engages closely with Gaelic tradition throughout the episode. *James Joyce and Nationalism* (London: Routledge, 1995), 96–112.

101. Perhaps of the kind advocated by contributors to Andrew Gibson and Len Platt, eds., *Joyce, Ireland, Britain* (Gainesville: University Press of Florida, 2006).

102. Treglown, *Romancing*, 122.

103. Louis MacNeice, *The Strings Are False: An Unfinished Autobiography* (London: Faber and Faber, 1965), 212.

FIVE Transit Writing

1. James W. Carey uses the term's double meaning to help establish the important distinction between "transmission" and "ritual" views of communication, which I refer to in Chapter 1. See Carey, *Communication as Culture: Essays on Media and Society* (Boston: Unwin Hyman, 1989), esp. pp. 14–23.

2. Louis MacNeice, "Train to Dublin," in *Collected Poems*, ed. Peter McDonald (London: Faber and Faber, 2007), 17–18, p. 17.

3. Valentine Cunningham, *British Writers of the Thirties* (Oxford: Oxford University Press, 1988), 356.

4. Enda Duffy, *The Speed Handbook: Velocity, Pleasure, Modernism* (Durham, NC: Duke University Press, 2009).

5. Dorthe Gert Simonsen, "Accelerating Modernity: Time-Space Compression in the Wake of the Aeroplane," *Journal of Transport History* 26, no. 2 (2005): 98–117, p. 98.

6. "'Listening-In' on a Motor Tour," *Times*, September 6, 1926, 11.

7. John Ruskin, *Works*, ed. E. T. Cook and Alexander Wedderburn, 39 vols. (London, Longmans, Green, 1907), 8:59.

8. Wolfgang Schivelbusch, *The Railway Journey: The Industrialization of Time and Space in the 19th Century* (Berkeley: University of California

Press, 1977), 24. There have been some useful challenges to the homogenizing rhetoric of "modernity" that take the railway in its global context as their focus: James A. Flath, "The Chinese Railroad View: Transportation Themes in Popular Print, 1873–1915," *Cultural Critique* 58 (2004): 168–90; Marian Aguiar, "Making Modernity inside the Technological Space of the Railway," *Cultural Critique* 68 (2008): 66–85.

9. Michel de Certeau, "Railway Navigation and Incarceration," in *The Practice of Everyday Life,* trans. Steven Rendall (Berkeley: University of California Press, 1984), 111–14, p. 112. The train's "inside" does interest de Certeau, but only in relation to its "outside."

10. Schivelbusch, *Railway Journey,* 64.

11. Lynne Kirby, *Parallel Tracks: The Railroad and Silent Cinema* (Durham, NC: Duke University Press, 1997).

12. Henri Lefebvre, *La vie quotidienne dans le monde moderne* (Paris: Gallimard, 1968), 104. My translation.

13. Colin Divall, "Civilizing Velocity: Masculinity and the Marketing of Britain's Passenger Trains, 1921–1939," *Journal of Transport History* 32, no. 2 (2011): 164–91.

14. Samuel Beckett, "Ding-Dong," in *More Pricks Than Kicks* (London: Pan Books, 1974), 35–43, pp. 36–37.

15. Steven Connor, "Slow Going," at http://www.stevenconnor.com/slow.htm, 2.

16. Paul Fussell, *Abroad: British Literary Traveling between the Wars* (Oxford: Oxford University Press, 1980).

17. Samuel Hynes, *The Auden Generation: Literature and Politics in England in the 1930s* (London: Faber and Faber, 1976), 227–31; Cunningham, *British Writers of the Thirties,* 341–76. The urgent preoccupations were of course to a large extent political: Bernard Schweizer, *Radicals on the Road: The Politics of English Travel Writing in the 1930s* (Charlottesville: University of Virginia Press, 2001).

18. Charles Burdett and Derek Duncan, introduction in *Cultural Encounters: European Travel Writing in the 1930s,* ed. Burdett and Duncan (New York: Berghahn Books, 2002), 1–8, p. 5. See also Helen Carr, "Modernism and Travel (1880–1940)," in *The Cambridge Companion to Travel Writing,* ed. Peter Hulme and Tim Youngs (Cambridge: Cambridge University Press, 2002), 70–86; Tim Youngs, "Travelling Modernists," in *The Oxford Handbook of Modernisms,* ed. Peter Brooker, Andrzej Gasiorek, Deborah Longworth, and Andrew Thacker (Oxford: Oxford University Press, 2010), 267–80; and David Farley, *Modernist Travel Writing: Intellectuals Abroad* (Columbia: University of Missouri Press, 2010).

19. Andrew Thacker, "Journey with Maps: Travel Theory, Geography and the Syntax of Space," in Burdett and Duncan, *Cultural Encounters,* 11–28, p. 25.

20. Graham Greene, *Journey without Maps* (Harmondsworth: Penguin Books, 1971), 21, 25.

21. Paul Eggert, introduction to *Twilight in Italy and Other Essays,* ed. Paul Eggert (Cambridge: Cambridge University Press, 1994), xxiii–lxxv, p. xxiii. Henceforth *TI.*

22. William Wordsworth, "Resolution and Independence," in *Poetical Works,* ed. Thomas Hutchinson and Ernest de Selincourt (Oxford: Oxford University Press, 1969), 155–57, p. 156.

23. Carr, "Modernism and Travel," 85. See also Howard J. Booth, "Making the Case for Cross-Cultural Exchange: Robert Byron's *The Road to Oxiana,*" in Burdett and Duncan, *Cultural Encounters,* 159–72.

24. Robert Byron, *The Road to Oxiana* (London: Vintage Books, 2010), 379–80, 383.

25. Robert Byron, *Europe in the Looking-Glass: Reflections of a Motor Drive from Grimsby to Athens* (London: George Routledge & Sons, 1926), 52, 103.

26. Byron, *Road to Oxiana,* 32–33, 298–99.

27. Philip S. Bagwell, *The Transport Revolution, 1770–1985* (London: Routledge, 1988), 218–19. See also Sean O'Connell, *The Car in British Society: Class, Gender, and Motoring, 1896–1939* (Manchester: Manchester University Press, 1998).

28. David Matless, *Landscape and Englishness* (London: Reaktion, 1998), 62–64.

29. Barbara Roscoe, "'Bradford-on-Avon but Shell on the Road': The Heyday of Motor Touring through Britain's Countryside," in *Rights of Way: Policy, Culture and Management,* ed. Charles Watkins (London: Pinter, 1996), 89–99. Roscoe's "heyday" is the period between 1950 and 1970.

30. Patrick Wright, *On Living in an Old Country* (Oxford: Oxford University Press, 2009), 58.

31. Steve Ellis, *The English Eliot: Design, Language and Landscape in "Four Quartets"* (London: Routledge, 1991), 81–82, 113.

32. Cunningham, *British Writers of the Thirties,* 228–30; Jed Esty, *A Shrinking Island: Modernism and National Culture in England* (Princeton, NJ: Princeton University Press, 2004), 42.

33. Matless, *Landscape and Englishness,* 66–67.

34. H. V. Morton, *In Search of England* (London: Methuen, 1927), 69–70. This conjunction of broadcasting and feudalism became a fairly common trope. The keenest listener-in of all, in Margery Allingham's *Look to the Lady* (1931), is the revered fount of local lore who lives in a remote, insanitary, moss-covered cottage. "A weed-grown brick path led up to the front door which stood open, revealing an old man in a battered felt hat

seated on a low wooden chair beside an atrocious loud-speaker which was at this moment murmuring a nasal reproduction of the advertising gramophone music from Radio Paris." *Look to the Lady* (New York: Felony and Mayhem Press, 2006), 155.

35. Sara Danius, *The Senses of Modernism: Technology, Perception, and Aesthetics* (Ithaca, NY: Cornell University Press, 2002), 124–46.

36. E. M. Forster, *Howards End* (Harmondsworth: Penguin Books, 1961), 185.

37. Virginia Woolf, *Dairy,* ed. Anne Oliver Bell and Andrew McNeillie, 5 vols. (London: Hogarth Press, 1977–1984), 3:147.

38. Ibid., 153.

39. Ibid., 157. Groombridge Place, on the Kent-Sussex border near Tunbridge Wells, was built toward the end of the seventeenth century, in the manner of Inigo Jones rather than Christopher Wren.

40. Makiko Minow-Pinkney, "Virginia Woolf and the Age of Motor-Cars," in *Virginia Woolf in the Age of Mechanical Reproduction,* ed. Melba Cuddy-Keane (New York: Garland, 2000), 159–82; Lorraine Sim, *Virginia Woolf: The Patterns of Ordinary Experience* (Farnham: Ashgate, 2010), 107–36.

41. Virginia Woolf, *Orlando: A Biography,* ed. Rachel Bowlby (Oxford: Oxford University Press, 1992), 293.

42. Woolf, *Diary,* 4:316.

43. Aldous Huxley, "Wanted, a New Pleasure," in *Music at Night and Other Essays* (London: Chatto & Windus, 1931), 248–57.

44. Duffy, *Speed Handbook,* 10.

45. D. H. Lawrence, *Lady Chatterley's Lover* (Harmondsworth: Penguin Books, 2006), 152–61, pp. 156, 159.

46. Hynes, *Auden Generation,* 317.

47. Edward Upward, "Sketch for a Marxist Interpretation of Literature," in *The Mind in Chains,* ed. C. Day-Lewis (London: Frederick Muller, 1937), 48, 40.

48. Edward Upward, *Journey to the Border* (London: Enitharmon Press, 1994), 20. Henceforth *JTTB.*

49. Arnold van Gennep, *Les rites de passage* (Paris: É. Nourry, 1909); Victor Turner, *The Ritual Process* (London: Pelican, 1974).

50. W. H. Auden, "Spain 1937," in *The English Auden: Poems, Essays and Dramatic Writings, 1927–1939,* ed. Edward Mendelson (London: Faber and Faber, 1977), 210–12, p. 212.

51. Hynes, *Auden Generation,* 321.

52. George Buchanan, *A London Story* (London: Constable, 1935), 174. Henceforth *LS.*

53. Paul Edwards, *Wyndham Lewis: Painter and Writer* (New Haven, CT: Yale University Press, 2000), 443–44.

54. Wyndham Lewis, *Men without Art*, ed. Seamus Cooney (Santa Rosa, CA: Black Sparrow Press, 1987), 232, 234.

55. Wyndham Lewis, *The Revenge for Love* (Harmondsworth: Penguin Books, 2004), 37. Henceforth *RL*.

56. Wyndham Lewis, *The Complete Wild Body*, ed. Bernard Lafourcade (Santa Barbara, CA: Black Sparrow Press, 1982), 83.

57. Wyndham Lewis, *The Art of Being Ruled* (London: Chatto & Windus, 1926), 279.

58. Lewis, *Complete Wild Body*, 17. See also, in the same volume, "Crossing the Frontier" and "A Spanish Household."

59. Lewis, *Men without Art*, 91–92.

60. Edwards, *Wyndham Lewis*, 452.

61. Fredric Jameson, *Fables of Aggression: Wyndham Lewis, the Modernist as Fascist* (Berkeley: University of California Press, 1979), 81–86.

62. Wyndham Lewis, *Snooty Baronet*, ed. Bernard Lafourcade (Santa Barbara, CA: Black Sparrow Press, 1984), 217–18.

63. Stevie Smith, *Over the Frontier* (London: Virago, 1980), 152–53.

64. Lesley Higgins and Marie-Christine Leps, "'Passport, Please': Legal, Literary, and Critical Functions of Identity," *College Literature* 25, no. 1 (1998): 94–138.

65. Rose Macaulay, *Crewe Train* (Leipzig: Bernhard Tauchnitz, 1926), 35.

66. Evelyn Waugh, *Labels: A Mediterranean Journey* (London: Duckworth, 1930), 26.

67. Eric Ambler, *The Dark Frontier* (London: Fontana, 1967), 66.

68. Buchanan, *Entanglement* (London: Constable, 1938), 57.

69. Woolf, *Diary*, 4:310–11.

70. Graham Greene, *Stamboul Train* (London: Vintage Books, 2001), 5.

71. Evelyn Waugh, *Vile Bodies* (Harmondsworth: Penguin, 1996), 11. Henceforth *VB*.

72. Evelyn Waugh, "People Who Want to Sue Me," in *Essays, Articles and Reviews*, ed. Donat Gallagher (London: Methuen, 1983), 72–73, p. 73.

73. Kate O'Brien, *Mary Lavelle* (London: Virago, 1984), xiii–xiv.

74. J. Hillis Miller, "The Critic as Host," in *The J. Hillis Miller Reader*, ed. Julian Wolfreys (Stanford, CA: Stanford University Press, 2005), 17–37, p. 18.

75. Gerard Genette, *Paratexts: Thresholds of Interpretation*, trans. Jane E. Lewin (Cambridge: Cambridge University Press, 1987).

76. Jacques Derrida, *The Truth in Painting*, trans. Geoff Bennington and Ian McLeod (Chicago: University of Chicago Press, 1987), 54, 64, 61.

77. Eric Ambler, *Uncommon Danger* (London: Hodder and Stoughton, 1952), 26.

78. Christopher Isherwood, *The Berlin Novels* (London: Vintage, 1992), 1. Henceforth *BN*.

79. Elizabeth Bowen, "Places," in *Pictures and Conversations* (London: Allen Lane, 1975), 34–57, pp. 41–42.

80. Maud Ellmann, *Elizabeth Bowen: The Shadow across the Page* (Edinburgh: Edinburgh University Press, 2003), 97–98.

81. Elizabeth Bowen, *To the North* (London: Vintage, 1999), 6. Henceforth *TTN*.

82. Elizabeth Bowen, *The House in Paris* (London: Vintage, 1998), 67. Henceforth *HiP*.

83. Elizabeth Bowen, "Notes on Writing a Novel," in *Pictures and Conversations*, 169–93, p. 169.

84. Siegfried Kracauer, "The Hotel Lobby," in *The Mass Ornament: Weimar Essays*, ed. and trans. Thomas Y. Levin (Cambridge, MA: Harvard University Press, 1995), 173–85, pp. 183, 177.

85. Elleke Boehmer, "Global and Textual Webs in an Age of Transnational Capitalism; or, What Isn't New about Empire," *Postcolonial Studies* 7, no. 1 (2004): 11–26, 13, 16, 23.

86. Elleke Boehmer, "Mansfield as Colonial Modernist: Difference Within," in *Celebrating Katherine Mansfield: A Centenary Volume of Essays*, ed. Gerri Kimber and Janet Wilson (Houndmills: Palgrave Macmillan, 2011), 57–71, p. 58.

87. Ruskin, *Works*, 5:370.

88. "Laws of the Air," *Times*, January 30, 1919, 4.

Conclusion

1. Henry Jenkins, *Convergence Culture: Where Old and New Media Collide* (New York: NYU Press, 2006).

2. Christopher Caudwell, *Illusion and Reality* (London: Lawrence and Wishart, 1946), 141, 218, 293–96. Caudwell's Marxism could be the starting point for a different approach to interwar British literary cool, one more compatible with Helmut Lethen's approach to Weimar culture in *Cool Conduct: The Culture of Distance in Weimar Germany*, trans. Don Reneau (Berkeley: University of California Press, 2002).

3. Christopher Caudwell, "D. H. Lawrence: A Study of the Bourgeois Artist," in *Studies in a Dying Culture* (London: Bodley Head, 1938), 44–72, pp. 67–69.

4. Caudwell, *Illusion and Reality*, 187.

5. W. H. Auden, *The English Auden: Poems, Essays and Dramatic Writings, 1927–1939*, ed. Edward Mendelson (London: Faber and Faber, 1977), 67.

6. Valentine Cunningham, *British Writers of the Thirties* (Oxford: Oxford University Press, 1988), 76.

7. Alison Light, *Forever England: Femininity, Literature and Conservatism between the Wars* (London: Routledge, 1991), 67–68, 73, 96, 81–82.

8. Ross McKibbin, *Classes and Cultures: England, 1918–1951* (Oxford: Oxford University Press, 1998), 484–86.

9. Light, *Forever England*, 90–91.

10. "Law of the Air," *Times*, March 5, 1918, 3.

11. Agatha Christie, *Death in the Clouds* (London: Harper, 2001), 34–35, 41–42, 109–16, 294–95.

12. Light, *Forever England*, 73.

13. Margery Allingham, *The Fashion in Shrouds* (London: Vintage, 2006), 110, 140–41, 212, 269, 124, 111, 220–36.

14. Christopher St. John Sprigg, *British Airways* (London: Thomas Nelson, 1934), 8.

15. Caudwell, *Illusion and Reality*, 294.

16. Christopher St. John Sprigg, *Death of an Airman* (New York: Sun Dial Press, 1937), 116, 265–66, 43–44.

17. Rose Macaulay, *Keeping Up Appearances* (Leipzig: Tauchnitz, 1928), passim.

18. For an informative survey, see David Welsh, *Underground Writing: The London Tube from George Gissing to Virginia Woolf* (Liverpool: Liverpool University Press, 2010).

19. T. S. Eliot, *Complete Poems and Plays* (London: Faber and Faber, 1969), 174.

20. Virginia Woolf, *The Waves*, ed. Gillian Beer (Oxford: Oxford University Press, 1992), 146, 148.

21. "The New Piccadilly 'Tube' Station: 'The Best in the World,'" *Illustrated London News*, December 15, 1928, 1145.

22. Woolf, *Waves*, 162.

23. Louis MacNeice, *Collected Poems*, ed. Peter McDonald (Faber and Faber, 2007), 103.

24. Louis MacNeice, *The Strings Are False: An Unfinished Autobiography* (London: Faber and Faber, 1965), 32.

25. Michel Serres, "The Origin of Language: Biology, Information Theory, and Thermodynamics," in *Hermes: Literature, Science, Philosophy*, ed. Josué V. Harari and David F. Bell (Baltimore: Johns Hopkins University Press, 1982), 71–83, p. 81. The key publications were Claude E. Shannon and Warren Weaver, *The Mathematical Theory of Communication* (Urbana: Illinois University Press, 1949); and Norbert Wiener, *Cybernetics: Or, Control and Communication in the Animal and the Machine* (Cambridge, MA: MIT Press, 1948).

26. Bruce Clarke, "From Thermodynamics to Virtuality," in *From Energy to Information: Representation in Science and Technology, Art, and Literature,* ed. Clarke and Linda Dalrymple Henderson (Stanford, CA: Stanford University Press, 2002), 17–33, p. 30.

27. Clarke and Henderson, introduction, ibid., 1–15, pp. 4–5.

28. Alan Liu, *The Laws of Cool: Knowledge Work and the Culture of Information* (Chicago: University of Chicago Press, 2004), 173.

29. James Beniger, *The Control Revolution: Technological and Economic Origins of the Information Society* (Cambridge, MA: Harvard University Press, 1986), 425.

30. Alex Goody, *Technology, Literature and Culture* (Cambridge: Polity Press, 2011), 73–77.

31. Julian Murphet, "Beckett's Televisual Modernism," *Critical Quarterly* 51, no. 2 (2009): 60–78, p. 67.

32. Elizabeth Bowen, *To the North* (London: Vintage, 1999), 137.

33. Thomas Elsaesser's recent essay on 3-D cinema includes some highly illuminating reflections on the ways in which an idea of the image as a "window to a view," as the occasion for contemplating or witnessing, has been replaced by an idea of the image as "a passage or a portal, an interface or part of a sequential process—in short, as a cue for action": "The 'Return' of 3-D: On Some of the Logics and Genealogies of the Image in the Twenty-First Century," *Critical Inquiry* 39, no. 2 (2013): 217–46, p. 241.

Index

www.ingramcontent.com/pod-product-compliance
Lightning Source LLC
Chambersburg PA
CBHW030641150426
42811CB00076B/2096/J